Controversies in Tourism

_____

Controversies in Tourism

Edited by

Omar Moufakkir

International Centre for Peace through Tourism Research (ICPTR),
School of Leisure and Tourism Management, Stenden University,
the Netherlands

and

Peter M. Burns

Centre for Tourism Policy Studies (CENTOPS),
Tourism and International Development, University of Brighton,
United Kingdom

www.cabi.org

CABI is a trading name of CAB International

CABI	CABI
Nosworthy Way	875 Massachusetts Avenue
Wallingford	7th Floor
Oxfordshire OX10 8DE	Cambridge, MA 02139
UK	USA
Tel: +44 (0)1491 832111	Tel: +1 617 395 4056
Fax: +44 (0)1491 833508	Fax: +1 617 354 6875
E-mail: cabi@cabi.org	E-mail: cabi-nao@cabi.org
Website: www.cabi.org	

A catalogue record for this book is available from the British Library, London, UK.

Library of Congress Cataloging-in-Publication Data

Controversies in tourism / edited by Omar Moufakkir and Peter Burns.
    p. cm.
  Includes bibliographical references and index.
  ISBN 978-1-84593-813-0 (alk. paper)
1. Tourism. 2. Tourism--Social aspects. I. Moufakkir, Omar. II. Burns, Peter (Peter M.) III. Title.

  G155.A1C658 2012
  338.4′791--dc23

                                        2011026536

ISBN-13: 978 1 84593 813 0

Commissioning editor: Sarah Hulbert
Editorial assistant: Alexandra Lainsbury
Production editor: Holly Beaumont

Typeset by SPI Publisher Services, Pondicherry, India.
Printed and bound by CPI Group (UK) Ltd, Croydon CR0 4YY.

Contents

Contributors

Dr Edward Addo, Assistant Professor, Tourism Department, Memorial University of Newfoundland, Grenfell Campus, Corner Brook, Newfoundland and Labrador, Canada. E-mail: eaddo@swgc.mun.ca

Dr Angela M. Benson, Tourism and Travel, University of Brighton, School of Service Management, Eastbourne, UK. E-mail: amb16@brighton.ac.uk

Dr Kalyan Bhandari, Nepal Centre for Tourism Research, Biratnagar, Nepal and School of Interdisciplinary Studies, University of Glasgow, Dumfries Campus, Scotland, UK. E-mail: k.bhandari.1@research.gla.ac.uk

Dr Nikolaos Boukas, The School of Business Administration, European University Cyprus, Cyprus. E-mail: N.Boukas@euc.ac.cy

Dr George Boustras, The School of Business Administration, European University Cyprus, Cyprus. E-mail: G.Boustras@euc.ac.cy

Dr Stephen W. Boyd, Professor, Department of Hospitality and Tourism Management, University of Ulster, Northern Ireland, UK. E-mail: sw.boyd@ ulster.ac.uk

Dr Peter M. Burns, Professor, Tourism and International Development, Centre for Tourism Policy Studies, University of Brighton, UK. E-mail: p.m.burns@brighton.ac.uk

Dr Don Craig, Professor, International Hotel Management, Stenden University, Leeuwarden, the Netherlands. E-mail: don.craig@stenden.com

Dr John Dobson, Senior Lecturer, Department of Tourism, Hospitality and Events Management, Cardiff School of Management, University of Wales Institute, Cardiff, UK. E-mail: jdobson@uwic.ac.uk

Dr Jorge Ferraz, Professor, Escola Superior de Hotelaria e Turismo do Estoril (Estoril Higher Institute for Hotel and Tourism Studies), Estoril, Portugal. E-mail: jorge.ferraz@eshte.pt

Dr Michael Guiry, Associate Professor, Coordinator of Marketing, International Business and Business Law, H-E-B School of Business & Administration, University of the Incarnate Word, San Antonio, USA.

Dr Don F. Holecek, Professor Emeritus, Michigan State University, East Lansing, Michigan, USA. E-mail: d.holecek@anr.msu.edu

Dr Raquel Huete, Senior Lecturer, Department of Sociology I, University of Alicante, Alicante, Spain. E-mail: R.Huete@ua.es

Brian Ipock, Center for Medical Tourism Research, University of the Incarnate Word, San Antonio, Texas, USA.

Dr Alejandro Mantecón, Department of Sociology I, University of Alicante, Alicante, Spain. E-mail: alejandro.mantecon@ua.es

Dr Sibel Mehter Aykin, Assistant Professor, Department of Economics, Faculty of Economics and Administrative Sciences (IIBF), Akdeniz University, Dumlupinar Bulvari, Campus, Antalya, Turkey. E-mail: sibelaykin@akdeniz.edu.tr

Dr Omar Moufakkir, Professor, School of Leisure and Tourism Management, Stenden University, Leeuwarden, the Netherlands. E-mail: omar.moufakkir@stenden.com

Dr Marina Novelli, Centre for Tourism Policy Studies, School of Service Management, University of Brighton, Eastbourne, UK. E-mail: M.Novelli@brighton.ac.uk

Anna E. Papanicolaou, Faculty of Humanities, Centre for Transnational Studies, University of Southampton, UK. E-mail: aep106@soton.ac.uk

Helen Pattison, Lancaster Environment Centre, Lancaster University, UK. E-mail: h.patisson1@lancaster.ac.uk

Alexandros Sinka, Cybarco Ltd, Nicosia, Cyprus.

Dr Craig Thompson, Academic Dean, International Hotel Management, Stenden University, Leeuwarden, the Netherlands. E-mail: craig.thompson@stenden.com

Anne Tisch-Rottensteiner, Beluga School for Life, Thailand. E-mail: Anne.Ti-Ro@gmx.de

Dr David G. Vequist IV, Center for Medical Tourism Research, University of the Incarnate Word, San Antonio, Texas, USA. E-mail: vequist@uiwtx.edu

Dr Stephen Wearing, Associate Professor, School of Leisure, Sport and Tourism, Faculty of University of Technology, Sydney, Kuring-gai Campus, Australia. E-mail: Stephen. Wearing@uts.edu.au

Dr Philip F. Xie, School of Human Movement, Sport and Leisure Studies, Bowling Green State University, Bowling Green, Ohio, USA. E-mail: pxie@bgsu.edu

Acknowledgements

I would like to thank Stenden University for giving me the opportunity to work on this book. I would also like to thank colleagues at the International Centre for Peace through Tourism Research. A special thank you goes to Julija Prigunova for her assistance through the journey. Also, our thanks to the following people at CABI for their support: Rachel Cutts, Holly Beaumont and Alexandra Lainsbury.

Introduction

Omar Moufakkir[1] and Peter M. Burns[2]
[1]*Stenden University, Leeuwarden, the Netherlands;*
[2]*University of Brighton, Brighton, UK*

Tourism is a dynamic global phenomenon: an agent of change, harbinger of controversy, and a significant factor in social, cultural and technical evolution. Such evolutions, especially those driven by tourism, are almost certainly followed by a variety of induced controversies. In order to gain further insight into how societies and cultures work and interact, critical analysis of the contexts, causes and consequences of the controversies is required. Failure to comprehend the basis of a tourism controversy may (more than not) produce myopic tourism development policies of the sort seen in countries ranging from Turkey to Kenya. At worst, failure to recognize and deal with controversy can lead to the systemic failure of tourism to meet the expectations of investors, politicians and citizens.

This book will make a substantial contribution to the understanding of tourism controversies. Its purpose is to provide a platform for open debate and intellectual discourse with a variety of views on perceived controversies or manifest conflicts firstly within tourism (endogenous controversies), but also in the multidimensional contexts of environment and civil society (exogenous contexts). The focus of the book is on **established** controversies in tourism and new and **emerging** conflicts, dilemmas, paradoxes and disputes within tourism contexts. As a caveat to the reader, no single volume can hope to deal with all the issues, so the contents of this book represent examples that set the stage for further cases to be identified and published.

The 'classic' controversies derived from, and rooted in, tourism such as dark/thanatourism, inappropriate tourism development, poor tourism planning, exploitative employment, malpractice with tourism statistics, appropriation of heritage for tourism, unsustainable tourism, sport and mega events that overwhelm locales, sex tourism, gaming linked with organized crime, commodification of culture, are well established in the tourism literature, whereas contemporary or emerging examples (such as medical tourism, political tourism, tourism related to poverty, volunteer tourism, wildlife tourism) are less documented and somewhat under-researched in academia.

Certainly, as there is a multitude of types of tourism, tourists and stakeholders, the controversies in tourism are both ample and widespread. For example, regarding development, Spretnak (1999) asks whether the discourse of development and action is simply a matter of economics rather than livelihood, positing that the real effect of modern development policies has been a substantive increase in the economic disparity between the minority economically rich countries and the economically disadvantaged world majority. If development advances only the materialism conception of the world, the questions become: what are the objectives and aims of development?

Tourism's alleged contribution to development is widely accepted but a number of fundamental questions remain unanswered (Butler, 1996). Reid (2003) states that 'Historically, however, tourism has not been a positive experience for all parties engaged in the development process, or treated all stakeholders in the enterprise equally. While trans-national corporations and entrepreneurs benefit greatly from tourism development, local people often bear the cost of that development without adequate reward' (p. 1). More interestingly, according to Swarbrooke (1999), investment in tourism by foreign entrepreneurs is sometimes seen as undesirable by the international community and may pose an ethical dilemma (although of course this flies in the face of the foreign direct investment argument put forward by development economists).

The controversies inherent in tourism development are also internal and external. External controversies are manifested in the development discourse that discusses the relational economic, cultural and environmental development interplay between the Majority World and Minority World (Burns and Novelli, 2008). Internal controversies are manifested inside the 'black box' of tourism policy and planning (Hall 1994; Veal, 2002). Policy and planning decisions in tourism are shaped by the complexity and diversity of the tourism environment (Holden, 2005), which encompasses interest groups beyond financial stakeholders, to also include residents, businesses, arts and humanities, cultural and natural resources, protection advocates, civil leaders, and professional designers and planners (Gunn and Var, 2002).

Looking at tourism through the sustainability prism, like many authors, Butler (1996), for example, has noted that its major binary divide, concept and practice are mired in contradictions and controversies, when discussing preservation and development issues. Among several others, Conlin and Baum (2003, p. 118) asked whether sustainability as a concept has been 'hijacked by the tourism industry through eco-labeling and eco-selling', and by 'the prevailing model of development and capitalism' (Mowforth and Munt, 2003, p. 113). While environmental and social impacts are not new to the tourism industry, they can be exacerbated by newly developed types of tourism supposedly developed as alternative to the most damaging mass tourism. One of these niches is adventure tourism. In the adventure tourism setting, due to the need for pristine environments, often intense connection with the local population and culture can stimulate tension between the adventurous and the nature and culture of the local community (Ewert and Jamieson, 2003).

The purpose of this brief overview is to lift the lid on the rather disorganized box of tricks that frames tourism's obvious and not so obvious controversies. To reiterate, many volumes would be needed to include all the existing controversies in tourism. The present volume then enables authors to present and discuss controversies with the idea of providing readers with a cohesive (if not fully comprehensive) perspective on tourism and its many controversies.

Content Overview

In the introductory chapter, Moufakkir sets the scene of the book by initiating a discussion about the nature of freedom in leisure and tourism. Discussing the moralization of tourism, he proposes that while some authors are enthusiastic about this moralizing drive for a more ethically oriented tourism, others have criticized the oversimplification of this moralization, maintaining that there is too much criticism of mass tourism while too much credit is given to alternative types of tourism, which are perceived to be but micro solutions to macro problems. The author stimulates a discussion about the controversies related to ethics in tourism in a style that will set the ground for the discussed controversies in this book.

In the first case (Chapter 2), Aykin examines controversies related to a common tourism policy of the European Union. Most of the studies addressing the extent of the European Union's involvement in tourism and the depth of its tourism policy argue that the European Union must play a proactive role in tourism, while the rest worry about centralization, claiming that the existing political framework is effectual and sufficient. This chapter attempts to assess approaches of various groups to a common tourism policy of the European Union from a historical perspective, with a special emphasis on the recent developments brought about by the Reform Treaty.

Moving from complex European politics to the equally complex controversy of tourism, social identity and culture, Papanicolau (Chapter 3) discusses the controversies surrounding tourism and the commodification of culture. She uses the case of tourism to Mexico's Mayan Riviera – the 130 km stretch of land situated directly beneath Cancun, in Mexico's Yucatan peninsula – to illustrate her analysis. Launched by state officials in the middle 1990s, the destination was designed to conjure up images of a 'Cote D'Azurian' sophistication blended with the 'culture' of one of the most celebrated civilizations of the Americas: the Mayans. Although Mayan communities have resided in the interior of the peninsula for centuries, they had been largely excluded from the tourist gaze until the end of the 1990s, when the 'selling' of culture, particularly authentic Mayan culture, began to gain ground. Drawing from fieldwork data gathered in 2009, this chapter examines this phenomenon, looking at issues of commodification, marketization and authenticity in the context of tourist attractions premised on the (re)presentation of culture, particularly Mayan culture.

In Chapter 4, Novelli and Tisch-Rottensteiner contribute a case study that focuses on the extent to which tourism leads to local development or whether the tourists' quest for authenticity holds back development. By using the hill tribes of Northern Thailand as a representative case, their study highlights the need for governmental institutions to recognize the substantial added value provided by the hill tribes to Thai tourism, tourists to be made more aware of what to expect, how to behave and how to interact when travelling to the locality, and finally, the need for tour operators to exercise their moral and ethical obligations to ensure that tourism truly benefits local communities.

Another sort of moral or ethical dimension is dealt with by Vequist, Guiry and Ipock (Chapter 5) who focus on the medical tourism industry and some of the interesting controversies that underlie the growth of this industry. Defined as individuals travelling outside of their immediate geographical area and even across international borders to obtain healthcare, medical tourism is a growing type of tourism. Medical tourism is suggested to be a rapidly growing industry and is affecting traditional healthcare delivery in many ways that are not yet fully understood. The authors provide insights into the controversies in the field of medical tourism and also determine what categories of controversies are well covered and which areas still need more research.

Discussing the controversies surrounding wildlife tourism and trophy hunting, Dobson (Chapter 6) offers an overview of the definitional dilemmas with which this 'leisure activity' is faced. He then presents arguments in support of this activity and arguments against it, and looks at trophy hunting from an ethical lens to analyse the trophy-hunting debate.

Definitional ambiguities also frame the ecotourism discourse even after 20 years of research. Issues related to definitions, the context and spaces in which ecotourism takes place frame Boyd's analysis of the controversies related to ecotourism in Chapter 7.

Returning to the question of social identity and cultural ethics, Xie (Chapter 8) argues that the popularity of aboriginal tourism has created a series of tensions and conflicts when ethnic culture is commoditized as a tourism resource. This chapter proposes a term 'ethnic panopticon' by using Foucault's eye-of-power to describe a controversy when aboriginal resources are used for tourism. Through the concept of ethnic panopticon, the participant/observer becomes the object to view and be viewed. The argument is that aboriginal tourism involves technologies of gazes in order to create, reify and reinvent a fantasy world of cultural difference for tourists' consumption. It has investigated an aboriginal folk village on Hainan Island, China, where tourism has become the major source of income.

Casinos have always attracted controversy and Chapter 9 sees Moufakkir and Holeck attempting to delineate major controversies surrounding casino gaming development, and discuss in-depth a set of important issues. The authors argue that despite the proliferation of casinos, especially in the USA, whenever and wherever casino gaming legislation has been introduced and discussed, heated debates arise between gaming's advocates and adversaries. This is partly because of the activity itself, which still connotes moral, religious, economic, political and social issues, and partly because of how the benefits are distributed. The authors conclude that it is, however, difficult, if not misleading, to discuss the impacts of gaming in general terms because different casino development models generate different outcomes.

While many of the chapters in this book are concerned with issues of culture and nurture, Chapter 10 takes on a major environmental issue with Boukas, Boustras and Sinka discussing the case of Golf Tourism in Cyprus. The overdependence of Cyprus on tourism, the decrease of tourist flows, and the recent economic crisis harming the Cypriot tourism sector are some of the major issues that have emerged as being in need of coping strategies. While Cyprus has been facing a water shortage for a number of years, the official tourism policy response aims to reposition the country in the global tourism market with the development of a number of world-class golf courses. This is inherently controversial, leading to strong disagreement between various parties. Although the construction of golf courses could be a solution for the economic recovery, there is no denying the potential ecological disaster resulting from this government policy decision. The chapter

aims to discover different views for this issue based on recent data from different perspectives: tourism and environmental planning, marketing and policy, crisis management and sustainable development. Finally, it gives alternative solutions in order to harmonize any possible contradictions resulting from this strategy.

The concept of residential tourism has been used since the late 1970s to explain the transformations brought about by the construction of property and expatriate homes in tourist areas, and the configuration of two types of human mobility: tourism and lifestyle migration. In Chapter 11, Huete and Mantecón present their research, which has been carried out in the Alicante province (Spain). A total of 872 face-to-face interviews in the respondents' homes were conducted. The operational classification presented here could become a useful tool in resource management and regional planning. It is worth noting that the towns where such process has been more intense experience great difficulties in explaining the complex system of residential mobility types with which they deal on a daily basis. The description of the mobility types here identified can also help to justify the resources necessary for the local administration of these areas where the boundaries between tourism and migration are blurred.

Addressing a major aspect of tourism controversies, Craig and Thompson (Chapter 12) examine the phenomenon of dark tourism, and, in doing so, distinguish different degrees of darkness and therewith seven destination categories: sites of mass murder and genocide, war museums and exhibitions, graveyards and cemeteries, simulated dungeons, battlefields, slavery tourism and re-enactments. To satisfy curiosity and its educational aspect are of utmost importance and to some degree Dark Tourism is financially beneficial to any destination. The chapter goes deeper into the contribution of media and how the so-called 'CNN phenomenon', global communications, social media and technology encourage death-related events to be reported in real-time, thus creating a frisson of excitement that has the potential to turn into tourism.

Furthermore, it clarifies why one experiences observing violence and death as 'enjoyment' and how this experience differs from time to time and from tourist to tourist.

Returning to the field of politics and tourism, Addo (Chapter 13) addresses the controversies surrounding the significance of events with a focus on Ghana's celebration of colonial independence. Celebrative events, like independence anniversaries and festivals, are ubiquitous in sub-Saharan Africa and often linked to European colonization and trade in commodities and slaves that characterized the sub-region over five centuries. Ghana, the first country to gain independence from colonial rule in the sub-region, celebrates the event and some Diaspora-related festivals. The 50th independence anniversary and Panafest, a Diaspora-related event, are the focus of this chapter. The events are economically, culturally and politically significant to Ghana's tourism industry. However, the experiential economic, political and ethnocentric controversies surrounding the events tend to overshadow their cultural significance.

The ideological role of intergovernmental organizations on the promotion of international tourism has caused controversies as governments try to balance regional objectives with national self-interest. In Chapter 14, Ferraz uses content analysis to investigate one of the most significant declarations and propositions of the main intergovernmental organizations regarding international tourism during the past 50 years: he assesses its ideological dimensions. His findings support the assumption that the discourses of intergovernmental organizations sustain the ideological nature of international tourism whilst promoting topics, products, practices and tourism models that contributes to an unequal interdependence between the different societies at stake, benefiting the most developed ones.

The tourist gaze will be familiar to tourism and cultural scholars in its original form set out by John Urry in his seminal work. However, in Chapter 15, Pattison turns the concept upside down by visiting the paradoxes of tourism encounters in The Gambia, with a focus on the host gaze instead of the tourist gaze. Exploring the complexity of becoming a 'host' in The Gambia, she has been able to (re)inscribe meaning to the term gaze with its (largely) one-dimensional utilization within tourism studies, and (re)conceptualize the traditional host–guest paradigm. In this chapter, binaries of 'us' and 'them', 'subject' and 'object' are deconstructed as the host's paradoxical gaze upon the West is manifested in host–tourist encounters that are dynamic, ambivalent and complex. The end result is the creation of a confused heterogeneous place.

Conservation has also been a significant controversy in tourism with conflicting interests at the heart of the matter. In Chapter 16, Bhandari reflects on whether tourism and conservation in Nepal's Chitwan National Park can exist in mutual harmony. His case study examines conflictual issues between tourism entrepreneurs and conservation activists. He looks into the case of the renewal of a 15-year contract to operate concessionaires within Chitwan National Park that became a national controversy and left more than half a dozen hotels (ecolodges) inside the park shut for 6 months. His chapter identifies four dimensions to understand this controversy and offers recommendations for policymakers and other stakeholders engaged in the tourism planning process.

In Chapter 17, Benson and Wearing argue that volunteer tourism has become a global phenomenon, with market predictions indicating growth in both size and value and with this growth has come the inevitable controversies that surround new trends or phenomena. They explain that in examining this phenomenon there is a need to examine a wider agenda beyond that of its size and growth. This chapter attempts to build around the ideas on the volunteer experiences from both their experiences and the experiences of the communities with which they interact. They also suggest that volunteer tourists cannot solely be aligned with neo-colonialism or neo-liberalism. Volunteer tourism sits at the intersection of a great many areas such as mass tourism, international development and sustainability, and as such it is essential that we do not isolate our ideas to singular theories, approaches or practices, as this would then limit our ability to research and appreciate this phenomenon. This chapter provides an overview of this area and attempts to provide the reader with an analysis of its function and characteristics.

References

Burns, P. and Novelli, M. (2008) *Tourism Development: Growth, Myths and Inequalities*. CABI Publishing, Wallingford, UK.

Butler, R.W. (1996) Problems and possibilities of sustainable tourism: the case of the Shetland Islands. In: Briguglio, L., Butler, R., Harrison, D. and Filho, W.L. (eds) *Sustainable Tourism in Islands and Small States: Case Studies*. Pinter, London, pp.11–31.

Conlin, M.V. and Baum, T. (2003) Comprehensive human resource planning: an essential key to sustainable tourism in small island settings. In: Cooper, C. (ed.) *Aspects of Tourism. Classic Review in Tourism*. Channel View Publications, Clevedon, UK, pp. 115–129.

Ewert, A. and Jamieson, L. (2003) Current status and future directions in the adventure tourism industry. In: Wilks, J. and Page, S.J. (eds) *Managing Tourist Health and Safety in the New Millennium*. Pergamon, Oxford, UK, pp. 67–84.

Gunn, C.A. and Var, T. (2002) *Tourism Planning: Basics, Concepts, Cases*. Routledge, London.

Hall, C.M. (1994) *Tourism and Politics: Policy, Power and Place*. Wiley and Sons, Chichester, UK.

Holden, A. (2005) *Tourism Studies and the Social Sciences*. Routledge, London.

Mowforth, M. and Munt, I. (2003) *Tourism and Sustainability: New Tourism in the Third World*, 2nd edn. Routledge, London.

Reid, D.G. (2003) *Tourism, Globalization and Development: Responsible Tourism Planning*. Pluto Press, London.

Spretnak, C. (1999) *The Resurgence of the Real: Body, Nature and Place in a Hypermodern World*. Addison-Wesley, New York.

Swarbrooke, J. (1999) *Sustainable Tourism Management*. CABI Publishing, Wallingford, UK.

Veal, A.J. (2002) *Leisure and Tourism Policy and Planning*, 2nd edn. CABI Publishing, Wallingford, UK.

1 Of Ethics, Leisure and Tourism: The 'Serious Fun of Doing Tourism'

Omar Moufakkir[1]

[1]*School of Leisure and Tourism Management, Stenden University, Leeuwarden, the Netherlands*

Introduction

It is no longer good enough to travel footloose and fancy free. Tourism is accompanied by constant warnings to limit one's behaviour and to be ethical. From the environmental group Arc's pamphlet 'Sun, Sea, Sand and Saving the World' to Friends of the Earth's advice to question whether you 'need' to travel at all, tourism is now the terrain of moral codes and not a little guilt-tripping. The often impulsive and reckless desire to strike out across Europe or further afield is no longer a good enough reason. A love of music, dancing and drinking provides no defence against the charge of immoral tourism. Excess moral baggage has to be lugged around if tourism is to be acceptable to some.

> Butcher (2002, p. 71)

Now the mass of mankind are evidently quite slavish in their tastes, preferring a life suitable to beasts.

> Aristotle (Book 1, Chapter 5)

In the words of poet Alexander Pope: 'Amusement is the happiness of those who cannot think.'

> Goodale and Witt (1991, p. 3)

The only lesson of morality appropriate to childhood, and the most important for every age, is never to harm anyone.

The very precept of doing good, if it is not subordinated to this one, is dangerous, false, and contradictory.

> J.J. Rousseau (Book 1, p. 104).

Like the cover, quotations do not necessarily do justice to the content of a book; neither do they justify the meaning of its thesis when taken out of their context. We use quotations, however, to give sense to our thinking, support our ideas and guide our reasoning. The selected quotations are profound in their meaning. They are complementary, yet different and possibly contradictory. They are used here to epitomize the controversies surrounding the theme of this chapter – tourism ethics. They are all concerned with freedom – the freedom to have, to be and to become.

Freedom and Tourism

Perceived freedom and intrinsic motivation are central to any definition of leisure (Iso-Ahola, 1999) and could also apply to definitions of tourism. Bregha (1991, 47) asks since leisure and freedom are in a profound relationship, 'does freedom, in fact, mean the ability of doing what one wants to do when one wants to? Is professional intervention in leisure services enhanced or limited by the ethos of freedom?' Many questions arise in relation to the moralization of tourism. To what extent are tourists free? Are mass tourists freer than those engaged in alternative tourism? To what extent is the moralization of tourism antithetical to freedom? Should tourists behave ethically in their tourism action? Leisure scholars have examined such concepts as leisure in one's life and education for leisure. Is tourism any different from leisure? What is freedom in this sense? Leisure scholars talk about deviant leisure or purple recreation (see, for example, Rojek, 1999). Is there something which might be termed deviant or purple tourism? Leisure scholars talk about the leisure ideal (see, for example, Goodale, 1991; Dustin and Goodale, 1999; Sylvester, 1999). Is there something like the tourism ideal? It is unfortunate that tourism academics have not yet taken full advantage of leisure studies, and that leisure academics themselves have not given the needed attention to tourism in their assemblage of importance.

This chapter is about the role of ethics in tourism. It is not about ethical tourism (Weeden, 2002), which may be defined as a type of niche tourism that has some ethical elements to it. If ethics is about right and wrong, then what is right and what is wrong about tourism, including mass/package tourism and its alternative types? The central question of this chapter is whether or not there is a place for moral considerations in tourism. I will argue that while some authors criticize the moralization of tourism (e.g. Butcher, 2002), paradoxically, tourism stakeholders do not seem to bother simply because this moralization is not sufficiently visible. I will then argue for more education about the ethics of tourism in tourism education. I have also asked many (normative) questions, but could not answer them all. After all, ethics is about wrong and right; who are we to decide what is and what is not?

The Moralization of Tourism

Tourism has an effect on people and the environment. Tourism is big business. Big business involves commercial enterprises organized and financed on a scale large enough to influence social and political decision making. Putting aside the social and political implications, production and consumption, and what comes with them, including possibly profit, competition, labour, exploitation and corruption, we can simply focus on tourism as big business from a demand perspective with the number of international tourists forecast to reach 1.6 billion by 2020. Most tourism commentaries regard this as a great achievement for tourism stakeholders. Others argue that 'Wariness rather than celebration typically accompanies accounts of the growth of travel for leisure' (Butcher, 2002, p. 7). To Butcher, it is 'this emphasis on tourism as a cultural and environmental problem that informs the moralization of tourism' (2002, p. 7). Should it not?

The concern here is not about the number of tourists per se, and neither is it about their behaviour, more than it is about the attitudes displayed in their tourism activities. Some would argue that tourists are human beings before they become tourists, and that human beings are guided by a set of moral principles that affect how they make decisions and lead their lives. These principles concern the past, present and future of humanity, and they forge our attitudes and behaviours towards becoming, if not more human, then a little less animal-like in our lives (Neulinger, 1990).

The concern of those who support such thinking is about moulding the behaviour of the 1.6 billion tourists who will be travelling the earth to visit famous, familiar and less familiar places. Some of them will stay close to home while others will boldly go where few have gone before. Some will follow in the footsteps of the explorers, taming the continents – their people, flora and fauna – and be driven by a constant need to find and cross new frontiers.

The Moralisation of Tourism by Jim Butcher (2002) has set the ground for this chapter, which is rooted in the ethical approach to leisure and leisure studies. Tourism is indeed an agent of change, for better or worse. 'Tourism produces change.

It changes the tourist, the tourist site, and the economy of the host community' (Godbey, 1994, p. 213). The nature of this change should not go uncriticized. Some have shown frustration with what is seen as exaggerated criticism of mass tourism (Butcher, 2002), others have sought to uncover the limitations of alternative types of tourism (e.g. Liu, 2003), while a few lament not only the ethical deficit in our tourism behaviour but in our lives (e.g. Smith and Duffy, 2003).

This is what Dea Birkett has to say on the cover of *The Moralisation of Tourism*: 'Don't go on your next holiday without it'. Certainly, others might say if you think about the future, this book is a 'must read', not only because of what it says, but also because of the opposite of what it says. Could something like the serious fun of doing tourism save the world – if not the day? Indeed, 'a noble task, yet also one that is bound to lead to confusion if performed by those who are not free themselves' (Bregha, 1985, p. 48).

The Paradox: The Ethical Deficit in Tourism

The ethical deficit seems to be a feature of many areas of modern society including public policy, scientific research and business practices. 'Some consumers even doubt the applicability of ethics to such areas at all' (Smith and Duffy, 2003, p. 8). Some authors lament the ethical deficit while others enthuse about the new ethical orientation of tourists. While some organizations have developed codes of ethics (e.g. WTO, WTTC, UNEP and the Tourism Industry Association of Canada), others have indicated their discontent with such endeavours, and oppose 'the vocabulary of the New Moral Tourist' (e.g. Butcher, 2002, p. 71).

In response to an early Tearfund (2002) report which indicated that tourists have become more interested in alternative types of tourism, Josephides (2002), the managing director of Sunvil Holidays, argued that 'British tourists have absolutely no interest in supporting a host country's economy, respecting local customs or acting responsible while on holiday … They also want it

cheap and to hell with who or what is exploited to get the price down.' A few authors have also indicated the irony that 'despite the frequency of our everyday use of ethical terms to describe certain states of affairs as right or wrong, good or evil, just or unjust, and so on, such evaluations often seem to carry little weight with key decision makers' (Smith and Duffy, 2003, p. 8). Moreover, forms of tourism that are alternatives to mass tourism and which claim to be more responsible have been criticized for an almost exclusive focus on localized, small-scale development projects which rarely transcend local or regional boundaries, or on particular industry sectors (Sharpley, 2000).

As tourism is a global phenomenon, critics of alternative types of tourism have indicated a need to go beyond niche marketing, and to incorporate ethics into tourism in general (e.g. Butler, 1998; Sharpley, 2000; Tribe, 2002; Liu, 2003). On the other hand, some commentators have argued that because of the problems associated with mass tourism, tourists are moving away from the 'traditional irresponsible' towards more responsible, 'green' (Krippendorf, 1987), 'new' (Poon, 1993), 'ethical', 'environmentally responsible', 'good' (Swarbrooke and Horner, 1999), 'enlightened' (Tearfund, 2002), and 'experiential' (King, 2002) types of tourism. This shift has reflected and enhanced recent interest in the ethical conduct of the tourism industry and tourists. For Krippendorf (1987) green tourism opposed development of an area without proper planning. Green tourism protects fine landscapes, reuses existing buildings and sets limits on the amount of development in an area. Where possible, only residents of the area operate as developers. The economic, ecological and social issues surrounding tourist development are all considered rather than just the economic ones. Traffic plans favour public transportation. Developers are required to bear the social costs of their development, and the architecture, historical sites and natural sites are retained even if they are an obstacle to tourism growth (Godbey, 1994, p. 213). Is there an element of moralization in this vision?

The argument that any form of responsible travel, if not tourism ethics in general, remains a myth (Josephides, 2002) is countered to some extent by those who claim that ethical principles create for tour operators who embrace them an opportunity for competitive advantage (Tearfund, 2001; Weeden, 2002; Goodwin and Francis, 2003). Tearfund's (2000) UK Market Research Report indicates that many consumers would opt for a tour company that offered positive guarantees, and would be willing to pay more for their holiday if necessary, and that tourists want more information about their destination so that they can behave responsibly and support the local economy. Similar research conducted by Tearfund in 2001 and more recently TUI (2010) shows a rising demand for ethical holidays.

The Irony of the Moralization of Tourism: Mass Tourism

Butcher is, *rightly*, infuriated by critics dehumanizing mass tourism while exaggerating the value of alternative types of tourism. The irony is that it is the democratization of leisure and tourism that has brought them to the masses, and that this so much desired achievement has become part of the problem rather than the solution. Paradoxically if we do not moralize tourism what can we do to minimize the problems emanating from its impacts? (see also Brian Wheeler, 1991, when he argued that responsible tourism is not the answer to tourism problems).

Many countries have adopted tourism as a strategy for economic development and increasingly have chosen to develop their tourism product and aggressively promote tourism resources to attract more tourists. However, tourism has also been recognized as having negative impacts on host communities, their cultures and natural environments (UNEP; UNWTO). Most of the negative impacts are attributed to mass package tourism. It is the most common type of tourism, perceived and criticized as 'crude, homogenous, insensitive to hosts, involving resorts that alter the landscape,

crowded, frivolous' (Butcher, 2002, p. 21). Mass tourists are criticized and caricatured as 'unthinking and blind to both the damage they do and the better time they could be having if only they would adopt more ethical practices' (p. 19).

While mass tourism is one of the outcomes of technological ingenuity, prosperity and democratization, it now carries more negative connotations than positive ones. However, if the negative impacts of tourism are generally attributed to visits to developing and economically poor countries, the outcry against mass tourism is ironic, considering the comparatively small number of tourists who visit Africa, South East Asia or Latin America, or even underdeveloped regions in Europe. In 2009, international tourist arrivals reached 880 million (Europe: 459.7; Asia and the Pacific: 181.2; the Americas: 140.7 with North America topping 92.1; Africa: 45.6; and the Middle East: 52.9). International tourism generated US$ 852 billion (€611 billion) in export earnings (Europe: 413; Asia and the Pacific: 203.7; Americas: 165.2, of which 118.9 goes to the USA; Africa: 28.9; and the Middle East: 41.2) (UNWTO, 2010). In 2020 the regions that will be receiving the lowest number of tourists are in developing countries. Why then should we warn people against visiting these places that are in desperate need of tourist flows, new dollars, investment and development?

Graburn (1989, p. 35) believes that mass tourists 'are likely to have the greatest impact on the culture and environment of the host peoples both by virtue of their greater numbers and by their demands for extensions of their home environments for which they are willing to pay handsomely'. Macleod (2004), however, argues that these tourists 'do not mix with local people and, therefore, are less likely to have deep cultural influence on them than the 'alternatives' who, although smaller in number, do actually interact with the host community at a more personal level' (p. 221).

Tourism is not only about business and development. It is also about discovery. Tourism can bring cultures together to benefit from each other. There are many studies of tourism encounters, cross-cultural behaviour and understanding in the tourism literature.

More recently, a revival of the tourism and peace proposition has been making progress in academia, politics and policy. Yet tourists are advised not to get too close to endogenous populations to safeguard local cultures and environments against culture contamination.

However, can the tourist ignore cultural diversity? How can we suppress the desire to visit other cultures and mingle with the locals, a motivation that is so much appreciated by the proponents of alternative tourism, and yet remain distant? How can we live in a rolling transparent bubble without guilt feelings, even when contact is minimal? Is tourism to blame for culture fluidity, a process which is praised by a lot of people?

It may be argued that the role of tourism in shaping, re-shaping and negotiating between cultures is negligible, considering that even remote parts of the world have access to television, the Internet or mobile phones. Where communication has no borders, one must seriously question the role of tourism – in both mass and alternative forms – and its impacts on shaping cultures for better or worse. There is one thing to acknowledge here: tourism does at least have the potential to bring people closer to the authentic, when the authentic is desired.

Butcher asks: 'But what is deemed to be so wrong with package [mass] tourism?' The development of the mass tourism

---

Box 1.1. Famous quotes depicting controversies in tourism (different sources).

'Traveling makes a man wiser, but less happy.' Thomas Jefferson

'The fool wanders, a wise man travels.' Thomas Fuller

'Your true traveler finds boredom rather agreeable than painful. It is the symbol of his liberty – his excessive freedom. He accepts his boredom, when it comes, not merely philosophically, but almost with pleasure.' Aldous Huxley

'Though there are some disagreeable things in Venice there is nothing so disagreeable as the visitors.' Henry James

'A man who leaves home to mend himself and others is a philosopher; but he who goes from country to country, guided by the blind impulse of curiosity, is a vagabond.' Oliver Goldsmith

'I am not much an advocate for traveling, and I observe that men run away to other countries because they are not good in their own, and run back to their own because they pass for nothing in the new places. For the most part, only the light characters travel. Who are you that have no task to keep you at home?' Ralph Waldo Emerson

'The traveler sees what he sees, the tourist sees what he has come to see.' Gilbert Keith Chesterton

'In travelling a man must carry knowledge with him, if he would bring home knowledge.' Samuel Johnson

'Life on board a pleasure steamer violates every moral and physical condition of healthy life except fresh air. It is a guzzling, lounging, gambling, dog's life. The only alternative to excitement is irritability.' George Bernard Shaw

'Tourism is like fire. You can cook your dinner on it; or it can burn your house down.' Anonymous

'Tourism is like being a little bit pregnant. It's fun getting there – but it poses increasing problems as the child grows and threatens to take over the parent.' Richard Butler

'Tourism is like a secularised or unconscious form of pilgrimage, and the attitude of the pilgrim, the 'intention to learn', should be consciously reinscribed into tourism.' Rupert Sheldrake

'Tourism is like seasoning on food. Some can make an improvement; a little more can make it perfect. A lot ruins it and makes a good thing disgusting.' Anonymous

'If you are motivated by a relief that tourism is prone to damage cultures and environments, wouldn't you be better off at home?' Jim Butcher

'Those who do travel are advised to 'travel well' –to seek out and revere the culture of your hosts ... but not to get too close, for fear of offending cultural sensibilities.' Jim Butcher

'Tourism is like a bridge. It connects our countries and it can connect people to each other.' Karen Chen

industry has brought needed development to many poor regions and poor countries. However, this positive aspect of mass tourism has been overshadowed by the negative aspects, which are too often exaggerated. In his book, he identifies many interesting facets of the exaggeration and the ironies that follow it.

Alternative Tourism

One response to these ethical tensions has been the recognition of the need for sustainable tourism, generally defined as management to ensure that its benefits can be enjoyed by consumers without adverse effects on the environment that maintains and nurtures the industry, and also that it can be enjoyed by future generations (Hawkes and Williams, 1993; Frank and Bowerman, 1994; WTO, 2001). Under the umbrella of sustainability, several forms of tourism have emerged as alternatives with the objective to minimize the negative impacts of tourism and optimize the positive ones. Liu (2003), however, suggests that so-called sustainable forms of tourism are not fulfilling their promise to transform the way in which modern conventional tourism is conducted, that they are mainly promoted for marketing rather than conservation purposes, and are 'at best a micro solution to what is essentially a macro problem' (Liu, 2003, p. 471). It is noted that even relatively small-scale niche types of tourism can have serious negative impacts (Smith and Duffy, 2003, p. 135).

> Ecotourism, sustainable tourism, green tourism, alternative tourism and most recently community tourism [and ethical tourism] have been presented as morally superior alternatives to package holidays. The package holiday revolution, celebrated by some, is increasingly condemned as destructive by a host of campaigns, academics and commentators.
>
> Butcher (2002, p.1)

Refuting the claim that mass tourism (e.g. Graburn, 1989; Smith, 1989) has a greater impact on the local community,

Mcleod (2004) argues that, despite their smaller numbers, alternative tourists such as backpackers can have a greater influence on a local community than mass package tourism, because of 'the propensity for alternative tourists to mix more with the locals, communicate with them, meet them on an equal level (not customer servant), spend money on services provided by local people (not owned by big business) and enter into emotional relationships with them' (Macleod, 2004, p. 221). This contrasts directly with the views of Smith (1989) and Graburn (1989) who attribute the greatest impact to mass tourists because of their numbers, economic clout and tendency to expect Western amenities.

The Irony of the Ironies

Criticizing the moralization of tourism and discussing the ironies surrounding this moralization is one thing; but the irony of these ironies is that this moralization dwells in books and journals and hardly ever reaches the target. So, the moralization of tourism and its critique is thus much ado about nothing. The majority of consumers have absolutely no knowledge about this moralization, ethical tourism or ethics in tourism. This tendency is also apparent in tourism education programmes. Some may even argue that this deficit is in itself immoral, knowing the effects that the negative impacts of tourism have on communities.

Consumers' knowledge about ethics in tourism

Most of the time, when we talk about the negative impacts of tourism, the term 'sustainability' emerges. According to a survey by TUI (2010) of 3887 respondents from eight countries, over one-half indicated their familiarity with the term sustainability. However, only a small number (20%) were familiar with the concept of sustainable holidays. Of these only a small portion

(26%) had actually taken such a holiday trip in the past four years. The strongest barriers to booking such holidays are perceived price and perceived lack of availability. The most important sustainability issues for holiday consumers were pollution, biodiversity and nature protection, climate change and carbon emissions. Of the total sample about one-half (45%) were interested in sustainability. Since sustainability is a concept hard to define, even among academics and practitioners, the statistics presented here, although somewhat revealing, remain inconclusive.

Ethics is as old as the history of humankind and it is certain that a concern with ethics in tourism is older than the concept of tourism sustainability, so one might expect the term tourism ethics to be more familiar to consumers. We randomly asked a sample of 200 people from four countries whether they were familiar with ethics in tourism, and the result was not surprising; only a small percentage answered in the affirmative (Table 1.1).

The question which arises is: is it possible for people to support, adopt and embrace sustainable tourism practices if they are not ethically aware? To be ethical in their tourism action, people need to be reminded again and again about the moral principles by which our lives should be guided.

Consumers' predispositions on ethical tourism

The general criteria for selecting a holiday seem to count for more than the ethics-oriented criteria (TUI, 2010). Our survey also supports the literature. The traditional criteria for selecting a holiday – price, weather, quality of accommodation and service – ranked greater in importance than the criteria directly related to ethical issues, such as a trip that presents less damage to the environment, booking with a company that has ethical policies, or holidays that provide opportunities to interact with local consumers.

Academic coverage of ethics in tourism

Lynn (2009) performed a content analysis on the tourism and hospitality literature for the period 1990–2008, and found that the results, for academic tourism journals in particular, are meagre compared to the attention that tourism ethics is given among academics (Table 1.2). For example, the Journal of Vacation Marketing features only two articles about tourism ethics, one in 2002 and the other in 2003. Tourism Geographies contains only one in 2008. Tourism Management includes only one in 1995. The Journal of Travel Research contains only three articles (1993, 1995, 1998). Tourism and Hospitality Research published only one in 2005. Tourism Analysis includes only one (2003). Annals of Tourism Research contained six articles, one appearing in each of these years: 1993, 1995, 1999, 2003, 2005 and 2008. Tourism Recreation Research published seven tourism ethics articles (2003, 2004, 2005, 2005, 2008, 2008 and 2008).

Furthermore, even with regards to research aspects, Tribe (2008), for example, found that critical tourism is still marginal in terms of the whole effort of tourism research. Key distinguishing feature of critical theory are its interest in: critical enlightenment; rejection of economic determinism; critical emancipation; critique of technical rationality; desire; ideology; hegemony; discursive power; culture, power and domination;

Table 1.1. Familiarity with ethics in tourism.

Are you familiar with ethics in tourism?	Swiss (N=200)	Dutch (N=200)	Lithuanian (N=200)	German (N=200)
Per cent 'No'	81.0	95.0	95.0	86.0

Table 1.2. A content analysis of tourism ethics articles in academic journals. (From Lynn, 2009).

Year	Total number of articles in the 12 ethics-related topics	Total number of articles categorized as 'tourism ethics'
1990	13	[a]
1991	14	
1992	22	
1993	11	
1994	13	
1995	5	
1996	8	
1997	7	
1998	8	
1999	13	
2000	8	0
2001	10	0
2002	32	5
2003	38	8
2004	53	9
2005	46	8
2006	32	4
2007	55	4
2008	83	10

[a]For the period 1990–1999 only six articles focused on tourism ethics. No detailed data available.

cultural pedagogy; and general domain of critical theory. These features of critical theory help us to be more critical in tourism, in that 'critical theory deliberately seeks to engage with normative questions of values and desired ends' (p. 247); ends towards the moralization of tourism.

Ethics in tourism programmes

Ring, Dickinger and Wöber (2009) performed a content analysis of 64 bachelor degree programmes taught in English, and their results show that there are discrepancies between existing programmes and what academics and industry professionals perceive as being important. Whereas 72% of the programmes focus predominantly on management, only 9% focus on environmental or nature tourism, ecotourism, or a related area. 'In addition, no tourism marketing program refers to sustainability. This is surprising since sustainability has become an increasingly

popular topic and is regarded as one of the most sensitive issues for the present and the future in various sectors' (p.110). Investigating what components of tourism programmes are most favoured by industry players and academics, the authors found ethics was given a very low priority. In support of the literature (e.g. Tribe, 2001, 2002; Inui *et al.*, 2006; Lynn, 2007) the authors conclude: 'tourism curricula should also offer students the chance to emerge as "future-shapers" equipped for the present but also able and willing to make a difference in the future' (p. 118). Perhaps it is no wonder that a gap exists between what the students think is ethical and what is really ethical (Lynn *et al.*, 2007). Lynn and colleagues bluntly put it:

> The literature states again and again that ethics must be taught in university hospitality programs. The inconsistent ethics instruction currently found in most hospitality programs does not adequately prepare students for the ethical demands of today's business environment. This study suggests that maturation alone will not make students ethically aware. They must be taught, and the literature supports an integrated case study approach. (p. 10).

Tribe (2001) explains that for worthwhile education, reflective philosophical method in hospitality and tourism curriculum design becomes necessary. In his vision for a worthwhile education he supports that a 'curriculum for tourism needs to develop a tourism society not just as society for business but one of society for all its Stakeholders' (p. 447).

Codes of conduct and consumers

Concerns about the negative impacts of tourism have led to the development of codes of ethics or conduct, aimed at enhancing the behaviour of consumers and providers of tourism experiences. It is suggested that they have become necessary in view of the extent and influence of tourism, the need to sustain the resources on which it depends, the sociocultural costs

---

Box 1.2. The Global Code of Ethics for Tourism.

The Global Code of Ethics for Tourism was adopted on 1 October 1999 at the General Assembly of the World Tourism Organization (WTO). The Code of Ethics is a set of basic principles whose purpose is to guide tourism development and to serve as a frame of reference for the different stakeholders in the tourism sector, with the objective of minimizing the negative impact of tourism on the environment and on cultural heritage while maximizing the benefits of tourism in promoting sustainable development. The Code of Ethics is not a legally binding instrument and therefore its acceptance is voluntary (WTO July 25, 2005).

---

involved and the service orientation of the industry. It is also submitted that, despite the disparate nature of tourism, a code of ethics may contribute to overall professionalism among those employed in the industry.

Malloy and Fennell (1998), in their analysis of tourism codes of ethics, distinguish between those that are deontological (i.e. prescribing behaviour according to a set of rules or procedures) and those that are teleological (i.e. aiming for the best outcomes and incorporating a rationale for particular actions). Codes of ethics have been criticized as platitudinous and developed for public relations purposes, too general to be applied in specific situations, and impossible to enforce. Despite WTO's call for the implementation of the principles of the Global Code of Ethics for Tourism by public and private stakeholders in tourism development and the monitoring of these principles and their effective application (WTO, 2001; see Box 1.2.), the dissemination of the code appeared to be minimal. For example, only 30% (29 countries) of the 94 countries who answered the WTO questionnaire about the implementation of the code to stakeholders indicated that they had disseminated the codes' material to tourists, a low figure compared to that of other stakeholders (WTO, 2005). The pattern distribution is shown in Fig. 1.1).

It seems rather doubtful that the moralization of tourism has had an impact on consumer behaviour. There is a need for research into the level of abidance and the effectiveness of code implementation. There is also a need for more explanatory information on the reasons for inclusion of code statements, and to ensure coordination among stakeholders in each destination.

The Morality of Tourism

While *The Moralisation of Tourism* is an expansive criticism of alternative tourism in all its forms and contradictions, the author of the book asserts that it 'is not a critique of morality of tourism, but of the *moralisation of tourism*' (Butcher, 2002, p. 3). The moralization of tourism as elaborated by Butcher concerns the act of moralizing about tourism, the act of dehumanizing mass tourism, and the act of exaggerating the moral values of alternative types of tourism. But what is morality of tourism? What is morality without moralization – a religion without scriptures?

Morality, originating from the Latin *moralitas* (manner, character, proper behaviour) is concerned with the distinction between good and evil or right and wrong; in tourism it concerns the distinction between right and wrong tourism actions. The morality of tourism may be said to be ingrained in the ten articles of the Global Code of Ethics for Tourism (see Box 1.3.).

Many of the problems faced by the tourism industry, including destruction of the environment, pollution, depletion of natural resources, economic imperialism, sexual exploitation (Payne and Dimanche, 1996; Holden, 2003) and working conditions of employees (Tearfund, 2002) have an ethical element and pose challenges to tourism stakeholders (WTO, 1999; Contour Sunday, 2003). The articles of the Code summarize ethics in tourism and these are reflected in what is now known as Responsible Travel.

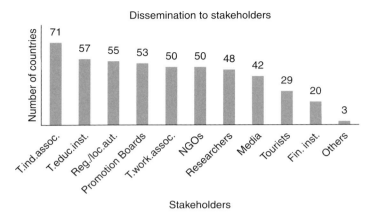

Fig. 1.1. Dissemination of the Global Code of Ethics for Tourism. According to the replies received, national tourism administrations (NTAs) have predominantly distributed the Global Code of Ethics for Tourism to tourism industry associations (mentioned in 71 cases). The dissemination of the Code was also carried out among tourism education institutes (in 57 cases); regional or local tourism authorities (in 55 cases); tourism promotion boards (in 53 cases); tourism workers' unions and non-governmental organizations (each category was mentioned in 50 cases); researchers/academics (in 48 cases); the media (in 42 cases); tourists and visitors (in 29 cases); and, lastly, financing institutions (only mentioned in 20 cases).

Box 1.3. Articles of the Global Code of Ethics for Tourism. (From WTO, 1999).

Tourism's contribution to mutual understanding and respect between peoples and societies;
Tourism as a vehicle for individual and collective fulfilment;
Tourism, a factor of sustainable development;
Tourism, a user of the cultural heritage of mankind and a contributor to its enhancement;
Tourism, a beneficial activity for host countries and communities;
Obligations of stakeholders in tourism development;
Right to tourism;
Liberty of tourist movements;
Rights of the workers and entrepreneurs in the tourism industry;
Implementation of the principles of the Global Code of Ethics for Tourism.

Responsible Travel (www.responsibletravel. com) offers tips to travellers before, during and after holiday trips, valuable enough to guide the most novice or tourism-ethics-conscious ones and detailed enough to irritate the least sensitive among the critiques of the moralization of tourism.

Tourism Education

Moral guidelines can be made operational in tourism education. Tribe (2002) calls for an ethical tourism education, where 'the discipline of philosophy and particularly its branches of ethics and aesthetics (…) must be included in the curriculum to underpin reflection for and in ethical tourism' (p. 320). What value do park, recreation, leisure and tourism associations, programmes and curricula have? Like many other scholars, Dustin and Goodale (1999) assert that leisure education is drifting away from its philosophical moorings. We speak of recreation business and leisure industry; we also speak of education as a business. 'Degrees and certificates have become commodities one buys because, like a car, they can get you somewhere and, like a suit, they make you presentable' (p. 483). Leisure and tourism education is about career orientation rather than education for citizenship and life: 'Broad and highly integrative thinking is sacrificed for narrow and highly technical thinking, and curricular offerings are shaped by market forces more so than by any particular quest for truth or understanding' (p. 483).

Education for tourism...

In the natural order men are all equal and their common calling is that of manhood, so that well-educated man cannot fail to do well in that calling and those related to it. It matters little to me whether my pupil is intended for the army, the church, [tourism] or the law. Before his parents chose a calling for him nature called him to be a man. Life is a trade I would teach him. When he leaves me, I grant you, he will be neither a magistrate, a soldier, nor a priest; he will be a man.

J.J. Rousseau (Book 1, 15).

To Rousseau, Emile [or every human] is born free. Yet, this freedom is challenged at the very moment the child was born. Human beings have the potential to become free again through education. The world environment has changed and so has tourism, and so too must the principles on which tourism is based. Tourists must become well-educated tourists, and through tourism education they have another opportunity to be *men*. What then is tourism education for?

Discussing tourism in the Grand Tours period as an ideal tends to ignore the continuous flow of development and new environments. In the beginning tourism was free from today's moralization. It was benign by the very nature of its numbers and impacts. Today, tourism is free no more. Tourism, in whatever form, has impacts on people and their environments, but it also has the power, not only to minimize those undesirable impacts, but to contribute to freedom, the freedom to become what we are supposed to be: humans – with the ability to use our left brain and to distance ourselves from other primates, to live the genuinely good life (Bregha, 1991). According to Bregha, acquiring the ability to experience leisure [in tourism] requires: (a) knowledge of what is available or permissible; (b) the ability to discriminate between what is good and what is wrong; and (c) the ability to acknowledge the various options and their consequences. 'Indeed were such knowledge absent, then every choice would of necessity be a blind one (...) This leisure is linked to knowledge and to wisdom, both of which form part of the ability to choose with intelligence and responsibility. Furthermore, this analysis suggests the need for education for leisure [and tourism]' (p. 48).

Bregha further argues that throughout history we have increasingly accepted education for work. History attests to human achievements in this domain of life, but 'Can humanity be left to its own devices in regard to leisure [and tourism] if we wish to occupy our leisure [and tourism] with intelligence and responsibility?' (p. 49).

In most instances, it is created needs that influence our ability to decide what we want to do or become. Our ability to be free is manipulated by 'the thousand and one mirrors used by politicians, salesmen and propagandists of all hues to disorient us' (Bregha, 1991, p. 49). It may be that if people genuinely knew what they wanted they would not want most of what they have. In this sense, in the absence of education, people's choices are limited, irrational, if not no choices at all. The exercise of freedom and hence of leisure may then be 'masked in the nurture of a false consciousness in which freedom to become is surrendered to marketplace consumption' (Kelly, 1987, p. 229).

Leisure education is not about learning new tricks; neither is it about adding 'another brick in the wall'. Rather, it is about drawing out of people the best they already have. Smith (1999), when discussing the difference between human and animals maintains: 'These are unpleasant words, but we must face the truth, even if unpleasant, if we are to progress as human beings. The truth is: members of Homo sapiens often engage in decidedly sub-human acts' (p. 78).

Therefore if a society holds the philosophy that the state exists to enable people to become as human as they can be, to emphasize and nurture good and enduring human values, then those social institutions that provide leisure services should take a careful look at their programs. Public recreation agencies, park departments, athletic leagues, youth groups, churches and schools (including universities) have the responsibility to evaluate their offerings in term of their location on the sub-human to human spectrum (pp. 78–79).

Turning to Greece and particularly the writings of Aristotle for discourse on leisure and its ideals, we find that leisure was seen as a basis for culture. Leisure provided a way of personal growth and social attainment of the 'good life' (Arnold, 1999, p. 12). Leisure for the Greeks centred on not only freedom from labour but also freedom from mundane *unleisure* activities; the freedom to reach the state of *arete* or virtue. 'Arete… symbolized the ideal for which all citizens must strive: attainment of the highest good of which humans were capable. Leisure, therefore was 'opportunity' for realization of that ideal'. This emphasizes the importance of educating people who will be able to make a difference in the future rather than just function in the current situation. 'In our rapidly evolving world, leisure is as much about the search for meaning as it is the search for pleasure' (Godbey, 1999, p. vii).

…Education for freedom

The conceptions of leisure as free time, idleness or enjoyment are prevalent in our definitions of leisure. Leisure is, however, also an opportunity for self-fulfilment or schooling in noble values (Cooper, 1999). 'When we do our best work we lift people up and out of their self-absorption to reveal the beauty, complexity, and mystery of the larger world (…) What better role for recreation, park and leisure studies to play as we voyage into the new millennium?' (Dustin and Goodale, 1999, p. 485).

Travel is need related. Studies of the different motivational factors, tourist typologies and markets attest to this. Generally, when we criticize tourism there is a tendency to focus more on the needs of the local community and less on the needs of the tourists themselves.

Tourism has been explained as:

> Novelty-seeking behavior, as play, as the seeking of the authentic, as relations among strangers, as a form of imperialism, as pleasure-seeking (sometimes called the four S theory of tourism – sun, sand, surf, and sex). It also may be motivated by the desire for anonymity or to fulfil fantasies. A study by Crompton (1981) of motivations for pleasure vacation found that such motivations included: escape from a mundane environment, exploration and evaluation of self, relaxation, prestige, regression, enhancement of kinship relations, social interaction, cultural motives, novelty, and certainly, many tourist experiences are undertaken due to a variety of motives.
>
> Godbey (1994, p. 209)

Are all these motives stimulated by needs or simply strong desires? A 'need is born out of a physical, psychological, emotional, spiritual, or social deficiency an individual is currently experiencing' (DeGraaf *et al.*, 1999, p. 76–78). Which ones are genuine needs and which are artificial needs created by clever marketing and promotion? DeGraaf and colleagues submit that many of us have difficulties in differentiating between needs and desires/wants. The latter are perceived as being needed but do 'not necessarily address the physical, psychological, emotional, spiritual, or social needs of a human being' (p. 78). Those who believe that most of the motives cited above address certain normative human needs may reject the idea of relinquishing proximate needs in order to guarantee the needs of others perceived as remote. Proximate needs may be defined as those needs that directly relate to personal benefits of the tourist, while remote needs may refer to benefits accruing to the host community. In a world in metamorphosis (Neulinger, 1990), to what extent is the natural selfishness of the individual stronger than social responsibility?

Viewing the changes taking place in our environment as a metamorphosis of the environment only, is taking us, human beings, out of the picture. It places us, once again, above and beyond nature. Reluctantly acknowledging a changing world, but not a changing human being, is perhaps the latest and hopefully last stand in this effort. We still cannot face the idea of being a slightly advanced species of apes desperately in need of progressing at least one step further.

Neulinger (1990, p. 11)

In the *Social Contract*, Rousseau discusses two types of freedom: personal freedom and social freedom. Is the latter too idealistic to achieve in tourism, despite the environmental metamorphoses? Is not the will to sustain humanity natural – also in tourism? Freedom in tourism is a means not an end. Tourism is also 'a search for meaning – a search to try and make sense of the entire world. While this idea seems to have some merit, it may be argued that many tourists are not interested in such broad objectives. They may, for instance, seek merely to find a warm beach or a good time in a new location' (Godbey, 1994, p. 209). What is amoral or immoral about fulfilling one's proximate needs (or having pleasure without happiness)? Cooper (1999, p. 3) asks: 'is the freedom of leisure [or tourism] the absence of causal determinism, as an undeterminist philosopher might suggest? Or is it the freedom to exercise one's faculties as one wants, without care for the instrumental values of doing so?'

People are consumers, education is a business, global warming is a reality, yet we do not only ignore the moralization of tourism, we are irritated by it. The shift from Fordist to post-Fordist society has marked progress from freedom to consume to the realization that consumer culture involves delusions relating to fulfilment and happiness (Rojek, 1999: 92). The social and moral categories of tourism constructed under Fordism (and 19th century Grand Tours) cease to have purchase in post-Fordist conditions. Coalter (1999) suggests that 'the concentration on individual satis-

factions and benefits present us with *leisure without society,* and recent debates identify a need for broader analyses based on a conception *of leisure in society'* (p. 510).

Education for tourism is education for freedom. To J.J. Rousseau freedom is the goal of education. To Aristotle the ultimate goal of life is happiness and true happiness comes only when we are free. Education is about becoming free to achieve the ultimate goal of happiness. 'Through the work we do we can equip people with the necessary education to make a difference in day-to-day lives' (Dustin and Goodale, 1999, p. 485).

If Tourism is to Matter

It is maintained that with the growth of tourism arrivals there is growing demand on the destination's infrastructure. The growth of infrastructure significantly alters the natural landscape and ecosystem, and puts much pressure on natural resources such as water and land. Coral reefs and other sensitive marine habitats are damaged by the sewage and wastes from tourist resorts. Recreational activities such as boating, diving, snorkelling and fishing have substantially damaged coral reefs in many parts of the world. Marine animals are disturbed by people approaching them closely. The examples of the negative impacts on destinations are substantial. On the other hand, some have argued that, in fact, mass tourism is less damaging to the natural environment and the host culture than alternative tourism. Mass tourists mostly engage in activities that keep them inside the bubble of packaged holiday tours. The back stage of local lives remains, if not inaccessible, of low or no interest to mass tourists. However, considering the large number of tourists, it is the physical mass that becomes a problem, because of the strains put on the community's infrastructure. Should people then refrain from travelling? If the mass is the problem, then small-scale tourism might offer several alternatives. Does it?

To many people who are inspired by Aristotle (and to those who will be), leisure is a useless notion if it is defined only in terms of free time, a time where one does what one wants to do without the exercise of virtue. Tourism, for this matter, despite the concerns of commentators who are against the moralization of tourism, can better meet its role as a noble human activity if it incorporates recognition of moral principles in its practices. To Goodale (1991), 'Well being and well doing are parts of a whole; complementary and synergistic' (p. 94). If tourism is to matter, that is, if we consider tourism as an activity that *should* help us develop as human being towards the ideal of who we ought to be/come, we need to move tourism from tourism in recreation to tourism in leisure. If tourism is to matter 'the happiness of all will be the goal of each, and the aspirations of each will be the concern of all' (Neulinger, 1990, p. 51). If tourism is to matter, then tourism should become a matter of serious fun. In its existential and social predicament (like leisure) tourism is a context and activity for being and becoming, for the self and society (Kelly, 1987).

Concluding Remarks

While some have argued against the ethical deficit in our lives and in our tourism action, others have criticized the moralization of tourism, and a few others have debunked the ethical claims of existing niche types of tourism. Ethics refers to standards of right and wrong that prescribe what humans ought to do, with the purpose to refrain from wrong actions. Doing what feels good in tourism is not necessarily right. Despite this consciousness, the reality of the actions of the tourist seems less promising. Perhaps, to some, this reality is closer to that of the vagabond: that who is struggling to lead *the good life* both outside and in tourism (Box 1.4).

At the heart of ethics in tourism is a concern about our environment and future generations. The question becomes not whether people are ethical in their tourism action, and subsequently whether our tourism freedom is contained. Rather, the question is about how to build character in and through tourism to bring freedom to our lives.

Box 1.4. Poem of a vagabond.

The vagabond
We like to play golf, we like to fly, we like to climb mountains, we like to swim in lakes and lie on sandy beaches, we like to take pictures of animals and people,
We are tired, we like to do things in summer, fall, spring and winter;
We like change, we like our comfort, we have made progress,
Transgressing into regression, we want to be closer to that which we want to become,
Humans... we want pleasure,
Pleasure in goodness, we want leisure, leisure in our lives before we rest,
Travellers in life we are, and happy is the traveller who is also a tourist
Lucky with this privilege he is another time enlightened in understanding the mystery of existence
But unhappy is the tourist who unlistens to the voices of nature when it is happy and when it is hurting
What would become of Life if life is a creation without purpose, a beginning without an end, empty when it starts and empty when it ends,
Freedom is the end. Relaxation, finally,
Hellas, only a traveller I still am: a vagabond who in tourism remains free,
Vagabonding, waiting for Godot..., asking: Freedom, is it too much to ask for, if it is not asking at all,
Free,
A free vagabond I want to be,
If not what needs be for a vagabond to remain free if he is not free at all?

References

Aristotle. Nicomachean Ethics, Book 1. Translated by Ross, W.D. Available at: http://www.constitution.org/ari/ethic_00.htm (accessed 15 October 2011).

Arnold, S. (1991) The dilemma of meaning. In: Goodale, T. and Witt, P.A. (eds) *Recreation and Leisure: Issues in an Era of Change*. Venture Publishing, State College, Pennsylvania, pp. 47–54.

Bregha, F.J. (1991) Leisure and freedom re-examined. In: Goodale, T. and Witt, P.A. (eds) *Recreation and Leisure: Issues in an Era of Change*. Venture Publishing, State College, Pennsylvania, pp. 47–54.

Butcher, J. (2002) *The Moralisation of Tourism: Sun, Sand… and Saving the World?* Routledge, New York.

Butler, R.W. (1998) Sustainable tourism: looking backwards in order to progress? In: Hall, C. M. and Lew, A.A. (eds) *Sustainable Tourism: A Geographical Perspective*. Addison-East Longman, Harlow, UK, pp. 25–34.

Coalter, F. (1999) Leisure sciences and leisure studies: the challenge of meaning. In: Jackson, E.L. and Burton, T.L. (eds) *Leisure Studies: Prospects for the Twenty First Century*. Venture Publishing, State College, Pennsylvania, pp. 507–522.

Cogswell, D. (2003) AST adds ethics code to tour operator program. *Travel Weekly* 62, 16.

Cooper, W. (1999) Some philosophical aspects of leisure theory. In: Jackson, E.L. and Burton, T.L. (eds) *Leisure Studies: Prospects for the Twenty-first Century*. Venture Publishing, State College, Pennsylvania, pp. 3–16.

DeGraaf, D.G. and Jordan, D.J. (1999) *Programming for Parks, Recreation, and Leisure Services: A Servant Leadership Approach*. Venture Publishing, State College, Pennsylvania.

Dustin, D.L. and Goodale, T. (1999) Reflections on recreation, park and leisure studies. In: Jackson, E.L. and Burton, T.L. (eds) *Leisure Studies: Prospects for the Twenty-first Century*. Venture Publishing, State College, Pennsylvania, pp. 477–486.

Frank P. and Bowerman, J. (1994) Can ecotourism save the planet? *Conde Nast* (December), 134–137.

Godbey, G. (1999) *Leisure in Your Life: An Exploration*. Venture Publishing, State College, Pennsylvania.

Goodale, T.L. (1991) Is there enough time? In: Goodale, T. and Witt, P.A. (eds) *Recreation and Leisure: Issues in an Era of Change*. Venture Publishing, State College, Pennsylvania, pp. 33–46.

Goodale, T. and Witt, P.A. (1991) *Recreation and Leisure: Issues in an Era of Change*. Venture Publishing, State College, Pennsylvania.

Goodwin, H. and Francis, J. (2003) Ethical and responsible tourism: consumer trends in the UK. *Journal of Vacation Marketing* 9, 217–284.

Graburn, N.H.H. (1989) Tourism: the sacred journey. In: Smith, V. (ed.) *Hosts and Guests: The Anthropology of Tourism*. University of Pennsylvania Press, Philadelphia, Pennsylvania, pp. 17–32.

Hawkes, S. and Williams, P. (1993) *The Greening of Tourism - From Principles to Practice, GLOBE'92 Tourism Stream: Case Book of Best Practice in Sustainable Tourism*. Sustainable Tourism, Industry, Science and Technology, Canada and the Centre of Tourism Policy and Research, Simon Fraser University, Burnaby, British Columbia.

Holden, A. (2003) *Environment and Tourism*. Routledge, New York.

Inui, Y., Wheeler, D. and Lankford, S. (2006) Rethinking tourism education: what should schools teach? *Journal of Hospitality, Leisure, Sport and Tourism Education* 5, 25–35.

Iso-Ahola, S.E. (1999) Motivational foundations of leisure. In: Jackson, E.L. and Burton, T.L. (eds) *Leisure Studies: Prospects for the Twenty-first Century*. Venture Publishing, State College, Pennsylvania, pp. 35–52.

Josephides, N. (2002) Ethics don't interest clients. *Travel Trade Gazette UK & Ireland* (2499), 33.

Kelly, J. R. (1987) *Freedom to Be: A New Sociology of Leisure*. Macmillan Publishing Company, New York.

King, J. (2002) Destination marketing organizations – connecting the experience rather than promoting the place. *Journal of Vacation Marketing* 8, 105–108.

Krippendorf, J. (1987) *The Holiday Makers*. Butterworth-Heinemann, Oxford, UK.

Liu, Z. (2003) Sustainable tourism development: a critique. *Journal of Sustainable Tourism* 11, 459–475.

Lynn, C. (2009) Review of hospitality ethics research in 2008. Available at: http://www2.nau.edu/~clj5/Ethics/ (accessed 15 October 2011).

Lynn, C., Howey, R. and Combrik, M.S. (2007) Students' response to ethical dilemmas. Available at: http://www2.nau.edu/~clj5/Ethics/ (accessed 18 May 2011).

Macleod, D.V.L. (2004) *Tourism, Globalisation and Cultural Change: An Island Community Perspective*. Channel View Publications, Bristol, UK.

Malloy, D.C. and Fennell, D.A. (1998) Codes of ethics and tourism: an exploratory content analysis. *Tourism Management* 19, 453–461.

Neulinger, J. (1990) *Eden, After All: A Human Metamorphosis*. Giordano Bruno, Culemborg, The Netherlands.

Payne, D. and Dimanche, F. (1996) Towards a code of conduct for the tourism industry: an ethics model. *Journal of Business Ethics* 15, 997–1007.

Poon, A. (1993) *Tourism, Technology and Competitive Strategies*. CABI Publishing, Wallingford, UK.

Ring, A., Dickinger, A. and Wöber, K. (2009) Designing the ideal program in tourism: expectations from industry and educators. *Journal of Travel Research* 48, 106–121.

Rojek, C. (1999) Deviant leisure: the dark side of free-time activity. In: Jackson, E.L. and Burton, T.L. (eds) *Leisure Studies: Prospects for the Twenty-first Century*. Venture Publishing, State College, Pennsylvania, pp. 81–97.

Rousseau, J.-J. *Emile*. The Echo Library, Teddington, UK.

Sharpley, R. (2000) Tourism and sustainable development: exploring the theoretical divide. *Journal of Sustainable Tourism* 8, 1–19.

Smith, D. and Duffy, M. (2003) *The Ethics of Tourism Development*. Routledge, New York.

Smith, S.L.J. (1999) On the biological basis of pleasure: some implications for leisure policy. In: Goodale, T. and Witt, P.A. (eds) *Recreation and Leisure: Issues in an Era of Change*. Venture Publishing, State College, Pennsylvania, pp. 73–85.

Swarbrooke, J. and Horner, S. (1999) *Consumer Behaviour in Tourism*. Butterworth-Heinemann, Oxford, UK.

Sylvester, C. (1999) The western idea of work and leisure: traditions, transformations and the future. In: Jackson, E.L. and Burton, T.L. (eds) *Leisure Studies: Prospects for the Twenty-first Century*. Venture Publishing, State College, Pennsylvania, pp.17–34.

Tearfund (2000) Tourism – an ethical issue. Available at: http://tilz.tearfund.org/webdocs/Website/Campaigning/Policy%20and%20research/Policy%20-%20Tourism%20Market%20Research%20Report.pdf (accessed 15 October 2011).

Tearfund (2001) Tourism: putting ethics into practice. Available at: http://tilz.tearfund.org/webdocs/Website/Campaigning/Policy%20and%20research/Policy%20-%20Tourism%20putting%20ethics%20into%20practice%20policy%20report.pdf (accessed 15 October 2011).

Tearfund (2002) Worlds apart. Available at: http://www.tearfund.org (accessed 27 November 2007).

Tribe, J. (2001) Research paradigms and the tourism curriculum. *Journal of Travel Research* 31, 442–448.

Tribe, J. (2002) Education for Ethical Tourism Action. *Journal of Sustainable Tourism* 10, 309–324.

Tribe, J. (2008) Tourism: A Critical Business. *Journal of Travel Research* 46, 245–255.

TUI (2010) TUI travel sustainability survey 2010. Available at: http://www.tuitravelplc.com/tui/uploads/qreports/1TUITravelSustainabilitySurvey2010-External.pdf (accessed 15 October 2011).

UNWTO (2010) Tourism highlights, 2010 edition. Available at: http://www.unwto.org/facts/eng/pdf/highlights/UNWTO_Highlights10_en_HR.pdf (accessed 15 October 2011).

Weeden, C. (2002) Ethical tourism: an opportunity for competitive advantage. *Journal of Vacation Marketing* 8, 141–153.

WTO (1999) Global Code of Ethics for Tourism. Available at: http://www.worldtourism.org/code_ethics/pdf/languages/Codigo%20Etico%20Ing.pdf (accessed 12 April 2006).

WTO (2001) The concept of sustainable tourism. Available at: http://www.world-tourism.org/sustainable/concepts.htm (accessed 25 February 2009).

WTO (2005) Activities of the World Committee on Tourism Ethics addendum 1: report on the WTO survey on the implementation of the Global Code of Ethics for Tourism. Available at: http://www.worldtourism.org/code_ethics/pdf/A_16_20%20Add1_e.pdf (accessed 25 February 2009).

2 A Common Tourism Policy for the European Union: A Historical Perspective

Sibel Mehter Aykın[1]

[1]*Department of Economics, Faculty of Economics and Administrative Sciences (IIBF), Akdeniz University, Antalya, Turkey*

Introduction

The European Union (EU) encompasses a vast area of both tourist-generating and tourist-receiving countries, and the involvement of EU member states in tourism, as well as their approaches to a common tourism policy at the EU level, varies a great deal. The views on the extent of the EU's intervention in tourism may be categorized into two groups. The first aspires to establish a tourism policy like other policies defined by the founding treaties, such as agriculture, transportation, the environment, and so forth. According to advocates of this opinion, any decision taken in any field at the EU level should somehow have an effect on the tourism industry. However, all decisions and measures are taken regardless of the needs of this industry. Yet, tourism enterprises – mostly small and medium enterprises (SMEs) – play prominent roles in achieving the objectives defined in the founding treaties and need support because of their tenuous business structures. The second group, however, argues that the problems in the tourism industry can be resolved by ensuring more collaboration and coordination among the parties within the existing structures, without introducing new regulations at the EU level. According to supporters of this viewpoint, there are three separate interest groups in the tourism industry that act under different motives; namely suppliers, consumers, and environmental and cultural enthusiasts. The expectations of each interest group are already met separately by the EU's various policies on enterprises, consumers, the environment and culture. The task of the EU should, according to the second group, be limited to ensuring coordination among these separate policies. The success of this approach depends on close collaboration and cooperation based on the principle of voluntarism among all related parties – i.e. representatives of public and private sectors, trade unions, voluntary agencies and so forth at local, regional and national levels. The history of the European tourism policy can be summarized as an impasse between these two opposing views. Nevertheless, the former prevailed as the European tourism policy and was finally put into writing with the Treaty of Lisbon, effective from 1 December 2009.

A great number of studies on the extent of the EU's involvement in tourism and the depth of its tourism policy have been undertaken. Most of these studies argue that the EU must play a proactive role in tourism (Akerhielm, *et al.*, 1990, 2003; Lickorish, 1991; Akerhurst, 1992, 1993; Greenwood, 1993; Davidson, 1998; Church *et al.*, 2000;

Mundt, 2000; Anastasiadou, 2006, 2007, 2008a,b), while the rest worry about centralization, claiming that the existing political framework is effectual and sufficient (Downes, 1997, 2000). Although each study contributed significantly to the literature during its own period, recent developments in the EU's approach to tourism require augmented studies on them.

Two methods are feasible in studies on tourism. The first method involves studying the practices that address tourism directly and reviewing the attempts to establish a common tourism policy in Europe and their results. The second method is to study the fields that influence tourism indirectly, such as consumer protection, public health, the environment, transportation, internal market and competition, and to identify the practices that affect tourism. To limit the scope, this study partially looks at EU policies that have an indirect influence on tourism and mainly lays emphasis on past actions to establish a common tourism policy in Europe. Accordingly, this study discusses approaches to tourism policies of stakeholders with different motives from a historical perspective and outlines the recently established common tourism policy.

Actions Directly Addressing Tourism Before 1990

A privileged activity of the elite in the 19th century, tourism gave birth to a popular global trend after World War II and was influenced by a number of improvements in the workforce, such as enlargement of the welfare state and the acknowledgement of the right to a paid vacation; increased disposable income and the rate of urbanization; and lower transportation costs and popular package tours. In the same period, Europe witnessed accelerated efforts to unite the continent under a single roof – having suffered through two world wars and hoping to prevent a third one. Following the founding of the European Coal and Steel Community by the Treaty of Paris, born out of the vision of 'peace through integration', the European

Economic Community (EEC) was brought into existence. Its aim was to rapidly raise the standard of living in Europe. However, this founding stage was too early to encounter any references to tourism activities in the Treaty of Rome.

In the late 1970s and the early 1980s, on the one hand Europe had achieved huge advances in the tourism industry, while on the other hand was facing serious dangers in terms of environmental pollution. During this period, views were put forward, one after the other, to prove the necessity of a comprehensive policy for sustainable growth in tourism. Accordingly, the European Commission (hereafter referred to as the Commission) (CEC, 1982) submitted a report outlining proposals for an EEC tourism policy. In turn, the Council of the European Union (hereafter referred to as the Council) (CEU, 1984a) welcomed the report and invited the Commission to launch the necessary actions explained in its resolution. Council Resolution stated that, since the tourism industries of member states differ in structure, the Community should not intervene with issues better resolved at national and regional levels. It should limit its actions in tourism matters to coordination of national policies, and this has been reflected in the EU's long-lasting viewpoint on tourism.

Pursuant to the provisions of the resolution, the Council directive on insurance that had been in force since the 1970s was revised and expanded to include tourist visits (CEU, 1984b). The Council then established an Advisory Committee on Tourism composed of member state representatives (CEU, 1986a). Functioning under the auspices of the Commission, the Advisory Committee was tasked to ensure cooperation and information exchange on tourism among member states. The Committee was responsible for reporting new measures enacted by member states, especially those affecting tourists, to the Commission and for convening at least once a year to discuss the reports. However, for effective involvement in decision making, neither the presence of a tourism unit in the Commission nor the establishment of the Advisory

Committee could provide an adequate basis for an institutional structure in which coordinated and cooperative tasks could be accomplished. In fact, ill-equipped with the necessary resources and power, the tourism unit failed to meet the interests of tourism enterprises (Greenwood, 1993).

As another step forward, the Council (CEC, 1986b) announced its resolution on improving the seasonal and geographical distribution of tourism, and made a recommendation on standardizing hotel information and charged the Commission with inquiring into the necessity of a central hotel classification system at the Community level (CEU, 1986c). Soon, the Council (CEC, 1986d) made another recommendation on hotel fire security, emphasizing that this recommendation should by no means lead to practices that could technically pose obstacles to trade in services. The argument that a harmonizing approach to the tourism industry at the European level would create the greatest threat to national and regional diversity caused tourism policy to fall behind all other Community policies, i.e. consumer protection, the environment, transport, to name a few.

Entered into force in 1987, the Single European Act envisaged comprehensive amendments to the founding treaties, but failed to include any such action on behalf of the tourism industry. In brief, the period from the 1970s to 1990s outwardly saw the predominant argument that the Community's intervention in tourism should be limited to coordination among national tourism policies; as a consequence, any action on behalf of this industry merely consisted of recommendations having no sanctions.

Actions Directly Addressing Tourism in the Decade from 1990 to 2000

First half of the 1990s: years of progress

The 1990s were the years in which significant steps were taken to establish a common tourism policy at the EU level. Throughout the preparatory work for the Maastricht Treaty, which catapulted the EEC beyond a mere economic entity, the Council (CEU, 1989) sought to benefit from tourism's ability to bring together subtly diverse cultures, therefore declaring 1990 as the 'European Year of Tourism'. This notion was to serve two essential purposes: first, to benefit from tourism's creative power in merging people from different cultural backgrounds into a 'People's Europe', thus building an expansive borderless area; and second to further increase tourism's contributions to economic and social policies, especially in terms of regional development and employment. A fund of 5 million European Currency Units (ECUs) was allocated from the Community budget and used for financing several projects involving tourism awards, promotional campaigns, and various pilot projects in cultural, rural and social tourism. However, lacking a coherent tourism strategy and policy, the projects funded throughout the European Year of Tourism were said to have marginal effects (Davidson, 1998). Worse than ever, during audits of the European Court of Auditors (1997), conducted between 1994 and 1996, irregularities were identified in the allocation and spending of the funds in the field of tourism. Resulting in the arrests of a number of people, including senior officers, this incident created a negative impression of tourism activities at the EU level.

With the declaration of the tourism year in Europe, a directive passed by the Council (CEC, 1990) came into focus. Stipulating the creation, pricing, proper announcement and sales of package tours and compensating for possible losses, the directive was considered a significant step in protecting the consumer and regulating the tourism industry. Protecting the health and economic interests of tourism consumers in the European internal market has always been easier and significantly more legitimate than protecting the interests of tourism entrepreneurs, in view of the provisions stipulated by the founding treaties (Maastricht Treaty, Articles 100, 129 and 129a; Amsterdam and Nice Treaties, Articles 94, 152 and 153).

Entered into force on 1 November 1993, the Maastricht Treaty (Treaty on European

Union O.J. C 191 of 29 July 1992) included provisions on the tourism industry for the first time, though inadequate. Nonetheless, the aims were defined in Article 2 of this founding treaty as follows:

> The Community shall have as its task, by establishing a common market and an economic and monetary union and by implementing common policies or activities referred to in Articles 3 and 4, to promote throughout the Community a harmonious, balanced and sustainable development of economic activities, a high level of employment and of social protection, equality between men and women, sustainable and non-inflationary growth, a high degree of competitiveness and convergence of economic performance, a high level of protection and improvement of the quality of the environment, the raising of the standard of living and quality of life, and economic and social cohesion and solidarity among Member States.

Moreover, Article 3(t) of the treaty (Amsterdam and Nice Treaties, Article 3(u)) stated:

> For the purposes set out in Article 2, the activities of the Community shall include, as provided in this Treaty and in accordance with the timetable set out therein: measures in the spheres of energy, civil protection and tourism.

The treaty also specified, in Article 235, the procedure to be followed in taking any action in the tourism industry (Amsterdam and Nice Treaties, Article 308), as follows:

> If action by the Community should prove necessary to attain, in the course of the operation of the common market, one of the objectives of the Community, and this Treaty has not provided the necessary powers, the Council shall, acting unanimously on a proposal from the Commission and after consulting the European Parliament, take the appropriate measures.

Further, with Declaration No. 1 attached to the treaty, it was stipulated that the inclusion of a 'Tourism' section in the founding treaty would be discussed at the forthcoming Intergovernmental Conference,

according to a report to be drawn up by the Commission and submitted to the Council not later than 1996. The Declaration indirectly referred to the principle of subsidiarity as defined in Article 3(b) of the treaty (Amsterdam and Nice Treaties, Article 5), as follows:

> The Community shall act within the limits of the powers conferred upon it by this Treaty and of the objectives assigned to it therein. In areas which do not fall within its exclusive competence, the Community shall take action, in accordance with the principle of subsidiarity, only if and in so far as the objectives of the proposed action cannot be sufficiently achieved by the Member States and can therefore, by reason of the scale or effects of the proposed action, be better achieved by the Community. Any action by the Community shall not go beyond what is necessary to achieve the objectives of this Treaty.

Obviously, Articles 2 and 3 of the Maastricht Treaty did not define tourism as a mere objective but as a means to achieve other objectives of the Community. Unfortunately, the principle of subsidiarity – whose practice was attempted under the unanimity clause – could not guarantee that EU institutions and bodies would competently or even conditionally enhance competitiveness of tourism enterprises. As Anastasiadou (2006) indicated, the principle of subsidiarity has been largely used as a restrictive mechanism on expansionist inclinations rather than supporting tourism undertakings.

Above mentioned provisions in the Maastricht Treaty as well as initiatives launched by ministers of tourism of the member states meeting at Gymnich provide the basis for significant steps towards establishing a European tourism policy. In effect, the first and only Tourism Action Plan (92/421/EEC) was accepted on 13 July 1992. The plan's objectives were defined as outlining a Europe tourism policy, tailoring Community instruments so as to assist the European tourism industry, and ensuring the industry's compliance with new circumstances arising from the creation of an internal market and the economic monetary union. Scheduled to be implemented over a three-year period starting 1 January 1993, and allocated 18 million ECUs, the action plan specified that the principle of *subsidiarity* would be observed and that coordination would be ensured among different Community policies. The action plan resolved in principle to support those initiatives that promote the development of tourism enterprises, especially SMEs; that improve the quality of tourism services; that encourage competition within the EU and enable tourism services to gain a competitive advantage in global markets; that protect natural environments, cultural heritages and local communities in their entirety; that contribute to improved delivery of information and services within the tourism industry; and that assure the safety and security of tourists. It was stipulated that upon expiration the Council could extend the plan upon delivery of a favourable report by the Commission (CEU, 1992).

According to Davidson (1998), the Tourism Action Plan was ineffective in many priority areas. In fact, expecting the plan to ensure anything beyond the provisions of the Maastricht Treaty would be foolhardy. As expected, in instances where EU institutions and bodies were not specifically commissioned, actions to facilitate the tourism industry's gaining a competitive advantage fell short of any legitimacy; in other words, legislatures did not pursue unsanctioned recommendations or resolutions pertaining to the tourism industry or any action plans beyond assistance that had no strategic or political legitimacy.

Green paper on the role of the European Union in tourism

Published in late 1993, a white paper on growth, competitiveness and employment identified strategies to provide 15 million new jobs on the eve of the 21st century (CEC, 1993). The implications of this white paper increasingly pointed to the contributions of tourism to economic growth and employment. In this period, various groups continuously expressed the necessity of a consistent tripartite policy: tourism enterprises, consumers, and natural and cultural heritage. The belief that decisions on tourism, as a horizontal policy area, would be more effective if made at the EU level rather than at the level of member states became widespread over time, leading to new initiatives. Following the Gymnich of tourism ministers held in Athens in 1994, the Commission (1995) published and submitted to all relevant parties a green paper on the role of the Union in the field of tourism to discuss the level of EU actions.

The green paper was composed of three main sections. The first section covered an overall assessment. Following an assessment of European tourism in light of recent worldwide developments, the paper considered both direct and indirect initiatives carried out and instruments used by the EU in tourism. The second section discussed potential advantages to be gained if a tourism policy were established at the EU level. In other words, by looking at the opinions of various groups, this section considered in detail how the tourism industry had contributed to attaining the objectives defined by the founding treaties and what potential roles the EU might undertake in tourism. Accordingly, tourism could be used as an important tool in achieving the basic objectives and targets of the EU: a balanced development of economic activities; non-inflationary and sustainable growth; improvement of economic performance, employment levels and the quality of life; and economic and social harmony among member states. The tourism industry contributed significantly both to the removal of borders among member states and to their transition to the economic monetary union.

Across the EU, tourism played a leading role in social and economic harmony together with the integration of interregional imbalances and the creation of new job opportunities. The presence and competitiveness of tourism was predicated on historical, cultural and environmental values. Therefore, sustainable growth formed the central pillar of tourism. Tourism established mutual tolerance and understanding among people from different backgrounds and created a substantial political influence in managing cultural diversity and in establishing a European awareness and identity. In brief, tourism could be employed as an essential tool in Europe's political and economic reorganization. The tourism industry comprised three separate players: suppliers, consumers, and natural and cultural heritages, all of which represented different interests. Consequently, actions related to the tourism industry could be planned around three poles: first, to improve service quality to protect the interests of consumers; second, to diversify activities to improve competitiveness and profitability; third, to juxtapose the concept of sustainable growth with tourism to protect natural and cultural heritages. Reconciling different interests or rather simultaneously fulfilling these three conditions was only possible if measures were taken at the EU level.

The third and last section of the green paper presented four options in terms of the scope and extent of EU actions and asked all related parties especially member states to deliver their opinions. These options were as follows:

The first option proposed to reduce or eliminate any specific EU actions on tourism. It argued that individual policies were established for each of the three separate interest groups within the tourism industry, however scattered they might be. Tourists were already supported under the consumer protection policy; tourism enterprises, under the enterprise policy; and natural and cultural heritages comprising tourist attractions, under environmental and cultural policies. The required financial tool was provided by structural funds. Under these circumstances, if the requirements of existing policies were met in areas such as consumer protection, the environment, culture, enterprises, competition, the internal market and so forth, tourism would not require additional action at the EU level.

The second option suggested that the current legal framework and level of intervention be retained. This option claimed that existing provisions on tourism in the founding treaties facilitated the implementation of the Tourism Action Plan, which in turn

provided the necessary basis for establishing dialogue, cooperation and coordination both among member states and within the industry. In consequence, a platform was created in which opinions were exchanged, experience and know-how shared, common projects implemented, and common strategies developed. Therefore, preserving the existing legal framework and the involvement level would be sufficient for growth in the tourism industry. The success of the system proposed by this option depended on instituting a strong climate of dialogue and cooperation among the parties, without interfering with each party's competence. Only if such a climate were created could the best practices in the areas of tourism be identified and models built. Moreover, the founding of partnerships would allow the tourism industry to further benefit from EU funds.

The third option recommended strengthening the EU's actions, without making any amendments to the founding treaties. This option maintained that the inadequacies of the tourism action plan could be overcome by integrating tourism into existing policies and by increasing fund allocations to tourism. Any attempts to grow the industry and enable tourism to gain a competitive advantage should be supported within existing rules stipulated by the founding treaties, with tourist security and safety guaranteed and protection of natural and cultural heritages encouraged. The greatest effort should be exerted to protect the interests of industry players in the EU's political practices in other spheres, while various other EU instruments could be used to support tourism. Finally, the existence of a powerful EU initiative to ensure the coordination of different policies and actions at different levels would create a multiplying effect on tourism with contributions from other policy areas.

The fourth option posed a number of questions, implying greater EU intervention to support tourism and aiming to pave the way towards establishing a tourism policy defined by the founding treaties. These questions required answers: Would the EU in its present state act as mediator to ensure mutual consultation, cooperation and coordination among all concerned parties at international, national, regional and local levels? Would the EU take any initiative it considered useful in duly performing this responsibility? Would the EU play a secondary role if European tourism were damaged as a whole or if national policies fell short? Following the logic of sustainable development, is it feasible to build a tourism policy – complementing national policies and based on other EU policies affecting tourism – that would supplement and reconcile the interests of all parties?

Following the publication of this green paper, 160 reports reflecting the opinions of various groups reached the Commission. While some of these reports are summarized in Fig. 2.1, the opinions of EU institutions were as follows: in its opinion, the European Parliament (European Parliament, 1995) expressed its belief in the necessity of including a section on tourism in a revised founding treaty. Similarly, the European Economic and Social Committee (ECOSOC, 1995) presenting its opinion emphasized the necessity of devoting an individual section to tourism in the treaty, believing that the EU must build an active policy in tourism. By contrast, in stating its opinion, the Committee of Regions (COR, 1995) considered it useless to change the EU's current legal framework to include the tourism industry. As Anastasiadou (2008b) specifically points out, as a result of the incompetency matter facing EU institutions, members of the European Parliament and the Commission had lost interest in tourism and were eventually caught up in a vicious circle.

Among professional organizations, the International Tourism Alliance and the International Automobile Federation (AIT & FIA, 1996) wrote a joint report and even went

The First Option: No advocates

The Second Option: Germany, Spain, the Netherlands, the UK, COR (Committee of Regions), IFTO* (International Federation of Tour Operators), FEG* (European Federation of Tourist Guide Associations)

The Third Option: Luxembourg, Austria, Portugal, Finland, IFTO* (International Federation of Tour Operators), EFCO (European Federation of Camping Site Organisations), CEMR (Council of European Municipalities and Regions), FEG*(European Federation of Tourist Guide Associations), ETC (European Travel Commission)

The Fourth Option: Belgium, Greece, Ireland, Italy, European Parliament, ECOSOC (Economic and Social Committee), AIT (Alliance Internationale de Tourisme), FIA (Fédération Internationale de l'Automobile), HOTREC (Hotels, Restaurants and Cafés in Europe), ETAG (European Tourism Action Group), EFCT (European Federation of Conference Towns), IATM (International Association of Tour Managers), FECTO (Federation of European Cities Tourist Offices), EUFED (European Union Federation of Youth Hostel Associations), ICCA (International Congress and Convention Association), ETOA (European Tour Operators Association), IAPCO (International Association of Professional Congress Organizers), EUROGITES (European Federation for Farm and Village Tourism), EUROTER (Tourisme en Europe Rurale), EUROPARKS (European Federation of Leisure Parks), BITS (Bureau International du Tourisme Social), ETLC (European Tourism Liaison Committee), WTTC (World Travel and Tourism Council), EUTO (European Union of Tourist Officers)

Abstention: Denmark, France, Sweden, ACI (Airport Council International), IRU (International Road Transport Union), EUROCHAMBERS (Association of European Chambers of Commerce and Industry)

* IFTO and FEG were in favour of both second and third options.

Fig. 2.1. Positions of the EU Institutions, the member states and the non-governmental organizations.

so far as to propose a draft document as a basis for a tourism section they wanted the founding treaty to include (available at http://europa.eu.int/en/agenda/igc-home/instdoc/industry/ait-en.htm). On the other hand, the Confederation of National Associations of Hotels, Restaurants, Cafés, and Similar Establishments in Europe (HOTREC, no date) stated that the best option would be a revision of Article 130 ('Industry'), if the EU agreed to include provisions on tourism in the treaty.

The preferences of member states regarding the options in the green paper were as follows: while no countries delivered an opinion in favour of the first option, Germany, Spain, the Netherlands and the UK favoured the second; Luxembourg, Austria, Portugal and Finland, the third; Belgium, Greece, Ireland and Italy, the fourth; and Denmark, France and Sweden abstained. Anastasiadou (2006, 2008b) categorizes the approaches of member states within a three-sided conceptual framework: financial, perceptual and pragmatic. The approaches of the member states vary depending on budget concerns, fear of centralization, their Euro-sceptic or Euro-enthusiast attitudes, and a decentralized or centralized administration of tourism.

Neither the green paper nor the Commission's welcomed report on strategic recommendations for the future of European tourism (CEC, 2001b; CEU, 2002) could provide a solid basis for establishing a common tourism policy in Europe. The limited actions carried out at that time were two-fold: the approval of two Council directives (CEU, 1995, 1994), the former on collecting statistical data on tourism and the latter on minimum requirements for timeshare contracts; and the creation of a system of 'tourism satellite accounts' in cooperation with the World Tourism Organization, the United Nations, and the Organisation for Economic Co-operation and Development.

The second half of the 1990s: years of recession

As previously stated, the Tourism Action Plan would last three years, expiring in early 1996, and the Council would decide whether to extend it depending on the Commission's report. Accordingly, the Commission, stating that a loophole existed in tourism and that to include provisions on a common tourism policy in the founding treaties would serve only to ensure consistency and effectiveness of EU actions, submitted a proposal on 'Philoxenia: The 1st Multiannual Programme to Assist European Tourism' to relevant parties for consideration and subsequent decision by the Council (CEC, 1996a). In its opinion, the ECOSOC found the goals of the programme consistent and well-defined but the allocated fund inadequate, but, nevertheless, approved it as a good starting point for Europe, which had yet to come up with a tourism policy (Bulletin EU 9-1996). The COR, also delivering its opinion as required by protocol, found the Commission's proposal favourable and listed all the issues that must be included in the programme (Bulletin EU 11-1996). Recommending a number of modifications in its first opinion (Bulletin EU 10-1996), the European Parliament stated, in its opinion on the modified programme, that a separate chapter on tourism should be introduced to the founding treaties. Further, the European Parliament summoned the Council to approve the Philoxenia Programme without any further delay (Bulletin EU 6-1997).

Planned for a four-year period starting on 1 January 1997, and allocated 25 million ECUs, the Philoxenia Programme aimed to contribute to economic growth and employment by improving the quality and competitiveness of European tourism through cooperation and coordination among relevant parties and policies. The priorities for achieving this aim were defined as the cumulative knowledge of tourism, improvement of the legal and financial frameworks, enhancement of the service quality, and the increase of the number of tourists from abroad. Consequently, the programme suggested that projects be endorsed that were in harmony with cost-benefit analyses and that would build international partnerships, yield noteworthy results in reorganizing the European tourism industry and comply with sustainable development (CEC, 1996b).

Meeting on 26 November 1997, the Council could not reach consensus on the Philoxenia Programme, thus the Commission had to withdraw its proposal. Similarly, another attempt to include a tourism section in the treaty, pursuant to Declaration I attached to the Maastricht Treaty, remained inconclusive. Failure to implement the Philoxenia Programme and to introduce a tourism chapter in the Amsterdam Treaty was interpreted in the industry as proof of non-compliance with the principle of proportionality in the treaty. The decision-making mechanism of the EU was primarily criticized for requiring a majority vote on decisions concerning policy areas that have effects on tourism – such as consumer protection, the environment and transportation – while decisions on tourism alone had to be taken unanimously (Mundt, 2000).

The Intergovernmental Conference convened at Turin in 1996, whereby amendments to the founding treaties were discussed, ending up with the signing of the Amsterdam Treaty that set the priority target of ensuring macroeconomic stability at the eve of economic and monetary union. Though unable to bring the expected results on behalf of tourism, the objective of achieving a high level of employment put on the EU agenda at the Amsterdam Summit and succeeding meetings on employment and tourism resulted in setting up a High-Level Group (HLG), composed of top tourism professionals commissioned to substantiate tourism's contribution to employment.

Based on the recommendations of the HLG, the Commission (CEC, 1999) submitted its own report to the Council. The report, which contained actions considered necessary by the Commission, could be summarized as follows: a common vision was not ascertained regarding the future of the European tourism industry, which encompassed a diffusion of national industries. Neither did the EU have a recognized and defined tourism policy. However, maximizing the contributions of European tourism to employment and balanced growth was viable by improving industry competitiveness. The EU should deal more profoundly with tourism and develop more

rational methods. Accordingly, EU instruments should be used more logically, procedures simplified and the impact of other EU policies identified more thoroughly. A consultancy and cooperation mechanism should be established among industry players at the EU level and cross-border partnerships encouraged. With implementing the General Agreement on Trade in Services (GATS), concluded at the Uruguay Round, tourism increasingly took an international dimension. EU candidate and partnership countries signed cooperation agreements in the sphere of tourism under the leadership and auspices of the EU. At this point, the need to create a comprehensive tourism vision became even more apparent. An innovative system, transparent in planning and legislation, became increasingly more necessary for setting targets through discussions and information exchange. The report had significant consequences in concerned circles. In its 2193rd session in 1999, a Council meeting on the internal market decided to set up special interest groups (SIGs) to examine various issues such as technology, environment, education and sustainable development in order to maximize tourism's contributions to employment and economic growth. The findings of these SIGs provided the basis of a report submitted by the European Commission to the Council in 2001.

International measures in tourism taken before 2000 included a joint action of the EU Council (European Council, 1997) that stipulated establishing a code of conduct in tourism under the leadership of the World Tourism Organization and in the struggle against human trafficking and child abuse. This same period distinguished itself with the inclusion of tourism projects in the Mediterranean Economic Development Area (MEDA) scheme, based on a Council resolution (CEU, 1996) envisaging the development of Euro-Mediterranean cooperation. In this period, current political instruments and practices were extended to include tourism instead of initiating special instruments and practices. In other words, reactive practices were followed based on changes in the EU agenda rather than adopting proactive approaches to set a new agenda on tourism.

Actions Directly Addressing Tourism After 2000

The Prodi period: years of collapse

Taking over the presidency of the European Commission from Jacques Santer, Romano Prodi grouped the strategic targets of the period 2000–2005 into four categories: promote new forms of European governance; stabilize Europe and boost Europe's global voice; set a new economic and social agenda meeting the requirements of the digital age; and ensure a better quality of life (CEC, 2000a). In his work programme for 2000, Prodi emphasized that sustainable development based on full employment, and social and territorial cohesion could be achieved only by setting a long-term strategy that would meet the requirements of a new economic and social order built on competition, innovation and information (CEC, 2000b).

The year 2000 started with rapid economic recovery but it was not sustained. Increased oil prices triggered an increase in inflation and interest rates in Europe. Food prices skyrocketed, and disposable income and individual consumption declined. Consequently, the economic recovery in early 2000 gradually gave way to recession in the second half of the year. The combined effect of the recession and the security concerns, stemming from the September 11 terrorist attacks, caused international tourism arrivals to experience a negative growth of − 0.6% in 2001 for the first time since 1982, as opposed to the outstanding growth of 6.8% in 2000. Similarly, international tourism revenue − with prices pegged to the US dollar − decreased by 5.2% worldwide in 2001, compared with that of the previous year (WTO, 2003). Europe was not exempt from this global trend. Not only cancelled business trips and incentive tours but a decreasing number of wealthy tourists from far distances such as Japan and the Middle

East affected European tourism industries at different levels. Circulation of the euro in 2002 and gaining more ascendancy encouraged trade with the USA to develop but to the detriment of the EU, causing the recession to deepen further in the euro zone. The use of a single currency also took effect in European travel markets and yielded two different results: the strong position of the euro against other currencies made Europe an expensive destination, thus impeding foreign tourism activities; on the other hand, the use of a single currency over a large geographical area made the euro zone attractive as an integrated destination for internal tourism activities. The economic downturn profoundly affected all tourism sub-industries, especially transportation. In particular, the airlines industry was on the verge of bankruptcy, failing to stand under the incremental costs of high insurance premiums and additional security measures, while yacht tourism companies operating in the Mediterranean region transferred their activities to the Caribbean (CEC, 2001a,c). These successive adverse events tended to thwart the goal of creating a global competitive economy based on the principle of sustainability and driven by knowledge and innovation, as suggested in the Lisbon Presidency Conclusions (European Council, 2000).

In light of these facts, the Commission (2001b) submitted a strategy paper to the Council outlining its recommendations on the future of the European industry based on opinions previously declared in early 2001 by the HLG. The report briefly listed actions to be taken to improve competitiveness in the tourism industry while contributing to employment and sustainable development as follows: a mechanism should be established to enable the priorities of all interest groups to be included on an equal basis in the EU's policy and actions under the cooperation and coordination of member states. A dialogue with the tourism industry should be reinforced by holding a yearly tourism forum with broader participation and by further extending the area of competency of the Advisory Committee on

Tourism. Volunteer partnerships and cooperative networks should be promoted among the different players on a local, regional and national basis. The tourism industry should be provided with consultancy services through specialist organizations to include monitoring, research and consultancy centres. The EU's financial instruments should be used in a rational way to serve the tourism industry, with the participation of local, regional and national agencies. Cooperation should be built among member states and all other concerned parties to create tourism satellite accounts. Awareness of sustainable development, to be created under the principles of Agenda 21, should be spread across Europe. An initiative of 'Tourism for All' should be developed to satisfy the needs of impaired citizens. 'Learning Areas' should be created, where theory and practice merge, and best practices should be identified and given precedence to develop models. Various methods and instruments should be designed to assess the quality of tourism services and destinations; accordingly, quality indicators should be defined, best practices identified, and a system of benchmarking disseminated.

Welcomed and fully endorsed, the Council (2002) acknowledged for the first time in its resolution as response to the Commission that the lack of a common tourism policy had caused the needs of the industry to be overlooked in decision-making processes. The Council further stated that this could be remedied only through greater coordination among different areas of policy and high-level involvement of all the players in the tourism industry and member states. The resolution strongly emphasized the necessity to observe the 'principle of subsidiarity' and use current structures and instruments according to the 'open method of coordination', all in one constituting a system that observed national competency to set policy while enabling EU policy making as well. Nonetheless, Council resolution did not provide the necessary basis for a road map

to establish a common tourism policy protecting the interests of the suppliers until the second half of the 2000s. Nor was the system, that seemed favourable to European tourism, properly managed during the Prodi period – a time that witnessed many failures.

The draft treaty establishing a constitution for Europe

Another failed initiative of the Prodi period was an attempt to implement a European constitution. Convened under the presidency of Valery Giscard d'Estaing to eliminate potential problems with the forthcoming enlargement of 2004 (i.e. central and southern European countries) the European Convention was entrusted with preparing a draft constitution. Although completed by mid-2003 and officially signed by the heads of governments and states in 2004, the ratification process of Draft Treaty establishing a Constitution for Europe (European Union, 2003), anticipated to end between 2004 and 2006, was suspended due to the 'no' votes of both the Netherlands and France.

The draft constitution, a highly controversial document, included neither a specific chapter on tourism nor Article 3(t) of the Maastricht Treaty composed of a single sentence. In the draft constitution, the EU's areas of activity were grouped into three categories: (i) exclusive competencies (as in the monetary policy for the euro zone, the establishing of competition rules, a common commercial policy, the customs union and conservation of marine biological resources); (ii) shared competencies (as in the internal market; freedom, security and justice; agriculture and fisheries; transportation and trans-European networks; energy; social policy; economic, social and territorial cohesion; the environment; consumer protection; public health; research and technology; space; development; and humanitarian aid); and (iii) supporting, coordinating or complementary actions (as in industry, public health, education, vocational training, youth and sports, culture, and civil protection).

Totally ignored in the draft constitution, tourism was considered a marginal subject that should be included under the EU policy on enterprise and industry. Anastasiadou (2008b) referred to the competencies exercised by the EU in tourism as 'creeping competency', since the tourism policy in Europe was largely set up by local authorities and even national governments were not generally involved in tourism. Article I-17 ('Flexibility Clause') of the constitution authorized the EU's institutions to take actions, for example, in tourism, even if the necessary power had not been granted, and conditions for such an authorization were defined in the 'Flexibility Clause'. Accordingly, the Council, acting unanimously on a proposal from the Commission and after obtaining consent from the European Parliament, would adopt appropriate measures, even if the constitution did not provide EU institutions with necessary powers or if action by the EU were deemed necessary to attain the objectives of various spheres of policy, such as the internal market and the economic monetary union. However, as was the case in the Philoxenia Programme, it was common knowledge that similar Articles previously inserted in the founding treaties could not have been easily executed to set a tourism policy that protected the supplier in the internal market. In the EU where involvement in tourism varied a great deal, the unanimity clause unfortunately denied the possibility to 'stretch' the treaty; therefore, tourism suppliers could not be adequately represented at the EU level.

Under these circumstances, the only way to set a common tourism policy was to amend the constitution in line with Article IV-7, a cumbersome process even calling forth convening an intergovernmental conference. The draft constitution, which did not consider tourism a primary policy area, was suspended without the need to actuate these processes; nevertheless, this was largely compensated for by

amendments to the Lisbon Treaty in the subsequent period.

Sustainable and competitive tourism

In the 2000s, the strategy papers on tourism began to cover the poles of sustainability and competitiveness inspired by the revised sustainable development strategy in addition to Lisbon strategy of growth and employment, purely complying with the EU's agenda. Emphasizing the necessity to ensure cohesion among various Community policies to make European tourism economically, socially and environmentally sustainable, the strategy paper of the Commission (2003a) soon led to the setting up of a Tourism Sustainability Group (TSG). Composed of representatives of member states, local authorities, trade unions, social partners and academics along with representatives from international organizations such as the United Nations World Tourism Organization and the United Nations Environment Program, the TSG was mandated to make concrete suggestions on the sustainability of European tourism and to schedule and monitor the efforts of all stakeholders. In its report, the TSG (2007) defined the role of tourism in sustainable development, challenges faced by European tourism, the roles of all stakeholders, and measures to be taken at the European level. Expanding the priorities on three axes, i.e. economic prosperity, social equality and cohesion, and environmental and cultural protection, and defining the roles of major players as well as suggesting a work schedule covering a period through late 2011, the TSG report provided the basis for a strategy paper by the Commission (2007). The Commission's strategy paper officially launched the medium- and long-term agendas processed from the bottom up.

This same period remarkably witnessed the issuance of the Commission's (2003b) decision that stipulated the requirements for tourist accommodations to be awarded the eco-label, defining two groups of criteria – 37 obligatory and 47 optional. On the other hand, 'Calypso' (social tourism), 'EDEN' (European Destinations of Excellence) and the 'Iron Curtain Trail' were three other instruments developed for raising awareness of sustainable tourism development. Efforts to ensure visibility of tourism at the EU level, dating back to the 1990s, gained momentum with attempts to revitalize the Lisbon process and the sustainable development strategy in the second half of the 2000s, finally reaching a happy ending with the Lisbon Treaty.

The Barroso period: the revival

Jose Manuel Barroso, who presided over the European Commission from 2005 to 2009, grouped the strategic targets of his mandate into four categories: prosperity, solidarity, security and freedom, and Europe as a world partner, and defined the revitalization of the Lisbon process as the new mission of the Commission (2005). Soon came the strategy paper by the Commission (2006) in which the aims of the renewed EU tourism policy were defined as improving the competitiveness of European tourism, ensuring strong and sustainable development, and thus providing better and more jobs. It would not be wrong to conclude that this strategy paper initiated the EU tourism policy materialized by the Lisbon Treaty.

Convening at the spring European Council in 2006, the heads of governments and states agreed on reinitiating the unfinished approval procedure of the constitution. In a revision of the draft constitution, previously rejected by the Netherlands and France, the Lisbon or Reform Treaty was officially signed by the heads of governments and states on 13 December 2007, and entered into force on 1 December 2009, pursuant to Article 6 of the treaty. Inserted for the first time into the founding treaties of the Community with the Maastricht Treaty, tourism was turned into a comprehensive sphere of policy and notably documented by the Lisbon Treaty.

The Lisbon Treaty: towards a consolidated tourism policy

Globalization, diverse demographics, climate change, demands for sustainable energy resources and new-found security threats all constitute the challenges Europe faces in an ever-changing and complex 21st century. Under these restrictions, Europe is believed to have attained through the Lisbon or Reform Treaty (European Union, 2010) a more democratic and transparent structure that ensures involvement and effectiveness in governance, guaranteeing rights, values, freedoms, solidarity and security, and enabling the continent to be a leading actor on the global stage. The treaty is considered a key factor in successfully turning the EU into a political integration rather than remaining a mere economic union. As Article 2 of the Treaty on EU specifies, commitment to the principles of protection of human rights, freedom, democracy, equality and the rule of law constitutes the keystone of 'the EU system of values'. These values put all member states on common ground in Europe where pluralism, struggle against discrimination, tolerance, justice, solidarity and gender equality dominate.

The aim of the EU is defined in such a way in Article 3 of the Treaty on EU to include various issues, such as home affairs and justice, socio-economic structure, foreign security and defence, and exercise of power. Accordingly, the EU is responsible for sustaining peace and basic values and for the welfare of its citizens within a borderless zone where freedom, justice and security are ensured. The EU will create an internal market across Europe. An internal market of sustained economic growth and price stability and a highly competitive social market economy will dominate, aiming at full employment and social progress. The EU will also exert every effort to ensure an eco-friendly sustainable development and support scientific and technological development. The union will struggle against social exclusion and discrimination, and make solidarity and economic, social and territorial cohesion dominant among member states. It will respect the enriched cultural and linguistic diversity and conserve and improve European cultural heritage. It will protect the rights of its citizens around the world, while contributing to peace, security and sustainable development. It will help to establish solidarity and understanding among people, and will contribute to the predominance of fair and free competition, to the struggle against poverty and to the protection of human rights. In the achievement of these objectives, the EU will act within the limits of power conferred, and will certainly abstain from actions contrary to its fundamental objective and to the provisions of the Treaty defining various policies including those on tourism.

The EU is responsible for exercising its delegated competency in fostering synergy among many targets and policies defined in the treaty, according to the 'community method'. Pursuant to Article 5 of the Treaty on EU, delegation and exercise of competencies evolve from three principles in the EU. According to the first, the 'principle of conferral', the EU acts within the sphere of competencies conferred upon it by member states to attain the objectives set out in the founding treaties. In areas where the EU does not have competencies, the right to act is reserved by member states. According to the 'principle of *subsidiarity*', in areas where the EU has not been given exclusive competencies, the EU can take action only if anticipated objectives cannot effectively be attained by member states (on a centralized, regional or local basis) but achieved at the EU level by reason of the scale and outcome of the proposed action. Finally, according to the 'principle of proportionality', the content and form of EU actions cannot exceed that which is necessary to achieve the targets of the treaties. These principles of conferral, *subsidiarity* and proportionality were inserted into the Maastricht Treaty; however, lacking a special chapter on tourism contrary to Lisbon compromise, they could not provide an adequate basis on their own to establish a comprehensive and coherent tourism policy at the EU level.

With Articles 2 and 6 of the Treaty on the Functioning of the EU, tourism is included in the EU's 'supporting, coordinating or complementary actions'. Accordingly, the EU is responsible for taking actions supporting, coordinating or complementing those of member states under conditions stipulated in the treaties and provided that the areas of competency are not transgressed. However, the binding secondary legal norms, such as European laws and framework laws pursuant to related provisions in the treaties, must not entail harmonization of member state laws and regulations. The treaty also validates ordinary legislative procedure in decision making on tourism (Articles 195, 289(1) and 294). Not requiring the unanimity clause in decision making is a significant improvement, which may be correctly interpreted as transforming the EU's competencies in tourism from what Anastasiadou (2008b) calls 'creeping competency' to literally 'complementary competency'.

Title XXII of the Treaty on the Functioning of the EU is devoted to the EU's tourism policy. Although Article 3(t) on tourism in the Maastricht Treaty was removed from the draft treaty establishing a constitution for Europe, Article 195 of the Treaty on the Functioning of the EU has restored significance to tourism. This Article finally led to the creation of a common standpoint supporting tourism entrepreneurs, for which tourism suppliers have been fighting since the 1990s. The Article reads as follows:

> 1. The Union shall complement the action of the Member States in the tourism sector in particular by promoting the competitiveness of Union undertakings in that sector.
>
> To that end, Union action shall be aimed at:
>
> (a) encouraging the creation of a favourable environment for the development of undertakings in this sector;
> (b) promoting cooperation between the Member States, particularly by the exchange of good practice.
>
> 2. The European Parliament and the Council, acting in accordance with the

ordinary legislative procedure, shall establish specific measures to complement actions within the Member States to achieve the objectives referred to in this Article, excluding any harmonization of the laws and regulations of the Member States.

Article 195 of the Treaty on the Functioning of the EU mandates that the EU take complementary actions to ensure competitiveness of tourism enterprises in the international market, by way of creating a favourable environment and promoting cooperation through sharing best practices, without ignoring the differences in the approaches of member states to tourism and their individual areas of competency. It also stipulates that the measures taken by the EU to complement the actions of member states will be resolved with a qualified majority vote. Consequently, this will accommodate an 'integrated tourism policy' at the EU level, while secondary legal norms will be legitimized to create a business environment that guarantees the tourism undertakings gain competitive power.

With the momentum created by the provisions of the Lisbon Treaty, the *Tourism Gymnich,* convening on 15 April 2010, signed the Madrid Declaration which contained a number of recommendations on implementing a 'consolidated EU tourism policy framework'. Subsequently, the European Commission (2010) issued a strategy paper outlining the tourism policy to be pursued and concrete actions to be taken. This strategy paper stated that in order to create a competitive, sustainable, modern and socially responsible European tourism industry, a concept of sustainable, responsible and high-quality tourism will be promoted throughout the EU, an integrated European image of sustainable and high-quality destinations would be created, and

EU's financial instruments would be utilized for the benefit of the tourism industry.

Conclusions

Although efforts to set up a common tourism policy in Europe date back as far as the 1990s, the concerned parties had to wait until the enforcement of the Lisbon Treaty that reformed the situation of tourism undertakings by putting producers on equal footings with consumers and environmental and cultural enthusiasts in the decision-making process. In fact, the Treaty does not imply a shift in the EU's standpoint on its tourism policy, but rather legitimizes action by the EU. Totally endorsing the motto of 'united in diversity', the EU recognizes the competencies of member states to set up tourism policies, while assuming the responsibility to take actions that would increase the competitiveness of European tourism, and documents this effort. In effect, this creates an expectation of the EU to henceforth identify strategic targets and priorities for increased competitiveness of tourism enterprises and to set up secondary legal norms directly addressing tourism, pursuant to the provisions of the Treaty. Achieving coordination among various European policies affecting tourism for the benefit of the industry as a whole, and consolidating the European tourism policy to accommodate considerations of all stakeholders would be the next stance of the EU. Apparently, getting prepared to introduce a number of complementary actions, the EU would create a more integrated, highly competitive and sustainable tourism industry, providing better and more jobs, and reinforce its position as a global actor in international tourism markets; thus would be attaining the 'Lisbon and Millennium goals' via tourism.

References

AIT & FIA (1996) Community tourism policy: the integration of tourism in the treaty - a proposal by the AIT & FIA to the Intergovernmental Conference. Available at: http://europa.eu.int/en/agenda/igc-home/instdoc/ industry/ait-en.htm (accessed 31 July 2000).

Akehurst, G. (1992) European community tourism policy. In: Johnson, P. and Thomas, B. (eds) Perspectives on Tourism Policy. Mansell, London, pp. 215–231.

Akehurst, G., Bland, N. and Nevin, M. (1993) Tourism policies in the European Community member states. *International Journal of Hospitality Management* 12 (1), 33–66.

Åkerhielm, P., Dev, C.S. and Noden, M.A. (1990) Europe 1992: neglecting the tourism opportunity. *Cornell Hotel and Restaurant Administration Quarterly* 31 (1), 104–111.

Åkerhielm, P., Dev, C.S. and Noden, M.A. (2003) Brand Europe: European integration and tourism development. *Cornell Hotel and Restaurant Administration Quarterly* 44 (5/6), 88–93.

Anastasiadou, C. (2006) Tourism and the European Union. In: Hall D., Marciszewska B. and Smith, M. (eds) *Tourism in the New Europe: The Challenges and Opportunities of EU Enlargement*. CABI Publishing, Wallingford, UK, pp. 20–31.

Anastasiadou, C. (2007) Group politics and tourism interest representation at the supranational level: evidence from the European Union. In: Burns, P.M. and Novelli, M. (eds) *Tourism and Politics: Global Frameworks and Local Realities*. Elsevier Science, Oxford, UK, pp. 59–70.

Anastasiadou, C. (2008a) Tourism interest groups in the EU policy arena: characteristics, relationships and challenges. *Current Issues in Tourism* 11, 24–62.

Anastasiadou, C. (2008b) Stakeholder perspectives on the European Union tourism policy framework and their preferences on the type of involvement. *International Journal of Tourism Research* 10 (3), 221–235.

CEC (1982) Initial Guidelines for a Community Policy on Tourism. COM (82)385 Final of 01/07/1982.

CEC (1993) Commission's White Paper on Growth, Competitiveness, and Employment: The Challenges and Ways Forward into the 21st Century. COM (93)700 Final of 05/12/1993.

CEC (1995) Commission's Green Paper on the Role of the Union in the Field of Tourism. COM (95)97 Final of 04/04/1995.

CEC (1996a) Proposal for a Council Decision on a First Multiannual Programme to Assist European Tourism "Philoxenia" (1997–2000). Document: 596PC0168.

CEC (1996b) Amended Proposal for a Council Decision on a First Multiannual Programme to Assist European Tourism - Philoxenia (1997–2000). Document: 596PC0635.

CEC (1999) Enhancing Tourism's Potential for Employment. COM (1999)205 Final of 28/04/1999.

CEC (2000a) Strategic Objectives 2000–2005: Shaping the new Europe. COM (2000)154 Final of 9/02/2000.

CEC (2000b) The Commission's Work Programme for 2000. COM (2000)155 Final of 9/02/2000.

CEC (2001a) Overview of EU Action in Response to the Events of the 11 September and Assessment of Their Likely Economic Impact. COM (2001)611 Final of 17/10/2001.

CEC (2001b) Working Together for the Future of European Tourism. COM (2001)665 Final of 13/11/2001.

CEC (2001c) Follow-up of the European Council of 21 September: the Situation in the European Tourism Sector. COM (2001) 668 Final of 13/11/2001.

CEC (2003a) Basic Orientations for the Sustainability of European Tourism. COM (2003)716 Final of 21/11/2003.

CEC (2003b) Commission Decision of 14 April 2003 Establishing the Ecological Criteria for the Award of the Community Eco-label to Tourist Accommodation Service (Notified Under Document Number C(2003)235), 2003/287/EC.

CEC (2005) Strategic Objectives 2005–2009 Europe 2010: A Partnership for European Renewal; Prosperity, Solidarity and Security. COM (2005)12 Final of 26/01/2005.

CEC (2006) A Renewed EU Tourism Policy: Towards A European Partnership for European Tourism. COM (2006)134 Final of 17/03/2006.

CEC (2007) Agenda for Sustainable and Competitive European Tourism, COM (2007)621 Final of 19/10/2007.

CEC (2010) Europe, the World's No 1 Tourist Destination – A New Political Framework for Tourism in Europe. COM (2010)352 Final of 30/06/2010.

CEU (1984a) Council Resolution on a Community Policy on Tourism. O.J. C 115, 30/04/1984, pp.0002–0027.

CEU (1984b) Council Directive of 10 December 1984 Amending, Particularly as Regards Tourist Assistance, the First Directive (73/239/EEC) on the Coordination of Laws, Regulations and Administrative Provisions Relating to the Taking-up and Pursuit of the Business of Direct Insurance Other Than Life Assurance. O.J. L 339, 27/12/1984, pp.0021–0025.

CEU (1986a) Council Decision of 22 December 1986 Establishing a Consultation and Cooperation Procedure in the Field of Tourism. O.J. L 384, 31/12/1986, pp.0052–0053.

CEU (1986b) Council Resolution of 22 December 1986 on a Better Seasonal and Geographical Distribution of Tourism. O.J. C 340, 31/12/1986, pp.0001–0002.

CEU (1986c) Council Recommendation of 22 December 1986 on Standardized Information in Existing Hotels. O.J. L 384, 31/12/1986, pp.0054–0059.

CEU (1986d) Council Recommendation of 22 December 1986 on Fire Safety in Existing Hotels. O.J. L 384, 31/12/1986, pp.0060–0068.

CEU (1989) Council Decision of 21 December 1988 on an Action Programme for European Tourism Year (1990). O.J. L 017, 21/01/1989, p.0053.

CEU (1990) Council Directive 90/314/EEC of 13 June 1990 on Package Travel, Package Holidays and Package Tours. O.J. L 158, 23/06/1990, pp.0059–0064.

CEU (1992) Council Decision 92/421/EEC of 13 July 1992 on a Community Action Plan to Assist Tourism. O.J. L 231 of 13/08/1992, pp.0026–0032.

CEU (1994) Directive 94/47/EC of the European Parliament and the Council of 26 October 1994 on the Protection of Purchasers in Respect of Certain Aspects of Contracts Relating to the Purchase of the Right to Use Immovable Properties on a Timeshare Basis. O.J. L 280, 29/10/1994, pp.0083–0087.

CEU (1995) Council Directive 95/57/EC of 23 November 1995 on the Collection of Statistical Information in the Field of Tourism. O.J. L 291, 06/12/1995, pp.0032–0039.

CEU (1996) Council Resolution of 13 May 1996 on Euro-Mediterranean Cooperation Regarding Tourism. O.J. C 155 of 30/05/1996, pp.0001–0002.

CEU (2002) Council Resolution of 21 May 2002 on the Future of European Tourism. O. J. C 135 of 21/05/2002, pp.1–3.

Church, A., Ball, R., Bull, C. and Tyler, D. (2000) Public policy engagement with British tourism: the national, local and the European Union. *Tourism Geographies* 2, 312–336.

COR (1995) Opinion of the Committee of Regions on the Commission Green Paper on the Role of the Union in the Field of Tourism. Available at: http://www.cor.eu.int/coratwork/comm5/english/3/6-95.htm (accessed 6 December 1999).

Davidson, R. (1998) *Travel and Tourism in Europe*. Addison-Wesley Longman Limited, Harlow, UK.

Downes, J. (1997) European Union progress on a common tourism sector policy. *Travel and Tourism Analyst* 1, 74–87.

Downes, J. (2000) EU legislation and the travel industry. *Travel and Tourism Analyst* 5, 49–71.

ECOSOC (1995) Opinion of the Economic and Social Committee on the Commission Green Paper on the Role of the Union in the Field of Tourism. Available at: http://eur-lex.europa.eu/Notice.do?val=310713:cs&lang=en&list=310713:cs,&pos=1&page=1&nbl=1&pgs=10&hwords=&checktexte=checkbox&visu=#texte (accessed 18 September 2011).

European Commission (2010) Declaration of Madrid Within the Scope of Informal Ministerial Meeting for Tourism Under the Spanish Presidency in April 2010 in Madrid Under the Motto 'Towards a Socially Responsible Tourism Model'. Available at: http://www.eu2010.es/export/sites/presidencia/comun/descargas/agenda/Cultura/abr15_declaracionrimturismoen.pdf (accessed 6 September 2010).

European Council (1997) 97/154/JHA: Joint Action of 24 February 1997 Adopted by the Council on the Basis of Article K.3 of the Treaty on European Union Concerning Action to Combat Trafficking in Human Beings and Sexual Exploitation of Children. O.J. L 063, 04/03/1997, pp.0002–0006.

European Council (2000) Presidency Conclusions. Lisbon, Portugal, 23–24 March 2000. Available at: http://www.europarl.europa.eu/summits/lis1_en.htm (accessed 12 October 2011).

European Court of Auditors (1997) Special Report No: 3/96 on Tourist Policy and the Promotion of Tourism, Together With the Commission's Replies. O.J. C 017, 16/01/1997, pp.0001–00023.

European Parliament (1995) Resolution of 17 May 1995 on the functioning of the Treaty on European Union with a view to the 1996 Intergovernmental Conference - Implementation and development of the Union. OJ C 151, 19.6.1995, p. 56, rapporteurs: Jean-Louis Bourlanges and David Martin, Doc. A4-102/95

European Parliament (1996) Briefing No.30: Tourism and the 1996 IGC. Available at: http://www.europarl.europa.eu/igc1996/fiches/fiche30_en.htm (accessed 12 October 2011).

European Union (1992) Treaty on European Union O.J. C 191 of 29 July 1992. Available at: http://eur-lex.europa.eu/en/treaties/dat/11992M/htm/11992M.html (accessed 12 October 2011).

European Union (1996a) Bulletin EU 9-1996 Enterprise Policy 2/2. Available at: http://europa.eu.int/abc/doc/off/bull/en/9609/p103046.htm (accessed 2 August 2000).

European Union (1996b) Bulletin EU 10-1996 Enterprise Policy 2/4. Available at: http://europa.eu.int/abc/doc/off/bull/en/9610/p103072.htm (accessed 2 August 2000).

European Union (1996c) Bulletin EU 11–1996 Enterprise Policy 6/6. Available at: http://europa.eu.int/abc/doc/off/bull/en/9611/p103079.htm (accessed 2 August 2000).

European Union (1997) Bulletin EU 6-1997 Enterprise Policy 4/4. Available at: http://europa.eu.int/abc/doc/
    off/bull/en/9706/p103122.htm (accessed 1 August 2000).
European Union (2003) Draft Treaty Establishing a Constitution for Europe, 20 June 2003, CONV 820/03.
European Union (2010) Consolidated Versions of the Treaty on European Union and the Treaty on the
    Functioning of the European Union O.J. C 38 of 30.3.2010.
Greenwood, J. (1993) Business interest groups in tourism governance. *Tourism Management* 14 (5),
    335–348.
HOTREC (no date) Recommendation for a Formulation of a Text Should the European Institutions Decide to
    Write Tourism Into the Treaty on European Union. Doc 96.170. Available at: http://www.hotrec.org/
    areas/tourism/suggestion.html (accessed 15 August 2003).
Lickorish, L.J. (1991) Developing a single European tourism policy. *Tourism Management* 12, 178–184.
Mundt, J.W. (2000) The European Union tourism policy. *Tourism* 48 (2), 125–134.
TSG (2007) Action for more sustainable European tourism. Available at: http://ec.europa.eu/enterprise/sectors/
    tourism/files/docs/tsg/tsg_final_report_en.pdf (accessed 30 August 2010).
WTO (2003) *World Tourism Barometer* 1 (1), Spain.

authenticity and commodification in the context of cultural and ethnic tourism. In the second section, I provide a brief history of the Mayan Riviera's development as a tourism destination. In the third and fourth sections, I introduce my two case studies. Here, I discuss how Mayan culture has been incorporated into the tourist-scapes of Xcaret and Alltournative by drawing on fieldwork data I collected in 2009. Additionally, in these two sections, I discuss how issues of authenticity and commodification relate to specific cultural attractions that are premised on the staging and selling of Mayan culture. Finally, in the conclusion I discuss the benefits and challenges that arise from this type of tourism, touching on some of the concerns related to the staging and selling of indigenous culture in the Mayan Riviera, particularly in the context of Xcaret and Alltournative's incorporation of 'Mayan culture' as a tourist attraction.

Authenticity, Commodification and the Selling of Indigenous Culture

When looking at the contemporary literature on authenticity and commodification in the context of a cultural tourism based on the selling of indigenous culture, two arguments become apparent. One of the most prevalent arguments that has been made in relation to ethnic or cultural tourism argues that tourism's promotion of indigenous culture and of indigenous communities as objects for touristic consumption is invariably detrimental to the culture's purity, authenticity, preservation and, ultimately, its intrinsic value. This is an idea that draws from MacCannell's theory of tourism as a quest for the authentic, as a search for the 'real' (1976).

According to MacCannell, modern Western societies have engendered a deep-seated sense of alienation in its members as a result of the all-pervasive nature of its pre-configured social forms (MacCannell, 1976). In an attempt to overcome this profound sense of detachment, he argued, people would travel to foreign lands hoping to experience authentic forms of cultural

Otherness 'elsewhere', 'in other historical periods and other cultures, in purer, simpler lifestyles' (MacCannell, 1976, p.3). However, this quest, he theorized, was too often jeopardized by the staging and the ensuing commodification of culture (MacCannell, 1976). In other words, as a result of a culture's authentic elements being staged and consequently 'commodified', local adaptations/ dependencies were generated and the culture's very authenticity was compromised. Watson and Kopachevsky (1994) argued that experiences, objects, activities and even the simple act of gazing are often commodified in tourism discourse and practice, i.e. they are turned into commodities to be bought and sold; commodities to be consumed. By being packaged, marketed and exchanged within a capitalist framework, they argue, the cultural elements that were initially sought-after for their authenticity cease to be authentic at all. Consequently, echoing MacCannell, they suggest that, as a result of the 'manipulations undertaken by many tourism establishments', 'the tourist rarely, if at all, achieves the sought after experience of authenticity' (Watson and Kopachevsky 1994, p.651). The idea that tourism represents a 'quest for authenticity' and the notion that, through tourism's commodification of culture, a culture's intrinsic authenticity can become endangered, though commonly debated, continue to run throughout the literature on tourism and commodification (see Mathieson and Wall, 1982; Cohen, 1988; Harrison, 1994; Tomaselli and Wang, 2001). In his study of ethnic tourism to San Cristobal de las Casas (in Mexico's state of Chiapas), Pierre Van den Berghe (1995) discussed how issues of authenticity and commodification, particularly in the context of ethnic tourism, related to the case of 'living Mayans' as cultural attractions. He argued that, once local entrepreneurs realized the marketability of the region's indigenous culture, they began to 'commodify' it by linking contemporary indigenous peoples to their Mayan ancestors, i.e. by making an 'explicit linkage between living and dead Mayas' (Van den Berghe, 1995, p.580). In San Cristobal de las Casas, he noted, this became a profitable venture owing to the fact that the 'mystique of living Indians as pure authentic descendants of an indigenous tradition appeals enormously to the tourist quest for authenticity' (p.576).

Critics have argued that the commodification and commercialization of indigenous culture, i.e. its treatment as a commodity to be bought and sold, is problematic, particularly when it involves the marketization of indigenous people, because it can result in the 'dilution' of their culture and the loss of authenticity (MacCannell, 1976; Shepherd, 2002). The categorization of indigenous groups as 'authentic' descendants of an ancient culture has also been criticized on the grounds that it cultivates a myth of 'purity' that is grounded in the obfuscation of wider socio-economic realities (MacCannell, 1976; Shepherd, 2002). Indeed, the argument goes that the very conceptualization of tourism as a 'polluting force' is controversial as it sustains what Frankland calls a kind of 'teleological conceit' which quintessentially relies on the idea that 'tourism causes dependency; dependency de-authenticates culture; culture is destroyed by tourism' (Frankland, 2009, p. 96). In other words, it is an idea that sustains the notion that 'any Eden found must soon be lost, precisely because it has been discovered; any Adam or any Eve will soon be polluted, their purity compromised by the very act of contact' (Frankland, 2009).

Many have argued that the conceptualization of tourism as a 'polluting agent' of authenticity is fundamentally problematic primarily because it commonly mobilizes a type of 'cultural cryonics' that discursively fixes indigenous peoples in an ancient, romanticized past. As Cole argues, 'following this logic, to preserve the tourism product, is to maintain the lack of economic development and hence to preserve poverty' (2007, p.495). Echoing Butcher (2001), she maintains that this type of tourism can create a 'straitjacket for communities' where economic development and inequality is preserved to maintain the 'authentic feel' of the 'tourism product' (Butcher, 2001; Shepherd, 2002, p.186; Cole, 2007). According to Cole, however, ethnic tourism

and the commodification of culture is not always detrimental to the indigenous communities in question. Indeed, she maintains, the selling and promoting of culture can contribute to their socio-economic empowerment and promote the revitalization of cultural traditions and ethnic identities.

Tourism to the Mayan Riviera

Records dating from the late 1990s that detail the transformation of the 'Cancun-Tulum corridor' into 'the Mayan Riviera' are few. According to Carmela, a local resident of Playa del Carmen who has been involved in tourism promotion to the region since the late 1990s, the mayor of the municipality of Solidaridad[3] and a marketing specialist came up with the name 'Mayan Riviera' as a way to re-brand the region by highlighting its natural and cultural resources (Carmela[4]; my translation). The Mayan Riviera's first resort was opened in 1995, paving the way for the development of dozens of other four- and five-star hotels along the coast. In 1998, there were 150 hotels in the Mayan Riviera; by 2007, that number had risen to 336 (SEDETUR, 2008). Tourist flows have since markedly increased: in 1998, 595,050 tourists visited the region; by the year 2007, that number rose to 2.8 million (SEDETUR, 2008).

Many of the Mayan Riviera's resorts are located miles apart from one another and, because of their relative seclusion, many resorts are 'all-inclusive', i.e. they enclose their own entertainment venues, restaurants, bars and shops, while offering exclusive access to the beach. In addition to all-inclusive resorts, a number of small towns in the region have undergone rapid development and have begun to offer their own 'alternative' accommodation in the form of small hotels and bungalows. Principal amongst these towns is Playa del Carmen, commonly known as the 'heart of the Riviera Maya' because of its central location and popularity with tourists. Notably, it was only 20 years ago that Playa del Carmen was a small and 'sleepy' fishing village inhabited by fewer than 100 people (Gonzalez, 2007). Today, it has more than 100,000 residents and attracts thousands of international tourists, especially 'alternative' tourists, who choose to forsake all-inclusive accommodation, opting for smaller-scale lodgings from which to explore the region's natural and cultural resources (INEGI, 2005; DATATUR, 2003).

The Mayan Riviera, however, as I discussed in the introduction to this chapter, was not envisioned, nor was it constructed, as an ethnic or cultural destination. Indeed, even today, it is a destination that continues to be chosen primarily for its luxurious facilities and breath-taking Caribbean setting. Although cultural or ethnic tourist attractions cannot be said to comprise the region's primary allure, the last decade has, however, witnessed a marked increase in the incorporation of 'Mayan culture' into the region's tourist landscapes. Indeed, as Torres notes, 'Mayan motifs' have been frequently employed to add a 'cultural dimension' and incorporate a 'Mayan aesthetics' to the Mayan Riviera's many hotels, restaurants and other tourist venues. What is more, she notes, 'Mayan hieroglyphics and images of ancient Maya Indians are displayed and sold on everything from coffee mugs to T-shirts' (Torres, 2002, p. 111). The incorporation of 'all things Mayan' into the Mayan Riviera's tourism industry and the celebration of contemporary Mayan culture in some of the region's tourist attractions has been widely recognized as adding value to the industry's product. Indeed, Mexico's Tourism Ministry (SECTUR) itself has noted the marketability of the region's Mayan culture. In 2004, in a report commissioned by SECTUR, the Mayan Riviera's main areas for tourism development were delineated (SECTUR, 2004). These included the region's natural and cultural assets. In relation to the latter, the authors wrote:

> Archaeological sites are among the cultural attractions [of the Mayan Riviera], among them those of Tulum and Coba, but [the Mayan Riviera] also counts with Mayan groups or communities distributed along the region, that is, with inhabitants who populate the actual territory and who are the depositories of a millenarian culture.
>
> SECTUR (2004, author's translation)

Here, SECTUR also highlighted the potential for a 'new type of tourist attraction', which had proven to be especially successful in promoting the region's natural and cultural attributes: thematic parks, also known as eco-parks. Principal among them, the authors argued, stands Xcaret, a park that 'highlights the spaces and manifestations of Mayan culture'; a park that, at the time the document was released, attracted 'more than one million people per year' (SECTUR, 2004).

The Case of Xcaret

Forty-five minutes south of Cancun and only 10 km from Playa del Carmen is Xcaret, a privately owned, self-enclosed, 'eco-archaeological theme park' that features its own underground rivers, lagoons and natural pools, a coral reef aquarium, turtle and butterfly pavilions, a mushroom farm and an orchid greenhouse. For US$69,[5] tourists can swim, snorkel and dive; they can admire the region's flora and fauna and mingle with dolphins. In addition to participating in these recreational activities, tourists can learn about the region's Mayan cultural heritage in a variety of ways: by visiting the park's 'Mayan Village', by taking a tour of the on-site archaeological Mayan ruins, or by watching Xcaret's widely renowned night show entitled 'Mexico Espectacular'[6]. Each of these sites and performances portrays Mayan culture in a different, albeit homologous, way. For example, when visiting the 'Mayan Village' tourists are invited to:

> Walk into the daily life of the Maya people and travel through time [by] visiting a replica of a Mayan Village... [where] you will be able to witness the everyday life of common Maya people at the time when the Maya civilization inhabited this land.
>
> XCARET (2010)

At the 'Mayan Village', tourists can also witness:

> The magical attraction of Mayan customs and traditions can be experienced through the work of their craftsmen and weavers [who] dressed in traditional Maya attire... will amaze you with their creativity as they carve Mayan sacred animals and god shapes in wood or make beautiful crafts the way they learned from their Mayan ancestors.
>
> XCARET (2010)

While the Mayan Village acts as a stage re/presenting purportedly 'authentic' Mayan life by its incorporation of 'Mayan' artisans and weavers, Xcaret's other Mayan cultural attraction, its archaeological ruins and their natural surroundings, remain imbued with an emptiness that is meant to stand for an extinguished, long-vanished, phantasmal civilization. When visiting this part of the park, the aim is not for tourists to discover the 'way of life' of the Mayan people, but to 'witness the traces' they left behind. With the assistance of a tour guide, they are invited to 'discover the vestiges of the rich cultural heritage that the Maya, these incredible mathematicians, astronomers, and architects left to mankind' (XCARET, 2010). 'Use your imagination', XCARET proceeds:

> To visualize, within the natural shelter of the Xcaret inlet, the arrival of hundreds of boats carrying their sumptuous feathers, incense, jade and gold ornaments, obsidian knives, furs, turtle eggs, shells, agricultural products and great quantities of salt, among other merchandise...[and] learn ...that Xcaret was also a very important religious center, where Maya people from all over the peninsula came to purify their bodies and souls in the waters of the cenotes.[7]
>
> XCARET (2010)

In addition to offering tourists the chance to 'learn' about Mayan culture by visiting its simulated Mayan Village and taking a tour of its archaeological ruins, XCARET presents a depiction of Mayan culture by way of choreographed dance and live music through its 'Mexico Espectacular night show'. In addition, en route to the theatre where the show takes place, tourists can witness 'Mayan culture' as they walk through an outside corridor where people dressed in pre-Hispanic outfits play the drums, sing or statuesquely stand as tourists pose for photographs to take as souvenirs of their encounter with cultural Otherness – however staged this may be. Inside the theatre, the show itself begins with a representation of indigenous life. This is followed by a depiction of the Spanish conquest and the Mexican Inquisition. By the third and final act, which represents contemporary Mexico's sociocultural diversity by way of regional music and dance, 'Mayan culture' ceases to be at all represented.

Scholars' reactions to Xcaret have been mostly critical. According to Walker, Xcaret 'is a highly controversial natural history theme park' (2005, p.70); it is a space enclosing authentic ancient archaeological ruins that, he argues, 'are treated as opportunities for amusement and unfettered exploration in the model of Disneyland theme parks' (2003, p.71); and a site where 'tourists are entertained by glamorized presentations of the Maya culture'. According to Walker (2005), Xcaret, like most attractions at the Mayan Riviera (excluding, he contends, the few operators who organize tours to contemporary Mayan communities in addition to visits to archaeological sites), leave tourists 'with the overall impression that the Maya are now extinct (sic.), despite the presence of more than a million Maya living there today' (Walker, 2005). The connection of Xcaret with 'Disneyland' is one that has been commonly made in relation to the park. Torres, for example, writes that Xcaret is 'commoditized and packaged' and represents:

> A classic example of Ritzer's McDisneyfication[8] mass tourist product, but ...[it] takes Ritzer's concept one step further by appealing specifically to a new breed of 'environmentally conscious' mass consumers with specialized tastes.
>
> Torres (2002, p. 110)

Moreover, many tourists I interviewed in the Mayan Riviera alluded to Xcaret as

'Disney-like'. Simon, for example, a tourist from the USA visiting Playa del Carmen, said that while Xcaret was an 'interesting place' it was 'too contrived', 'not cultural in any way', and 'too Disney'. Reflecting on this, he added:

> I've just been all over a lot of places in the world and have been able to witness very genuine sort of cultural experiences where you're just witnessing daily life, daily rituals or a ceremony that's not put on your behalf and you haven't purchased some ticket to go see it, you know... whenever you purchase a ticket to see culture you know you can pretty much be sure to be seeing culture lite.
>
> Simon (2009)

For Simon, 'culture lite' ensued whenever a cultural product or performance was created exclusively for tourists' consumption, a process that resulted in its commodification and the consequent loss of its cultural authenticity (Simon, 2009).

It is important to add, however, that not all tourists considered the staging of culture problematic or conducive to a loss of genuineness or authenticity. Carly, a US tourist who was staying at an all-inclusive resort in the Mayan Riviera, commented that 'Xcaret is the best way to get to know the history of the country and Mayan culture' (Carly, 2009). Regardless of whether Xcaret's display of culture was deemed authentic or not, its commodification of culture was not necessarily received negatively by all of its consumers. Indeed, its influence on tourists' appraisal of the culture being staged was by no means uniformly critical. For example, Maria, a local resident of Playa del Carmen involved in the tourism industry, considered Xcaret 'commercialized' but nevertheless she added that:

> The show of Xcaret makes me cry... I love it; it gives me goose bumps... yes, it is commercialized, and on a mass-scale, but how amazing that we have a park like that!
>
> (Maria, 2009, author's translation)

Overall, Xcaret makes few overt associations between ancient and contemporary Mayans. Indeed, it is not uncommon for tourists to leave the park with the impression that Mayans continue to abide by ancient customs. Xcaret's Mayan Village, a simulacrum of 'Mayan life', allows for no interaction to unfold between those performing it and those gazing at its performance. The Xcaret night show's portrayal of Mayan culture similarly focuses exclusively on Mayan peoples as having lived in pristine environmental symbiosis prior to their 'defeat' by Spanish forces, leaving no room for the representations of Mayans living in Mexico today.

The Case of Alltournative

In the mid-1990s, Carlos Marin, a native of Mexico City, envisioned the idea of creating a tourism venture that would combine outdoor recreational activities with visits to archaeological ruins and contemporary Mayan villages in the Mayan Riviera (Jones, 2007). In 1999, this idea became a reality and Alltournative, one of the region's first 'ecotourism'[9] companies, was founded. I interviewed Roger[10], who was involved with Alltournative's establishment. He talked about the company's mission, its early years, and its impact on local Mayan communities. When discussing Alltournative's founding, Roger remembered the initial trepidation with which local tourist agencies approached the idea:

> They said to us, 'you guys are crazy, we're not going to let you people take our clients out into the jungle'... no, they didn't want to do it at all... 'We're not going to let you take them, and rope them and lower our clients down into a hole into the water down below where they can swim... No way'.
>
> (Roger, 2009)

Although convincing them 'took a long while', he added, 'once it took off, it just boomed'. Alltournative's annual growth in tourist customers was considerable, he notes: 'we went from attracting 6,000 clients in 1998, to 19,000 in 1999, to 42,000 the following year, to 58,000 the next year, to 87,000 the next year, to 99,000 the following year'

(Roger, 2009). Since its inception in the late 1990s, Alltournative has provided a series of tours. From its very beginning, however, the most popular tour has been its 'Coba Maya Encounter Expedition'. Here, for US$119, tourists can follow up a trip to the ancient city and archaeological ruins of Coba with a series of recreational activities (e.g. zip-line flying, swimming, rappelling and canoeing) and a visit to an 'authentic Mayan village'. Here, they can 'See how the Mayas live and experience with these wonderful people an adventure in their natural world' (Alltournative, 2010b). It is after admiring and reflecting upon the achievements of the ancient Mayans therefore (by taking a tour of the ancient archaeological ruins of Coba and hearing a historical account of the rise and fall of the Mayan civilization) that tourists are introduced to contemporary Mayan peoples as 'authentic' descendants of ancient Mayan culture. It is this connection between the past and the present that, after all, comprises the primary allure of Alltournative's 'Maya Encounter Expedition'.

Mauricio, one of Alltournative's tour guides who frequently leads these tours, argues that the 'encounters' between tourists and Mayan community members are very important because of their impact on tourists' imaginaries of Mayan culture and Mayan peoples. In fact, he exclaimed, 'a lot of people think that Mayan people no longer exist!' (Mauricio, 2009; author's translation). The 'encounter' includes a purification ritual conducted by a Mayan shaman in a Mayan dialect prior to the tourists' descent into the community's cenote. This is followed by the recreational activities mentioned above which take place within the Mayan community and finally, tourists are invited to enjoy a traditional Yucatecan meal where they can interact with the Mayan women who have prepared it and with the Mayan community members who have been providing assistance in their tour.

According to Roger, one of the primary goals of Alltournative's 'Maya Encounter Expeditions' is to expose tourists to contemporary forms of Mayan culture and educate them about the socio-economic conditions of present-day Mayan communities:

> We said, 'hey, let's go into the forest, and let's walk around and let's see how Mayan people are living today. How they used to be before, we're not going to try to keep them that way. They are after all, like we, a culture in transition. And they're changing as we change, and you're going to see what that looks like today. In two years' time, it's going to be different. They may have concrete houses instead of wooden houses, because suddenly they have access to money, and they can build concrete houses'.
>
> Roger (2009)

Alltournative's impact on the socio-economic conditions of the Mayan communities they work with is worthy of note. Once forced to commute long hours to work in the resorts, hotels and restaurants of Cancun and the Mayan Riviera, members of the Mayan communities that work with Alltournative can remain 'at home' earning 'about 900 to 1000 percent more than what they did before started with us' (Roger, 2009). In addition to increasing the income received by Mayan communities, Alltournative seeks to 'improve the life quality' of its inhabitants by creating jobs within Mayan communities, protecting the environment, preserving local customs, encouraging education in 'ecotourism practices', providing community members with skills training and fomenting 'respect for traditional customs within the community' (Alltournative, 2010a).

Today, the company supports six different communities and employs 220 people (Roger, 2009). According to Mauricio, Mayan community members have embraced tourism:

> They are very happy to be working with Alltournative... they are like, 'now we can stay at home and look after our family, look after our land and our animals, and work'.
>
> Mauricio (2009, author's translation)

The Mayan villages that Alltournative includes in its tourist portfolio have experienced considerable socio-economic development. While, to some, changes could be perceived as detrimental to the product's 'authenticity', Roger makes a point of emphasizing the company's non-interventionist approach to the way in which communities develop. This being said, however:

> We come with our intention to develop them, along the lines that they want to develop in, not that we want to impose... [but] there are certain things that we do suggest, especially in terms of uses of natural resources, training ...and certain social processes like education, child labor, gender equality and access to education.
>
> Roger (2009)

According to Mauricio, there have been considerable positive changes in the Mayan communities Alltournative works with. 'Children begin to know more things and gain more education, become healthier', he said. And while exposure to mainstream tourism is 'a crash' he proceeded, for them to come into contact with tourists and in many cases with an outside world that until that point was unknown to them:

> Is a crash that has been good for the Mayan communities... it is incredible to see how people adapt to computers and start doing different things and they like that...something completely different is being created.
>
> Mauricio (2009, author's translation)

To this, Roger added that:

> These Mayan communities that were marginalized before we met up with them and who have been treated very badly throughout the ages have signed exclusive usage contracts with us, i.e. given Alltournative the exclusive right to use their natural and cultural resources in a tourism-based economy. They're not allowing anybody else in there. And the fact that they still sign these contracts with us and are happy to do so now for longer and longer periods of time, I think is pretty clear. It clearly reflects their trust in our company and the acceptance of the way we work, which is totally transparent and honest and positive in terms of the impact we're bringing to their regions.
>
> Roger (2009)

In contrast to the 'Mayan Village' staged at Xcaret, most people I interviewed who visited both tourist attractions, felt that Alltournative's 'Mayan Encounter Expeditions' were more 'authentic'. Mauricio argues that this is because:

> Xcaret... shows you an ancient Mayan world not the contemporary one... not the one we are living in now which has nothing to do with the one you see at Xcaret...they don't tell you; they say this is Mayan culture this is what Mayans are like... then people leave and for example they come with us and they say 'ah what a difference! I thought Mayan people continued painting themselves and hunting'.
>
> Mauricio (2009, author's translation)

Jeremy, a US citizen who visited Playa del Carmen five years ago and decided to become a full-time resident, argued that the growth of companies like Alltournative is indicative of tourists' interest in experiencing something other than the many 'culture-less' activities available in the region. He claimed that:

> Once tourists have done Cancun and they have done the Pirate Ship [i.e. a popular dinner cruise in Cancun] and they've done the Catamaran [which involves a series of recreational water activities], you know, then what else are they going to do? I guess the Mayan thing is the new thing.
>
> Jeremy (2009)

When asked about 'the Mayan thing', particularly in relation to Alltournative's Maya Expeditions, Jeremy said that while tours like those of Alltournative can be 'a little touristy, a little contrived', a lot can be learned by taking part in them and 'experiencing' the reality of how many Mayan communities live:

> Out there in the villages you know once you get off the [tourist] strip it's... I hate to use the term 'third world' because a lot of people consider 'third world' is almost like an insult to some of the indigenous people ...but it really is 'third world' if you go away from here two or three hours inland you come into the wild ...I think that the culture there is very different and very strong.
>
> (Jeremy, 2009)

Ryan, a US tourist who has been visiting Playa del Carmen for the last seven years, argued that tours like those offered by Alltournative are a positive addition to the region's tourism industry because, 'Mayan culture here is very prevalent but not in Playa [del Carmen]' (Ryan, 2003). In other words, he said, tours like those offered by Alltournative served to 'open tourists' eyes to the region's real social environment' (Ryan, 2003).

Conclusion

The issue of authenticity and commodification, in the context of Mayan culture in the Mayan Riviera is undeniably complex. While Xcaret and Alltournative both engage in the commodification of Mayan culture, the way in which they re/present otherness, influence individuals' imaginaries of Mayan culture, and engage with Mayan local communities dramatically differs. For example, while the cultural re/presentations of Mayan culture offered by Alltournative are premised on the selling of the 'real' – that is, the 'reality' of contemporary Mayan peoples – Xcaret offers a staged, performed and generic re/presentation of Mayans, one that scholars and critics have equated to a 'Disneyfied' version of Mayan culture: sanitized, simulated, romanticized and packaged.

The way in which tourist attractions sell Mayan culture is by no means inconsequential. It can, for instance, contribute to the maintenance of a myth, one that maintains that Mayan culture is 'extinct' and, by definition, worth exploring only within the confines of staged or performed representations of an idealized past. Essentialized re/presentations that discursively tie contemporary Mayans to ancient Mayan culture can also contribute to the wider obfuscation of Mayan communities' recent history by disregarding the 'political, economic, and cultural relations that integrate them... albeit in a marginal and subordinate position, in a much larger world of modern Mexico and beyond' (Van den Berghe, 1995,

p. 583). Conversely, tourism that is based on the promotion of cross-cultural 'encounters' can be conducive to the social and economic inclusion of a people who have long been excluded from taking advantage of the region's many opportunities for socio-economic development. Alltournative, for example, while only impacting a small proportion of the region's Mayan communities[11], has managed to bring substantial socio-economic benefits to the communities that they work with (CEIDAS, 2009). At the same time, they have expanded tourists' imaginaries of contemporary Mayan realities by bringing them into contact with indigenous people who they would otherwise never have encountered. However, it is important to remember that Alltournative's 'Maya Encounter Expeditions', much like Xcaret's stagings and performances of Mayan culture, are structured on the presentation of a particular set of commercialized and romanticized images of Mayan culture created not by Mayan groups, but by the companies in charge of selling them.

Both Xcaret and Alltournative are, after all, tourist attractions that must compete with those around them in order to attract tourists. Although the images they sell, as I argued above, markedly differ, both Xcaret and Alltournative are structured around the idea of Otherness as a marketable commodity. When assessing their treatment of culture and looking at the discourses through which Mayan culture and indeed Mayan peoples are promoted, companies like Xcaret and Alltournative mobilize tropes of authenticity and the exotic. Pereira et al. argue that, with the advent of globalization, 'primitive' cultures - cultures that have been excluded from the 'homogenizing forces of globalization' - have gained value because they 'provide tourists with a "truly authentic" and "intimate" experience with another culture' (2002, p. 79; author's translation). This idea is consistent with the statement made by Ramirez who noted that, ethnic or 'indigenous tourism' to rural communities in the Mayan Riviera has a great potential for development, especially within foreign markets who find ethnic tourism 'greatly appealing because they do not have that kind of tourism [at home]' (Noticaribe, 2007; author's translation). The increasing 'desire on the part of tourists to experience the exotic and primitive "other" embodied in Mayan culture' (Torres, 2002, p. 111), in the context of the Mayan Riviera, can by no means be denied. Indeed, this is evident in the rise in popularity of both Xcaret and Alltournative.

Although forms of indigenous culture in the region have become increasingly popular in the last decade, the vast majority of re/presentations of Mayan culture in the Mayan Riviera continue to be consumed within the confines of mainstream entertainment venues such as those of Xcaret and do not involve any meaningful interaction with contemporary Mayan peoples. The representations encountered here, as a result, do not have a transformative effect on tourists' imaginaries of Mayan culture nor do they socially or economically benefit the many Mayan communities located in the interior of the peninsula, far from the ever-growing tourist-scapes of the Mayan Riviera and the lavish backdrops of their resorts.

On the whole, the analysis of the way in which Mayan culture is packaged and sold by tourist companies like those examined in this chapter points to the complex issues surrounding ethnic or cultural tourism in the Mayan Riviera. Today, issues of authenticity and commodification continue to represent an essential component of tourist discourses – both within and outside the confines of academia. Assessing tourism from the angle of whether or not it sustains 'authentic' culture, whether it transforms it into a 'commodity' and subsequently 'pollutes' it, or whether it altogether 'destroys' it, is problematic because such an assessment relies upon the presumed idea that authenticity can be fixed and is not subject to contestation. In this context, one must ask: authenticity for whom? In the words of Cole, 'who has the right, authority, or power to define what is authentic?' (Cole, 2007, p. 495).

Questions of authenticity and commodification, as the literature attests, are intertwined with questions of representation. In the context of the Mayan Riviera, it is essential to widen the discussion to include the voices of the re/presented, the imagined, and the subsequently consumed. Because tourism's integration of Mayan cultural forms and Mayan people as objects of the touristic interest in the Mayan Riviera is relatively recent, research in this area is still in its nascent stages. Undoubtedly, the selling of Mayan culture in the Mayan Riviera is a controversial phenomenon that interweaves many voices, imaginaries and representations. Although challenging, the incorporation of Mayan culture into the region's tourist circuits can assist in the transcendence of the socio-economic disparities that have, since their inception, characterized Cancun and the Mayan Riviera. The terms of its inclusion, however, are important. While Alltournative's approach, for example, does not resolve all the contradictions of ethnic or cultural tourism, their 'Maya Encounter Expeditions' have the potential to expand tourists' understanding of Mayans' present-day realities while also contributing to the socio-economic development of the communities with which they are involved. Xcaret's representations of Mayan culture, on the other hand, do little to challenge monolithic representations of Mayans as 'authentic' paragons of primitive Otherness, maintaining thus the type Otherness that is commonly promoted in both Cancun and the Mayan Riviera – an Otherness that can be gazed at, consumed, but never truly 'encountered'.

Notes

[1] Though definitions for both 'ethnic' and 'cultural' often differ, in this chapter, I use 'ethnic' and 'cultural' tourism interchangeably, combining van den Berghe and Keyes' definition of ethnic tourism as 'tourism wherein the prime attraction is the cultural exoticism of the local population and its artifacts' (Keyes and van den Berghe, 1984, p344) with McKercher and Du Cros' definition of cultural tourism as 'a form of

special interest tourism where culture forms the basis of either attracting tourists or motivating people to travel' (2002, p. 4).

[2] It is important to bear in mind that, in the literature, 'commodification' and 'commoditization' are often used interchangeably to describe the objectification of intangible culture and its concurrent treatment as a commodity that can be bought and sold in the tourism market.

[3] The municipality of Solidaridad, in Quintana-Roo, includes most of the Mayan Riviera's territory.

[4] For confidentiality reasons, I have replaced the names of personal contacts and interviewees with pseudonyms.

[5] Today's price for a general admission ticket (see: www.Xcaret.com)

[6] For a critical analysis of this show in relation to its re/presentation of Mexican culture, see Guerrero, 2010.

[7] Cenotes are groundwater-filled sinkholes; they can be found above ground, underground (inside caves or caverns), or partially underground.

[8] 'McDisneyfication' is a concept developed by George Ritzer and Allan Liska to represent commoditized, mass produced, hyperreal 'non places' which lack authenticity and relish in a post modern vacuum of simulacra; it is a fusion of Ritzer's concept of McDonalidization and with that of Disneyfication (See: Ritzer and Liska, 1997).

[9] According to Alltournative, 'ecotourism is of special interest to many travellers because of its relationship with conservation, sustainability, and biological diversity. As a developmental tool, ecotourism can advance two basic goals: [the conservation of]... biological and cultural diversity, by strengthening protected area management systems (public or private) and increasing the value of sound ecosystems... [and the promotion of] sustainable use of biodiversity by generating income, jobs and business opportunities in ecotourism and related business networks' (see Alltounative.com, 2010a). In addition, they add 'the purpose of ecotourism is to allow tourism to develop in a way that is fair and equitable for host communities'.

[10] All Interviewees have been given a pseudonym.

[11] Alltournative works with six communities and employs around 220 people in a state which (according to a local census in 2007) houses 282 rural communities and thousands of indigenous people living in acute poverty and with a 'high, or very high degree of marginalization' (CEIDAS, 2009, p.15; INEGI, 2007).

References

Alltournative (2010a) Ecotourism. Available at: http://www.alltournative.com/sustainable/tourism/ecotourism.asp (accessed 1 October 2010).

Alltournative (2010b) Coba Maya encounter expeditions. Available at: http://www.alltournative.com/tours-expeditions/coba_maya_encounter.asp (accessed 6 October 2010).

Butcher, J. (2001) Cultural baggage and cultural tourism. In: Butcher, J. (ed.) *Proceedings of the 5th ATLAS International Conference: Innovatory Approaches to Culture and Tourism, Rethymnon, Crete, Greece.* ATLAS, Arnhem, The Netherlands, pp. 2–25.

CEIDAS (2009) Pobreza y marginación: el rostro indígena. *Excelsior*, 4.

Cohen, E. (1988) Authenticity and commoditization in tourism. *Annals of Tourism Research* 15, 371–386.

Cole, S. (2007) Beyond authenticity and commodification. *Annals of Tourism Research* 34, 943–960.

DATATUR (2003) Reporte semanal centros turisticos seleccionados. Available at: http://datatur.sectur.gob.mx/work/docs/6_reporte_mensua/men092003.pdf (8 October 2009)

Frankland, S. (2009) The bulimic consumption of pygmies: regurgitating an image of otherness. In: Robinson, M. and Picard, D. (eds) *The Framed World: Tourism, Tourists and Photography*. Ashgate Publishing, Farnham, Surrey, UK, pp. 95–116.

Gonzalez, J.M. (2007) *Playa del Carmen, Aquella Villa de Pescadores*. El Fondo Editorial del Honorable Ayuntamiento de Solidaridad, Playa del Carmen, Mexico.

Guerrero-Rodriguez, R. (2010) Mexico for sale: the creation and manipulation of a cultural identity for tourism. The case of Xcaret night show. *Proceedings of the Tourism and the Seduction of Difference Conference, 9–12 September 2010. Lisbon, Portugal.* TOCOCU, Lisbon, Portugal.

Harrison, D. (1994) Tourism, capitalism and development in less developed countries. In: Sklair, L. (ed.) *Capitalism and Development*. Routledge, London, pp. 232–257.

Hiernaux-Nicolas, N. (1999) Cancún bliss. In: Judd, D. and Fainstein, S. (eds) *The Tourist City*. Yale University Press, New Haven, Connecticut, pp. 124–139.

INEGI (2005) Conteo de población y vivienda 2005, Instituto Nacional de Estadística, Geografía e Informática, Available at: http://www.inegi.gob.mx (accessed 7 February 2010).

Jones, L. (2007) Dollars and cenotes. *The Alcalde* 95, 72–73.

Keyes, C.F. and van den Berghe, P.L. (1984) Tourism and re-created ethnicity. *Annals of Tourism Research* 11 (3), 343–352.

MacCannell, D. (1976) *The Tourist: A New Theory of the Leisure Class.* Schocken Books, New York.

McKercher, B. and du Cros, H. (2002) Cultural Tourism: The Partnership Between Tourism and Cultural Heritage Management. Hawthorn Press, New York.

Marti, F. (1985) *Cancún, Fantasía de Banqueros: La Construcción de Una Ciudadturística a Partir de Cero.* Editorial Uno, Mexico.

Mathieson, A. and Wall, G. (1982) *Tourism: Economic, Physical, and Social Impacts.* Longman, London.

Noticias Caribe (2007) Piden involucrar a comunidades para arraigar el turismo rural. Available at: http://www.noticaribe.com.mx/rivieramaya/2007/10/piden_involucrar_a_comnidades_para_arraigar_el_turismo_rural.html (accessed 2 October 2010).

Ritzer, G. and Liska, A. (1997) McDisneyization and post-tourism. In: Rojek, C. and Urry, J. (eds) *Touring Cultures: Transformations of Travel and Theory.* Routledge, London, pp. 96–109.

SECTUR (2004) El Turismo en la Riviera Maya. Boletin Cuatrimestral de Turismo. SECTUR, Mexico.

SEDETUR (2008) Boletin Turistico de Cancun. SECTUR, Mexico.

Shepherd, D. (2002) Commodification, culture, and tourism. *Tourist Studies* 2, 183–201.

Tomaselli, K.C. and Wang, C. (2001) Selling myths not culture: authenticity and cultural tourism. *Tourism Forum Southern Africa* 1, 271–289.

Torres, R. (2002) Cancun's tourism development from a Fordist spectrum of analysis. *Tourist Studies* 2, 87–116.

Urry, J. (1990) *The Tourist Gaze: Leisure and Travel in Contemporary Societies.* Sage Publications, London.

Van den Berghe, P. (1995) Marketing Mayas: ethnic tourism promotion in Mexico. *Annals of Tourism Research* 22, 568–599.

Walker, C. (2005) Archaeological tourism: looking for answers along Mexico's Mayan Riviera. *NAPA Bulletin* 23, 60–73.

Watson, G.L. and Kopachevsky, J.P. (1994) Interpretations of tourism as commodity. *Annals of Tourism Research* 21, 643–660.

XCARET (2010) Mayan village. Available at: http://www.xcaret.com/Culture/MayanVillage.html (accessed 20 October 2010).

4 Authenticity Versus Development: Tourism to the Hill Tribes of Thailand

Marina Novelli[1] and Anne Tisch-Rottensteiner[2]
[1]*Centre for Tourism Policy Studies, School of Service Management, University of Brighton, Eastboune, UK;* [2]*Beluga School for Life, Thailand*

Introduction

This chapter examines whether the increasing demand for authenticity by tourists contrasts with the proclaimed efforts to use tourism as a development tool. By using the hill tribes of Northern Thailand as a representative case, this chapter focuses on the extent to which tourism benefits local people, leads to local development or whether the tourists' quest for authenticity holds back development.

Development is a multifaceted process with tourism gradually being influenced by various theories and emerging as a widely recognized development tool. At the same time, while tourists have increasingly been seeking what they consider to be authentic experiences, a growing demand for new forms of tourism such as ethnic/indigenous tourism has come to light, with several micro-level implications (Wheeler, 1992; Burns and Figurova, 2005).

Results from the fieldwork revealed that tourists who visit the hill tribes in Northern Thailand generally expect an authentic experience, but their expectations are often not met as the hill tribes are increasingly being influenced by Western lifestyles and progress, a natural development process reinforced by globalization.

Furthermore, it became evident that tourism impacts both positively and negatively on local indigenous communities. The study also concluded that while there is an urgent need for governmental institutions to recognize the substantial added value provided by the hill tribes to Thai tourism, tourists have to be made more aware of what to expect, how to behave and how to interact when travelling to the locality, with tour operators having the responsibility and moral obligation to ensure that tourism truly benefits local communities.

Development and (New) Tourism: Theories and Issues

During the four decades prior to the new millennium, import and export were satisfactorily seen as the main influencing factors in the economic development of a country (Mamoozadeh and McKee, 1990). However, as economic growth is just one aspect of development (Sharpley, 2000; Clayton, 2003; Marcouiller *et al.*, 2004), it became obvious that 'the classical approach to the study of development derives from neoclassical economics and totally [Western] dominated thinking for a period close on forty years' (Potter *et al.*, 2008). This is linked to the modernization theory, which is founded on the belief that a country can be 'developed' through modernization, often based on Western principles (Rostow, 1960; Scheyvens, 2002; Potter *et al.*, 2008). More recently, while neo-liberalist structures exist among multinational companies, often criticized for creating uneven power relationships, inequalities and dependencies through their policies (Amin, 1996; Scheyvens, 2002; Higgins-Desbiolles, 2006), modernization and economic growth continue to be considered the main contributors to the development of a destination (Sharpley, 2002; Jamal and Stronza, 2008).

Since 'there is probably no other economic activity which transects so many sectors, levels and interests' (Cater, 1995, p. 21), tourism has been increasingly recognized as a promising tool for development in many countries (Mamoozadeh and McKee, 1990; Hunter, 1995; Sharpley, 2000; Telfer, 2002; Crick, 2003; de Oliveira, 2005; Brown and Hall, 2008). However, tourism has often been criticized as a new form of colonialism, since the industry is characterized by uneven power relationships and leakages (Brohman, 1996; Hall and Brown, 2006; Higgins-Desbiolles, 2006; Burns, 2008a, 2008b; Potter *et al.*, 2008; Pattullo, 2009). Based on the controversial issue that 'tourism development not only enhances the ability of the elite to control dissident voices, but encourages the development of hegemonic consensus that makes control cheaper and capital investment more profitable' (Smith 1997, p. 204), the need for tourism to become better integrated into broader development plans (Hunter, 1995; Brohman, 1996; Boxill, 2003; Karagiannis, 2003; Zezza *et al.*, 2009), the requirement of involving all stakeholders (Clayton, 2003) and the need for plans to be long-term rather than short-term (Karagiannis, 2003) are part of an ongoing debate. Indeed, tourism can lead to an increase in foreign exchange and investment, job creation, infrastructure development (Mamoozadeh and McKee, 1990; Burns and Holden, 1995; Sharpley, 2002; Hjalager, 2007) and potentially a multiplier effect emerging from the sector's linkages

and networks with positive implications for the entire destination (Mamoozadeh and McKee, 1990; Brohman, 1996); but, tourism can also lead to reverse multipliers as the costs for local people increase due to tourism (Chambers, 2000). Other negative consequences of tourism include '...foreign domination and dependency, socioeconomic and spatial polarization, environmental destruction, cultural alienation, and the loss of social control and identity among host communities' (Brohman, 1996, p. 48). Economic leakages through the predominantly foreign ownership of most tourism businesses are also a major problem (Chambers, 2000; Knowles *et al.*, 2004; Dodman, 2009). Taking those issues into account, 'scholars have posited a shift from a predominately Fordist model of capitalistic development to the emergence of post-Fordist and neo-Fordist modes of production and consumption' (Torres, 2002, p. 87), which has led to a set of new sustainable development approaches and new forms of tourism.

New development approaches and new forms of tourism have progressively increased over the past 30 years, aiming at '[...]a more realistic possibility of contributing positively to the lives of people in the Third World' (Brown and Hall, 2008, p. 843). Development strategies started looking beyond economic growth, by focusing on the environment and social issues (Schuurman, 1990; Sharpley, 2000; Telfer, 2002; Northcote and Macbeth, 2006). 'Since the late 1980s, sustainable development has become a buzzword in development studies in general and in tourism research in particular' (Liu, 2003, p. 459). In 1990, Schuurman (1990, p. 22) had noted that 'the term sustainable development encompasses development strategies which range from light-green to dark-green, from romantic and nostalgic conservatism to utopian socialism, from absolute-zero growth in the economy to maintaining the present world economic growth rate. As a result, the "green" notion of sustainable development could be incorporated without effort into both the "blue" development model (neo-liberal) and the "red" development model (socialist, and these days social democratic). In a number of cases one can therefore hardly speak of an alternative development model'. In effect, some may add that sustainability can be regarded as a luxury that the poor cannot afford, when it comes to the daily survival of their families (Cater, 1995). In line with sustainable development principles, new forms of tourism have emerged with a set of debatable implications for the host destination (Wheeler, 1992; Lane, 1994; Brohman, 1996; Weaver, 1999; Butcher, 2003; Liu, 2003; Beeton, 2006; Fennell, 2006; Hall and Brown, 2006; Fennell and Malloy, 2007; Brown and Hall, 2008; Higgins-Desbiolles, 2008; Pattullo, 2009). The controversy is that while there is a tendency to refer to those new forms of tourism as 'better' options than mass tourism, most are practiced on a small scale, therefore with 'small scale impact and contribution to the local economy' (Wheeler, 1992, p. 233).

Implementing sustainable tourism is not easy, due to the number and variety of stakeholders (Lane, 1994). For instance, more recently, '[t]he importance of tourism for poor countries is a widely discussed issue in international development' (Carbone, 2005, p. 559) leading to the emergence of concepts such as pro-poor tourism as a strategy to engage the poor, guarantee a more equal distribution of the benefits resulting from tourism and alleviate poverty (Valdés and Stoller, 2002; Carranza Carbone, 2005; Hawkins and Mann, 2007; Brown and Hall, 2008; Higgins-Desbiolles, 2008; Mowforth et al., 2008). In this regard, increasing emphasis has been placed on the value of community-based tourism (CBT) (Cheong and Miller, 2000; Tosun, 2000), often led by foreign interests (Tosun, 2000; Mowforth and Munt, 2008) with some severe implementation challenges, such as the lack of local capacity, which adds to the debate on the controversy of tourism and development. One of the dilemmas is that local people often lack expertise, which makes it hard to fully incorporate the community into a tourism operation, with approaches often remaining top-down and tokenistic (Tosun, 2000; Timothy and Ioannides, 2002; Novelli and Gebhardt

2007; Moscardo, 2008). Moreover, debates on green tourism and ecotourism have become very popular (Wheeler, 1992; Liu, 2003; Higgins-Desbiolles, 2008), leading to the fact that ecotourism is often controversially used as a marketing tool and at times practised on the same scale as mass tourism (Wheeler, 1995; Buckley, 2002; Wagner, 2005). There is therefore a need for revisiting the concept of ecotourism (i.e. carrying capacity) as, in some cases, it has contributed even more negatively than mass tourism on some of the more exotic, unspoilt (Weaver, 1999; Scheyvens, 2002; Liu, 2003; Mowforth and Munt, 2008) and fragile places in which it takes place.

Globalization and Authenticity in Tourism

Potter et al. (2008, p. 131) state that 'globalisation is seen by those subscribing to modernisation theory as the outward flow of Western know-how, capital and culture to the rest of the world'. Since globalization and development are interrelated, many authors agree that tourism is both a driving force and consequence of globalization (Fayed and Fletcher, 2002; Freyer, 2006; Azarya, 2007; Hjalager, 2007; Cooper and Hall, 2008; Potter et al., 2008).

Within the last few decades, new concerns over the consumption of goods have emerged (Urry, 2002; Knowles et al., 2004), which Inglehart and Flanagan (1987) described as post-materialistic. The new consumers are '[...]living in economies where their basic needs are quickly and easily satisfied[...] As a result they tend to reject mass-produced and mass-marketed commodities in favor of products and services that can claim to be in some way authentic' (Lewis and Bridger, 2001, p. 4). Many agree that tourists have therefore become more demanding, travel to less well-known and unspoilt places and are ever more in search of authenticity (Diamantis, 1998; Medina, 2003; Smith and Duffy, 2003; Salazar, 2005; Azarya, 2007; van Egmond, 2007;

Brown and Hall, 2008; Cole, 2008; Gonzalez, 2008; Telfer and Sharpley, 2008; Pattullo, 2009).

What is perceived as being authentic depends on the perception of each individual and his/her cultural background and experiences. In fact, '[…]in Western societies, what is and is not authentic is largely the consequence of replicated interpretations, which although contested by professionals, are commodified for mass consumption' (McIntosh and Prentice, 1999, p. 590). Taylor (2001, p. 9), for example, argues that 'within cultural tourism, and wherever else the production of authenticity is dependent on some act of (re)production, it is conventionally the past which is seen to hold the model of the original'. Therefore, authenticity stands in contrast to our modern world and that past often has to be artificially recreated to attract tourists (Teo and Yeoh, 1997), what MacCannell (1973) referred to as staged authenticity, through which tourists experience a superficiality of performances on a front stage, while the real traditions are kept (in the back) for the local population. In any case, as tourists often cannot distinguish between the real and the set up performances, 'it may be necessary to discount the importance, and even the existence, of front and back regions except as ideal poles of touristic experience' (MacCannell, 1973, p. 597). Moreover, tourism can be seen as a way to conserve traditions, since local people continue to pass them on to the next generations as a tourist product (Azarya, 2007).

'Globalization, with its new forms of production, transportation and universalized mass media, has led to major cultural changes and thus transformations of identity… Some identities wane, and others are transformed' (Langman, 2003, p. 244). As social identity changes naturally over centuries (Schirato and Webb, 2003; Scholte, 2005) so does culture (Skelton, 1996; Mowforth and Munt, 2008) and as Langman (2003, p. 223) states 'globalization creates forces that both homogenize and differentiate identity', with the preservation of culture becoming a predominant tourism-focused activity (Azarya, 2007; Cole, 2008; Medina,

2003; Schirato and Webb, 2003). Undoubtedly, 'there is a growing desire by millions of travellers for access to "primitive" societies, a hunger to taste if only briefly their traditional ways of life, a wish to see, experience and photograph their "exotic" practices'. (Sofield and Birtles, 1996, p. 396) and the assumption that 'to develop is to modernise' becomes controversial in the tourism arena as 'if a remote cultural tourist destination modernises, it is no longer "primitive" and it loses its appeal' (Cole, 2008, p. 22). In effect, 'the critical point to such arguments is that commodification and modernization place tradition and "authenticity" in jeopardy' (Taylor, 2001, p.13).

In the context of the above, if development was to be regarded as modernization and authenticity as conservation of culture, one could simplistically argue that the increasing demand for authentic experiences on the part of tourists may hold back the development of destinations, which may find (or not) expression in ethnic/indigenous tourism scenarios.

Ethnic/Indigenous Tourism

Yang and Wall (2009, p.235) define ethnic tourism as 'motivated primarily by the visitor's search for exotic cultural experiences through interaction with distinctive ethnic groups'. They furthermore state that it is hard to separate an ethnic tourist from the masses since an ethnic activity can also be part of a mass tourist attraction (Yang and Wall, 2009). Ethnic tourism involves what is often referred to as indigenous people, which are defined as those that are traditionally native to a country (Hinch and Butler, 1996). Weaver (2009) argues that almost all indigenous people are nowadays more or less involved in tourism activities, often leading to the controversial issues regarding the use of land between tourism businesses and indigenous populations (Wall, 1999). The increasing demand for ethnic and indigenous tourism originates from tourists' increasing search for more authentic experiences, with tourism seen as an additional source of income for indigenous people. Smith (1996, p. 287) talks about the four 'Hs' of indigenous tourism, namely 'the geographic setting (habitat), the ethnographic traditions (heritage), the effects of acculturation (history), and the marketable handicrafts' and 'the exposure which many tourists now have to indigenous cultures and peoples is [often] limited to a master/servant relationship, or to fleeting, often staged and inauthentic representations of traditional life styles' (Hinch and Butler, 1996, p. 3).

In 2004, the UN declared the 'International Decade of the World's Indigenous People', with the aim of empowering indigenous people (United Nations, 2008). In 2009, the 'Guidelines on Indigenous Peoples' proposed ways of 'promoting or reinforcing sustainable development, areas such as cultural tourism, and/or cultural and creative industries, where desired by the community' (United Nations, 2009, p. 34) to benefit indigenous people and contribute to development. In contrast, in the name of authenticity, tourism may hold back development because indigenous people's marginality is seen as the unique selling proposition for the tourists. Where they are no longer 'different from the tourists', they would loose their attractiveness and 'to sustain such commodity, continue attracting customers, they have to maintain their difference' (Azarya, 2007, p. 961).

The experience of the tourists depends on their expectations. In this regard, the management of expectations takes shape in what Burns and Figurova (2005, p.107) describe as 'honest and clear communication'. Tourism can give marginalized indigenous populations a rediscovered sense of self-esteem through the outsiders' recognition of the value of their culture and traditions (Ryan, 2005). Despite the criticism on staged authenticity, Cohen (1995) argued that staged cultural performances can be the way forward to keep tourists outside the real life of indigenous people, who on their part have to adapt to the pressure of globalization in order to survive (Ryan, 2005; McCaskill et al., 2008). On reflection, an adequate preparation of the tourist on what to expect at the hand of trained local tour guides becomes essential in order to guarantee a positive experience for both hosts and guests (Millman, 1995).

Tourism in Thailand: Development Implications

Thailand was among the first countries in South-east Asia to emerge as a tourist destination. Mass tourism began to develop under Marshal Sarit Thanarat's premiership in the 1950s, and in 1959, the Tourist Organisation of Thailand (TOT) - currently Tourism Authority of Thailand (TAT), was established (Peleggi, 1996). 'Thailand began national level tourism planning in 1976 in the interest of developing the tourism industry and based on maximization of the benefits of national attractions' (Leepreecha, 1997, p. 271). The Vietnam War led to an immense investment boom in the country; however, the image of the country started to reshape into that of a sex tourism destination (Boniface and Cooper, 2001). Thailand faces increasing competition from its neighbouring countries such as Vietnam, Laos and Cambodia, but despite the 2004 Tsunami and the political unrest of 2010, which led to a decline in tourist numbers that has not yet recovered (Bangkok Post, 2010), it remains a well-established tourism destination (Forsyth, 1995), generally enjoying 'a very good reputation and...a safe country for foreign tourists' (Cohen, 2009, p. 185).

In response to competition and the negative connotation of sex tourism, the Thai government is increasingly focusing on the development of more sustainable forms of tourism. Most recently, the TAT published a booklet called 'Learning Through Travelling', featuring 48 projects in different regions of the country where tourists can experience Thailand away from the traditional tourist routes (TAT, 2008). Additionally, since indigenous communities and their culture emerged as one of the main reasons why people travel to Thailand, CBT became increasingly recognized as a way forward to

preparation of data collection tools supported by extensive desk research in order to become familiar with the topic, choose appropriate interviewees and design appropriate questions. The interviewees had been contacted well ahead of time and they were given the choice of being interviewed either at the ITB in Berlin or in a familiar location in Thailand. Triangulation was applied by using data collected via a questionnaire conducted with 81 randomly selected tourists and the interviews.

At times due to language barriers some questions had to be simplified and rephrased during the interview, and a translator used during the interviews with hill tribes villagers, leading to possible misunderstandings or inadequate interpretation of responses. However, the recording proved to be useful to revisit some of the dialogues.

Since this research involved people, ethical considerations became essential. All respondents were informed about the purpose of the research and asked for permission to record the interviews. Anonymity was granted to those who chose to; however, for the purpose of this study respondents were all coded with 'R' followed by a number. The research did not aim for replicability in terms of specific findings, but rather for a set of specific qualitative information to contribute to the ongoing debate on tourism, authenticity and development. In this sense, an empirical case study has been developed that can be compared with others.

Findings: Hill Tribes and Thai Respondents

When asked about defining 'development', respondents became hesitant, but agreed on it as an improvement of a current situation. Surprisingly none of them mentioned specifically economic gain as main contributor to development. While one respondent specifically expressed that development means not only development of material things, but it is also a 'mental' state (R10), others pointed out that: 'development means

change...the assumption is that it is change for the better' (R3); 'it is all about giving people opportunities' (R6) and 'it can be through economic development, social development so development is a broad sort of term [...] it can mean obviously better quality of life, better standards of living... also education and knowledge about the world and other aspects as well' (R4).

That tourism has the potential to lead to development of a country emerged as a common understanding. However, it became obvious that it largely depends upon the way tourism is practised. A general consensus about the economic benefits of tourism emerged with specific emphasis placed on the potential for reinvesting the money spent by tourists in projects within the country (R10), a controversial issue given the leakages produced by foreign dominated tourism businesses (Hall and Brown, 2006; Potter et al., 2008, Pattullo, 2009).

Different levels of concerns about tourism were expressed, from the extensive changes that it produces to a destination (R4), to defining it as 'a really dangerous thing' (R8). The recognition of ecotourism as a new form of tourism and its potential to 'develop and help [...] if it's done the right way' was matched by the desire to use CBT as a development tool (R1). While emphasis was placed on the distinction between the development of a country (economic contribution) and the development of a community, tourism was certainly seen as a tool to improve communities' livelihood (R3).

The emergence of new consumers with greater concern about their behaviour and interest in authentic experiences, the surfacing of alternative approaches in tourism development and the materialization of new forms of tourism are aspects of the changing face of Thai tourism too, with an increasing number of visitors interested in niches such as ecotourism and opportunities to get involved with local communities (R1).

The connection between tourism and globalization was drawn by referring to the role of multimedia bringing the world 'into our lounges every day [...] people are no longer frightened to travel, going through airports, different cultures, different customs, etc. there is less of a barrier nowadays so the interest, in special interest tourism – in getting away from the mainstream is becoming greater' (R6). On the increase is the demand for responsible tour operators because 'people [have] become more ethically minded and more green and more conscious about their choices, not just through travel, but in shopping, through anything now, people become more aware of the consequences of how they behave[…] I think more than ten years ago you didn't see signs or adverts for eco tours, things like that, so it's definitely come about within the last ten years or so – whether they are real eco tours or not is another thing' (R4).

It appeared that tourists did more research as they show interest in the daily life of locals and are eager to share experiences and knowledge with them (R8, R5). They 'ask for [a] kind of more authentic or traditional community experience' (R7) and the increasing demand for CBT may reinforce these views (R11). Furthermore, 'where people can give something back to the community is getting more and more popular […] people just don't want to stay two weeks in a beach resort, lie at the pool or lie at the beach and then go back to their country again, but they want to give something back and I think [that] the interaction between the local people and the tourists is getting more and more popular' (R2).

This, however, neglects the fact that alternative tourists travelling to unspoilt places may damage the environment at times even more than conventional mass tourists (Wheeler, 1992; Scheyvens, 2002; Mowforth and Munt, 2008) as there is more demand for 'off the beaten path areas, so travellers are getting more adventurous, they wanna explore aside of the main tourist spots' (R4).

Tourism versus Development: Thailand and the Hill Tribes

The adaptation of Western ideas into the local culture (Schirato and Webb, 2003; Cohen, 2007; Cole, 2008) emerged as a generally accepted and natural ongoing evolutionary and imitative process, as '[…]one of the charms of Thailand, for example, is that you have the western infrastructure […] but it also has this chaotic Asian atmosphere, it is not as organised and structured like for example in Singapore. They take the good things from western countries and try to adapt [them], but of course you have your traditions' (R2).

Tourists who visit Thailand for the first time focus on its major landmarks and attractions. About a decade ago, the TAT started to promote sustainable tourism projects (i.e. the Green Leaf Foundation) also catering for the large number of repeat visitors by giving them new reasons to visit (R2). However, many tour operators in Thailand still believe that sustainable tourism is a frivolous concept and is harming their business (R11).

As in many other destinations, the general inclination of the governor of the TAT is to increase the numbers of tourists by also looking at more sustainable options including ecotourism (TAT Press Conference, ITB 2010). The potential for ecotourism was further recognized in the fact that 'when you balance the access and the other amenities and the Thai people, the culture and [the rest], the strategic location of Thailand in global terms, when you […] benchmark it, Thailand was far ahead, Northern Thailand was far ahead' (R6), with clear reference made to the hill tribes.

Expectations of Tourists

Of the 81 randomly selected tourists (46 female and 35 male) who completed the questionnaire, 67 were between 20 and 30 years old, 58 were in Thailand for the first time and 23 had already visited the hill tribes. Of the 58 travellers that had not been to the hill tribes yet, 37 were considering going there, and only 20 people indicated that they were not planning to go there. Thirty-six people stated that they were organizing their visit to the hill tribes individually, while 19 were planning their visit as part of a package tour.

When asked about their expectations, many people referred to the visit to the hill tribes as a 'traditional life-style' and a 'real-life' experience. One respondent stated that he/she expected 'houses without electricity, no running water, kind people, different language, peaceful and quiet environment and happy, with no material stuff' and another one 'friendly people who live with no modern technology and are still happy'. These views support the rather 'romantic' and 'nostalgic' view of the hill tribe villages mentioned by Lewis and Lewis (1984) and Wang (1999), which may have been influenced by the media since one stated 'It will be remote and like we see on the TV'. On reflection, the expectations of one of the respondents had not been met as he/she 'expected the people to be pretty isolated, not really affected by Western culture, but found that they were quite influenced by the outside world…televisions, non-hill tribe clothing, etc.'

One person, for instance, claimed to have expected a 'relatively authentic [village] but tainted by tourism – slightly, probably accustom[ed] to tourists…I think tourism will hinder development as for the tribe. [It] may develop them…but exposure to "modern" values may corrupt their authenticity and make them value money, superficial things more'. Other tourists recognized some level of staged authenticity, by indicating that 'it doesn't seem very authentic to me, more a mass tourism activity, with people wearing traditional clothes for the pictures'.

In general, it became obvious that most tourists expected an authentic experience typically expressed as 'a self-sufficient community that is not influenced by western culture and technologies (no electricity) and not yet touristic'. One respondent stated, for example, 'I'd hoped there wouldn't be anyone wearing an Adidas T-shirt there' (which, in fact, was seen), with some consensus that Western influences and tourism change and mostly harm the hill tribes.

Most tourists had a possibly distorted image of what a hill tribe village would look like, which may be linked to the romanticized description of the TAT website, which describes them as 'isolated', 'remote' and 'exotic' (TAT, 2010). When asked about their most impressive experience, most tourists stated that the friendly welcome of the locals left a positive picture in their mind. Those who stayed overnight seemed to have the most profound experiences: 'Our guide and people from the village were sitting together at the fire and singing songs and playing guitar, and that was so happy and authentic'. In contrast, many who visited the tribes for a short visit felt 'extremely uncomfortable in the bazaar pseudo-village that was set up in order to support tourism'. Several tourists pointed out that they were not willing to visit the long-neck hill tribes and described them as a 'human zoo'.

The expectations of the tourists emerged during the observations at the villages. During the 'mass tourism' trip, tourists mainly took pictures of what they considered to be 'authentic', by avoiding satellite antennas, motorbikes, mobile phones and electricity posts in their pictures. The idyllic picture of villages untouched by civilization remains a nostalgic representation of the postcards sold in Bangkok. As in many other developing destinations, '[t]he tourism industry showed interest in and started working with ethnic minorities years ago, but never made them stakeholders' (R6), which was worsened by the fact that many hill tribe people do not have Thai citizenship, making it even harder for them to exercise their rights (R10, R9, R13, R8, R12), with no bargaining power except to accept existing business practices (R7). The lack of citizenship means restricted land rights (R6, R9, R5, R8, R12), no access to healthcare systems, restricted ability to move (R8), and therefore no recognized status in Thai society (McCaskill, 1997; Cohen, 2000). Another controversial issue is that while the 'nationalism process of the government' (R7) of providing educational opportunities to ethnic minorities may be seen as a positive step towards integration, local languages are not allowed in school to the loss of cultural identity, as 'the bulk of the hill tribes […] only have an oral history, they don't have a written language, only the Mien in this area have a written language - you go through one or two generations of people who aren't willing [or able] to learn about the history [and language], their history can be lost' (R8). It was raised that the negative image of hill tribes associated with the cultivation of poppies and the language barriers (Lewis and Lewis, 1984; Chandraprasert, 1997; McCaskill, 1997; Vater, 2006) 'can be changed through CBT also as a way to provide alternative livelihood to people', but the lack of cooperation between companies and local people hinders progress in this direction (R9). As a common denominator with other developing country destinations, the supply chain emerged as the real problem (R1, R6, R5) as '[…]it is very difficult to tell where the money goes when tourists book a package tour to the hill tribes' (R7), 'the locals hardly benefit from conventional tours to their villages' (R9). During the high season, about 100 tourists daily visit a local Akha village and an income of about 400 Thai Bath (THB) per day is generated on average from the sale of handicraft. The village does not get any money from the tour operators, with mass tour operators not even asking for permission to visit the village (R13).

As highlighted by Hinch and Butler (1996), tourism can bring additional income to indigenous people, but this has to be organized in a way that is fair to those who hold the attractiveness, who provide the product – the hill tribes. For example, while the home stay at a local Akha village produces substantial revenues that go to a community fund, which is used for infrastructure development and education for the children (R13), Lisu Lodge directly works with the hill tribe village nearby and is able to generate about 4 million THB (some US$132,000) per year, that goes directly to the local people (R9). However, these good practices cannot be generalized, as in several other cases the unequal distribution of revenues has caused inequalities amongst villagers and changes in the hierarchical tribal structure (R6).

The risk of tourism creating false expectations, conflicts of uses and operation beyond carrying capacity, with customs and nature being destroyed to cater for tourists

are a reality of Northern Thailand (R1). For instance, there was an example where elephant owners and local farmers came into conflict due to the unsustainable number of elephant camps opened near a hill tribe village so both attractions could be combined on a day trip, with the animals increasingly destroying the crops of local farmers (R7).

In contrast, that tourism could restore villagers' pride, dignity and reputation in Thai society was a given fact, but the loss of identity, the increased adversity towards or dependency on tourism was observed when villagers hid in their houses and children followed the visitors even to the next village incessantly trying to sell their handicrafts, which are now competitively mass produced in Bangkok (Fig. 4.1) and displayed in fair-trade shops all over Thailand (Fig. 4.2).

As handicraft and tour guiding produce insufficient revenues, prostitution and drug dealing become ways to make extra money, which is encouraged by some tourists' desire to try opium as an 'authentic' experience, worsening local habits. The discussion on the ethics of the visits to the longneck tribes was characterized by a clear differentiation with other hill tribes as the longneck people are strongly controlled by outsiders forcing them to wear traditional costumes, sell handicrafts that are not produced in the village and often 'held' in restricted areas for tourism purposes (R8, R1). Further controversy emerged when reflecting upon the ethics of tourism consumption and their interest in viewing and photographing people with physical conspicuousness (i.e. long neck, big ears) as a tourism attraction (Fig. 4.3).

Authenticity versus Development

The dichotomy between the hill tribes aspiring to profit from a modern life and tourists wishing to encounter authenticity was clear throughout the study. In Lisu village things have changed: a truck has been bought and villagers can enjoy some comforts of modern life (Fig. 4. 4), but traditions are still maintained (R12). On the other hand, a local woman from an Akha village clearly stated

that she would prefer the traditional self-sustaining lifestyle to a monetary one. Each village has different priorities and attitudes, 'that people must live in bamboo houses because it's traditional and must wear traditional clothing, because that's how they should be and, you know, not ride on motorbikes or have mobile phones or anything like that. They should be able to do what they wanna do, as long as they have the information about the pros and cons of doing it[...]' (R8).

On the relationship between development and authenticity, the general view was that tourism accelerates change and tourists should accept that globalization and progress have reached the hill tribes of Thailand too. 'In its current format, it [tourism] holds back the development. But I think if we sort of change the model of tourism [...] whether or not the current stakeholders in tourism want it or not, purely because of the power of the internet and the social media [...] and enough people willing to change it, there's enough people who want special interest travel [...] I think that [this] will bring about massive change far faster than we would normally expect, I can see that happening over the next 5–10 years' (R6). It is the responsibility of the tour operators to inform tourists about progress in destinations as 'a lot of people are a little bit disappointed when they go to a hill tribe village and they see that not everybody is wearing the traditional costumes anymore. There are people who walk in jeans, they have TV, they have satellite, they have radio, they have internet' (R11). The challenge is that '[...]if a remote cultural tourist destination modernises, it is no longer "primitive" [...] it loses its appeal' (Cole, 2008, p.22), which is what has been happening all over Thailand: as soon as remote villages change to be more 'like other lowland Thai people then the trekking route tends to shift to more primitive or authentic cultures' (R7). In response to this, some may say that staged authenticity is a good thing if it makes tourists visit and motivates younger generations to learn traditional dances and other skills (R7), it may be a good way to preserve traditions (Azarya, 2007), '[...]it's like a performance, some people like it and some people don't[...]' (R4).

As immigrants from neighbouring countries, the hill tribes have been a great draw for tourism to Northern Thailand; however, for many years they have been marginalized by Thai society. It has long been debated that the government should start recognizing the value that these tribes bring to Thailand as a tourism destination (R10, R6, R7, R8) and attribute them a status in Thai society (R9) by accepting them as Thai citizens (R9). If this became the case, reconsideration over land rights and full recognition of their role as stakeholders should emerge (R6). On the other hand, '[T]ourism is really only to supplement them in terms of money, but also in terms of knowledge, information, education, ideas from foreigners' (R4). Viable secondary revenue streams for ethnic rural communities should be sought in order to avoid becoming dependent on a single sector (R6).

Conclusions

The data reported above tell us at least three things. Firstly, that there is an ongoing contradiction between the promotion of tourism as a pro-poor development tool and the evident limited benefit of tourism for indigenous communities such as the hill tribes. Secondly, that the quest for unspoiled locations, authentic settings and unique experiences remain amongst the most controversial contributors to socio-economic and environmental changes of visited localities. Thirdly, that despite years of empirical research on the effects of globalization on tourism, society and culture and of progress and change on communities' identity in Thailand, the role of indigenous people such as the hill tribes remains marginal.

The evidence also confirmed that, in this particular case, tourists were indeed looking for an authentic experience while travelling, and more interaction with local people. However, from the hill tribe side, findings indicated feelings of interference with local customs and lifestyle.

This study highlighted the failing role of tour operators in properly managing such encounters. As much as tour operators have to adapt to the changing needs of tourists, they should change their attitude towards hill tribes and become more responsive to their needs and avoid exploitative practices. For instance, despite the limited sample of hill tribes visited, the findings contributed further to the controversies surrounding tourist expenditure and local benefit: in the case under study (though limited to two tribes) the money still does not reach hill tribe members.

Although the involvement of the community in alternative management of resources (i.e. the natural environment) is a widely debated multidisciplinary issue, the challenge remains in the fact that the hill tribes should be enabled through capacity building to better engage with the tourism development and management process and acquire a set of business skills to operate responsibly in such a complex sector. If after so many decades of tourism, in a country like Thailand, rural communities are still marginalized from the tourism planning process and are unable to 'control who is coming to their village, when, and how many people' (R3), it is obvious that community empowerment remains a preached rather than practised reality, which would benefit from better cooperation between government, local people and tour operators.

Over the course of this study, while it became evident that tourism and the quest for authenticity cannot hold back development from the hill tribes of Northern Thailand, changes in their way of life can be regarded as a natural process accelerated by globalization and tourism. It is therefore important for tourists to receive correct information about current developments and modernization processes occurring in the hill tribes' villages, so that they know what to expect and how to behave if they decide to visit. Ultimately, it would remain a decision of those travelling whether to accept staged authenticity or not, with some arguing that this may be the only way to preserve traditions and generate additional income through tourism.

References

Amin, S. (1996) Reflections on the international system. In: Golding, P. and Harris, P. (eds) *Beyond Cultural Imperialism: Globalization, Communication and the New International Order*. Sage, London, pp. 10–24.

Azarya, V. (2007) Globalization and international tourism in developing countries: marginality as a commercial commodity. *Current Sociology* 52, 949–967.

Bangkok Post (2010) TCC: bombing hurt tourism sector. Available at: http://www.bangkokpost.com/breaking-news/188482/tcc-bombing-hurts- tourism-sector (accessed 11 August 2010).

Beeton, S. (2006) *Community Development Through Tourism*. Landlinks Press, Collingwood, Australia.

Boniface, B. and Cooper, C. (2001) *Worldwide Destinations: The Geography of Travel and Tourism*. Butterworth-Heinemann, Oxford, UK.

Boxill, I. (2003) Towards an alternative tourism for Belize. *International Journal of Contemporary Hospitality Management* 15, 147–150.

Brohman, J. (1996) New directions in tourism for third world development. *Annals of Tourism Research* 23, 48–70.

Brown, F. and Hall, D. (2008) Tourism and development in the global south: the issues. *Third World Quarterly* 29, 839–849.

Buckley, R. (2002) Tourism ecolabels. *Annals of Tourism Research* 29, 183–208.

Burns, P. (2008a) Tourism, political discourse and post-colonialism. *Tourism and Hospitality Planning & Development* 6, 61–73.

Burns, P. (2008b) Some reflections on tourism and post-colonialism. In: Babu, S., Mishra, B. and Parida, B. (eds) *Tourism Development Revisited: Concepts, Issues and Paradigms*. Sage Publications, London, pp.64–75.

Burns, P.M. and Figurova, Y. (2005) Tribal Tourism. In: Novelli, M. (ed.) *Niche tourism: Contemporary Issues, Trends and Cases*. Elsevier Butterworth-Heinemann, Oxford, UK, pp. 101–110.

Burns, P.M. and Holden, A. (1995) *Tourism: A New Perspective*. Prentice Hall, London.

Butcher, J. (2003) *The Moralisation of Tourism: Sun, Sand... and Saving the World?* Routledge, London.

Carbone, M. (2005) Sustainable tourism in developing countries: poverty alleviation, participatory planning, and ethical issues. *The European Journal of Development Research* 17, 559–565.

Carranza Valdés, J. and Stoller, R. (2002) Culture and development: some considerations for debate. *Latin American Perspectives* 29, 31–46.

Cater, E. (1995) Environmental contradictions in sustainable tourism. *The Geographical Journal* 161, 21–28.

Chambers, E. (2000) *Native Tours: The Anthropology of Travel and Tourism*. Waveland Press, Long Grove, Illinois.

Chandraprasert, E. (1997) The impact of development on the hilltribes of Thailand. In: McCaskill, D. and Kampe, K. (eds) *Development or Domestication? Indigenous Peoples of Southeast Asia*. Silkworm Books, Chiang Mai, Thailand, pp. 83–96.

Cheong, S.M. and Miller, M.L. (2000) Power and tourism: a Foucauldian observation. *Annals of Tourism Research* 27, 371–390.

Clayton, A. (2003) Policy coherence and sustainable tourism in the Caribbean. *International Journal of Contemporary Hospitality Management* 15,188–191.

Cohen, E. (1995) Contemporary tourism – trends and challenges: sustainable authenticity or contrived post-modernity? In: Butler, R. and Pearce, D. (eds) *Change in Tourism: People, Places, Processes*. Routledge, London, pp. 1–29.

Cohen, E. (1996) Hunter-gatherer tourism in Thailand. In: Butler R. and Hinch, T. (eds) *Tourism and Indigenous Peoples*. International Thomson Business Press, London, pp. 227–254.

Cohen, E. (2000) *The Commercialized Crafts of Thailand: Hill Tribes and Lowland Villages: Collected Articles*. Curzon Press, Richmond, UK.

Cohen, E. (2009) Death in paradise: tourist fatalities in the tsunami disaster in Thailand. *Current Issues in Tourism* 12, 183–199.

Cohen, E. (2007) From benefactor to tourist – Santa on cards from Thailand. *Annals of Tourism Research* 34, 690–708.

Cole, S. (2008) *Tourism, Culture and Development: Hopes, Dreams and Realities in East Indonesia*. Channel View Publications, Clevedon, UK.

Cooper, C. and Hall, C.M. (2008) *Contemporary Tourism: An International Approach*. Elsevier Butterworth-Heinemann, Oxford, UK.

Crick, A.P. (2003) Internal marketing of attitudes in Caribbean tourism. *International Journal of Contemporary Hospitality Management* 15, 161–166.

Cummins, P. (2002) Hill tribe children: empowered and impressive. Available at: http://www.chiangmai-mail.com/004/features.shtml (accessed 10 February 2010).

De Oliveira, J.A. (2005) Tourism as a force for establishing protected areas: the case of Bahia, Brazil. *Journal of Sustainable Tourism* 13, 24–49.

Diamantis, D. (1998) Consumer behavior and ecotourism products. *Annals of Tourism Research* 25, 515–528.

Dodman, D. (2009) Globalization, tourism and local living conditions on Jamaica's north coast. *Singapore Journal of Tropical Geography* 30, 204–219.

Dusik, R. (2008) Den bergmenschen ganz nah. *Asien* 2, 48–51.

Fayed, H. and Fletcher, J. (2002) Report: globalization of economic activity: issues for tourism. *Tourism Economics* 8, 207–230.

Fennell, D.A. (2006) *Tourism Ethics*. Channel View Publications, Clevedon, UK.

Fennell, D.A. and Malloy, D.C. (2007) *Codes of Ethics in Tourism: Practice, Theory, Synthesis*. Channel View Publications, Clevedon, UK.

Forsyth, T.J. (1995) Tourism and agricultural development in Thailand. *Annals of Tourism Research* 22, 877–900.

Freyer, W. (2006) *Tourismus: Einführung in die Fremdenverkehrsökonomie*. Oldenbourg Wissenschaftsverlag GmbH, Munich, Germany.

George, S. (2007) A short history of neo-liberalism: twenty years of elite economics and emerging opportunities for structural change – conference on economic sovereignty in a globalising world. Available at: http://www.globalexchange.org/campaigns/econ101/neoliberalism.html (accessed 31 October 2009).

Gonzalez, M.V. (2008) Intangible heritage tourism and identity. *Tourism Management* 29, 807–810.

Hawkins, D.E. and Mann, S. (2007) The World Bank's role in tourism development. *Annals of Tourism Research* 34, 348–363.

Higgins-Desbiolles, F. (2006) More than an 'industry': the forgotten power of tourism as a social force. *Tourism Management* 27, 1192–1208.

Higgins-Desbiolles, F. (2008) Justice tourism and alternative globalisation. *Journal of Sustainable Tourism* 16, 345–364.

Hinch, T. and Butler, R. (1996) Indigenous tourism: a common ground for discussion. In: Butler, R. and Hinch, T. (eds) *Tourism and Indigenous Peoples*. International Thomson Business Press, London, pp. 3–19.

Hjalager, A.M. (2007) Stages in the economic globalization of tourism. *Annals of Tourism Research* 34, 437–457.

Hunter, C.J. (1995) On the need to re-conceptualise sustainable tourism development. *Journal of Sustainable Tourism* 3, 155–165.

Inglehart, R. and Flanagan, S.C. (1987) Value change in industrial societies. *The American Political Science Review* 81, 1289–1319.

Jamal, T. and Stronza, A. (2008) Dwelling with ecotourism in the Peruvian Amazon: cultural relationships in local global spaces. *Tourist Studies* 8, 313–335.

Jantakad, P. and Carson, S. (1998) Community based natural resource management from villages to an inter-village network: a case study in Pang Ma Pha District, Mae Hong Son Province, Northern Thailand. Paper presented at the International CBNRM Workshop, Washington, DC, pp. 1–14.

Karagiannis, N. (2003) Tourism, linkages, and economic development in Jamaica. *International Journal of Contemporary Hospitality Management* 15, 184–187.

Knowles, T., Diamantis, D. and El-Mourhabi, J.B. (2004) *The Globalization of Tourism and Hospitality: A Strategic Perspective*. Thomson Learning, London.

Lane, B. (1994) Sustainable rural tourism strategies: a tool for development and conservation. *Journal of Sustainable Tourism* 2, 102–111.

Langman, L. (2003) Culture, identity and hegemony: the body in a global age. *Current Sociology* 51, 223–247.

Leepreecha, P. (1997) Jungle tours: a government policy in need of review. In: McCaskill, D. and Kampe, K. (eds) *Development or Domestication? Indigenous Peoples of Southeast Asia*. Silkworm Books, Chiang Mai, Thailand, pp. 268–288.

Lewis, D. and Bridger, D. (2001) *The Soul of the New Consumer: Authenticity - What we Buy and Why in the New Economy*. Nicholas Brealey, London.

Lewis, P. and Lewis, E. (1984) *Peoples of the Golden Triangle: Six Tribes in Thailand*. Thames and Hudson, London.

Liu, Z. (2003) Sustainable tourism development: a critique. *Journal of Sustainable Tourism* 11, 459–475.

MacCannell, D. (1973) Staged authenticity: arrangements of social space in tourist settings. *The American Journal of Sociology* 79, 589–603.

McCaskill, D. (1997) From tribal peoples to ethnic minorities: the transformation of indigenous peoples: a theoretical discussion. In: McCaskill, D. and Kampe, K. (eds) *Development or Domestication? Indigenous Peoples of Southeast Asia*. Silkworm Books, Chiang Mai, Thailand, pp. 26–60.

McCaskill, D., Leepreecha, P. and Shaoying, H. (2008) Globalization, nationalism, regionalism, and ethnic minorities in the greater Mekong subregion: a comparative analysis. In: McCaskill, D., Leepreecha, P. and Shaoying, H. (eds) *Living in a Globalized World: Ethnic Minorities in the Greater Mekong Subregion*. Mekong Press, Chiang Mai, Thailand, pp. 1–57.

McIntosh, A.J. and Prentice, R.C. (1999) Affirming authenticity - consuming cultural heritage. *Annals of Tourism Research* 26, 589–612.

Mamoozadeh, A. and McKee, D.L. (1990) Development through tourism. *Tijdschrift voor Economie en Management* 35, 147–157.

Marcouiller, D.W., Kim, K.K. and Deller, S.C. (2004) Natural amenities, tourism and income distribution. *Annals of Tourism Research* 31, 1031–1050.

Medina, L.K. (2003) Commoditizing culture - tourism and Maya identity. *Annals of Tourism Research* 30, 353–368.

Millman, R. (1995) Tourism and minorities' heritage: rediscovering the vernacular. In: Burns, P. (ed.) *Tourism and Minorities' Heritage: Impacts and Prospects*. University of North London Press, London, pp. 13–17.

Moscardo, G. (2008) *Building Community Capacity for Tourism Development*. CABI Publishing, Wallingford, UK.

Mowforth, M. and Munt, I. (2008) *Tourism and Sustainability: Development, Globalization and New Tourism in the Third World*. Routledge, Oxford, UK.

Mowforth, M., Charlton, C. and Munt, I. (2008) *Tourism and Responsibility: Perspectives from Latin America and the Caribbean*. Routledge, Oxford, UK.

Northcote, J. and Macbeth, J. (2006) Conceptualizing yield: sustainable tourism management. *Annals of Tourism Research* 33, 199–220.

Novelli, M. and Gebhardt, K. (2007) Community based tourism in Namibia: 'reality show' or 'window dressing'? *Current Issues in Tourism* 10, 1–37.

Pattullo, P. (2009) Under an ethical sky. In: Pattullo, P. (ed.) *The Ethical Travel Guide,* 2nd edn. Earthscan, London, pp. 1–41.

Peleggi, M. (1996) National heritage and global tourism in Thailand. *Annals of Tourism Research* 23, 432–448.

Potter, R., Binns, T., Elliott, J. and Smith, D.W. (2008) *Geographies of Development: An Introduction to Development Studies.* Prentice Hall, Harlow, UK.

Richards, G. and Hall, D. (2000) The community: a sustainable concept in tourism development? In: Hall, D. and Richards, G. (eds) *Tourism and Sustainable Community Development.* Routledge, Oxford, UK, pp. 1–13.

Ryan, C. (2005) Who manages indigenous cultural tourism product – aspiration and legitimization. In: Ryan, C. and Aicken, M. (eds) *Indigenous Tourism: The Commodification and Management of Culture.* Elsevier, London, pp. 69–73.

Rostow, W.W. (1960) *The Stages of Economic Growth: A Non-Communist Manifesto.* Cambridge University Press, Cambridge, UK.

Royal Project Foundation (1996) The Royal Project Foundation in the north of Thailand. Available at: http://www.royalprojectthailand.com/general/english/index.html (accessed 11 August 2010).

Salazar, N.B. (2005) Tourism and glocalization: 'local' tour guiding. *Annals of Tourism Research* 32, 628–646.

Scheyvens, R. (2002) *Tourism for Development: Empowering Communities.* Prentice Hall, London.

Schirato, T. and Webb, J. (2003) *Understanding Globalization.* SAGE Publications, London.

Scholte, J.A. (2005) *Globalisation – A Critical Introduction.* Palgrave Macmillan, Basingstoke, UK.

Schuurman, F.J. (1990) Introduction: development theory in the 1990s. In: Schuurman, F.J. (ed.) *Beyond the Impasse: New Directions in Development Theory.* Zed Books, London, pp. 1–48.

Sharpley, R. (2000) Tourism and sustainable development: exploring the theoretical divide. *Journal of Sustainable Tourism* 8, 1–19.

Sharpley, R. (2002) Tourism: a vehicle for development. In: Sharpley, R. and Telfer, D.J. (eds) *Tourism and Development: Concepts and Issues.* Channel View Publications, Clevedon, UK, pp. 11–34.

Skelton, T. (1996) Globalization, culture and land: the case of the Caribbean. In: Kofman, E. and Youngs, G. (eds) *Globalization – Theory and Practice.* Pinter, London, pp. 318–328.

Smith, M. and Duffy, R. (2003) *The Ethics of Tourism Development.* Routledge, London.

Smith, M. E. (1997) Hegemony and elite capital: the tools of tourism. In: Chambers, E. (ed.) *Tourism and Culture – An Applied Perspective.* State University of New York Press, New York, pp. 199–214.

Smith, V.L. (1996) Indigenous tourism: the four Hs. In: Butler, R. and Hinch, T. (eds) *Tourism and Indigenous Peoples.* International Thomson Business Press, London, pp. 283–307.

Sofield, T.H. and Birtles, R.A. (1996) Indigenous peoples' cultural opportunity spectrum for tourism. In: Butler, R. and Hinch, T. (eds) *Tourism and Indigenous Peoples.* International Thomson Business Press, London, pp. 396–433.

TAT (2008) *Learning Through Traveling.* Tourism Authority of Thailand, Bangkok, Thailand.

TAT (2010) *Where to Go.* Available at: http://www.tourismthailand.org/where-to-go/ (accessed 13 August 2010).

Taylor, J.P. (2001) Authenticity and sincerity in tourism. *Annals of Tourism Research* 28, 7–26.

Telfer, D. (2002) The evolution of tourism and development theory. In: Sharpley, R. and Telfer, D.J. (eds) *Tourism and Development: Concepts and Issues.* Channel View Publications, Clevedon, UK, pp. 35–80.

Telfer, D. and Sharpley, R. (2008) *Tourism and Development in the Developing World.* Routledge, Oxford, UK.

Teo, P. and Yeoh, B.S. (1997) Remaking local heritage for tourism. *Annals of Tourism Research* 24, 192–213.

Timothy, D.J. and Ioannides, D. (2002) Tour-operator hegemony: dependency, oligopoly, and sustainability. In: Apostolopoulos, Y. and Gayle, D.J. (eds) *Island Tourism and Sustainable Development – Caribbean, Pacific, and Mediterranean Experiences.* Praeger, Westport, Connecticut, pp.181–198.

Torres, R. (2002) Cancun's tourism development from a Fordist spectrum of analysis. *Tourist Studies* 2, 87–116.

Tosun, C. (2000) Limits to community participation in the tourism development process in developing countries. *Tourism Management* 21, 613–633.

Tourism Concern (2008) Burmese refugees trapped by tourism. Available at: http://www.tourismconcern.org. uk/index.php?mact=News,cntnt01,detail,0&cntnt01articled=29&cntnt01origid=96&cntnt01returnid=72 (accessed 18 October 2009).

Tourism Concern (2009) Kayan museum ordered to close. Available at: http://www.tourismconcern.org.uk/ index.php?mact=News,cntnt01,detail,0&cntnt01articleid=132&cntnt01origid=96&cntnt01returnid=72 (accessed 18 October 2009).

UNFF (2005) National report to the fifth session of the United Nations Forum on Forests. Thailand. Available at: http://www.un.org/esa/forests/pdf/national_reports/unff5/thailand.pdf (accessed 29 December 2009).

United Nations (2008) Second international decade of the world's indigenous people. Available at: http:// www.un.org/esa/socdev/unpfii/documents/brochure_2nd_decade.pdf (accessed 16 August 2010).

United Nations (2009) Guidelines on indigenous peoples' issues. Available at: http://www.un.org/esa/socdev/ unpfii/documents/UNDG_guidelines_EN.pdf (accessed 29 December 2009).

Urry, J. (2002) *The Tourist Gaze*. Sage, London.

van Egmond, T. (2007) *Understanding Western Tourists in Developing Countries*. CABI Publishing, Wallingford, UK.

Vater, T. (2006) *Kultur Schock – Thailands Bergvölker und Seenomaden*. Reise Know How, Bielefeld, Germany.

Wagner, C.G. (2005) The conscientious tourist. *The Futurist* (September–October), 14–15.

Wall, G. (1999) Partnerships involving indigenous peoples in the management of heritage sites. In: Robinson, M. and Boniface, P. (eds) *Tourism and Cultural Conflicts*. CABI Publishing, Wallingford, UK, pp. 269–286.

Wall, G. and Mathieson, A. (2006) *Tourism – Change, Impacts and Opportunities*. Prentice Hall, Harlow, UK.

Wang, N. (1999) Rethinking authenticity in tourism experience. *Annals of Tourism Research* 26, 349–370.

Weaver, D.B. (1999) Magnitude of ecotourism in Costa Rica and Kenya. *Annals of Tourism Research* 26, 792–816.

Weaver, D. (2009) Indigenous tourism stages and their implications for sustainability. *Journal of Sustainable Tourism* 17, 1–18.

Wheeler, M. (1992) Applying ethics to the tourism industry. *A European Review* 1, 227–235.

Wheeler, M. (1995) Tourism marketing ethics: an introduction. *International Marketing Review* 12, 38–49.

Yang, L. and Wall, G. (2009) Authenticity in ethnic tourism: domestic tourists' perspectives. *Current Issues in Tourism* 12, 235–254.

Zezza, A., Carletto, G., Davis, B., Stamoulis, K. and Winters, P. (2009) Rural income generating activities: whatever happened to the institutional vacuum? Evidence from Ghana, Guatemala, Nicaragua and Vietnam. *World Development* 37, 1297–1306.

5 Controversies in Medical Tourism

David G. Vequist IV[1], Michael Guiry[2] and Brian Ipock[1]
[1]Center for Medical Tourism Research, University of the Incarnate Word, San Antonio, Texas, USA; [2]H-E-B School of Business & Administration, University of the Incarnate Word, San Antonio, Texas, USA.

Introduction

In this chapter, the authors examine the 'medical tourism' phenomenon and some of the interesting controversies that underlie the growth of the sector. According to a report by Frost and Sullivan (Anonymous, 2011) the thought leadership and consulting firm, the medical tourism sector reached US$78.5 billion in revenues by 2010 and was expected to grow to US$100 billion by 2012. They also estimated that more than three million patients travelled around the globe for medical care in 2010. The predicted growth rate for this sector was 20–30% annually and seems to be a sustainable trend that is bound to continue in the years to come. According to this report 'The Middle East is one of the latent source markets of patients and it is estimated that 20 per cent of healthcare seekers worldwide are from Gulf and Arab states'. In addition, a separate megatrends report on healthcare by Frost and Sullivan in 2011 suggested that nearly 870,000 Americans travelled overseas for surgery in 2010, and those numbers were expected to grow to more than 1.5 million by 2012.

Vequist, Teachout and Galan (2012) suggest that factors that have led to the increasing popularity of medical tourism include 'the high cost of health care, long waiting times for certain procedures, the ease and affordability

of international travel, and improvements in both technology and standards of care in many countries'. Currently, more than 50 countries have identified medical tourism as a national sector, although historically, it can be argued that medical tourism is as old as civilization itself. More than 2000 years ago, affluent citizens of Rome would often travel to the areas now known as Switzerland and Turkey to take advantage of therapeutic mud baths and hot-springs found in those areas.

Although very little hard evidence exists of the number of medical tourists, procedures performed and/or size of the market (Vequist and Valdez, 2009), there is enough evidence of a massive disruptive trend in the form of the increasing consumerism and globalization of healthcare. We do have some evidence of the fact that millions of patients are travelling to other countries for various healthcare procedures and these medical tourists are spending billions of dollars (estimated US dollars) on treatments all over the world typically on a fee-for-service, cash basis.

Controversies

It has been argued by Cohen (2010) that:

> Medical tourism is itself part of a larger move towards healthcare globalization,

encompassing among other things the re-importation of drugs from Canada and elsewhere, the importation of healthcare providers through medical migration (the 'brain drain'), research tourism (where clinical trials by U.S.-based pharmaceutical companies are performed abroad), and telemedicine (e.g. teleradiology) where both the patient and provider stay put in their respective countries but the service is provided remotely.

Cohen (2010, p. 1476)

According to Vequist (in press), increasing access to technology (defined as hardware, software and equipment) around the world has a escalating effect on globalization, which then creates more choices for consumers, or greater amounts of consumerism behaviours. Because the field of medical tourism is growing so rapidly (it is truly a nascent sector), it has created new controversies that cut across fields as diverse as healthcare, international business, the law and civil procedures, intellectual property, politics, philosophy and ethics (Fig. 5.1).

Taxonomies and Categories of Controversies

In the following sections, we lay out some of the controversies that have been created by the growth of this sector, sorted by some pre-existing categorizations gathered from the literature. Also, examples from the

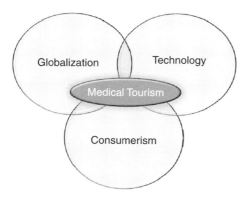

Fig. 5.1. Drivers of medical tourism (Vequist, 2010).

academic literature that touch on these controversies will be highlighted so that current readers and future researchers can build upon this foundational-level work to expand upon our understanding of this sector.

In Gray and Poland's (2008) '*Medical tourism: Crossing borders to access health care*', which was featured in the *Kennedy Institute of Ethics Journal*, the authors suggested there were three major categories of ethical issues involved in medical tourism, as described below.

Gray and Poland's Three Categories of Controversies in Medical Tourism

Economic considerations

Controversies that are listed under this category include: (i) regarding the ultimate role of government and private business in healthcare, or how should government be involved in what is primarily a business trend brought on by the privatization of healthcare; (ii) the assumed (although not well quantified) argument that medical tourism creates an uneven access to health resources (sometimes referred to as a 'two-tiered' system; see also controversy (xi) in this category below) in the countries where medical travel is being performed (Connell, 2006); (iii) the possible economic impact of medical tourism to local medical centres, which, according to Dunn (2007), could be 'significant or even devastating' if the trend continues to flourish; (iv) the legal, ethical and financial implications of the increasing international healthcare workforce in countries worldwide, which is correlated with medical tourism (Fried and Harris, 2007); (v) the economic development issues regarding the transfer of healthcare management expertise and intellectual property (IP) from developing country's medical centres to international sites (primarily in the developing world) that then compete with them for patients (Schroth and Khawahja, 2007); (vi) Douglas (2007) points out how American businesses are considering medical tourism, as an option to provide cost-effective and high-quality healthcare for employees, even though it would take money and opportunities away from the local community (in terms of local medical facilities and personnel); (vii) Wieners (2007) also suggests that medical tourism shares many of the controversial attributes with the outsourcing model in the technology sector; (viii) the controversy of medical tourists not 'waiting patiently in the queue' for access to healthcare (like the majority of their compatriots), and the further obligations (pre and post) of the primary-care physician to medical travellers, as discussed in Horowitz and Rosensweig (2007); (ix) Lee (2007) emphasizes the continuing need for regulation and monitoring of the medical tourism sector, including eventual certification of staff involved in treating international visitors; (x) Milstein and Smith (2006) offer that this 'solution' (referring to medical tourism) for obtaining affordable healthcare is a symptom of bad healthcare systems in the developed world (and not necessarily a positive fix); (xi) Ramirez de Arellano (2007) focuses on the controversy of national resources being consumed on care for foreigners, which leads to the possibility of the host country denying its own citizens equitable access to care (which promotes a two-tiered health system defined by the economic means of the patients); and finally (xii) the controversial possibility that medical tourism will remain essentially an unregulated global sector despite concerns over health quality and data protection, as raised by Terry (2007).

Legal and public policy issues

The rapid growth of international health travel has created many fascinating new controversies and many of them have a legal or regulatory component. Interestingly, this sector has grown so quickly that it has not generated enough case law to support the needs of legal and policy analysts who can then point to precedents as guidelines. This makes writing specific regulations or suggesting possible legislation much more difficult.

Instead, at this time we are still relying, to a major extent, on academic legal and public policy scholars and thought leaders to work through the logic of probable scenarios and draw from findings in other fields (comparative analysis) to try to suggest some much needed policy recommendations.

Controversies that are suggested under this category include the following examples: (i) Brady (2007) offers the possibility that if American private insurance companies and health maintenance organizations (HMOs) were to offer medical outsourcing, they would be in violation of the Employee Retirement Income Security Act (ERISA) of 1974 (a US federal law); (ii) an issue raised by Derckx is that medical tourism could be considered, by some, as the inhuman treatment of sick people (sending them to potentially less-qualified overseas providers), which would run counter to legal systems that focus on human dignity (2006); (iii) Howze (2007) believes that there are liability issues involving medical negligence in medical tourism (he then goes on to suggest that these issues should cause it to be limited as a regular aspect of the present US healthcare system); (iv) Klaus (2006) raises the controversial fact that medical travellers may bear the costs of medical errors, which is a practice that lacks in social justice standards; (v) Mirrer-Singer (2007) states that 'the level of paternalism reflected in medical-tourism regulations should parallel the transparency of the industry', highlighting the current controversy that there is currently not enough valid information available to protect the rights of medical tourists; and (vi) it is a significant possibility that only imposed restrictions (possibly implemented because of some of these controversies), through government regulations and oversight, will slow the growth of this sector (Pennings, 2007).

Applied areas: assisted reproduction and organ transplantation

Controversies in this area include the following examples: (i) Morris (2008) criticizes the European Directive on Tissues and Cells passed in 2004 that she suggests is a weak regulation that is more focused on regulation based on science without fully considering bioethical thinking or having the proper amount of public discourse; (ii) the controversial possibility that the harmonization of legislation (which seems to be a natural outgrowth of medical tourism) is a bad thing for society because it does not allow private ethical matters to be handled by national legislative bodies (Pennings, 2004); (iii) in an early article by Scheper-Hughes (2002), the author argues that the problem with healthcare and free markets (such as medical tourism) is 'that they reduce everything – including human beings, their labor, and their reproductive capacity – to the status of commodities' which promotes gross injustices in economic and human terms; (iv) authors such as Mulay and Gibson (2006) have suggested that these specific trends have had a negative impact on public health in the receiving countries (in this case, India) and on reproductive rights and women's health; and finally (v) Shimazono (2007), in an analysis of international organ trading, suggests that there may be dire consequences for local healthcare systems as resources are drained away to support the foreign markets.

Cohen's Categorization of Controversies in Medical Tourism

Another taxonomy that is offered, from a legal standpoint, is from Cohen (2010) who suggests that the most useful categorization of medical tourism controversies 'is to separate medical tourism for services that are *legal* in both the patient's home country and the destination country, from medical tourism for services that are *illegal* in both countries, from medical tourism for services that are *illegal* in the patient's home country but *legal* in the destination country'.

In the first category, offered by this author, some possible controversies would include: (i) although a procedure is legal in both countries, there may be patient-protective concerns, particularly around the welfare of the medical tourist patient (usually involving the quality of care and concerns about medical malpractice recovery in the event of a medical error); (ii) concerns from stakeholders (such as practitioners and policy makers), in the home country of the possible traveller, of the possible impact of medical tourism on the price and access to healthcare among non-tourist patients still seeking healthcare through traditional methods (the author suggests these could be labelled protectionist concerns); and (iii) concerns about the effect of international medical travel on patients in the destination country, using theories of international justice, and having a better understanding of all stakeholder's moral obligations to avoid causing harm (even if unintended) by their actions.

The second category is obviously the most rich, in terms of debate, because it includes many controversies that are striking and perhaps requiring more regulatory and statutory frameworks in place to help prevent these behaviours and ultimately prosecute offenders. Some examples include: (i) if a citizen from one country were to travel to another to engage in an organ transplant using illegally obtained organs (by laws in both the home and in visited country), where should the jurisdiction fall for the prosecution of this lawbreaker; (ii) the difficulty of nations and intra-governmental organizations regulating businesses that exist between 'two worlds' in terms of their legal, ethical, moral and legal responsibilities (performing illegal procedures in international waters such as could be found in medical cruise ships programmes); and even (iii) how to handle brokerages that solicit patients (usually through the internet) to engage in illegal activities (again, in both the home and visited country) while the broker itself is in another, third, country that may or may not have legal repercussions to prevent them from continuing these behaviours.

In the third category that Cohen (2010) suggests, there are controversies such as: (i) in reproductive tourism, securing a surrogate from India (commercial surrogacy is legal in India) and bringing this child back to Massachusetts, USA, where paid surrogacy is illegal and surrogacy agreements are unenforceable, raising the issue of whether the state should step in and prosecute; (ii) in the case of 'death tourism' or 'physician-assisted suicide' (see Vequist and Barnes, 2010) where a patient (and possibly surviving co-conspirator or spouse/partner/family member) travels across sovereign boundaries to Switzerland (where this activity is allowable) and commits what would amount to a felony (enforceable with possible fines and/or a jail sentence for both the 'patient' and the co-conspirator) in their home country; or (iii) when a patient is barred from joining a clinical trial of an experimental drug because they do not meet the inclusion criteria, and are therefore prohibited by law from purchasing the unapproved drug, though international availability can circumvent governmental regulation and enable the patient to travel to another country, where the drug is available for purchase, and use it for treatment there.

The controversies offered, in all three of these categories, raise more interesting questions than they suggest answers. For example, in the surrogacy case, Cohen suggests that a country's legal and political stakeholders need to think through the issue of whether they should 'respect a country's sovereignty in deciding that this form of "exploitation" is not worthy of legal condemnation' and if 'the exploited group were sufficiently enfranchised' and had a choice in the process (2010). Other supporting legal research around these controversies (in all three categories) can be found in the works of Anonymous (2008), Hunter and Oultram (2010), an additional piece by Tan, (2007), Glenn Cohen (2009) and Moncrieff, (2009). An example, from Hunter and Oultram (2010) focuses on a subset of medical tourism that they dubbed 'rogue medical tourism', which is where the patient is motivated 'not to access something that is unavailable/affordable on the grounds of cost in the patient's own country but instead to access a medical technology or procedure, which is unavailable because the government has

decided to ban or not legalize the intervention'. This presents a clear and present challenge to governments that wish to control their citizen's access to particular medical technologies or treatments. Typically, this limit in access occurs because of one or more of these three reasons, as suggested by the authors: (i) concerns about the safety of the intervention; (ii) concerns about evidence of the effectiveness of the intervention; and finally (iii) concerns about the moral acceptability either about the intervention itself or the implications of the intervention.

Hadi's Framework for Controversy in Medical Tourism

Finally, the last controversy categorization framework for medical tourism comes from a conceptual framework for this sector from Hadi (2009). This framework was used as a starting point for categorizing the remaining ethical issues, mentioned in the literature, that were not mentioned in the two previous taxonomies (Fig. 5.2). Some of the other controversies, listed by area, in this framework are outlined below.

Health outcomes

Kangas (2007), who is the first researcher to have performed a dissertation on medical tourism, concluded in a piece for the *Journal of Anthropology and Medicine* that 'people who travel abroad for medical care do not do so necessarily because they can afford it. They are not buying a treatment vacation package, as "medical tourism" would suggest. Rather, they are pursuing the hope of a better situation than they now have, at whatever the cost.'

In an article by Svantesson (2008), the author reviews the medical tourism sector and the different legal alternatives for seeking damages if a medical procedure goes wrong. McCallum and Jacoby (2007) look at the possibility of financial planners working with their clients to reduce their healthcare

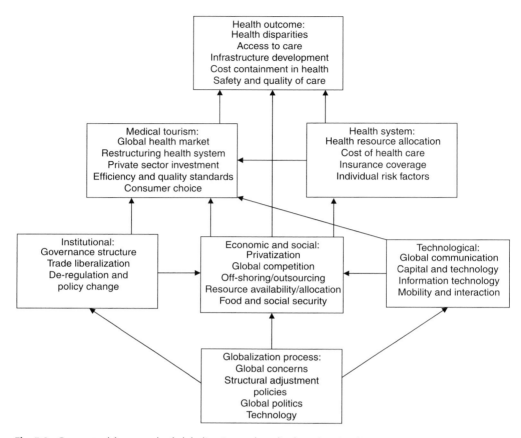

Fig. 5.2. Conceptual framework of globalization and medical tourism (Hadi, 2009).

costs, increase their access and have quality options, but they also caution that there are liability issues to be considered by these planners before suggesting healthcare outsourcing. Also, in a very thorough article, Nathan Cortez (2008), a law professor at SMU, analyses the various medical malpractice laws of many medical tourism countries and suggests how countries can balance both risks and benefits to international patients. The article by Burkett, from 2007, represents one of the most thorough texts on medical tourism at this time. It is a well written piece that covers a wide swathe of research but most of it is concerned with the legal implications of medical travel overseas. She suggests that:

> Any regulation addressing the social, economic and health system issues posed by medical tourism should work on three

fronts: (A) increased emphasis on the accreditation of international hospitals; (B) regulation of health insurance that covers medical tourism; and (C) restriction on travel for medical tourism to approved destination hospital countries. Such regulations would work to achieve the legitimate governmental goal of ensuring that the health care Americans receive overseas is of high quality. At the same time, such regulations would serve the second legitimate governmental interest of protecting the American health care system from increased competition and further economic instability.
>
> Burkett (2007, p. 242–243)

In a recent article, Guiry and Vequist (2011) found that the medical tourism service provided to US tourists was not completely up to the expectations of these travellers. Therefore a suggested controversy is that the level of service in these locations may need to be improved (or at least the visitor's expectations may have to be re-adjusted). In addition, the trend of medical tourism brings up the question of how service quality differs in different cultures and how this then impacts the expectations of service received in international venues by visitors from other countries. If perceptions of quality are not met by the medical tourism facility then the patients may not be receiving care that is up to the traveller's perception of quality.

Medical tourism

Brown and Hall (2008) point out that some new forms of tourism have emerged recently that have an ethical dimension 'as a result of a shift from a product-driven to a consumer-driven approach.' They believe that this trend is a new manifestation of old-style tourism and that medical tourism has the look of 'neo-colonialist exploitation' and has manifest ethical issues because medical tourists 'consume resources at the expense of local populations, but they also create revenues which could be used to benefit said populations.' English *et al.* (2006) also suggest that this trend creates many ethical issues and Parker (2006) suggests that medical tourism may even be at odds with the sustainability of national health-care systems. In one of the most detailed pieces on medical tourism and the ethics of the trend, Widdows (2007) suggests that 'medical tourism presents a clear example of the inability of local laws and ethics to regulate current practices and prevent exploitation and injustice'. She believes that 'other areas of bioethics present at least equally compelling reasons for ensuring ethics is global.'

Health system

In an article about the nursing systems in place in India, Abraham (2007) is quoted as believing that:

International experience tells us that there is no single correct answer for shaping a country's health system. Within India, the priority of issues and the choice of options should vary according to the conditions prevailing in various states and districts. The reliance on private spending on health in India is among the highest in the world. Paying for health puts Indians at risk of financial ruin when they become ill. More than 40 percent of Indians need to borrow money or sell assets when they are hospitalized. However, private health care in India is on par with the best in the world with the latest equipment, highly qualified doctors and nurses, and high standards of care, yet this is accessible only to a privileged few. As a result of the technology and skills, India has become a destination for medical tourism.

> Abraham (2007, p. 80)

Leng, in 2010, suggested that historically healthcare 'was considered a crucial component of governmental responsibility, as expressed in the 1978 Declaration of Alma-Ata (WHO-UNICEF, 1978); and health services are not readily seen as a marketable commodity despite the existence of an international trade.' This author argues that entitlement to healthcare was (and should continue to be) 'a cornerstone of social citizenship, conceptualized within the framework of nation, and citizenship rights and obligations.' Therefore, this suggests that some possible controversies in this area are: (i) determining if there is an inherent conflict between the state's obligation to ensure healthcare access for its citizens on the one hand and its advocacy of medical tourism on the other; (ii) what the state's responsibilities are regarding cross-border health-care utilization (particularly foreign visitors' utilization of national health services); and (iii) the attempts to 'divert these patients to the private sector', which the author describes as outright 'marketing'.

Institutional

An article by Dumont and Zurn (2007) summarizes the impact of the liberalization of trade and The General Agreement on Trade in Services (GATS; the legal framework of the World Trade Organization or WTO) and particularly how that has affected international health-related services. GATS allows WTO members to choose which service sectors to open up to trade and foreign competition. According to the authors 'to date, only 50 WTO Members have made some type of commitment on health services under GATS, much less than in financial services (100 Members).' GATS has four different modes that affect the trade of health services: (i) Mode 1: Cross-border supply. Health services provided between countries, usually via interactive audio, visual and data communication. The controversy here is whether or not these medical-tourism-like interactions are appropriate for telephony applications; (ii) Mode 2: Consumption abroad. This covers incidents when patients seek treatment abroad or receive care while they are abroad. The authors point out that although it can generate a foreign exchange, it can also have the impact of crowding out local patients and act as a drain on local resources; (iii) Mode 3: Foreign commercial presence. These are health services supplied in another country through a commercial presence. Although this can make new services available (possibly even driving up quality and creating employment opportunities), it can also lead to the creation of a two-tier health system and even to a possible 'brain drain' of healthcare assets out of the country; and finally (iv) Mode 4: Movement of people. The controversy here is when healthcare personnel work in other countries (although this mode of GATS speaks to the movement on a temporary basis) and accentuate 'brain drain'. This 'brain drain' occurs when the differences in wages paid, demand fluctuations and host country facility quality results in culturally skilled and knowledgeable healthcare professionals to seek employment in other countries (particularly controversial when these providers shift from less developed to more developed countries). Overall, the main controversy in GATS according to the authors (Dumont and Zurn, 2007) is that 'the capacity of states to regulate health-related services will be

eroded', although they admit that 'there is a lack of empirical data on the level of international trade in health-related services, as well as on the effects of liberalization in specific countries.'

Economic and social

Health tourism has at least two concerns when viewed in terms of sustainability, according to Bristow (2009). First is the concern that access to medical care in health tourism communities will be limited to wealthy foreigners who can afford to pay more than the local prevailing wages. The ethical implications are more complicated when it is, for example, a medical doctor's attention that is being outsourced. Further, since health tourism clinics are often private facilities, nearby public services may be strained beyond operational capacity to meet the needs of the indigenous population. Poorer local citizens are particularly threatened since private clinics are financially out of reach (George, 2009).

Technological

Jones and Keith (2006) suggest that reproductive technologies involved in medical tourism 'may challenge the limits of ethics, policy and legality'. Also, Leahy (2008) believes that 'in addition to the safety issues raised by medical tourism, there are potential damaging effects on the provider countries. The emphasis on technology driven tertiary care for foreigners may impact on basic healthcare for citizens of developing countries.' Another possible controversy is that foreign direct investments (FDIs) in healthcare facilities, particularly in technologically more intensive facilities, may not be equally impactful to the local community's health status because investors have no vested interest in the low margin care usually provided to disadvantaged citizens within the local region.

In a thorough article by Martin (2010) about the ethical issues around medical travel and the purchasing of human biological materials (HBMs), which is arguably driven by the availability of healthcare technologies, the author suggests that there are the following general concerns (especially with respect to the use of living vendors): (i) potential HBM sellers are frequently drawn from communities in developing countries suffering extremes of poverty. Even when this occurs in more developed countries, the potential sellers are somewhat better off but are nevertheless often at a disadvantage with respect to recipients of the materials; (ii) medical travel for HBM may lead to coercion of potential HBM sellers, such as found in human trafficking, and the possible subjection of sellers to undue risks of harm; (iii) when payment is provided to potential sellers, their autonomy may be impaired, and they may suffer exploitation or inappropriate commodification due to impaired decision-making capacities through the appeal of an excessive inducement; (iv) HBM providers risk a variety of social consequences, economic costs, physical discomforts, medical sequelae, and the potential social or emotional impact of donation on donor lives including significant social stigma; (v) exploitation becomes a major possibility in HBM sales because the transaction usually involves relatively wealthy customers purchasing goods or services from suppliers in developing countries (Martin points out that the exploitation occurs because someone in a position of relative power uses that power to make the weaker person agree to an unfair deal in which the weaker party undeservedly receives an unequal share of benefits); (vi) HBM potential sellers may be motivated by desperate economic circumstances which may lead to vulnerable individuals agreeing to sell biological materials due to a lack of alternative employment options (which may leave them only marginally and not sustainably better off); (vii) even when fair payment is offered, this may potentially represent an instance of 'omissive coercion'. It is suggested that omissive coercion occurs when a person agrees to do something in exchange for another person fulfilling their pre-existing obligations; (viii) trade in HBM may override humanitarian duties to provide basic human rights to potential sellers (which Martin suggests should precede any involvement in HBM trading); (ix) medical tourism for HBM exploits wider gaps of inequity (both financial and possibly legislative or standards of care) between foreign patients and potential HBM sellers in the destination country; (x) HBM, as part of medical tourism, may actually be failing to respect the dignity of potential sellers as human beings and instead they become commoditized: rather than being individuals with the recognized rights, obligations and roles that are attributed to humans, they become commodities to be sold, even when acting as free moral subjects in deciding to sell their biological materials and pursuing their own ends. Martin further suggests that primarily in poor communities 'a price may become synonymous with human bodies, whence it is easy to envisage a progression to recognition of humans as a living source of financial capital that may be "cashed in" as required'; and finally (xi) medical travel for HBM may further impair access to domestic resources by citizens of the destination country (as well as limit economic growth of structures in the travellers' home country that facilitate necessary HBM procedures).

Globalization process

In an interesting opinion piece, Shearmur (2008) argues that it may make sense to have liberal regulations on organ sales and transplant medical tourism, and Mattoo and Rathindran (2005) even offer that the 'outsourcing' of healthcare may ultimately be beneficial to both the sending and receiving countries. Also, as medical tourism grows around the world and the awareness of its economic impact becomes better understood, there is the very real possibility that future country politics and antagonism could lead to an embargo being imposed on the flows of patients travelling between countries, as a political tool for leverage on other agendas.

Summary and Review
of the Controversies

After reviewing most of the academic literature on controversies in medical tourism, it
seems that there are several 'themes' that
continue to come up frequently. They are as
follows: (i) the possibility of healthcare
access becoming differentiated by economic
ability; (ii) the issue of the utilization of
local resources by foreign nationals (thus
limiting local access to care); (iii) legal
issues surrounding the situation of services
offered in one country that may not be
allowable or ethically appropriate in the
patient's home country; (iv) the possibility
that medical tourism represents lesser care
for medical travellers; (v) the increasing
emphasis on healthcare as a business (which
is exaggerated by medical tourism); and (vi)
the sustainability of international healthcare flows and trends (such as the brain
drain of personnel that occurs partially as a
result of the sector).

We suggest that more empirical evidence of the impacts of these trends need to
be carried out (whether through true quantitative studies or with qualitative and/or
case analysis). There is still a sincere lack of
substantial research in many areas in this
sector (see also Vequist, in press). The
importance of this research cannot be over-
stated; this sector and its ancillary impacts
could well change much about what we
consider sacred in traditional domestic
healthcare throughout the world.

Conclusion

Medical tourism is a very important phenomenon that may affect traditional healthcare in ways that researchers have not even
begun to consider; for example, Cohen
(2010) suggests that the newly passed
American healthcare reform which introduces an individual mandate may actually
further stimulate the entry of lower-cost
insurance plans containing some amount of
incentivized/required   insurer-prompted
medical tourism, unless specific steps are

taken legislatively to prevent it. So, it is
important that there is more research around
how this trend will impact both the medical
tourism patients themselves and the various
stakeholders involved (such as the sending
and receiving countries and the various
care-givers providing services to these
patients, both pre- and post-medical
tourism).

Another weakness in this sector is that
we don't know what we don't know yet.
The growth of this trend has occurred so
fast that the prerequisite research on the
possible impacts and outcomes has not
matured yet. Therefore, the categorizations
mentioned in this chapter may not adequately describe all the possible future controversies that are emerging as this text is
being written. In a recently released special
topic (medical tourism) version of the
*International Journal of Behavioural &
Healthcare Research*, edited by Teachout
and Vequist (2010), a categorization for the
articles is offered that was based on a framework used for the preparation of the first
annual   Medical   Tourism   Research
Conference in January 2010. This research
framework was developed by the Center for
Medical Tourism Research (CMTR) and
shaped the scholarly contributions and the
conference programme. The main topics
and subtopics are:

1. Genesis and drivers of medical tourism
   a. economic, regional, political, social,
      cultural and cross-cultural issues
   b. medical tourism insurance/re-insurance
      and reimbursement models
2. Legal and ethical issues in medical tourism and the globalization of healthcare
   a. technological and privacy issues (e.g.
      confidentiality and security)
   b. economic and social impact on coun-
      tries, industries and jobs
   c. adequacy of quality of care at medical
      tourism facilities
   d. care and responsibility (e.g. international
      malpractice and risk management)
3. Assessments or evaluations of medical
   tourism practices (including accreditation)
   a. independent provider credentialing
      and qualification

Milstein, A. and Smith, M. (2006) America's new refugees – seeking affordable surgery offshore. *New England Journal of Medicine* 355, 1637–1640.

Mirrer-Singer, P. (2007) Note: medical malpractice overseas: the legal uncertainty surrounding medical tourism. *Law and Contemporary Problems* 70, 211–232.

Moncrieff, A. (2009) Federalization snowballs: the need for national action in medical malpractice reform. *Columbia Law Review* 109, 844.

Morris, E. (2008) Reproductive tourism and the role of the European Union. *Chicago Journal of International Law* 8, 701–713.

Mulay, S. and Gibson, E. (2006) Marketing of assisted human reproduction and the Indian State. *Development* 49, 84–93.

Parker, T. (2006) The future of medicine: Natural Doctors International. *Journal of the American Herbalists Guild* 6, 32–34.

Pennings, G. (2004) Legal harmonization and reproductive tourism in Europe. *Human Reproduction* 19, 2689–2694.

Pennings, G. (2007) Ethics without boundaries: medical tourism. In: Ashcroft, E., Dawson, A., Draper, H., McMillan, J., Ashcroft, R.E., Dawson, A., Draper, H. and McMillan, J.R. (eds) *Principles of Health Care Ethics*, John Wiley and Sons, London, pp. 505–510.

Ramirez de Arellano, A. (2007) Patients without borders: the emergence of medical tourism. *International Journal of Health Services* 37, 193–198.

Scheper-Hughes, N. (2002) The ends of the body: commodity fetishism and the global traffic in organs. *SAIS Review* 22, 61–80.

Schroth, L. and Khawahja, R. (2007) Globalization of health care. *Frontiers of Health Services Management* 24, 19–30.

Shearmur, J. (2008) The real body shop, part 2: spare parts. *Policy* 24, 25–29.

Shimazono, Y. (2007) The state of the international organ trade: a provisional picture based on integration of available information. *Bulletin of the World Health Organization* 85, 955–962.

Sood, A. and Cox, E. (2008) Medical tourism – a strategy for containing health care cost increases and immigration pull. *Working Papers in Global Studies* 2, 1–8.

Svantesson, D. (2008) From the airport to the surgery to the courtroom – private international law and medical tourism. *Commonwealth Law Bulletin* 34, 265–276.

Tan, K. (2007) Aesthetic medicine: a health regulator's perspective, clinical governance. *An International Journal* 12, 13–25.

Teachout, M. and Vequist, D. (2010) Editorial. *International Journal of Behavioural and Healthcare Research* 2, 1–4.

Terry, N. (2007) Under-regulated health care phenomena in a flat world: medical tourism and outsourcing. *Western New England Law Review* 29 (2), 421–72.

Vequist, D. (2012) Medical tourism research: the unfortunate lack of valid data. *Journal of Health and Human Services Administration* (in press).

Vequist, D. and Barnes, R. (2010) Assisted suicide tourism: wish fulfillment? Paper presented at the International Conference on Ethical Issues in Medical Tourism, June 25, 2010, Simon Fraser University, Vancouver, Canada. Available at: http://www.sfu.ca/medicaltourism/2010_conference_archive/presentations/VequistBarnes.pdf (accessed 31 December 2011).

Vequist, D. and Valdez, E. (2009) The correlation between medical tourism and biotechnology. *Journal of Commercial Biotechnology* 15, 287–289.

WHO-UNICEF (1978) Declaration of Alma-Ata. International Conference on Primary Health Care, Alma-Ata, USSR, 6–12 September, 1978. Available at: http://www.who.int/hpr/NPH/docs/declaration_almaata.pdf (accessed 30 March 2011).

Widdows, H. (2007) Is global ethics moral neo-colonialism? An investigation of the issue in the context of bioethics. *Bioethics* 21, 305–315.

Wieners, W. (2007) Going global: delivering health care services in a 'flat' world. *Frontiers of Health Services Management* 24, 41–43.

6 Ethical Issues in Trophy Hunting

John Dobson[1]

[1]*Department of Tourism, Hospitality and Events Management,
Cardiff School of Management, University of Wales Institute, Cardiff, UK*

Introduction

Hunting other animals has underpinned human development as the dominant species on planet Earth. It was a central activity for early hunter–gatherer societies and is still considered, by some, to be an essential human activity even in industrial societies today. However, in the West, hunting has experienced a transformation away from being an urgent activity that is necessary in order to survive, to being an activity that is largely undertaken for pleasure and has led to its emergence as a leisure and tourism activity. The period of colonial expansion by Western powers during the 19th century was significant in helping to link hunting and tourism. Tiger shooting became an important leisure activity in British colonial India with Hamman (2008) noting 'many Western visitors came to India to visit friends and relatives and engaged in the "sport" of tiger shooting as part and parcel of their tour' (p. 99). Colonial expansion in Africa led to the 'Era of Big Game Hunting' that took place in East Africa between 1900 and 1945 – perhaps one of the most well-known and most documented examples of tourist travel for hunting purposes (Akama, 2008). Hunting tourism was not solely limited to colonial possessions; British tourists were travelling to hunt and fish in Scandinavia for more than 170 years (Sillanpää, 2008) and hunting and fishing has been embedded in American culture through the early settlers and continues to be an important leisure activity (Dunlap, 1988).

Travelling for the purpose of hunting and fishing is not without controversy. Both Hamman (2008) and Akama (2008) note the devastating impact that unregulated hunting had on tiger populations in India (Hamman, 2008) and the big five in East Africa (Akama, 2008). Hunting animals for pleasure as a prime motivation, rather than for essential food, has caused much debate as illustrated by a conversation that Ernest Hemingway (2004) recalls he had with fellow traveller named Kandisky regarding his hunting activities in Africa.

> Kandisky: 'What are you doing here?'
> Hemingway: 'Shooting.'
> Kandisky: 'Not ivory I hope?'
> Hemingway: 'No. For kudu.'
> Kandisky: 'Why should any man shoot a kudu? You, an intelligent man, a poet, to shoot kudu.'
> Hemingway: 'I haven't shot any yet.... But we've been hunting them hard now for ten days...'
> Kandisky: 'But you should hunt for a year. At the end of that time you have shot everything and you are sorry for it. To hunt for one special animal is nonsense. Why do you do it?'

Hemingway: 'I like to do it.'
After a short discussion on the merits of
the poetry of Rilke the conversation again
returns to hunting.
Kandisky: 'Well at least you do not kill
elephants.'
Hemingway: 'I'd kill a big enough one.'
Kandisky: 'How big?'
Hemingway: 'A seventy pounder. Maybe
smaller.'
Kandisky: 'I see there are things we do
not agree on.'

Hemmingway (2004, p. 6)

The disagreement between Hemmingway and Kandisky regarding killing animals
for sport, and the pleasure involved in doing
so, provides an introduction to the arguments that have emerged within wildlife
literature regarding the merits of hunting
and in particular trophy hunting as a touristic activity. Trophy hunting is a form of
hunting that can be carried out by tourists
where the prime motivation for undertaking
the activity is the acquisition of a permanent reminder of the experience in the form
of a trophy. Trophies are defined by Novelli
and Humavindu (2005) as 'any part of an
animal that can be displayed as a sign of the
catch' (p. 172); trophies can include heads,
horns or skins with the quality depending
on size or weight, with trophies from older
males being particularly prized (Novelli
and Humavindu, 2005). This chapter will
provide an overview of the arguments for
and against trophy hunting as a touristic
activity and will also evaluate these issues
through a number of different ethical lenses.
Before these issues can be fully explored it
is necessary to evaluate the dualistic notion
that has emerged that defines hunting as
consumptive wildlife tourism and wildlife-
watching activities as non-consumptive
wildlife tourism.

Blurred Boundaries: Problems in Defining Consumptive Wildlife Tourism

Tourism that involves hunting and fishing
activities are often categorized as a form of
consumptive wildlife tourism. Sinha (2001,
p. 4) defines consumptive wildlife tourism

as involving 'the capture or killing of
target animals. It can be in the form of:
(i) recreational hunting of waterfowl and
big game (may also be valued for meat);
(ii) recreational fishing (fish may be released
after catching or valued for food); or (iii)
trophy hunting and fishing (the trophy
itself may be valued as well as the thrill of
hunting itself).' Shackley's (1996) conceptualization of wildlife tourism comple-
ments Sinha's view of hunting and fishing
as a form of consumptive wildlife tourism;
she identifies the killing of animals as a
central concept in what she identifies as
'destructive tourism'. The act of killing or
causing harm to target animals is therefore
a central aspect of consumptive wildlife
tourism; conversely, non-consumptive
wildlife tourism is conceptualized as activities that involve the use of animals but do
not result in either the species being permanently affected or killed by the tourism
interaction (Duffus and Dearden, 1990).
A dualism has therefore been established
within wildlife tourism between activities
that involve causing harm to target species,
i.e. hunting and fishing, and those activities such as wildlife watching that are not
perceived to cause harm to target species.
This dualism has also helped to establish
the foundations for ethical judgements to
be made about what should be considered
to be wildlife tourism. Newsome *et al.*
(2005) deliberately exclude hunting and
fishing from their conceptualization
of wildlife tourism on moral grounds.
They state:

> we neither condone nor accept this practice
> and have deliberately delimited our
> definition of wildlife tourism to exclude
> any activity which results in the killing of
> wildlife as it does not sit comfortably with
> the ecocentric worldview that engenders
> respect for all living creatures.
>
> Newsome *et al.* (2005, p. 20).

They go on to add:

> By extension the culling (killing) of
> 'overabundant' species by tourists is also
> excluded from the authors' view and
> definition of wildlife tourism.
>
> Newsome *et al.* (2005, p. 20).

However, those who advocate hunting and fishing as legitimate tourist activities have increasingly argued against the labelling of only these activities as consumptive wildlife tourism. There is concern that defining wildlife-related tourism is becoming problematic as this type of tourism expands and diversifies and that use of the term 'consumptive' to distinguish and advocate between different types of wildlife tourism is inconsistent, contradictory and flawed (Tremblay, 2001). Within wildlife tourism literature the term 'non-consumptive' is frequently and uncritically applied to certain wildlife-related activities such as photography and viewing, which are seen as more desirable forms of wildlife use (Tremblay, 2001).

The central tenet of their argument is that the term consumptive implies causing a negative impact upon the target species, which, it is argued, is not restricted to only hunting and fishing activities. Wildlife viewing is considered to be a non-consumptive use of wildlife by many because the activity 'does not require the killing of individual animal' (Tremblay, 2001, p. 82). The definition of non-consumptive use of wildlife as described by Duffus and Dearden (1990) is more complex and moves beyond the act of killing and includes any activity which avoids the target species being 'purposefully removed or permanently affected by the engagement' (Duffus and Dearden, 1990, p. 15). It is this widening of the scope of consumptive activities, from killing to permanently affecting, which has caused some to question just how benign activities such as wildlife viewing are and just how different they are to activities such as hunting and fishing. Lovelock (2008) makes the point that wildlife viewing can also cause negative impacts for the target species involved. He points to a number of impacts that wildlife watching can cause, such as the disruption to essential activities (such as breeding and feeding), the introduction of potentially harmful pathogens and problems of habituation of animals to humans through continued exposure and feeding (Lovelock, 2008). Baker (1997) goes so far as to suggest that wildlife-viewing tours can

actually be more detrimental to the targeted species and their wider habitat than activities such as hunting and fishing. Baker (1997) also argues that this is due to the more commercial orientation of wildlife-viewing activities, which rely on high tourist volumes and the resultant need for significant infrastructure developments which ultimately degrade the environment.

The defence of hunting and fishing activities as legitimate forms of wildlife tourism has expanded to include a critical examination of the type of experience that is provided and the resulting relationship with the environment that can be generated. For Franklin (2002), both hunting and fishing provide an embodied experience, in that these activities allow participants to reconnect with nature unlike other forms of visual wildlife tourism in which participants are 'set off to one side, nervously hoping to have as little impact as possible' (Franklin, 2002, p. 218). Despite objections towards hunting and fishing which have risen in recent years, Franklin (2002) identifies that the enduring popularity of hunting and fishing demonstrates their importance and role of getting people back into nature. He links the desire to hunt with Neo-Darwininsm and the concept of the killer ape, which attempts to reverse the negative impact of urban living on the (male) human body, which is vulnerable to 'weakening and pathology' (Franklin, 2002, p. 219). For Franklin, hunting and fishing: 'the antidote to metropolitan physical malaise was the frequent return to nature, the ultimate test of which was to join battle with natural predators or fight an enormous fish' (Franklin, 2002, p. 219). It is the embodied experience provided by hunting and fishing that allow humans to get back to nature which both Franklin (2008) and Lovelock (2008) use as a defence of these activities and also to criticize wildlife viewing. Protected areas such as national parks and wildlife reserves are politically fragile and rely on the support of users. Franklin (2008), however, considers that non-consumptive users are not effective long-term supporters as their experiences are not as intense or embodied as hunters, who he believes are much more likely to be engaged in rural local affairs and therefore more likely to provide long-term support. To support this he cites the UK's largest ever political-based rally that took place in August 1997 to protest against the ban on foxhunting. Franklin (2008) suggests that the size of this rally helps to show that hunters are engaged with issues of their environment and are willing to become politically involved at a national level to ensure the protection of local areas.

Caution is needed here as it can be argued that the comparisons being made here do not seem to compare like with like. Both Franklin (2002, 2008) and Lovelock (2008) utilize local hunting examples (wildlife leisure activities) where the participants have developed an intimate knowledge of their local environment over a long period of time against wildlife tourists who travel to unfamiliar locations in order to view exotic species for pleasure. There are two potential problems with this line of argument, the first is that there are also those who undertake wildlife viewing in their own local environment (for example birdwatchers, ramblers and those who photograph wildlife) who may have just as an embodied experience, have developed intimate knowledge of their local environment and care just as much about its protection. A second problem arises in ignoring the problems that can arise when hunters choose to travel outside of their local environment to hunt and fish, especially if one of their main motivations is to acquire trophies.

Before the arguments both for and against trophy hunting as a tourist activity can be explored fully it is essential to distinguish between different types of hunter. Gunn (2001) notes that there are a variety of hunter types identified within the literature and that '[d]efenders of hunting invariably contrast what they regard as "true" sport hunting, with hunting for some other purpose, and especially with hunting just for the sake of killing something' (Gunn, 2001, p. 74). This distinction between sport hunting and hunting for other purposes is supported by both Causey (1989) and Vitali (1990). Positive human character traits such

as patience, discipline and the desire to be at one with nature are used by both authors to distinguish sports hunters from others who engage in hunting. Sports hunting is also associated with the principles of fair chase, which ensures that an animal has a significant chance of escaping from the hunter and that the hunter will not engage in unfair means to achieve a kill (e.g. shooting from vehicles, hides or using traps). Fair chase principles also emphasize the need for hunters to achieve a clean kill and to avoid causing the animal to suffer excessively (Lovelock, 2008). The sports hunter is therefore linked to the type of hunting that Franklin (2008) identifies as being more embodied and in-touch with nature. A second type of hunter described in the literature is the shooter. The shooter participates in hunting through necessity rather than to gain any intrinsic pleasure from the experience or to acquire an extrinsic reward such as a trophy. Shooters therefore hunt for food or in order to eradicate pests. The third category of hunter is the trophy hunter who is dealt with much less sympathetically within hunting literature. Trophy hunting is also identified as plastic hunting and slob hunting (Loftin, 1988). Unlike the sports hunter, trophy hunters are often attributed with negative characteristics, such as being deceitful or engaging in cheating. Causey (1989) condemns both the participant for using semi-automatic weapons, vehicles or hides to gain nothing more than a 'head to decorate their office wall' (Causey, 1989, p. 340) and the operators for running operations which require little in the way of skill to achieve the trophy. Interestingly Gunn (2001) notes that 'nowhere in the literature, so far as I am aware, is the hunting for fun, for the enjoyment of killing, or for the acquisition of trophies defended' (p. 68). Although there is little defence put forward for participants who engage in trophy hunting and they are widely criticized, the actual activity and benefits that can be produced from it are more widely supported. This next section will outline the key arguments that are put forward to both support and criticize trophy hunting as a tourist activity.

Arguments in Support
of Trophy Hunting

For some, trophy hunting has undertaken an extraordinary transformation in recent years. It has been noted above that recent history has recorded trophy hunting as being a prime cause in pushing numerous species, such as the tiger in India and the big five in southern and eastern Africa, to the brink of extinction. However, in some parts of the world trophy hunting has been reinvented as the saviour of many species and a central argument in defence of trophy hunting has been to show that it has the potential to generate revenue streams that can be channelled into the conservation of both the natural environment and some individual species that are threatened with extinction.

A number of authors have discussed the economic value that trophy hunting can have for local economies, particularly in southern Africa. Damm (2005) estimates that trophy hunting is worth between US$65.6 and US$137 million to the South African economy and Novelli and Humavindu (2005) placed a value of US$26.3 million on the Namibian trophy hunting industry, which they estimate to be 14% of the whole tourism industry in the country. Zimbabwe's Communal Areas Management Program for Indigenous Resources (CAMPFIRE) scheme has been widely regarded as an example of how trophy hunting can be successfully integrated into the local economy. The scheme was designed to empower local communities and provide them with control over how natural resources in their area were managed. Wildlife tourism was a cornerstone of the scheme and the selling of hunting permits was one of the most significant ways in which local communities could generate a sustainable income. This income was then reinvested in local community schemes such as the building of schools or the drilling of boreholes for water. The scheme also provided a direct income for local households that were involved (Mbaiwa, 2008). CAMPFIRE is also credited with helping to conserve wildlife as animals were protected from poachers by local people due to their value as a tourism resource (Frost and Bond, 2008).

Perhaps one significant aspect of trophy hunting's potential to contribute towards local economic development in Africa is its ability to attract hunters not only to the more well-known and more developed eastern and southern African hunting destinations but also to more marginal areas (both in terms of political stability and environmental quality) where other forms of wildlife tourism have not been able to develop (Lindsey et al., 2006). Therefore areas that have lower densities of watchable wildlife or areas where livestock is dominant can still be attractive to the trophy hunters as long as there are trophy species available. Perhaps more significantly is the ability for trophy hunting to take place in countries that are deemed to be politically unstable or that have poor tourism infrastructure. Wilkie and Carpenter (1999) identify that despite being located in a politically unstable region both the Cameroon and Republic of Congo have developed successful trophy-hunting industries. They believe that trophy hunters are more prepared to travel to these potentially risky locations in search of new trophies and therefore have helped to develop a niche tourism product that brings revenue that has the potential to contribute towards environmental protection. The political instability in Zimbabwe provides a further example of the resilience of trophy hunting compared to more traditional forms of tourism. The land seizures and subsequent social and economic instability had a devastating impact on the country's tourism industry; however, Novelli and Humavindu (2005) reported that the trophy-hunting industry was largely unaffected and Lindsey et al. (2006) highlight that the trophy-hunting industry only experienced a 12% reduction in revenues compared to a 75% reduction for the traditional tourism industry.

In terms of contributing to species conservation Leader-Williams et al. (2005) cite the important role that trophy hunting has had in the conservation of the white rhino

(*Ceratotherium simum*). White rhino populations have seen their numbers dramatically decrease due to illegal poaching (rhinos are targeted for their horns which are used in some aspects of traditional Chinese medicine) and were listed on Appendix 1 of the Convention on International Trade in Endangered Species (CITES) in 1977 (Appendix 1 contains a list of the world's most threatened species and all international trade in these species is prohibited). Since its initial CITES listing in 1977 the white rhino population has experienced a recovery and is now listed as near-threatened. However, Leader-Williams *et al.* (2005) point out that this important population recovery had less to do with the listing of the white rhino by CITES and more to do with the fact that small populations were protected on state and privately owned land in some areas of southern Africa. This enabled populations to recover and this recovery was assisted by the introduction of limited trophy hunting (Leader-Williams *et al.*, 2005). Trophy hunting became a viable proposition as the breeding programmes became more successful and the carrying capacity of the protected areas was reached and something needed to be done about excess males within the population. Controlled hunting of these males (the removal of excess population numbers is often referred to as the management of offtakes) therefore allowed the population to be effectively managed and a revenue stream generated which fed into the conservation programme (Leader-Williams *et al.*, 2005). The success of this approach to the conservation of white rhino populations has led Leader-Williams *et al.* (2005) to call for the same approach to be applied to black rhino (*Diceros bicornis*) populations, which as yet have not experienced the same level of population growth as the white rhino and are still listed as critically endangered.

Arguments against Trophy Hunting

There is one essential element in order for a successful trophy hunt to take place, a dead animal, and the kill is often seen as being truly essential for an authentic hunt (Gunn, 2001). It is the act of killing the trophy specimen and the manner in which it is done that form the central criticisms of hunting and trophy hunting in particular. The suffering (both physical pain and emotional stress) that can be caused to individual animals, through the chase and the final act of killing, underpins much of the case against hunting and Loftin (1984) acknowledges that animal suffering is one of the most serious arguments that can be levelled against the hunting community. Animal suffering and whether humans have a duty to minimize it is a contentious point and the ethical position will be explored later in this chapter. The extent to which animals suffer during hunting is difficult to assess but Gunn (2001) acknowledges that suffering for some animals is inevitable and that it is probably impossible to kill without pain. The extent and duration of that pain will generally depend on the skill of the hunter and the ability to ensure a clean kill. Van Emmenes (2007) provides a window into the problems of ensuring a clean kill through his account of hunting blue wildebeest (*Connochaetes taurinus*) in South Africa. He recounts several instances where despite his experience and skill it was impossible to ensure a clean kill. In one instance, having shot a female wildebeest, Van Emmenes (2007) observed that 'Although she had taken a sure killing shot through her lungs, she stayed on her feet and mobile, for several minutes' (p. 56) and it took a second shot to eventually bring her down. In a second incident a male wildebeest was shot in the lung but did not die immediately. This led to a protracted search of the African bush which had to be called off at night. Van Emmenes (2007) recalls 'It was getting late and we were losing concentration. Rapula was losing the spoor more often and we decided to return in daylight. We were no longer sure that the bull would die anytime soon' (p. 58). The male wildebeest was recovered the next day, having finally succumbed to its wound 6 km from where it was initially shot.

Some forms of trophy hunting do not necessarily require a kill but can still result in the suffering of the targeted animal. Sport fishing is one such example of this, where anglers will attempt to catch a trophy species but, increasingly, will then release the fish back into the wild, so-called catch-and-release fishing. In catch-and-release fishing the trophy takes the form of a photograph of the angler with a fish. This approach is now being considered to be a more ethical approach to sports fishing. However, despite the adoption of catch-and-release practices in some areas, Fennell (2000) criticizes one type of sports angling, billfishing, arguing that it still has the potential to cause the suffering of animals during the initial catch and subsequent handling of the fish. Fennell (2000) also expressed concerns about the survival prospects of the fish once they were released.

Although advocates of trophy hunting extol its potential to make positive contributions to the conservation of the wider environment and individual species (such as the case of the white and black rhino discussed above), there is also concern that trophy hunting can have a negative impact on some populations of species that are targeted by trophy hunters, especially in areas where populations are wild or in areas where regulation governing quota limits and so on are not enforced. The argali sheep (*Ovis ammon*), which are found throughout central Asia, are hunted as trophies due to their distinctive horns. The sheep are considered to be endangered throughout their range due to habitat loss and also poaching. As with the white rhino, trophy hunting was seen as a method of ensuring the long-term survival of the species. Unfortunately, this initiative has not achieved the same success as that of the white rhino in southern Africa. A controlled trophy-hunting programme was introduced in Gansu Province of the People's Republic of China aimed at generating revenue that could feed back into the conservation of the sheep (Harris and Pletshcer, 2002). Unfortunately Harris and Pletshcer (2002) found that, although the scheme had potential to generate significant amounts of revenue, which

they estimated to be approximately US$60,000, little of the money reached the local level and their overall assessment of the scheme to the conservation of the argali sheep was minor. Unfortunately for the argali sheep this was not an isolated failure. Across the border in Mongolia the argali sheep were facing similar problems and as in China a trophy-hunting scheme was established to assist in the conservation of the species (Amgalanbaatar *et al.*, 2002). This scheme proved to be controversial; the number of hunting licences significantly increased over a 10-year period generating high levels of revenue but again, as with China, little money found its way into funding direct conservation activities. The scheme was also mired in controversy with allegations of corruption and local communities complaining that they received little benefit from the hunting industry, which caused resentment and a growth in local opposition (Amgalanbaatar *et al.*, 2002).

The inevitable focus on the trophy in trophy hunting can also have further implications for wild populations that are targeted by hunters. As highlighted by Novelli and Humavindu (2005), trophy hunters tend to focus on males as these tend to have the more developed features (horns, tusks, antlers, manes, etc.), which make the best trophies. The targeting of these males can have evolutionary consequences for the remaining population as the prime breeding stock is removed. Coltman *et al.* (2003) studied the evolutionary consequences of the removal of male bighorn rams (*Ovis Canadensis*) by trophy hunting over a 30-year period. They concluded that the best trophy rams were also the best genetic breeding stock and that as these rams were removed before fulfilling their full breeding potential this resulted in the production of a population of lighter rams with smaller horns, a problem both for the wild population and the sustainability of the hunting industry. In a separate study, Singer and Zeigenfuss (2002) observed the effect of trophy hunting on three species of mountain sheep: Dall sheep (*Ovis dalli*), Rocky Mountain bighorn (*Ovis Canadensis canadensis*) and the desert bighorn (*Ovis Canadensis nelsoni*). They compared populations that were hunted with those that were not hunted. In hunted populations they found increased evidence that ewes were harassed by young rams compared to unhunted populations where more older rams were present and therefore there was 'a more orderly, hierarchical and less disruptive mating system present' (Singer and Zeigenfuss, 2002, p. 696).

Some mature male animals can also develop celebratory or iconic status within the area that they live and their removal by trophy hunting can cause public outrage. An example of this was the killing of the 'Emperor of Exmoor', by an alleged trophy hunter in October 2010. The Emperor was a red deer stag (*Cervus elaphus*) that lived in Exmoor National Park in South-west England and had become well known among wildlife enthusiasts. The stag was estimated to be nine feet tall, weighing approximately 300 pounds and had a set of antlers that were worth in the region of £10,000 (Knight Bruce, 2010). His killing in the middle of the rutting (breeding) season resulted in significant amounts of media coverage, public anger and criticism, particularly of the trophy-hunting industry, when it emerged this may have been the reason that the animal was killed (even though the stag was killed by a licence holder and was therefore legal). Despite the legality of the killing and experts putting forward ecological-based arguments that the stag was in its last breeding year and would have eventually died a slower and more painful death, public reaction was overwhelmingly negative. Newspaper message boards were dominated by comments such as:

> I can't understand the mentality of anyone who would do such a thing as a hobby.

and

> You would think that in the 21st century we would, as a species, have evolved beyond killing animals for sport. Apparently not.

One person who claimed to be a member of the hunting community also felt the killing was wrong and interestingly noted that this act of trophy hunting would further undermine support for hunting in the UK:

> I belong to the British Association for Shooting and Conservation, BASC and I belong to two game shooting syndicates. I do not by choice shoot deer. I understand that deer herds need to be managed, the old and weak animals removed and numbers kept to a healthy population for the environment where they are to be found. However, this stag was healthy and moreover an iconic symbol recognised, honoured and respected by many folk. My own feelings are that whoever shot him and those that permitted it, are miserable bastards with very little humanity and certainly no understanding of public relations. If shooting as a sport loses public support and ends up under pressure to be banned, it will be as a result of the actions of the morons who ended the existence of this magnificent beast. I can't remember when a story upset and angered me as much as this one.

A further criticism that is levelled against trophy hunting is the manner in which it can be undertaken. Put-and-take hunting involves animals being bred specifically to be hunted and clients can pre-order the species that they want to kill before they arrive in their destination. There is some concern that this can lead to a focus on the introduction and breeding of exotic species rather than a focus on breeding native species as these are the animals that hunters want to kill. Canned hunting is perhaps the most extreme and heavily criticized form of trophy hunting and has been a common form of hunting in both the USA and South Africa. Trophy animals are kept within confined areas (although the size of the enclosure can vary from a few feet to over a thousand acres) and according to the Born Free Foundation (undated) some animals have been hand reared making them trusting of humans and so making them extremely easy to kill. The controversy of canned hunting of lions in South Africa led to this particular form being banned by the South African government in 2009

(Anonymous, 2009), although an appeal by breeders to lift the ban was being heard at the time of writing this chapter. Canned hunting and to some extent put-and-take hunting goes against the philosophy of the sports hunter as the key elements of fair chase and being at one with nature are removed from the experience and are replaced by a focus on shooting the animal and gaining the desired trophy.

Trophy Hunting: Through an Ethical Lens

The controversy that surrounds trophy hunting and the arguments that both support and criticize it as a tourist activity provide a useful window to help explore ethical issues pertaining to the environment and more specifically how humans use other animals for pleasure. This section will now use a number of different ethical perspectives to analyse the trophy-hunting debate and explore how both sides of the controversy can be considered to be ethical depending upon various human beliefs. This section will also revisit the debate concerning the impacts of wildlife watching and trophy hunting on target species. It will apply the Doctrine of Double Effect (DDE) theory to try to explore one possible way of differentiating between them ethically.

From an ethical perspective the main difference between those who defend hunting and those that criticize it lies in whether they consider animals to have any moral rights. Some of those who defend hunting consider that individual animals do not have rights and therefore do not deserve any moral consideration; a perspective described by Midgley (1983) as absolute dismissal. This absolute dismissal perspective has been dominant in Western philosophical thought on animals and has been shaped by dualistic thinking where the mind and body are considered separate. Three key factors emerged from this line of thinking leading to humans being placed above all other animal life; the first, only humans possessed souls; the second, only humans were

capable of rational thought; and the third, that only humans could command language. In the West, dualistic thinking dominated religious belief; a number of pronouncements within the Old Testament classified animals as mere instruments to help satisfy human interest (DeGrazia, 2002; Fudge, 2002). A number of notable philosophers were also influenced by this line of thinking and also viewed animals as being below humans and therefore we had no duty towards them. Notably, Immanuel Kant dismissed animals from moral consideration on the grounds that they were not rational beings and Rene Descartes was also similarly dismissive of animals describing them as organic machines that could not suffer pain (Dobson, in press). In his defence of hunting as an ethical activity, Vitali (1990) adopts this type of reasoning stating '[s]ince only humans manifest such powers of reflection and choice, …, it follows that only humans can and should be regarded as moral agents having moral rights. Consequently, only humans should be regarded as having natural (as opposed to legal) rights to life, freedom from harm, and freedom from non-consensual interference.' (p. 75). In relation to animals, Vitali (1990) goes on to claim that they 'have no natural rights and thus no claim upon a principle of constraint that limits how, when or why they may be treated by human beings' (p. 75). For Vitali, there is no moral reason why animals should not be hunted as they are not included in the sphere of moral consideration as they are incapable of rational thoughts and therefore cannot act as moral agents. From this perspective Vitali (1990) also emphasizes that due to the experiential benefits that hunting can have for humans (in terms of psychological and physical health) hunting is a natural good and a morally worthy activity.

Not all defenders of hunting ignore the need to widen the sphere of moral consideration beyond humans. The prime defence of hunting lies in what is commonly referred to as an 'environmental ethic'. In its simplest form the environmental ethic concedes that anything can be done to a component of an ecosystem (e.g. animal or plant), provided that the action does not place the whole ecosystem at risk (O'Neil *et al.*, 2008). Trophy hunting is therefore morally permissible provided that any individual species that is targeted does not belong to an endangered species (and hunting them would put the species further at risk) or that the activity does undue damage to the ecosystem.

Unfortunately for Vitali (1990), his defence of hunting from the absolute dismissal perspective is flawed. It is widely accepted that not all human beings are capable of rational thought or can command language (notably human infants and those humans with severe learning difficulties) and excluding them from moral consideration can be troubling. Even though some categories of humans and all animals cannot act as moral agents, as they are unable to make moral decisions, they can be affected (both positively and negatively) by such decisions and are therefore often referred to as moral patients (Regan, 2004; Franklin, 2005). In order to include such moral patients into the sphere of moral consideration, the boundary for consideration has been extended beyond the limits of rational thought and the command of language. The boundary is now commonly set to include all sentient beings, i.e. all those that are capable of experiencing pain, most notably mammals, birds and (perhaps) some fish. This stance has been supported by notable philosophers including Mary Midgley (1983) and Peter Singer (1993, 1995). Singer (1993, p. 57) wrote 'If a being suffers, there can be no moral justification for refusing to take that suffering into consideration'. For those who acknowledge sentience as the basis for moral consideration, hunting can be seen as immoral as it can cause suffering to animals through the stress of the chase, injury and ultimately death.

Loftin (1984) proposes a form of utilitarianism as a third way in which the ethics of hunting can be evaluated. Utilitarianism is an ethical perspective which makes judgments as to what is the right thing to do based on the consequences of an action (a so called teleological approach to ethics) and ensuring that the greatest good is achieved for the greatest number of those with interests in the action (Dobson, in press). From a hunting perspective utilitarianism has the potential to combine elements of the environmental ethic (i.e. concern for the ecosystem) with concerns for individual animals. Hunting can be considered ethical and a sentient animal can be killed provided that there are proven beneficial consequences that are derived from the death of the animal. These benefits can include the continued survival of the species (as with the white rhino example) or the wider protection of the ecosystem which can be made possible through mechanisms such as the revenue gained from selling hunting permits, the advocacy for conservation practices promoted by the hunting lobby and financial benefits that can be derived for local communities in places such as the Congo or Cameroon. In his utilitarian reasoning Loftin (1984) recognizes that animals deserve moral consideration but concludes that certain animals can be hunted for the greater good, describing those animals who die as 'martyrs' (p.248).

A final objection to hunting and especially trophy hunting that is often raised by opponents to these activities relates to the underlying motivation of participants. As outlined above many sports hunters engage in hunting to reconnect with nature and trophy hunters to gain an extrinsic reward from their experience. Issues of human pleasure/enjoyment are therefore underlying the motivations to take part in hunting. For some this is perfectly acceptable, for example, Vitali (1990) considers that only persons have rights, there is nothing wrong with hunting for food or trophies so long as the ecosystem is not jeopardized (as this can have negative consequences for human well-being) and he defends the pleasure that can be derived from hunting as a moral good as it has a benefit to human health. Midgley (1983) identifies that all sentient beings have 'interests' which she differentiates between 'trivial' and 'urgent'. Trivial interests can be considered to be interests that may be beneficial to sentient beings but are not necessary for the avoidance of pain or long-term survival. Urgent interests may be considered to be those that relate to the avoidance of pain or suffering by sentient beings. Midgley (1983) highlights 'however far down the queue animals may be placed, it is still possible in principle for their urgent needs to take precedence over people's trivial ones' (p. 17). There is therefore a question of whether hunting and especially trophy hunting is providing only for a trivial human interest which can be met in other ways, whilst impinging on an urgent interest of the target animal, its life.

Inevitably this line of argument returns us to the fact that it is not only hunting that can cause animals to suffer; so-called nonconsumptive wildlife tourism activities also have the ability to cause suffering to animals. An ethical theory known as the Doctrine of Double Effect (DDE) may help unpack the subtle ethical differences between hunting and wildlife watching. Central to DDE is that it makes a moral distinction between what is an intended outcome of an action and what is merely foreseen as a side effect (Driver, 2007). This distinction can therefore help to distinguish between hunting and many forms of wildlife watching. Within hunting there is an explicit intention to kill the animal and the kill is central to the hunter's experience and without it the experience is not the same (Vitali, 1990). An added issue within trophy hunting is that there is an explicit intention to take some aspect of the dead animal to display as a trophy. It can be argued that it is this intention to cause harm that sets hunting apart from many wildlife-watching activities where although the activity can cause problems for the target animal (e.g. disturbance or stress) it is not necessarily intentional.

Conclusion

Hunting has played a central role in humans becoming the planet's dominant species. However, during the past 100 years, hunting has undergone a transformation in Western societies, moving away from being an activity born of necessity to one that is undertaken for pleasure. This transformation has been controversial and has raised a number of ethical questions regarding the way humans utilize animals. It has been shown that defining hunting and fishing activities as consumptive users of wildlife and those that watch wildlife as non-consumptive users is problematic and this dualism is considered too simplistic by those who defend hunting activities.

Those hunters who travel outside of their local environment with the purpose of killing an animal to gain a trophy are widely derided in hunting literature and are contrasted against sports hunters who are often considered to be both at one with their environment and strong advocates for its protection. Despite this, some argue that the trophy-hunting industry has an important role to play in the economic development of less-developed countries and can also help in environmental protection and species conservation. Opposed to this are critics of trophy hunting who argue that taking pleasure from killing an animal is morally wrong and that, in some cases, the trophy hunting can have more negative than positive impacts.

The issue of trophy hunting provides a useful issue through which to apply different ethical viewpoints regarding human/ environment/animal relationships. Those who defend trophy hunting do so either from a perspective of absolute dismissal or from an environmental ethic, defending their actions on the basis that it is the ecosystem that has moral worth. Those who criticize trophy hunting tend to ascribe animals with some form of moral rights and argue that killing an animal for a trophy violates the urgent interest of the animal (i.e. by taking its life) to satisfy a trivial interest of the hunter (i.e. taking pleasure from the kill and the gaining of a trophy). Even within hunters there can be conflicting and confusing emotions felt at the moment of the kill as O'Kelly (2007) highlights:

Relief, sadness, satisfaction – those mixed emotions that hunters experience at the conclusion of a successful hunt – flooded through me. Relief at having found my ram, relief that my shot had been good and my ram hadn't suffered. Sadness that this ram would never again graze on the banks of that little river. Satisfaction that the hunt had played a small part in ensuring that his offspring would feed on the banks of that little river. And also hope that the area would be protected for future generations of bushbuck – and hunters.

O'Kelly (2007, p. 47).

The arguments relating to trophy hunting are difficult to resolve and will no doubt carry on into the future. Should we place the rights of individual animals above human pleasure or should we accept that it is a necessary evil that, in the long term, can bring about positive enhancements for the natural environment and the local communities in which it takes place?

References

Akama, J.S. (2008) Controversies surrounding the ban on wildlife hunting in Kenya: an historical perspective. In: Lovelock, B. (ed.) *Tourism and the Consumption of Wildlife: Hunting, Shooting and Sport Fishing*. Routledge, London, pp. 73–86.

Amgalanbaatar, S., Reading, R.P., Lhagvasuren, B. and Batsukh, N. (2002) Argali sheep Ovis ammon trophy hunting in Mongolia. *Pirineos* 157, 129–150.

Anonymous (2009) Canned hunting of captive lions banned in South Africa. Available at: http://www.telegraph.co.uk/news/worldnews/africaandindianocean/southafrica/5516764/Canned-hunting-of-captive-lions-banned-in-South-Africa.html (accessed 27 December 2010).

Baker, J. (1997) Development of a model system for touristic hunting revenue collection and allocation. *Tourism Management* 18, pp. 273–286.

Causey, A.S. (1989) On the morality of hunting. *Environmental Ethics* 11, 327–343.

Coltman, D.W., O'Donoghue, P., Jorgenson, J.T., Hogg, J.T., Strobeck. C. and Festa Bianchet, M. (2003) Undesirable evolutionary consequences of trophy hunting. *Nature* 426, 655–658.

Damm, G. (2005) Hunting in South Africa: facts, risks and opportunities. *African Indaba* 3, 1–14.

DeGrazia, D. (2002) *Animal Rights: A Very Short Introduction*. Oxford University Press, Oxford, UK.

Dobson, J. (in press) Towards a utilitarian ethic for marine wildlife tourism. *Tourism in Marine Environments* (in press).

Driver, J. (2007) *Ethics: The Fundamentals*. Blackwell Publishing, Oxford, UK.

Duffus, D.A. and Dearden, P. (1990) Non-consumptive wildlife-oriented recreation: a conceptual framework. *Biological Conservation* 53, 213–231.

Dunlap, T.R. (1988) Sport hunting and conservation, 1880–1920. *Environmental Review* 12, 51–60.

Franklin, A. (2002) *Nature and Social Theory*. Sage Publications, London.

Franklin, A. (2008) The 'animal question' and the 'consumption' of wildlife. In: Lovelock, B. (ed.) *Tourism and the Consumption of Wildlife: Hunting, Shooting and Sport Fishing*. Routledge, London, pp. 31–44.

Franklin, J.H. (2005) *Animal Rights and Moral Philosophy*. Columbia University Press, New York.

Fennell, D.A. (2000) Ecotourism on trial – the case of billfish angling as ecotourism. *Journal of Sustainable Tourism* 8, 341–345.

Frost, P.G.H. and Bond, I. (2008) The CAMPFIRE Programme in Zimbabwe: payments for wildlife services. *Ecological Economics* 65, 776–787.

Fudge, E. (2002) *Animal*. Reaktion Books, London.

Gunn, A.S. (2001) Environmental ethics and trophy hunting. *Ethics and the Environment* 6, 68–95.

Hamman, K. (2008) Shooting tigers as leisure in colonial India. In: Lovelock, B. (ed.) *Tourism and the Consumption of Wildlife: Hunting, Shooting and Sport Fishing*. Routledge, London, pp. 99–111.

Harris, R.B. and Pletscher, D.H. (2002) Incentives toward conservation of *Argali Ovis ammon*: a case study of trophy hunting in Western China. *Oryx* 36, 1–9.

Hemmingway, E. (2004) *Green Hills of Africa*. Arrow Books, London.

Knight, B.R. (2010) Death of the Exmoor emperor. Available at: http://www.telegraph.co.uk/earth/wildlife/8089207/Death-of-the-Exmoor-Emperor.html (accessed 27 December 2010).

Leader-Williams, N., Milledge, S., Adcock, K., Brooks, M., Conway, A., Knight, M., Mainka, S., Martin, E.B. and Teferi, T. (2005) Trophy hunting of black rhino *Diceros bicornis*: proposals to ensure its future sustainability. *Journal of International Wildlife Law and Policy* 8, 1–11.

Lindsey, P.A., Alexander, R., Frank, L.G., Mathieson, A. and Romañach, S.S. (2006) Potential of trophy hunting to create incentives for wildlife conservation in Africa where alternative wildlife-based land uses may not be viable. *Animal Conservation* 9, 283–291.

Loftin, R.F. (1984) The morality of hunting. *Environmental Ethics* 6 (3) 241–250.

Loftin, R.F. (1988) Plastic hunting and real hunting. *Behavioural and Political Animal Studies* 1, 317–323.

Lovelock, B. (2008) An introduction to consumptive wildlife tourism. In: Lovelock, B. (ed.) *Tourism and the Consumption of Wildlife: Hunting, Shooting and Sport Fishing*. Routledge, London, pp. 3–30.

Mbaiwa, J.E. (2008) The success and sustainability of consumptive wildlife tourism in Africa. In: Lovelock, B. (eds). *Tourism and the Consumption of Wildlife: Hunting, Shooting and Sport Fishing*. Routledge, London, pp. 141–154.

Midgley, M. (1983) *Animals And Why They Matter*. The University of Georgia Press, Athens, Georgia.

Newsome, D., Dowling, R. and Moore, S. (2005) *Wildlife Tourism*. Channel View Publications, London.

Novelli, M. and Humavindu, M.N. (2005) Wildlife tourism – wildlife uses vs. local gain. Trophy hunting in Namibia. In: Novelli, M. (eds) *Niche Tourism Contemporary Issues, Trends and Cases*. Elsevier, London, pp. 171–182.

O'Kelly, W. (2007) Beginner's Luck. *Magnum* (April), 46–47.

O'Neil, J., Holland, A. and Light, A. (2008) *Environmental Values*. Routledge, London.

Regan, T. (2004) *The Case for Animal Rights*. University of California Press, Los Angeles.

Shackley, M. (1996) *Wildlife Tourism*. International Thomson Business Press, London.

Sillanpää, P. (2008) The Scandinavian sporting tour, 1830–1914. In: Lovelock, B (ed.) *Tourism and the Consumption of Wildlife: Hunting, Shooting and Sport Fishing*. Routledge, London, pp. 59–72.

Singer, F.J. and Zeigenfuss L.C. (2002) Influences of trophy hunting and horn size on mating behaviour and survivorship of mountain sheep. *Journal of Mammalogy* 83, 682–698.

Singer, P. (1993) *Practical Ethics,* 2nd edn. Cambridge University Press, Cambridge, UK.

Singer, P. (1995) *Animal Liberation:* 2nd edn. Pimlico, London.

Sinha, C.C. (2001) Wildlife tourism: a geographical perspective paper presented at the Geography Curriculum Inservice Conference, *Tourism Geography: Issues, Challenges and the Changing Nature of Contemporary Tourism,* University of Western Sydney, Hawkesbury Campus, 27 July 2001. Available at: http://www.hsc.csu.edu.au/geography/activity/local/tourism/LWILDLIF.pdf (accessed December 2010).

Tremblay, P. (2001) Wildlife tourism consumption: consumptive or non-consumptive? *International Journal of Tourism Research* 3, 81–86.

Van Emmenes, F. (2007) Blue wildebeest blues. *Magnum* (April), 56–58.

Vitali, T. (1990) Sport hunting: moral or immoral? *Environmental Ethics* 12, 69–82.

Wilkie, D.S. and Carpenter, J.F. (1999) The potential role of safari hunting as a source of revenue for protected areas in the Congo Basin. *Oryx* 4, 339–345.

tourism, protection for the environment, the creation of jobs for local people, and offering environmental education – has shaped much of the discussion on how ecotourism has been defined over the years, and is reflective in some of the earlier definitions during the 1990s (see Table 7.1).

Table 7.1 also illustrates the divergence of opinion as to what the key tenets of the term are. Diamantis (1999) noted that most of the early definitions described the characteristics of the destination and trip taken. He offered a detailed critique of these early definitions (not something this author plans to do here), assessing each on the extent to which it emphasized what he viewed as the three key components of ecotourism:

natural based, sustainable and educational. He concluded that it was 'more appropriate to treat ecotourism as a concept and illustrate the components and issues implied by ecotourism rather than the issues of ecotourism', noting that most of the early definitions contained these three essential components (Diamantis, 1999, p. 116). His work would later form the basis of more detailed examination of what were the key tenets of ecotourism.

A number of important early works emerged that provided some useful simplification over the definition that allows the term to have practical relevance. Early work by Wight (1993) argued that it was best if ecotourism was viewed as a spectrum that

Table 7.1. Evolving discourse over defining the term 'ecotourism'.

1989	'Ecotourism is a form of tourism inspired primarily by the natural history of an area, including its indigenous cultures. The ecotourist visits relatively undeveloped areas in the spirit of appreciation, participation and sensitivity. The ecotourist practices a non-consumptive use of wildlife and natural resources and contributes to the visited area through labour or financial means aimed at directly benefiting the conservation of the site and the economic well-being of the local residents…' Ziffer (1989, p. 6).
1991	'Ecotourism is nature tourism that contributes to conservation, through generating funds for protected areas, creating employment opportunities for local communities, and offering environmental education' Boo (1991, p. 4).
1991	The Ecotourism Society definition: 'The purposeful travel to natural areas, to understand the cultures and natural history of the environment, taking care not to alter the integrity of the ecosystem, while producing economic opportunities that would make the conservation of natural resources beneficial to local people…' Epler Wood et al. (1991).
1993	'Travel to remote or natural areas which aims to enhance understanding and appreciation of the natural environment and cultural heritage, avoiding damage or deterioration of the environment and the experience for others.' Figgis (1993, p. 8).
1994	'Nature-based tourism that is focused on provision of learning opportunities while providing local and regional benefits, while demonstrating environmental, social, cultural, and economic sustainability' Forestry Tasmania (1994, p. ii).
1994	'Nature-based tourism that involves education and interpretation of the natural environment and is managed to be ecologically sustainable' Australia Department of Tourism (1994, p. 4).
1996	'A responsible nature travel experience, that contributes to the conservation of the ecosystem while respecting the integrity of host communities and, where possible, ensuring that activities are complementary, or at least compatible, with existing resource-based uses present in the ecosystem' Boyd and Butler (1996a, p. 386)
1996	'Ecotourism is a form of tourism which fosters environmental principles, with an emphasis on visiting and observing natural areas' Boyd and Butler (1996b, p. 558).
1996	'Low impact nature tourism which contributes to the maintenance of species and habitats either directly through a contribution to conservation and/or indirectly by providing revenue to the local community sufficient for local people to value, and therefore protect, their wildlife heritage area as a source of income' Goodwin (1996, p. 288).
1997	'Ecotourism is tourism and recreation that is both nature-based and sustainable' Lindberg and McKercher (1997, p. 67).

From Diamantis (1999).

included a variety of products as opposed to defining it from a narrow, product specific perspective. Steward and Sekartjakrarini (1994) stated that a definitional structure of ecotourism was based on two approaches: (i) the activity-based perspective of ecotourism; and (ii) the definition regarding ecotourism as an industry. The former would see ecotourism defined according to what ecotourists do or should do and the value dimension behind the activity in terms of its benefit to that particular setting, whereas the latter focused on what ecotourism could offer communities as a tool for conservation and local development. Perhaps of all the early scholars writing on ecotourism, Wall (1994) was the most critical suggesting that ecotourism was essentially just nature travel that currently exists, and that the term was merely a repackaging exercise of an old product but in a new way; 'old wine in new bottles'. In the case of North America, the characteristics between ecotourism in natural settings were argued to be broadly similar to the concept of wilderness recreation (Boyd and Butler, 1996a).

Continua are a useful way to illustrate diversity of opinion and possibilities, and Orams (1995) provided us with what he termed 'a continuum of ecotourism paradigms' where an ecotourism spectrum may be positioned between two extreme poles: a low human responsibility pole against which it may be argued that all tourism could be viewed as ecotourism and a high human responsibility pole where ecotourism was considered impossible as an activity. Oram's ecotourism spectrum ranged from 'passive' as one moved toward the low human responsibility pole end where ecotourism activity seeks to minimize damage to 'active' where ecotourism contributes toward resources protection. Diamantis (1999) assessed early definitions against the continuum, arguing that, for example, Ceballos-Lascurain's definition was best viewed as passive, positioned toward the low responsibility pole, whereas Boo's (1990) definition could be seen to be situated in the active position toward the high responsibility pole; in short it demonstrated

that the body of researchers engaged in ecotourism research were a broad church where differing positions could be accommodated. In contrast, Blamey (1997) argued that there was a need to make the distinction between intentions and outcomes as well as between normative and descriptive perspectives, preferring a minimalist definition that involved a mixture of intentions and outcomes. He cites the Australian Commonwealth Department of Tourism (1994, p. 7) definition within their National Ecotourism Strategy (NES) whereby ecotourism is reduced to three components or dimensions: that it is nature based (supportive of the position taken by Boo (1990)); environmentally educated (supportive of Ceballos-Lascurain's (1987) thinking), and is sustainably managed and/or conservation supporting (supportive of the position taken by Buckley (1994)). Blamey (1997, p. 115) quickly came to the conclusion that there exists no quick-fix to arriving at an 'operational' definition of ecotourism and that '...different definitions will be suited to different circumstances. Compromise will have to be made...as the choice of definition is inherently subjective'. He noted that ecotourism may represent a distinct segment of the nature-based tourism market and suggested that any movement toward an operational definition of ecotourism would involve a subset of four main dimensions, namely size of operation (small groups/personalized), education/interpretation, sustainability in intention (demand) and sustainability in outcome (demand plus supply). He listed ten factors that were relevant to be considered in arriving at a definition:

1. The combination that best describes current demand
2. Purpose of market research
3. The combination that is preferred from a normative growth perspective
4. The combination that is preferred from a normative sustainability perspective
5. Scale of market research
6. Focus of market research
7. Measurement issues associated with any given combination

8. Nature of attractions, current management practices and tourist population
9. Funds available for market research
10. Need for consistency with other research.

Blamey's research led to the conclusion that attempting to provide a single definition of ecotourism that is suitable for all applications was a futile exercise. The preferred course of action is to focus on an appropriate minimalist definition based on just the nature-based and educative/experiential dimensions; hence a return to the position adopted by Ceballos-Lascurain himself.

Developments toward identifying key tenets of the term were seen in the work by Fennell (2001) who undertook a content analysis of 85 ecotourism definitions. He found five variables that were most common within the definitions:

- A reference to where ecotourism occurs, e.g. natural areas
- Conservation
- Culture
- Benefits to locals
- Education.

Fennell identified that most definitions emerged between 1991 and 1996 with the most comprehensive of these emerging between 1994 and 1996, as seen in Table 7.1. He noted a changing emphasis in how ecotourism was conceptualized over time, stating that beyond 1996 there was greater emphasis on variables such as conservation, education, ethics, sustainability, impacts and local benefits. In highlighting these aspects, he built on the three key components of Diamantis (1999). Donohoe and Needham (2006) made further progress toward clarifying key tenets. They developed a useful framework to assist in the development of ecotourism policy and applications by disentangling the various sets of themes that had evolved in the definitional debate over ecotourism. Their framework was based on key tenets of ecotourism, where tenets represent a set of established fundamental beliefs central to ecotourism. They identified the following six as central to what they saw as an evolving contemporary definition:

1. Nature based
2. Preservation/conservation
3. Education
4. Sustainability
5. Distribution of benefits
6. Ethics/responsibility/awareness.

The sixth tenet listed above was emergent across ecotourism discourse and has provoked some heated debate and opinion, as described later in the present chapter.

A number of broad conclusions may be arrived at with respect to the definitional controversies. First, maybe there has been too much attention given to defining the term. Fennell's (2001) work would attest to this; but this is to be expected among the emergent paradigm/school of researchers interested in this topic. Second, the debate has been more one of discourse as opposed to one of major controversy as many definitions have emerged where the number of emergent themes or dimensions has varied between scholars. Recent work by Fennell (2001), following on from that by Donohoe and Needham (2006), has provided what Weaver and Lawton (2007, p. 1170) see as almost 'near consensus...that ecotourism should satisfy three core criteria: (i) attractions should be predominantly nature based; (ii) visitor interactions with those attractions should be focused on learning or education; and (iii) experience and product management should follow principles and practices associated with ecological, sociocultural and economic sustainability'. But to what extent is this reflected in the voluminous collection of research published on ecotourism? The information compiled in Table 7.2 clearly demonstrates the exponential growth in published works on ecotourism over successive decades, starting in the 1980s up to the current time.

What clearly emerges from Table 7.2 is that if you take what seem to be accepted criteria of ecotourism, namely that it is nature based, occurring predominantly in protected areas, that it generates impacts, is connected to sustainability and has some learning component, some of these criteria get more attention within the published literature than others. For instance, most

Table 7.2. Growth in cited works on ecotourism and occurrence of key defining criteria.

Year/period	Ecotourism	Protected areas	Nature	Impacts	Sustainability	Learning	Nature+ learning+ sustainability
1980–1989	3	1	2	0	0	0	0
1990–1999	567	114	460	226	278	16	9
2000–2009	1871	329	1325	585	840	93	34
2010–present	179	41	141	41	73	3	3
Total	2620	485	1928	852	1191	112	46

Based on author's analysis of CAB Direct.

works emphasize it to be nature based, followed by a connection to sustainability, with the learning dimension getting the least mentions. When three dimensions are combined (nature, sustainability and learning), what emerges is that very few of the cited works name all three, suggesting that there exists a plethora of published work on ecotourism that either deliberately or coincidentally place emphasis on certain tenets over others, that author(s) do not see the value of a detailed discourse on definition, or maybe it is the outcome of limitations of combining certain dimensions and relying on a database where definition criteria need to be cited as keywords. This is not a futile exercise here as it may just illustrate that broad consensus around defining ecotourism is based on acceptance of very few main criteria.

Understanding the Ecotourist

The controversies regarding the term ecotourism has been matched by the concomitant term 'ecotourist', with their characteristics and values coming into the spotlight. Much of the discussion has focused on developing typologies, ranging from early work of Wilson and Laarman (1988) with the emphasis on extremes: 'hard' through to 'soft', where the former related to dedicated natural history ecotourists, and the latter equated to those travellers that combined nature-oriented travel with other mass tourism activities.

Variants of this spectrum were offered, for example, by Ziffer (1989) who presented a typology of four types: hard-core, dedicated nature, mainstream nature and casual nature; Boyd and Butler (1996b) who produced a three-type typology: ecospecialists (individuals, high knowledge, little infrastructure, limited impact), intermediate (small groups use basic transport, rely on pre-arranged facilities) and ecogeneralists (large groups, organized tours, high level of comfort and facilities); and Weaver (1998) who simplified the spectrum thinking to two broad categories: primary purpose (PP) and popular, casual, passive and diversionary (PCPD). These are all based on the hard–soft model. An interesting departure from this position was offered by Weaver and Lawton (2002) through what they termed the 'structured ecotourist' who acted both hard and soft depending on how they interacted with nature and the type of food and accommodation sought, respectively. While the discussion over how the ecotourist market has been segmented in terms of motivation, attitude and behaviour has focused on typology development, Weaver (2008, p. 47) noted that the difficultly of developing a universally agreed model around the soft–hard continuum is addressing the wider question of 'whether ecotourism classifications should be based on individuals or products, or a combination of both?'. Part of the remaining challenge is the need to accept that ecotourism, and hence ecotourists, are linked to other types of tourism and tourists.

Ecotourism and Linkages to Other Terms

While the focus in the previous sections was on defining the term and the participant, an argument may be made that the term 'ecotourism' is not, in fact, the preferred term used in the literature. Based on CAB Direct as a database, nature tourism recorded substantially more mentions than ecotourism, 14,095 compared to 2620, respectively, and as Table 7.3 reveals other related terms are clearly favoured or reflect more accurately what the research was focused on. It is perhaps not surprising the preference to nature tourism or nature tourists as Table 7.2 illustrated that most mentions on ecotourism stated its nature component.

An alternative argument is that the term 'ecotourism' is an industry label and that the term gives the industry legitimacy but that outside of industry much of academia prefers to talk of nature tourism, recognizing what they are writing about the industry sees as ecotourism.

Table 7.4 illustrates that linkage between ecotourism, alternative tourism and sustainable tourism in publications in the period 1980–2010. A number of trends emerge. First, there exist more publications where ecotourism is linked with sustainable tourism as opposed to linkages between ecotourism and alternative tourism; a trend that is present for all decades examined; second, while the number of works that make reference to all three terms are evident from the 1990s, the trend is that the number of mentions increases over time; third, sustainable tourism is more researched than any of the other two terms, but that publications/mentions increase for all three as one moves through the decades. A final point to note from the table is that research into alternative tourism preceded that on ecotourism, and that the former was more established by the time work emerged on the latter. Caution needs to be exercised here into over-reading the figures as a quick search shows citing of work on nature tourism was well established in the 1980s (3444 mentions) and that research that was focused on ecotourism took place under the wider term of nature tourism until ecotourism as a term was first coined. It should, however, be also pointed out that mentions/publications on nature tourism over the 1990s and 2000s remained considerable,

Table 7.3. Ecotourism and related terms.

Term	Mentions (1980–2011)
Ecotourism	2,620
Eco-tourism	198
Ecotourists	230
Nature tourism	14,095
Nature tourists	5,378
Nature-based tourism	399
Wildlife watching	119
Whale watching	82
Wildlife tourism	1,877
Alternative tourism	2,490
Sustainable tourism	6,068

Author's analysis of CAB Direct search.

Table 7.4. Ecotourism and related terms.

Period of time	Ecotourism	Alternative tourism	Sustainable tourism	Ecotourism + alternative tourism	Ecotourism + sustainable tourism	Ecotourism + alternative tourism + sustainable tourism
1980–1989	3	451	133	0	0	0
1990–1999	567	604	1426	73	278	46
2000–2009	1871	1280	3838	153	840	82
2010–present	179	155	671	14	110	9
Total	2620	2490	6068	240	1228	137

Author's analysis of recorded mentions in CAB Direct.

2793 and 6762, respectively, and from the start of the current decade more than 1000 publications on nature tourism are recorded.

Research on alternative tourism was a response to industry recognizing the need to act in a responsible manner to the impacts and change that tourism can bring to destinations and the emergence of a body of research that formed the base for Jafari's (2001) adaptancy and knowledge-based platforms mentioned above. As Table 7.4 demonstrates, alternative tourism was not always about ecotourism; much was focused on cultural tourism, adventure tourism and community-driven tourism. While ecotourism had a role, to some, it formed a hybrid between nature and cultural tourism. Fennell (2001) refers to it as ACE tourism, a term that has not been widely embraced by scholars (see comments in Weaver and Lawton, 2007). Alternative tourism was the challenge to be an alternative to the mass tourism that had emerged under the modern era of tourism with its preference for sun and sea/beach environments. Early commentators were, however, quick to challenge the benefits of alternative tourism. In particular, Butler (1990) argued that in many cases the negative impacts from alternative forms may be greater in certain settings than what may result from traditional and mass tourism activity. Characteristics of ecotourism are similar to those of alternative tourism: small scale, local benefits, controlled leakage, positive impacts and, while some commentators view ecotourism to be a subset of alternative tourism (Fennell, 2003), others (Weaver, 2001, 2005) see the merits of destinations providing forms of mass ecotourism where a strong regulatory environment is in place. This latter development leads to another area of controversy: what places and spaces should be considered as ecotourism environments?

Broadening Ecotourism Environments

In an early paper, Boyd and Butler (1999) argued the existence of a tiered structure of ecotourism destinations: 'primary' destinations that conveyed the images of being exotic, unique, having diversity of flora and fauna, tropical, often found in the less developed countries (LDCs) and predominantly set within protected landscapes as opposed to private developments; 'secondary' destinations and the attraction of ecotourism to the economies of peripheral areas such as Australasia, Canada and the remote landscapes of polar regions; and 'tertiary' destinations of the less exotic temperate landscapes of the more advanced economies where ecotourism often takes place in areas with a long tradition of extractive industries. During the past decade there has been limited change in the broad development of ecotourism spaces. However, in some 'secondary' destinations such as Canada, Australia and New Zealand, ecotourism has become a significant tourism niche. Publicly protected landscapes are preferred over private protected reserves, the former because of the formal environmental protection they offer (Weaver, 2008). However, there are a number of well recognized and visited private protected reserves in South Africa and Kenya, as well as the famous Monteverde Cloud Forest Reserve in Costa Rica. As of late, some authors have challenged the assumption of ecotourism as a non-consumptive activity and one focused on natural environments, thereby broadening our understanding of what constitutes an ecotourism environment (Novelli et al., 2006).

In the context of southern Africa, a debate is emerging as to whether or not ecotourism can and should embrace forms of consumptive tourism such as sport or trophy hunting, which can be beneficial to a region's economy, environments and local communities (Novelli and Humavindu, 2005; Novelli et al., 2006). The argument that these authors make is that sport and trophy hunting are important uses of wildlife; they are low-volume, high-value activities that bring greater benefit compared to non-consumptive viewing and the taking of photographs. Furthermore, these activities occur alongside non-consumptive activities, are both part of conservation arguments and policies, and that, in many cases, although trophy hunting is viewed as very controversial (Hofer, 2002), it has been the impetus for wider legislation, protection strategies and reallocation of monies by government agencies toward management, protection and nature conservation (Novelli and Humavindu, 2005).

Less controversial is the emergence of research supportive of urban ecotourism (Higham and Luck, 2002; Weaver, 2005). Weaver (2005) outlined potential urban spaces, ranging from remnant natural habitat to downtown high rises. Higham and Luck (2002) noted that the established definition of ecotourism has, within its definition, contradictions and challenges for urban ecotourism, as such environments were neither unmodified spaces (Boyd and Butler, 1996b; Blamey, 1997) or pristine, and that ecotourism visitor operations and activities be low in impact (Acott *et al.*, 1998; Honey, 1999). Citing three New Zealand urban case studies, Higham and Luck (2002) suggest that urban ecotourism is not a contradiction in terms as it takes place in environments that offer some degree of naturalness, the transport costs are low and preferable in terms of the environmental impacts of transportation, offer opportunity for mass education, and capture a larger audience than ecotourism in remote locations. As such, urban ecotourism offers a financially viable business option. Their work points to the weaknesses inherent in definitional criteria that are narrow in focus that have been imposed on the ecotourism term, something of which the author of the present chapter is equally guilty!

Although not focused on a specific environmental context, there has emerged some debate as to the relationship between the size of an ecotourism business operation and the term ecotourism: is large-scale ecotourism an oxymoron? Much of the early literature on defining the characteristics of ecotourism claimed it to be small-scale tourism; something which is now being challenged. Luck (2002) demonstrated how several large tour companies implemented policies and actions that minimized the impacts on destinations. Weaver (2001) argues that mass ecotourism can be harmonious with the environment and considers the implications of this claim for the tourism sector and for ecotourism spaces. In some ecotourism destinations, such as Kenya, the most visited national parks are within one day's drive of the coastal tourism belt north and south of Mombasa. Most tourists take in that whole-day experience as part of a traditional and predominantly 'mass' beach holiday. What this example may allude to is that perhaps much, if not most, of ecotourism may be viewed as mass tourism. Provided ecotourism adheres to established criteria, Weaver (2008, p. 22) argues that 'it is not impossible to visualize a sophisticated nature-based interpretation centre and surrounding high-tech trails that are capable of supporting and educating a large number of visitors in an environmentally sustainable and profitable way'.

It would not be contentious to state that the vast majority of ecotourism is focused on terrestrial (protected spaces) and marine settings (reefs, parks). What new regions/frontiers have ecotourism potential? Weaver (2011) makes a case for viewing the sky as a new horizon for nature-based tourism, referring to this opportunity as celestial ecotourism, including travel to observatories and observation of the aurora borealis and australis. He states that celestial ecotourism exists only as an ideal rather than as reality but that the ecotourism industry should embrace this opportunity with the start toward designation of dark sky reserves, which are currently not for tourism purposes but rather community and scientific benefit.

Part of the foregoing discussion on the broadening of the places and spaces in which ecotourism occurs raises ethical concern over consumptive practices and activities and has challenged whether or not the ecotourist can be ethical in the activities in which they participate or observe.

Ethical Ecotourists?

Ethics can be a very controversial issue, and there has emerged healthy academic discussion that raises the challenge of defining ecotourists by ethical as opposed to behavioural considerations. It is well established within the ecotourism literature that if an activity is to be considered as ecotourism, there has to be an element of education, often where clients are given guided interpretation, resulting in the industry putting in place codes of conduct and behaviour for specific destination regions. Some of the early discussion on this topic noted the need for ecotourism to be based on principled values and ethics (Malloy and Fennell, 1998; Honey, 1999). Fennell (2004) argued that if a region's ecotourism sector wishes to be perceived as responsible, it needs to be underpinned by morals where there exists a practical reverence and respect by tourists for nature. Buckley (2005, p. 129), while agreeing philosophically with this position, argued on practical terms that it was extremely difficult to incorporate an ethical test 'into operational criteria for any practical application of ecotourism', and thereby it is not realistic to define ecotourism in ethical terms. His case study of viewing narwhal of the northern tip of Baffin Island in the Canadian High Arctic raised the issue of how an ethical ecotourist should behave given that alongside the ecotourism experience the local Inuit communities are involved in hunting the narwhal not for subsistence but for cash. Buckley (2005) concludes that perhaps it is best that we define ecotourism without reference to ethical criteria, but that we expect ecotourists to act ethically. Buckley's research note in 2005 resulted in a direct response by Malloy (2009) who made the case that a 'genuine' ecotourist cannot be unethical if they truly value the tenets of ecotourism and thereby act upon these values. He concludes that ecotourism must have ethical principles to avoid it becoming what he calls 'yet another inauthentic moral cloak that the marketplace will exploit' (p. 73). This response by Malloy resulted in a reply by Buckley (2010, p. 169) where he defends his initial stance, stating 'there are practical difficulties in defining an industry subsector in terms of its intentions of its customers', especially when balancing concerns over the conservation of endangered species with the concerns over the rights and responsibilities of indigenous communities to engage in traditional harvesting activities. Such a discourse between scholars is rare in tourism academia, but more of this is warranted and vital within any community of scholars if it helps in advancing the field of inquiry (see Fennell and Malloy (2007) for a detailed discussion of ethics in tourism).

Indigenous Stewardship

The discussion over ethical behaviour raises the wider issue of responsibility for stewardship of the ecotourism resource base, in particular when indigenous communities are involved. Zeppel (2006) points out the strong association between indigenous peoples, their culture and ecotourism on the basis of argued links existing between their cultures and the natural environment. As noted earlier in the present chapter, Aboriginal ecotourism was the topic of the *Journal of Ecotourism*'s only special edition (the term Aboriginal favoured over indigenous). It was rich with case studies from both the northern and southern hemisphere, which outline the many challenges associated with Aboriginal ecotourism. Fennell (2008, p. 129) questioned what he saw as the legitimacy of ecological stewardship as an innate characteristic of traditional societies, arguing 'there may be serious philosophical and operational problems inherent in packaging aboriginal ecotourism as having a superior environmental ethic'. Literature on ecotourism and traditional societies is framed around the three concepts of control, traditional values and an environmental ethic. However, Fennell (2008) concluded that this sentiment lacks empirical evidence and that history is replete with evidence where indigenous people are associated with over-hunting, consumptive activities and lack a conservation ethic. He concludes that given the consumptive practices of many indigenous ecotourism operators, it would be preferable to position their activity as part of nature-based tourism, free from the ethical restrictions on behaviour that are imperative to ecotourism. As such, Fennell (2008) called for models showing the sustainable implementation of indigenous ecotourism. Higgins-Desbiolloes (2009) challenged some of the assertions of the 'myth of indigenous stewardship' raised by Fennell (2008) and offered a critical perspective on the capacity of indigenous ecotourism to foster more sustainable life-ways by transforming the ecological consciousness of participants and stakeholders in ecotourism. Writing about a case study of Camp Coorong in South Australia, she points out that some indigenous communities are using ecotourism to teach indigenous values in the hope of fostering transformations in consciousness.

A similar case is made by Colton and Harris (2007) who, in a study of First Nation people's ecotourism development for Lennox Island, applied the four Cs of aboriginal community development. These are: community economic development; community empowerment; community learning; and community wellness. The authors were able to demonstrate the four Cs in action, arguing that utilizing this type of framework helps communities begin to explore how 'tourism might intentionally or unintentionally impact them both positively and negatively' (Colton and Harris, 2007, p. 233). What both these cases illustrate, as do many within the ecotourism literature, is the necessity to accurately assess the value that ecotourism can bring to local regions and communities.

Valuing Ecotourism

The ecotourism literature abounds with discussion over the benefits and costs (Page and Dowling, 2002; Fennell, 2003; Weaver, 2008). Focus has often been on the effects of human observation on wildlife where ecological impacts are concerned. Where sociocultural impacts are concerned, the focus has been on community-based ecotourism operations and the need to empower communities, in particular indigenous communities. As for economic impacts, attention has been on identifying what monetary value ecotourists are willing to pay for the experience itself (Weaver and Lawton, 2007). The extensive body of case studies that focus on the impacts of ecotourism is not surprising as the topic of impacts has garnered more research in tourism circles with perhaps the exception of sustainable tourism development, of which mitigating impacts is a key component.

Not so much a controversy but rather a neglect has been the limited study undertaken on the concept of natural capital (nature, scenery) toward valuing ecotourism as sustainable tourism. There are a few exceptions. Muller (2000) approached ecotourism from the position that it was an economic concept for ecological sustainable tourism, outlining a number of instruments to achieve it (environmental impact assessment, eco-auditing). He cautioned that ecotourism cannot be considered as a panacea for conservation and the protection of biodiversity, nor can it alone be an economic saviour to lift local people out of a condition of poverty. Butcher (2006), focusing on rural settings in the LDCs, considers the role of natural capital in the advocacy of ecotourism as sustainable tourism using evidence from a number of non-governmental organizations (NGOs) that are developing ecotourism as integrated conservation and development. He concludes that there is a clear emphasis on the non-consumption of natural capital in the advocacy of tourism as sustainable development. Equally the conservation of natural capital can be justified as an environmental imperative and as worthy as an economic resource for local communities through the revenues ecotourism generates. Butcher (2006) concludes that despite important differences existing within the advocacy of ecotourism as sustainable development, he is able to point to a shared strong sustainability approach where limited capacity exists for natural capital to be substituted by human capital. Stronza (2007) challenges the economic promise that ecotourism offers for conservation of natural resources. In a study of community involvement in Peru, the social and economic changes were measured over the history of their involvement with the build and co-management of an ecotourism lodge. Stronza noted that despite low economic return, many in the community had a willingness to be involved in ecotourism work, and that ecotourism was not perceived as a narrow economic tool for conservation, but that it encouraged new values and social relations to form. Her findings illustrate the limitations of measurement of value on the basis of economic return as empowerment within communities to be involved can often be of greater value to them. However, the extent to which local participation is present within ecotourism projects is often limited or downplayed.

Absence of Local Participation in Ecotourism Discourse

Garrod (2003) noted the relative absence of any effective discussion of local participation within the established ecotourism literature; exceptions being Drake (1991) and Brandon (1993) who stress that there is a moral issue to involve those people who will be most affected by ecotourism operations, as well as an economic benefits issue that if local people are to buy in to the development of ecotourism they must achieve genuine and long-lasting benefits from it. Garrod, in developing a model to involve local participation in the planning and management of ecotourism, argues that elements of successful participatory planning of ecotourism include the need for leadership, empowering the local community, linking economic benefits to conservation, involving local stakeholders at every stage of the project cycle, and to have local participation in project monitoring and evaluation. He argued that on a more fundamental level local participation should be pivotal in the construction of the concept of ecotourism. Honey (2008) in espousing the 'stakeholder theory', recognized this, contending that if ecotourism is to be viewed as a tool for rural development, economic and political control must also be shifted to local communities, villages, cooperatives and entrepreneurs.

Central to this theme is the idea that people will protect assets from which they receive value. Stronza's (2007) research, noted above, observed, however, that the efficacy of the stakeholder theory as an incentive for conservation has largely been assumed rather than empirically evaluated and thus remains a largely untested hypothesis. It is worth noting that there were other factors that influence ecotourism's success as a conservation strategy beyond the connection between increased income and increased conservation. In light of the need to research non-economic considerations of successful conservation, there is an emergent discourse concerning the socio-cultural context within which interventions occur (Fletcher, 2009). He argues the merit of viewing ecotourism as a discursive process that embodies a culturally specific set of beliefs held by those that practice and promote ecotourism (predominantly white, professional-middle-class members of post-industrial Western societies) where local people's response to ecotourism promotion may depend on how this particular cultural perspective resonates with their own understandings of the world. As such, this ecotourism discourse challenges the stakeholders' theory and raises a new avenue for debate.

Ecotourism, Quality Control and Certification

Weaver (2008) noted the relative absence of research on quality control in ecotourism. Quality control measures can range on a scale from weak and informal (quotas, fees, codes of conduct) to strong and formal (certification-based ecolabels). Movement along this continuum from weak to strong reflects increased professionalism and creditability. The relative absence of research here is all the more surprising as there have been a number of well-established accreditation programmes developed, the most notable being the National Ecotourism Accreditation Program (NEAP) introduced as early as 1996 in Australia. Honey and Stewart (2002) noted that over 100 certification or eco-labelling programmes have been developed, where the debate has focused on their potential positive and negative impacts. Sharpley (2001) questions whether the market for certified tourism products is sufficiently large enough for certification programmes to become economically viable and that the proliferation of schemes has generated confusion among consumers, hence impacting on the effectiveness of the programmes. While research has addressed the key elements of certification-based ecolabels (Black and Ham, 2005), others (Medina, 2005) have raised concern that the broad parameters of ecolabels have been based on meeting sustainable tourism standards and not ecotourism standards, namely that it must benefit local communities.

Certification has been seen as a means of moving ecotourism beyond conceptualization to codification and for distinguishing genuine ecotourism from greenwashing (Honey, 2002). The challenge exists to create and implement ecotourism certification schemes with criteria for assessing benefits to local communities that take into account meanings such as 'local', 'participation' and 'benefit', while recognizing universal terms can often have multiple and contested meanings within and across local and international arenas. Medina (2005) argues that divergent perspectives on such issues such as the extent to which benefits accrue to local communities must be recognized and accommodated in the standardization of certification criteria for ecotourism. Jamal et al. (2006) in their observation of the institutionalization of ecotourism, argue that certification programmes have been dominated by what they call an economic–conservation paradigm over a social–cultural one, where social responsibility is absent and where focus is on self-control and self-regulation over formal regulation. It is part of a broader case for the need to de-centre and re-situate ecotourism as a more equitable paradigm oriented toward well-being that sees ecotourism re-visioned around the notions of cultural equity, participatory practice and researcher praxis (Jamal et al., 2006). They argue the need for cultural equity in order to ensure fair consideration of the changes being brought to the community's cultural fabric, participatory practice to put in place effective certification schemes, and researcher praxis to ask why ecotourism organizations feel they have the duty to self-regulate and decide what should be considered appropriate forms of ecotourism and conservation behaviour.

Conclusions

The intention of this chapter was predicated on the assumption that a healthy discourse has taken place within the academic community during the past quarter of a century, and that debate has not always been shaped around controversy. Perhaps too much time was given in early years toward finding a universally accepted definition of ecotourism, which was futile given that many areas of tourism remain mired by definitional paradoxes. Moreover, the emergence of the tenet of ethics late in this debate has thrown up the behavioural controversy: to what extent do the ethical actions and behaviours of ecotourists have to be considered within the concept of ecotourism? Analysis undertaken by the present author, in searching for keywords, has revealed that there exists a paucity of work embracing ecotourism as defined by a common set of tenets. Equally, how beneficial was the time devoted to defining the participant, namely the ecotourist, given that the vast discourse concerned itself with the developments of continuums ranging from soft to hard? Another issue that has emerged was whether or not nature-based tourism is the preferred term over ecotourism, the latter used by industry to give itself legitimacy. Debate is emerging around what constitutes an ecotourism environment, where the traditional narrow base of protected and private reserves has broadened to include consumptive and urban spaces, as well as the extent to which mass forms of ecotourism are becoming established practices in a number of destinations.

Controversy, however, remains within ecotourism discourses over defining the ecotourist by ethical considerations, over the quality of stewardship of resources by indigenous peoples, how we value ecotourism that takes in economics, ecological and sociocultural benefit, the relative absence of local participation in planning and managing of ecotourism, and the need to develop better governance within the industry to ensure that benefits accrue to local communities. In light of this, there exists much scope and need to build on the research that has taken place over the past quarter of a century in order to enrich the discourse and gain deeper insight into the relationship between ecotourism and indigenous landscape and culture as the danger exists for ecotourism places and spaces to be constructed solely as playgrounds for the rich!

References

Acott, T.G., La Trobe, H.L. and Howard, S.H. (1998) An evaluation of deep ecotourism and shallow ecotourism. *Journal of Sustainable Tourism* 6, 238–253.

Australia Department of Tourism (1994) *National Ecotourism Strategy*. Government Publishing Service, Canberra, Australia.

Black, R. and Ham, S. (2005) Improving the quality of tour guiding: towards a model for tour guide certification. *Journal of Ecotourism* 4, 178–195.

Blamey, R.K. (1997) Ecotourism: the search for an operational definition. *Journal of Sustainable Tourism* 5, 109–130.

Boo, E. (1990) *Ecotourism: The Potentials and Pitfalls*. World Wildlife Fund, Washington, DC.

Boo, E. (1991) Ecotourism: a tool for conservation and development. In: Kusler, J.A. (ed.) *Ecotourism and Resource Conservation: A Collection of Papers* 1. Omnipress, Madison, Wisconsin, pp. 54–60.

Boyd, S.W. and Butler, R.W. (1996a) Seeing the forest through the trees: using geographical information systems to identify potential ecotourism sites in Northern Ontario, Canada. In: Harrison, L.C. and Husbands, W. (eds) *Practicing Responsible Tourism: International Case Studies in Tourism Planning, Policy and Development*. John Wiley and Sons, Chichester, UK, pp. 380–403.

Boyd, S.W. and Butler, R.W. (1996b) Managing ecotourism: an opportunity spectrum approach. *Tourism Management* 17, 557–566.

Boyd, S.W. and Butler, R.W. (1999) Definitely not monkeys or parrots, probably deer and possibly moose: opportunities and realities of ecotourism in Northern Ontario. *Current Issues in Tourism* 2, 123–137.

Brandon, K. (1993) Basic steps toward encouraging local participation in nature tourism projects. In: Lindberg, K. and Hawkins, D.E. (eds) *Ecotourism: A Guide for Local Planners*. The Ecotourism Society, North Bennington, Vermont, pp. 134–151.

Buckley, R. (1994) A framework for ecotourism. *Annals of Tourism Research* 21, 661–669.

Buckley, R. (2005) In search of the narwhal: ethical dilemmas in ecotourism. *Journal of Ecotourism* 4, 129–134.

Buckley, R. (2010) Ethical ecotourists: the narwhal dilemma revisited. *Journal of Ecotourism* 9, 169–172.

Butcher, J. (2006) Natural capital and the advocacy of ecotourism as sustainable development. *Journal of Sustainable Tourism* 14, 529–544.

Butler, R.W. (1990) Alternative tourism: pious hope or Trojan horse? *Journal of Travel Research* 28, 40–45.

Ceballos-Lascurain, H. (1987) The future of ecotourism. *Mexico Journal* (January), 13–14.

Colton, J. and Harris, S. (2007) Indigenous ecotourism's role in community development: the case of the Lennox Island First Nation. In: Butler, R.W. and Hinch, T. (eds) *Tourism and Indigenous Peoples: Issues and Implications*. Butterworth-Heinemann, London, pp. 220–233.

Diamantis, D. (1999) The concept of ecotourism: evolution and trends. *Current Issues in Tourism* 2, 93–122.

Donohoe, H.M. and Needham, R. (2006) Ecotourism: the evolving contemporary definition. *Journal of Ecotourism* 5, 192–210.

Drake, S.P. (1991) Local participation in ecotourism projects. In: Whelan, T. (ed.) *Nature Tourism: Managing for the Environment*. Island Press, Washington DC, pp.132–163.

Epler Wood, M.E., Gatz, F. and Lindberg, K. (1991) The ecotourism society: an action agenda. In: Kusler, J.A. (ed.) *Ecotourism and Resource Conservation: A Collection of Papers (Volumes 1 and 2)*. The Ecotourism Society, North Bennington, Vermont. pp. 75–79.

Fennell, D.A. (2001) A content analysis of ecotourism definitions. *Current Issues in Tourism* 4, 403–421.

Fennell, D.A. (2003) *Ecotourism: An Introduction*. Routledge, London.

Fennell, D.A. (2004) Deep ecotourism: seeking theoretical and practical reverence. In: Singh, T.V. (ed.) *New Horizons in Tourism: Strange Experiences and Stranger Practices*. CABI Publishing, Wallingford, UK, pp. 109–121.

Fennell, D.A. (2008) Ecotourism and the myth of indigenous stewardship. *Journal of Sustainable Tourism* 16, 129–149.

Fennell, D.A. and Dowling, R. (2003) *Ecotourism Policy and Planning*. CABI Publishing, Wallingford, UK.

Fennell, D. A. and Malloy, D.C. (2007) *Tourism Ethics*. Channel View Publications, Clevedon, UK.

Figgis, P.J. (1993) Ecotourism: special interest or major direction? *Habitat Australia* (February), 8–11.

Fletcher, R. (2009) Ecotourism discourse: challenging the stakeholders theory. *Journal of Ecotourism* 8, 269–285.

Forestry Tasmania (1994) *Guided Nature-based Tourism in Tasmania's Forests: Trends, Constraints and Implications*. Forestry Tasmania, Hobart, Tasmania, Australia.

Garrod, B. (2003) Local participation in the planning and management of ecotourism: a revised model approach. *Journal of Ecotourism* 2, 33–53.

Goodwin, H. (1996) In pursuit of ecotourism. *Biodiversity and Conservation* 5, 277–291.

Higgins-Desbiolles, F. (2009) Indigenous ecotourism's role in transforming ecological consciousness. *Journal of Ecotourism* 8, 144–160.

Higham, J. and Luck, M. (2002) Urban ecotourism: A contradiction in terms? *Journal of Ecotourism* 1, 36–51.

Hofer, D. (2002) *The Lion's Share of the Hunt. Trophy Hunting and Conservation: A Review of the Eurasian Tourist Hunting Market and Trophy Trade under CITES*. TRAFFIC Europe Regional Report, Brussels.

Honey, M. (1999) *Ecotourism and Sustainable Development. Who Owns Paradise?* Island Press, Washington, DC.

Honey, M. (2002) *Ecotourism and Certification: Setting Standards in Practice*. Island Press, Washington, DC.

Honey, M. and Stewart, E. (2002) The evolution of green standards for tourism. In: Honey, M. (ed.) *Ecotourism and Certification*. Island Press, Washington, DC, pp. 33–71.

Jafari, J. (2001) The scientification of tourism. In: Smith, V.L. and Brent, M. (eds) *Hosts and Guests Revisited: Tourism Issues of the 21st Century*. Cognizant Communications, New York, pp. 28–41.

Jamal, T., Borges, M. and Stronza, A. (2006) The institutionalisation of ecotourism: certification, cultural equity and praxis. *Journal of Ecotourism* 5, 145–175.

Lindberg, K. and McKercher, B. (1997) Ecotourism: a critical overview. *Pacific Tourism Review* 1, 65–79.

Luck, M. (2002) Large-scale ecotourism – a contradiction in itself? *Current Issues in Tourism* 5, 361–370.

Malloy, D.C. (2009) Can one be an unethical ecotourist? A response to R. Buckley's 'In Search of the Narwhal'. *Journal of Ecotourism* 8, 70–73.

Malloy, D.C. and Fennell, D.A. (1998) Ecotourism and ethics: moral development and organizational structures. *Journal of Travel Research* 26, 47–56.

Medina, L.K. (2005) Ecotourism and certification: confronting the principles and pragmatics of socially responsible tourism. *Journal of Sustainable Tourism* 13, 281–295.

Muller, F.G. (2000) Ecotourism: an economic concept for ecological sustainable tourism. *International Journal of Environmental Studies* 57, 241–251.

Novelli, M. and Humavindu, M. (2005) Wildlife tourism: wildlife use vs local gain – trophy hunting in Namibia. In: Novelli, M. (ed.) *Niche Tourism: Current Issues, Trends and Cases*. Elsevier, Oxford, UK, pp. 171–182.

Novelli, M., Barnes, J.I. and Humavindu, M. (2006) The other side of the ecotourism coin: consumptive tourism in Southern Africa. *Journal of Ecotourism* 5, 62–79.

Orams, M.B. (1995) Towards a more desirable form of ecotourism. *Tourism Management* 16, 3–8.

Page, S.J. and Dowling, R.W. (2002) *Ecotourism*. Prentice Hall, Harlow, UK.

Sharpley, R. (2001) The consumer behaviour context of ecolabelling. In: Font, X. and Buckley, R.C. (eds) *Tourism Ecolabelling*. CABI Publishing, Wallingford, UK, pp. 41–55.

Stewart, W.P. and Sekartjakrarini, S. (1994) Disentangling ecotourism. *Annals of Tourism Research* 21, 840–841.

Stronza, A. (2007) The economic promise of ecotourism for conservation. *Journal of Ecotourism* 6, 210–230.

Wall, G. (1994) Ecotourism: old wine in new bottles. *Trends* 31, 4–9.

Weaver, D.B. (1998) *Ecotourism in the Less Developed World*. CABI Publishing, Wallingford, UK.

Weaver, D.B. (2001) Ecotourism as mass tourism: contradiction or reality? *Cornell Hotel and Restaurant Administration Quarterly* 42, 104–112.

Weaver, D.B. (2005) Mass and urban ecotourism: new manifestations of an old concept. *Tourism Recreation Research* 30, 19–26.

Weaver, D.B. (2008) *Ecotourism*. Wiley, Milton, Queensland, Australia.

Weaver, D.B. (2011) Celestial ecotourism: new horizons in nature-based tourism. *Journal of Ecotourism* 10, 38–45.

Weaver, D.B. and Lawton, L.J. (2002) Overnight ecotourist market segmentation in the Gold Coast Hinterland of Australia. *Journal of Travel Research* 40, 270–280.

Weaver, D.B. and Lawton, L.J. (2007) Twenty years on: the state of contemporary ecotourism research. *Tourism Management* 28, 1168–1179.

Wight, P. (1993) Ecotourism: ethics or eco-sell? *Journal of Travel Research* 31, 3–9.

Wilson, M.A. and Laarman, J.G. (1988) Nature tourism and enterprise development in Ecuador. *World Leisure and Recreation* 29/30, 22–27.

Zeppel, H. (2006) *Indigenous Ecotourism: Sustainable Development and Management*. CABI Publishing, Wallingford, UK.

Ziffer, K.A. (1989) *Ecotourism: The Uneasy Alliance*. Conservation International and Ernst and Young, Washington, DC.

8 Ethnic Panopticon:
A Controversy in Aboriginal Tourism

Philip Feifan Xie[1]

[1]*School of Human Movement, Sport and Leisure Studies, Bowling Green State University, Bowling Green, Ohio, USA*

Introduction

Ethnicity is arguably the most fundamental basis of perceived distinction between human groups, which can be generally defined as 'the existence of culturally distinctive groups within a society, each asserting a unique identity on the basis of a shared tradition and distinguishing social markers such as a common language, religion, or economic specialization' (Winthrop, 1991, p. 94). A variety of terms, such as 'aboriginal', 'indigenous', 'tribal' and 'native', are extensively used in the tourism literature to describe the original inhabitants of a country. Although usage of the terms is elastic and often vague, scholars normally choose a specific term to describe a particular group, which reflects its ethnic identity and the potential responses of the readers with respect to the research studies (Hinch and Butler, 2007).

The advent of aboriginal tourism started as the pursuit of the exotic 'other', the differentness, and the authentic experience. It is commonly regarded as part of cultural tourism, which is a form of recreation combining cultural and natural resources that is marketed to the public in terms of 'quaint' customs of indigenous and often exotic peoples. Cole (2006) distinguished aboriginal and cultural tourism as the former is used

for the 'primitive other' and the latter for the high arts in the developed nations. Aboriginal tourism also refers to tourism activities in which ethnic people are directly or indirectly involved either through control and/or by having their culture served as the centre of the attraction. The modern explosion of interests in aboriginal tourism is multifaceted in cause, ranging from supply factors (such as heritage planning, economic need and cultural revival), to demand factors (such as the desire for creative, cultural pride, authentic experiences and entertainment by and for visitors). It is assumed that, as the people in the majority, who are usually the tourists, observe and experience aboriginal cultures, their understanding and appreciation of aboriginal positions on major issues may improve (Xie and Lane, 2006). Increased understanding can result in changed attitudes and behaviours that lead, in turn, to a more just and equitable relationship between aborigines and non-aborigines (Cohen, 2002).

The popularity of aboriginal tourism has also created a series of tensions and conflicts when ethnic culture is commoditized as tourism source. The anthropologist Van den Berghe (1994, p.8) described aboriginal tourism as activities in which 'the tourist actively searches for ethnic exoticism'. Aboriginal tourism has traditionally been viewed as 'utopia of difference', a by-product of imperialism or the new product of neo-colonialism (Hall and Tucker, 2004). Historically, meetings with aboriginal group members became the stuff of romanticized visions and the basis of conscious or unconscious oppression by colonizers or members of the majority society. The process of aboriginal tourism could create acculturation and value changes undermining the core of aboriginal traditions (Morgan, 1994). Examples such as the cultural assimilation of aboriginal people in Australia until the early 1970s, and the authentic 'noble savage' of African countries under the British rule where 'spectatorial lust' (Erlmann, 1999, p. 109) motivated the tours of African landscapes are typical in the early stage of aboriginal tourism. Numerous studies (Zeppel, 1998; Mason, 2004; Butler and Hinch, 2007) have implied that aboriginal tourism may not serve as a catalyst for the changing relationships between the minority and majority; rather, it tends to undermine the indigenous places and identities intentionally and unintentionally (Bhabha, 2004; Said, 2003). Hall and Tucker (2004) write that:

> The role that [aboriginal] tourism can play in transforming collective and individual values is inherent in ideas of commoditization, which implies that what were once personal 'cultural displays' of living traditions or a 'cultural text' of lived authenticity become 'cultural products' that meet the needs of commercial tourism, as well as the construction of heritage. Such a situation may lead to the invention of tradition and heritage for external consumption that meet visitor conceptions of the other.
> Hall and Tucker (2004, p.12)

This chapter proposes a term 'ethnic panopticon' by using Foucault's (1980) eye-of-power to describe a controversy when aboriginal resources are used for tourism. Through the concept of ethnic panopticon, the participant–observer becomes the object to view and be viewed. Aboriginal peoples' interactions with tourists are controlled by the business practice that tourism produces, rather than reduces, difference. The controversy is that aboriginal tourism involves technologies of gazes in order to create, reify and reinvent a fantasy world of cultural difference for tourists' consumption. These differences can be aestheticised and intentionally exaggerated to create a sense of quaintness. The result is a form of 'asymmetry', described by Ghai (2000, p. 12), as the power inequity played by different stakeholders. 'Touristic ethnicity' (Wood, 1998, p. 771) is established through the invisible expectations from these stakeholders; often ethnic communities are excluded during the process of aboriginal tourism.

The Concept of Ethnic Panopticon

Michel Foucault's exploration of the relationship between knowledge and power in his book 'Discipline and Punish: The Birth of the Prison' marks a shift in the traditional research in the social sciences. The metaphoric idea of 'technology' and internalized disciplinary practice, as demonstrated by Foucault (1980), posits a control, which combines both detachment and mastery of forces. A number of 'technologies' manage and discipline prisoners who are under the continual surveillance of a gaze that has the power to punish them. The technologies of powers encompass the relationships between individuals, the organizations, and even the States. Foucault draws upon the work of 18th-century philosopher Jeremy Bentham's prison concept of panopticon, to conceptualize the interactions among power, technology and observation. Foucault (1980, p. 147) described Bentham's panopticon as: 'a perimeter building in the form of a ring. At the centre of this a tower, pierced by large windows opening on to the inner face of the ring. The outer building is divided into cells each of which traverses the whole thickness of the building. These cells have two windows, one opening onto the inside, facing the windows of the central tower, the other, outer one allowing daylight to pass through the whole cell.

All that is then needed is to put an overseer in the tower and place in each of the cells a lunatic, a patient, a convict, a worker or a schoolboy. The back lighting enables one to pick out from the central tower the little captive silhouettes in the ring of cells. In short the principle of the dungeon is reversed; daylight and the overseer's gaze captures the inmate more effectively than darkness, which afforded after all a sort of protection.'

As one can imagine, panopticon is a remarkable prison model in which the power of the gaze results in self-control and self-regulation by the prisoner. The panopticon is *dispositif* (apparatus), a 'machine of the visible' based upon a 'brutal dissymmetry of visibility' (Friedberg, 1994, p. 17) which permeates the guard–prisoner relationship. The structure of the panopticon is designed to permit the guards to see their prisoners without their being seen. Even though there might be no guards working in the central tower, Foucault pointed out the effect of lighting and the carefully placed blinds prevent prisoners from knowing that at the given moment they feel they might be under observation. This combination of observation and power dominance gives the gazer (guards) a sense of omnipresent voyeurism and the gazee (prisoners) with a feeling of inescapable surveillance.

Foucault's conception of *le regard* has induced a special type of gaze, 'panoptic gaze', wherein the subject is placed in a condition of inescapable visibility. The subject thus can only imagine that everything he does is viewed by the guard. The panopticon's purpose is to create a highly efficient mechanism to control prisoners, and has reflective impact on the prisoners' psychological behaviour. Strain (2003, p. 27) characterized the technology of panoptic gaze as 'the constant push and pull of distanced immersion, by the desire to be fully immersed in an environment yet literally or figuratively distanced from the scene in order to occupy a comfortable viewing position'. Foucault's discernment is that the creation of a gazer-'gazee' relationship characterized by an imbalance of power and distance between the two results in an immensely powerful control system. Surveillance ought to occur involuntarily whenever the distance separates the functioning of the subjugated (i.e. those supposedly receiving the power) and the dominating (i.e. those supposedly wielding the power). The distinctiveness of the roles reinforces the sense of identity because each must fit in the designated construct. The process prompts the prisoners in the cells to self-regulate consistent with the rules or the standards of conduct set by the prison. Foucault called this conformity with the rules *practique de soi*, a self-directed process designed to meet societal expectations. An advantage of the panoptic model is that it tends to make corporal punishment unnecessary because confinement can be successfully maintained by just the structure of the prison and the prisoners' expectation that they may always be under scrutiny.

The significance of the gazer–gazee construct has had a profound impact on research in many fields. Almost all institutional settings can, as Hollinshead (1999) has suggested, be conceptualized from a panopticon perspective; that is the eye-of-power/eye-of-authority/the new-power-of-universal-surveillance. For example, the surveillance cameras hidden in the corners of the streets echo the meaning of panopticon to that people are being watched. The concept has also been adapted to the centre–periphery theory to explain the socio-cultural identity in the context of post-colonialism. When explaining Englishness, Hall (1997, p.174) pointed out that the colonized other was constituted within the regimes of representation of a 'metropolitan centre' while colonized persons were placed in their otherness, in their marginality, by the nature of the 'English eye'. In other words, English identity is strongly centred 'knowing where it is, what it is, it places everything else'.

The gazer–gazee perspective entered discourse of tourism studies with the publication of John Urry's book 'The Tourist Gaze' in 1990. Urry masterfully applied Foucault's *le regard* to the context of modern tourism by problematizing the interrelated complex roles: tourists and tourees. The eye-of-power construct has become institutionalized within the tourism industry by viewing the tourist role as the dominant one, driven by the expectation of receiving pleasurable (through distance) experience with less advanced tourees. From a distance, tourists cast a privileged 'eye' on tourees as they see, understand and appropriate desired things, although there is a clear segregation between 'front stage' and 'back stage'. Tourees are encouraged to act or behave exactly according to what tourists expect so that smiling faces are shown and photos can be snapped.

Most importantly, the gaze of tourists ensures the sustainability of power structures since various stakeholders stay involved in tourism development. Urry suggested that tourees as aboriginal minorities are aware of being observed by tourists and they are requested to 'perform' in ways that emphasize their difference from tourists. The tourist–touree relationship centres on 'romantic gazes' that are systematically constructed on the participants' beliefs that there are racial, linguistic, cultural and historical differences between the two groups. The ocularcentrism in tourism, as proposed by Urry (2002), authenticates tourist gazes in order to allow tourists to gratify their needs.

Foucauldian *le regard* can serve to highlight two critical aspects of aboriginal tourism, which I call 'ethnic panopticon': (a) the Other as a distant object within a structured power relationship; and (b) the structuring of the Other as a consumable product spatially and temporally. The first of these aspects involves defining some behaviour as normal and some as deviant by the gazers. There is a tendency for gazee–gazer (or host–tourist) relationships to be unequal and unbalanced in character. The panopticon as a model for incarceration is based upon perspectives of power and the 'subject of power' (Foucault, 1980) to control the relationship between gazers and gazees. Tourists (the Self) and the aboriginal minorities (the Other) are allowed to interact within a matrix of a rational-disciplinary relation characterized by time–space compression.

The life of ethnic minorities is viewed as remote, exotic, sensual, primitive and servile, and dependent upon tourists for survival and modernization.

Nagel (2003, p. 14) suggested that ethnicity and sexuality are interrelated in the process of commercialization. Erotic locations and exotic destinations such as ethnic folk villages are 'surveilled and supervised, patrolled and policed, regulated and restricted, but that are constantly penetrated by individuals forging sexual links with ethnic Others across ethnic borders'. Aboriginal tourism uses the technologies of gaze to enable tourists to take possession of ethnic minorities from a distance. It can be noted that the distance between tourists and ethnic minorities can be perceived, imagined, reconstructed and phantasmagoric. Aboriginal tourism provides an excellent opportunity to compress time–space in order to validate a healthy definition of Self through visiting ethnic villages and attractions. The socio-cultural gap between tourists and the host cultures is clearly manipulated since distinct differences are required to define social relationships, history and identities.

According to Bauman (2000), the voyeuristic gaze on the Other is deemed to be optimal since tourist–host interactions tend to be fleeting and fluid. Such transience of contact favours and promotes distance and casts the Other as an aesthetic object to be viewed from different angles. To some extent, the tourists and the Other come together, though at a distance in an artificial space. In this sense, tourists are like the prison guards in the central tower of the panopticon whilst aborigines are the prisoners confined in the cells, the objects of an imagined scrutiny, where the internalized expectation of surveillance changes the imposition of external power, in this case, tourism. The eye-of-power can exist due to the perceived distance where both tourists and tourees consciously and effectively follow the *practique de soi*. Bruno (1993, p. 201) described tourism as 'lust of the eyes'. Curiosity about the Other motivates tourists to visit the division between the ordinary (mainstream culture) and the extraordinary (minority culture). However, the vigour of that curiosity reinforces the notion that 'such gazes cannot be left to chance. [Tourists] have to learn how, when and where to "gaze"' (Urry, 2002, p. 10). Borrowing Foucault's concept of heterotopias (places outside of all places), aboriginal tourism fosters the location of tourists' contact with ethnic minorities in settings different from the tourists' everyday experience. Globalization and commodification of ethnic culture, as tourism impinges on the communities, induces tourists to superimpose their imagination upon the Other, and to create nostalgic representations of the past for contemporary consumption.

The simulation of Other as a consumable product closely resembles the lighting effect in the panopticon: the prisoners are prevented from seeing the guards in the central tower but believe they are regularly watched perennially. Such one-way vision works perfectly well in the context of power and dominance. Tourism turns out to be an imagined landscape including sensescape, soundscape, smellscape, tastescape and dreamscape manufactured for consumption (Spang, 2000; Strain, 2003). The Other may be unaware of social change or tourist tastes (as obstructed by the lights and blinds in the panopticon); however, it goes without saying that an exotic 'Other' is most likely to attract tourism business. Romanticized primal or undeveloped ethnic people are most effective in stimulating the fantasy of tourists. In modern society, the mobility of tourism allows tourists to travel to distant ethnic destinations, many of which are not ready to accommodate them. Through the gaze, aboriginal tourism, in this case, becomes marked and ritualized as an open text, hence evoking 'the idea of dynamic construction, of an open and complex organization' (Casetti, 1998, p. 8). Ethnicity henceforth becomes the decoded message whilst tourists become the spectator and the decoder. As a decoded message, the meaning of ethnicity is 'read' by many tourists from different cultures, languages, genders, races, social classes, to name just a few. Hunter (2001, p. 43) suggested that the tourists in a panopticon setting are 'trapped in an invisible glass cage, able only to gaze out at the "other's" body, an indecipherable text, a confusing, foreign combination of signifiers'. The tourist–host relationship is context-bound and embedded in barriers of differences. Aboriginal performance is socially and spatially regulated to varying extents. The 'encountering space' between tourists and tourees is staged and contrived for the convenience of consumption. Aboriginal culture should be frozen since museumified heritage will arouse the interests of the tourists. Tourism as an industry manipulates social power and is a key factor for the construction of culture and heritage.

The research for this chapter investigated an aboriginal folk village on Hainan Island, China, where tourism has become the major source of income. A brief history of the Island is introduced. The Island's largest aboriginal community, Li, was used as a case study to understand the concept of ethnic panopticon. Their aboriginal folk villages are purpose-built to cater to tourists interested in Li culture and heritage. The Baoting Areca Manor, established in 1995 and located along the central highway of Hainan, was chosen as a longitudinal study from 1999 to 2009. It is the pioneer village to draw the attention of tourists and to serve as a model for aboriginal tourism development on Hainan.

Hainan Island and Aboriginal Li

Hainan is arguably the most unique island in China. It is the only tropical province in China and is located by the South China Sea. It was described by ancient Chinese as 'Tianya Haijiao' (the end of heaven and sea) because it is far from the heart of the Mainland. Geographically, Hainan has a land area of 34,087 km^2 and a coastline of 1584.8 km, and is located in the central part of the Pacific Economic Circle, lying at the same latitude as Hawaii. The western coast of the island borders the Gulf of Tong Kin, with Vietnam visible in the distance. The eastern portion of the island is near Hong Kong, Taiwan is to the north, and the Philippines is located to the south-east. From the perspective of location, Hainan is strategically located in the South China Sea.

The majority of Hainan's inhabitants are Han Chinese who migrated from the mainland as early as the Han dynasty (200 BC to 220 AD) when Hainan was first incorporated into China's territory. The aboriginal inhabitants are the Li, Miao, Zhuang and Hui tribes, of which Li is the largest ethnic group. By 2007, the total population was about 8.19 million and the ethnic Li population about 1.26 million, which was about 15% of the total population (Statistics Bureau of Hainan, 2008). The ethnic distribution is disproportionate, with most of the Han residents concentrated along the coastal plains, while in the central–south mountainous areas, aboriginal Li and other minorities clustered in scattered, low density, Li and Miao Autonomous Regions.

Outsiders tend to view the ethnic Li minority as exotic for its unique culture and heritage. They are widely viewed as 'mystical beings' by people in Mainland China. In particular, the Han majority population is fascinated by the traditional Li marriage ceremony and the tattooing customs. The former remains a relic of a maternal clan society, in which women were in charge of the selection of the men and the rearing of children. The Li wedding ceremony is different from the Han Chinese practice in which the woman leaves her family to move to her husband's natal village or to live with her husband's family. When a Li girl reaches puberty around 12 to 13 years old, a single room called a Liao is built beside the family house. The girl can start to see any man she likes. Shortly thereafter the wedding (marriages are arranged by the parents when their children are still young), the bride goes back to live with her own parents. She can have relationships with other men until she becomes pregnant. This marriage custom, prohibited by the Communist government as a corrupt practice, had virtually disappeared; however, the onset of tourism has rejuvenated 'staged' ethnic wedding ceremonies in recent years. Tourists from China, mostly Han men, view non-Han minority women as feminized exotic Others so that

the re-enactment of the wedding ceremony provides an instant, voyeuristic opportunity to view 'sexually promiscuous, erotically titillating, and available' ethnic women (Schein, 2000, p. 70–71). The mock wedding ceremony with the participation of the tourists is typically used for entertainment in which expressions of sexuality are highlighted.

In contrast, tattooing is a vanishing tradition in the Li communities. Historically, Li tattoos signified that a woman was eligible to be married and the ritual was accompanied by an elaborate puberty ceremony in the village centre. Li women tattooed on such bodily surfaces as the face, neck and legs believed their tattoos not only made them beautiful, but allow them to be recognized by their ancestors after death. It was a practice handed down from the ancestors to connect with the myths and heritage of the Li. Krutak (2007) documented the history of Li culture and found that all Li groups tattooed and the practice was more common amongst women, although men tattooed three blue rings around their wrists for medicinal purposes. Furthermore, tattoo designs and motifs differed between each tribe, and sometimes they differed within families. Tattooing served as an important cultural marker amongst Li communities providing an identity differentiating each village. Currently, however, it is rarely practised given Hainan's close integration into the Chinese state.

Although the Li minority populations are not heavily involved in tourism, their existence is widely publicized in the tourism brochures. The tourism industry capitalizes on aboriginal culture in a way that brings members of the Li minority into mainstream development. Ethnicity on Hainan has become a popular and marketable resource. The Li minority generally participates in the informal tourism sector by selling craft souvenirs and local fruit. However, a small proportion of the population works in the hotel and hospitality industry. Since there is a growing interest from Mainland China in the aboriginal island cultures, the most visible manifestation for ethnic employment is in the tourist folk villages where Li work as dance performers and staff (Xie, 2003). A number of folk villages have been established on Hainan where song and dance shows, the enactment of ceremonies and the availability of ethnic foods and souvenirs provide opportunities for visitors to become acquainted with ethnic cultures.

It can be noted that the situation of the Hainan folk villages is very different from those in North American and Australian contexts. The primary difference is that the issue of aboriginal land claims by ethnic minorities does not exist on Hainan. All lands belong to the national government and the Li minority has no control of the territory where the village is located. The central government has set up a number of 'Autonomous Regions' populated primarily by an ethnic minority. However, the state's definitions of aboriginal space were seldom in keeping with the perceptions of the aboriginal groups themselves. Ironically, the creation of an Autonomous Region was not designed to foster independence for ethnic people, but rather to initiate the process of socialist transformation and to establish spatial relations between the centralized cultural, political and economic power of the Han Chinese and the disenfranchised ethnic minorities on the periphery. The Li believe that they are joined inseparably with nature and see the Earth as their 'root' rather than viewing it as a resource to be used only for their short-term advantage. However, since the government controls all land, the population has to relocate their homes if development occurs in their communities. Many of the attempts by the local government to integrate ethnic minorities into prevailing wage economies have led to the alienation of these groups from the land with resulting negative impacts (Xie, 2010).

The Changing Phases of the Areca Manor

The Manor was established in October 1995, when tourism was just starting on the island. The site was located in the lush green forest of the central route of Hainan. Historically,

most Li communities have been located in this region. From 1995 to 2004, the objective of the Manor was to 'faithfully portray the life, customs, and conditions of the Li minority'. The 'inhabitants' in the folk villages were all of the Li ethnicity. They demonstrated such traditional skills as the manufacture of embroidery, the singing of traditional Li songs in their own languages, playing a range of traditional musical instruments, folk dancing and the presentation of Li folklore. The village benefitted from geographic proximity to Li communities which supplied both labour and services. The concept of the Manor was, by and large, a living community designed to help tourists understand everyday life of Li. It also had a small and primitive showroom to introduce Li culture and history in the area. The façade of the Manor was designed based upon traditional Li boat-shape housing. The Li who had tattoos were all old women who have been used as a promotion in the villages. The tattooed faces have even been published in the leaflets and tourism brochures to emphasize the uniqueness of Li culture. Although the Manor was never a top tourist attraction on the central route, it nonetheless attracted a significant number of tourists who were truly interested in experiencing Li culture. The Manor expanded faster than almost any other village during the past decade.

In 2005, Areca Manor decided to change its business model from portraying pure aboriginal Li culture to one that would present a combined focus on wilderness and ethnicity. Part of the reason for these changes was the result of the wide support of the local government which wanted to develop 'ecotourism' and 'wilderness' given that the area is located in the forests. The most important issue was the demands from tourists and tour guides that they need to have a 'fun' experience in the village.

A new ethnic tribe called the 'Chiyou tribe' was deliberately created. This artificial tribe was supposed to have come from Northern China. Similar to Kombai tribe in Papua New Guinea, the Chiyou were described as primitive tree people of the Stone Age. Tools were made from stone, and men and women dressed in grass skirts and hunted to catch wild animals. In a typical event offered to tourists, soon after the tour group arrives, a troupe of 'Chiyou' dressed and acted in a stereotyped 'tree dweller' fashion, and came out from the jungle. Then they used spears to kill a pig that had been tied up at the performance hall. Thus, the Manor evolved from being a living museum focused on the Li people, to a theme park centred on the life of a cultural group found only in Chinese folklore. The central purpose of the Manor became offering spectacular and attractive entertainment. A poster at the Manor's entrance offered the following description of the park:

> This is a Forest Kingdom where Chiyou tribe lives. These people are primitive and still live in Stone Age. They live in trees and wear deep blue clothing to cover most of their bodies. You can learn bow-drill fire-making with Chiyou individuals, and you can experience how they eat raw and bloody meat. Don't forget they are the lost people and you shouldn't miss this opportunity to visit them.

The shift of the aboriginal theme has profound impacts: previous Li had been presented authentically, but the shift in direction for the Manor was intended to create a new tourism product in order to attract more tourists as they were on the way to the beach resort. The change of the Manor's theme has also altered the remaining programmes performed by Li. The Li dance hall and the showroom were moved to the edge of the Manor. The size of the dance hall was greatly reduced and the performance was shortened from 30 minutes to 10 minutes. The Li performances have been gradually marginalized. In 2008, the Manor decided to lay off all full-time Li performers, and hire part-time performers from neighbouring areas. These part- timers are paid per show and do not have any fringe benefits provided by the Manor. As suggested by the village managers, the layoff decision reinforced the declining tourist interests in Li performance. On the other hand, the decreased focus on Li culture confirms that

the new tourist attraction, the Chiyou tribe show, is working extremely well.

The Manor has become a world of 'kitsch'. Two separate shows were observed in the dance hall. The first performance, supposedly centred on Li culture, was titled 'the matchmaker'. A female master of ceremonies (MC) introduced twin girls dressed in beautiful Li costume. She told the audience that these twin Li girls had just reached puberty, that they were eager to find 'prince charming' and to have romantic trysts with the audience. The audience roared and several male tourists stood up and made catcalls to the twin girls. Two tourists were finally chosen, one was old, another was young, and both started to learn how to hold the girls' hands like a 'lover' in a traditional Li way. Some off-colour jokes were cracked by the MC and the twin girls obviously blushed. However, enthusiasm in the dance hall was palpable, as the show continued to demonstrate how Li women 'empower' a man in the bedroom. Another presentation was of a supposed fire ritual of the Chiyou tribe. The actors dressed and behaved like New Zealand Maori fire poi spinning and dancing with fire. At the end of the performance, one of the actors was invited to put out fire with his bare feet. The audience cheered as the fire became only smoke and ashes, but nobody knew if the bare feet of the actor were unharmed or actually burned.

During the interview, the village managers constantly reminded me that tourists on Hainan do not actually want the truth but want to be entertained. In other words, why should the Manor spoil this enjoyment for them? Flying in the face of these managers' comments is the unavoidable realization that the difference between authenticity and commodification means little in the running of the village. One of the managers pointed out to me that using Li as a tourism product has increasingly become a passé and anachronistic remnant of pre-modern authenticity. Tourists, in fact, are looking for something new and stimulating. The Manor faces fierce competition from numerous theme parks recently built in the Sanya area (the beach resort located in the southern tip of the Island). Most of those parks have a section devoted to such aboriginal Li performance as the bamboo-beating dance; therefore, it has become extremely difficult to attract tourists who have already watched the performance in Sanya. There was a strong need to find an interesting product to draw tourists for day excursions. The combination of a wilderness setting and performance by a caveman-like tribe became an instant hit for tourists who wanted to escape beach life in Sanya. An authentic village like the Areca Manor can be commoditized to the point where the balance between historical and socio-cultural veracity has been lost.

Conclusions

The case study of the folk village on Hainan Island presents a contentious issue in aboriginal tourism that ethnicity has been viewed as a marketable resource to sell for tourists. Instead of presenting authentic Li culture, the aboriginal identity has increasingly become hybrid and diluted for commercial purpose. Tourists' 'fun gaze' (Ooi, 2002, p. 87) accepts kitsch, commercialism and cultural inauthenticity. Attractions centred on the 'fun gaze' are understood as constructed spectacles, in which tourists are in a playful search for enjoyment. In this approach, the main concern is the illusion of authenticity rather than a definitive reality (Wang, 1999; Yang and Wall, 2009).

Ethnic panopticon reflects that aboriginal communities tend to be powerless in the process of tourism planning, that is, the gazers (tourists, village businesses and governments) control the views of gazees (aboriginal communities). The majority of problems associated with the tourist industry stem from 'hegemony' and 'asymmetry'

of the power domination. The salient feature of aboriginal tourism is how aborigines' involvement rests on using their 'exoticness' as part of the commodities they sell. Unfortunately, due to the unequal positioning, the manipulation of aboriginal performance programmes and other cultural events to serve economic interests resulted in the loss of authenticity and educational value: spectacle and entertainment seem to have been valued more highly in the aboriginal folk village. Since the businesses depended on the number of tourist arrivals, mass tourism was used to exploit ethnicity for economic gain of the enterprises. Tourists often expected that the Li in the villages would be quaintly traditional and in a state of 'museumification', that is, viewed through the lens of 'panopticon'.

On a theoretical level, the panopticon system is played out by gazee's roles of perpetuating and buying into constructed misconceptions of aboriginal culture. Aboriginal identities are defined by the views of the gazers and their expectations. Aboriginal tourism can be conceptualized as an 'ethnic panopticon' set in a changing social and economic milieu. Each stakeholder has an opportunity to gaze and be gazed by others and strives to find an optimal viewpoint, which I called 'positioning'. Positions and counter-positions are named and arranged as individuals negotiate their identities while in interaction with others. Hall (1997) concluded that self-definitions are complicated by cultural registers and social coordinates, which over time become concretized and situated between the centre and the periphery. The realm of the gaze applies temporal and spatial distance between subject and object in an effort to present something culturally 'authentic' in order to make the products valuable and unique.

References

Bauman, Z. (2000) *Liquid Modernity*. Polity, Cambridge, UK.

Bhabha, H. (2004) *The Location of Culture*. Routledge, London.

Bruno, G. (1993) *Streetwalking on a Ruined Map: Cultural Theory and the City Films of Elvira Notari*. Princeton University Press, Princeton, New Jersey.

Butler, R. and Hinch, T. (2007) *Tourism and Indigenous People*. Elsevier, Oxford, UK.

Casetti, F. (1998) *Inside the Gaze: The Fiction Film and its Spectator*. Indiana University Press, Bloomington, Indiana.

Cohen, E. (2002) Authenticity, equity and sustainability in tourism. *Journal of Sustainable Tourism* 10, 267–276.

Cole, S. (2006) Cultural tourism, community participation and empowerment. In: Smith, M. and Robinson, M. (eds) *Cultural Tourism in a Changing World: Politics, Participation and (Re)presentation*. Channel View Publications, Clevedon, UK, pp. 89–103.

Erlmann, V. (1999) *Music, Modernity, and the Global Imagination: South Africa and the West*. Oxford University Press, Oxford, UK.

Foucault, M. (1980) *Power/Knowledge: Selected Interviews and Other Writings, 1972–1977*. Pantheon Books, New York.

Friedberg, A. (1994) *Window Shopping: Cinema and the Postmodern*. University of California Press, Berkeley, California.

Ghai, Y. (2000) Ethnicity and autonomy: a framework for analysis. In: Ghai, Y. (ed.) *Autonomy and Ethnicity: Negotiating Competing Claims in Multi-ethnic States*. Cambridge University Press, Cambridge, UK, pp. 1–24.

Hall, C.M. and Tucker, H. (2004) *Tourism and Postcolonialism: Contested Discourses, Identities and Representations*. Routledge, London.

Hall, S. (1997) The local and the global: globalization and ethnicity. In: McClintock, A., Mufti, A. and Shohat, E. (eds) *Dangerous Liaisons: Gender, Nation, and Postcolonial Perspective*. University of Minnesota Press, Minneapolis, Minnesota, pp. 173–187.

Hinch, T. and Butler, R. (2007) Introduction: revisiting common ground. In: Butler, R. and Hinch, T. (eds) *Tourism and Indigenous Peoples: Issues and Implications*. Butterworth-Heinemann, Oxford, UK, p. 1–14.

Hollinshead, K. (1999) Surveillance of the worlds of tourism: Foucault and the eye-of-power. *Tourism Management* 20, 7–23.

Hunter, W. (2001) Trust between culture: the tourist. *Current Issues in Tourism* 4, 41–67.

Krutak, L. (2007) *The Tattooing Arts of Tribal Women*. Bennett and Bloom, London.

Mason, K. (2004) Sound and meaning in aboriginal tourism. *Annals of Tourism Research* 31, 837–854.

Morgan, M. (1994) *Mutant Message Down Under*. HarperCollins Publishers, New York.

Nagel, J. (2003) *Race, Ethnicity, and Sexuality: Intimate Intersections, Forbidden Frontiers*. Oxford University Press, Oxford, UK.

Ooi, C. (2002) *Cultural Tourism and Tourism Cultures: The Business of Mediating Experiences in Copenhagen and Singapore*. Copenhagen Business School Press, Copenhagen, Denmark.

Said, E. (2003) *Orientalism*. Penguin Classics, New York.

Schein, L. (2000) *Minority Rules: The Miao and the Feminine in China's Cultural Politics*. Duke University Press, Durham, North Carolina.

Spang, L. (2000) *The Invention of the Restaurant*. Harvard University Press, Cambridge, Massachusetts.

Statistics Bureau of Hainan (2008) Published Data Issued From Statistics Bureau of Hainan, Haikou, China.

Strain, E. (2003) *Public Places, Private Journeys*. Rutgers University Press, Piscataway, New Jersey.

Urry, J. (2002) *The Tourist Gaze*. Sage Publications, London.

Van den Berghe, P. (1994) *The Quest for the Other: Ethnic Tourism in San Cristobal, Mexico*. University of Washington Press, Tacoma, Washington.

Wang, N. (1999) Rethinking authenticity in tourism experience. *Annals of Tourism Research* 26, 349–370.

Winthrop, R. (1991) *Dictionary of Concepts in Cultural Anthropology*. Greenwood Press, Westport, Connecticut.

Wood, R. (1998) Bali: cultural tourism and touristic culture. *Annals of Tourism Research* 25, 770–772.

Xie, P. (2003) The bamboo-beating dance in Hainan, China: authenticity and commodification. *Journal of Sustainable Tourism* 11, 5–17.

Xie, P. (2010) *Authenticating Ethnic Tourism*. Channel View Publishing, Clevedon, UK.

Xie, P. and Lane, B. (2006) A life cycle model for aboriginal arts performance in tourism: perspectives on authenticity. *Journal of Sustainable Tourism* 14, 545–561.

Yang, L. and Wall, G. (2009) Authenticity in ethnic tourism: domestic tourists' perspective. *Current Issues in Tourism* 12, 235–254.

Zeppel, H. (1998) Come share our culture: marketing Aboriginal tourism in Australia. *Pacific Tourism Review* 2, 67–81.

9 Gaming in the USA: Historical Development, Controversies and Current Status

Omar Moufakkir[1] and Don F. Holecek[2]

[1]*School of Leisure and Tourism Management, Stenden University, Leeuwarden, the Netherlands;* [2]*Michigan State University, East Lansing, Michigan, USA*

Introduction

In 2008, 54.6 million people visited casinos in the USA (American Gaming Association, 2009). In the same year, 233 Indian tribes in 28 states operated casinos that generated nearly US$26 billion in gross gaming revenues (National Indian Gaming Association, 2009). That same year, 445 commercial casinos and 44 'racinos' (racetrack-based casinos) in 20 different states generated another $39 billion in gaming revenues (American Gaming Association, 2009). This translates into an average of about $600 wagered at casinos by each American household in 2008 (Mallach, 2010). Despite the proliferation of casinos and the popularity of gaming, gaming remains a contested recreational and economic development activity, because of the numerous controversies that surround gaming development. Communities have embraced casino gaming for two main reasons: the first is to generate revenue and employment by attracting more tourists; the second is to keep local gaming money at home (Moufakkir, 2002).

Although more than half of the states have introduced legislation related to gaming since the late 1980s, whenever and wherever casino gaming legislation has been introduced and discussed, heated debates have arisen between advocates and adversaries of gaming because it is perceived as a moral, religious, economic, political and social issue (Boger, 1994; Eadington, 1996; National Gaming Impact Study Commission, 1999; Moufakkir, 2002).

The increase in local opposition to gambling is apparent through the defeat of more than 25 gambling initiatives since 1991 (Chadbourne and Wolfe, 1997). Growing questions regarding its social side effects and ability to deliver on its economic promises led Congress in 1996 to create a national commission to study gambling. The National Gaming Impact Study Commission (NGISC) undertook a national and comprehensive study focusing on the impact that gambling has on people and communities. The database of the study covered the period of 1980–1996. For each community (about 100 were selected), data were assembled on social problem indicators which include per capita crime levels (by crime type), unemployment rates, divorce rates, child abuse and domestic violence cases, and welfare caseloads; and economic indicators including employment levels, unemployment rates, average earnings, government revenues and bankruptcy rates, government expenditures on criminal justice and related services (NGISC, 1999). The NGISC issued its research report in June 1999, concluding that the 'metamorphosis' of gambling in general – from an amoral activity to a recreational activity – clearly has had significant economic and social impacts on individuals, communities and the country at large. The Commission unanimously acknowledged the complexity of the gambling issues, and pointed out that 'along with the real benefits of gambling come equally undeniable and significant costs' (p. 7–2). More than a decade later, the same simple yet complicated question persists: to what extent is casino gaming development a viable economic catalyst for the community? Or simply, do the benefits of casinos outweigh the costs? Operationalizing such a complex question is even more challenging because: although an impact sometimes can be distinguished as 'economic' or 'social', it is not possible to make a clear distinction between the two because their interactions are numerous and complex. Clearly, social pathologies can have significant economic costs, while economic effects, such as changes in labour force activity, also have social implications (Mallach, 2010, p. 6). The purpose of this chapter is to delineate and discuss controversies surrounding gaming development.

Gaming is certainly not a new human activity. The game of craps/dice is believed to have been played in ancient Egypt with the dice carved from animal bones. Even today, dice are commonly called 'bones' by craps players. At which point in human history wagering became associated with games of chance and what was wagered is open to speculation, but such games certainly date back to the earliest known civilizations. Gaming is popular even in certain regions of the world where it is not legal or regulated and where heavy penalties can often be imposed if one is caught gambling.

With very few exceptions, legal gaming functions as a government-controlled monopoly across the USA and in most other countries where gaming is legal. It does not operate in a free-market environment where supply and demand dictate what gaming opportunities are offered and consumed. Hence, understanding the role governments play in gaming and why is critical to assessing the history, current status and future of gaming. A brief encapsulated history of gaming in the USA will set the scene for discussing the controversies surrounding gaming development.

It is important to highlight two limitations to keep in mind in reviewing what follows. First, the focus of the discussion is on the real and perceived social and economic impacts of gaming that arise when new casinos or major expansions of existing casinos are proposed. These impacts seldom, if ever, include the recreation benefits patrons derive from their visits to casinos. Hence, while the literature introduced herein stresses a benefit/cost theme, it is largely focused on social and economic impact analysis which is a materially different type of economic analysis. For example, one issue of concern in new casino development is displacement of existing businesses. Significant displacement is generally viewed as negative in social economic impact analysis. However, in a benefit/cost analysis, displacement would be viewed as a positive since consumers receive net benefits from shifting spending from existing businesses to casinos. Second, while there is an abundant amount of literature on the topic of social/economic impacts of casinos, it ranges from being 'sound science' to 'expert opinion' to 'pure propaganda'. Unfortunately, the amount of 'sound science' available to draw upon is limited, especially that directly relevant to a new casino development proposal. Even much of what seems to be 'sound science' has been characterized as 'work that has been done…under the auspices of either proponents or opponents of casino gambling' (Mallach, 2010, p. 7). To fully grasp the range and depth of the issues associated with casino development, it is necessary to introduce literature that is 'expert opinion' and even some that approaches being undocumented 'pure propaganda'. Given the many issues involved, the differences across individual cases, and the necessarily murky foundation of 'facts' to draw upon, the objective for this chapter is to introduce readers to casino development issues and their related pros and cons. It is not our objective to assume a position in support of or in opposition to casino development in general.

Development of Gambling in the USA

The history of gaming varies from country to country and within regions in individual countries. Capturing the global history, current status and future of gaming is not feasible in the context of this short chapter. However, there are more similarities than differences across gaming venues in the nature of gaming enterprises, why they exist (or do not), their costs and benefits and governments' links to them. Thus, focusing on gaming in the one country with which we are most familiar, the USA, will serve to illustrate most of the issues one would find in most other gaming venues across the globe. Readers interested in a more in-depth history of gaming in America may want to review Durham and Hashimoto (2010) and Thompson (2001).

The history of gaming in the USA is older than the country itself. The Pilgrims were among the first to travel from England to establish a colony in the New World in the region which in time became part of the USA. At the time, voyages to the New World were not only risky, a big gamble on their part, but also expensive. The Pilgrims are reported to have raised the money for their transport and necessities to establish a successful colony in America through a lottery.

After several difficult years, the original colonies became well established. Spreading awareness of opportunities to be exploited in the New World fuelled an expanding flow of emigrants to settle across the eastern region of North America. Several decades of war between and among British and French settlers and Native American tribes eventually ended with 13 English colonies in what is now the USA. Over time, the residents of these colonies became unhappy with their British rulers, especially taxes levied on imported tea. To protest the imposition of this tax, colonists in Boston organized what we now know as the Boston Tea Party, which marked the beginning of the American Revolutionary War with the British.

The colonists quickly recognized that the British, arguably the most powerful country in the world at the time, were determined to retain control of their 13 New World colonies and that revolutionary spirit alone was not sufficient to set themselves free from British rule. They would need financial resources, but, with no taxing authority and colonists' demonstrated dislike of taxes, how could they raise money to fund the war? Like the Pilgrims, leaders in the rebellious colonies established a lottery to fund the American Revolutionary War. As will become evident as you read on in this chapter, the theme in these events early in US history that 'governments need revenue but their citizens revolt against taxes' recur over and over in the history of gaming in the USA.

Gambling and lotteries were illegal in the original 13 US colonies (now US states) for the next couple of centuries. Their governments required only limited resources to pay for the minimal services that citizens expected of them, and their small annual revenue requirements were easily met by means other than from some form of gaming. At this time in early US history, negative perception of gaming dominated the views of the majority of the population due to lack of fairness of the games offered and the costs of gaming (e.g. problem gamblers), which remain evident today. Most religious leaders stood in opposition to gambling and were prone to chastise members of their congregations that were drawn to this form of illegal and 'sinful' entertainment. Still, gambling remained popular in private and the underground economy with minimal government efforts to bring violators to justice. Lax law enforcement was often tied to bribes paid to police to turn a blind eye to the gaming venues in their jurisdictions.

The gaming environment was much friendlier on the developing western US frontier where government, law and regulation were in their infancy. Gamblers were the frequent travellers of the day, travelling on river boats along the Mississippi river and other waterways that served as the dominant means of transport in much of the region prior to development of railroads. These gamblers held a well-deserved reputation for cheating their customers out of their hard-earned money. Many moved west with the railroads and set up shop in saloons that were built to slake the thirst of those attracted to the new opportunities opening with expansion into unsettled areas 'claimed' from their Native American residents. Either through skillful play or by simply cheating, they continued to take the hard-earned money of mostly young and inexperienced cowboys (most were in fact boys), miners and ranchers who were captured in their webs.

In the early 1900s, gambling in the USA began to shift from being the domain of individual riverboat gamblers or games (the majority illegal) offered by an individual business/saloon. When the Federal Government made the production and consumption of alcoholic beverages illegal in the USA, existing criminal groups emerged to capitalize on the opportunity to supply alcohol to the thirsty masses. To maximize their profit opportunities, these criminal groups became more organized, often through a considerable amount of bloodletting. In cities where several dozen gangs operated and controlled illegal activity in their neighbourhoods, prohibition resulted in only one or two organized gangs controlling illegal markets in their city. They in effect merged to capture economies of scale in the manufacturing, distribution and sale of alcoholic beverages.

When selling alcoholic beverages became illegal, organized crime had to develop drinking establishments (commonly referred to as 'speakeasies') where drinks could be served. Soon thereafter, management of speakeasies introduced gaming into their product offering to grow their profits. These began to frame what have become the legal casinos that exist in many US states today.

When the USA repealed the law that led to prohibition, legal drinking establishments quickly reemerged across most states. Individual states, as in the case of casino gaming, control and regulate alcohol sales

and distribution. While the repeal of prohibition led to legal drinking establishments, gaming, also legal at the Federal level, did not accompany them because gaming was not legal in the states. This was largely because gaming in saloons and speakeasies was rightly perceived negatively by most Americans due to its close association with organized crime, inherent negative aspects and image as being unfair to gamblers.

Current Status of Commercial Casino Gaming in the USA

Las Vegas became a city in 1905. It was a small town in the middle of the Nevada desert that survived largely because of being a stop along an intracontinental rail line. In the early 1930s, it became a boom town fuelled by thousands of construction workers employed in building the Hoover Dam. It was the largest dam in the world when completed. The rapid increase in population in Las Vegas and across Nevada was a two-edged sword for governments. They welcomed the economic development but lacked revenues required to expand infrastructure (e.g. roads) and public services (e.g. police and fire). Imposing higher taxes on the general population was not considered to be politically viable. On the other hand, a form of sin tax levied on gambling surfaced as being a satisfactory revenue generator since it would be paid by 'sinners', tourists and visiting construction workers. Longtime residents, in essence the voting population, could avoid paying the tax by not gambling in a casino. This suited them since a significant percentage of permanent residents didn't gamble for religious reasons.

The state of Nevada legalized and began to tax casino gaming in 1931. It is a perfect example of the public's tax policy preferences: tax him and the guy behind the tree but not me. For about the first decade after being legalized and taxed, Las Vegas casinos were saloons with modest gambling areas. But, in 1941, casinos began to be built with gambling opportunities as their dominant feature, often with attached lodging and restaurants. In the 1930s, gambling profit was of secondary importance to alcoholic drink sales. In the new casinos that emerged in the 1940s, gambling profit was not only dominant, but free food, drinks and lodging were provided to gamblers who wagered larger amounts of money in these new casinos. This pattern of compensating 'high rollers' remains a practice in casinos across the USA today.

By the mid-1940s, organized criminal elements began to invest heavily in Las Vegas casinos. Although they generally offered relatively fair games to their customers as a good business practice, they did little to help problem gamblers to break their addictive behaviour and employed threats of serious harm, including death, to collect gambling debts. Beyond the attractive house advantage in casino games, organized crime was attracted to legal casinos in Las Vegas and eventually Reno as well because they could use them to launder money generated in their illegal businesses such as drugs and prostitution. Throughout the 1950s and 1960s, federal and state governments struggled to drive the criminal element out of Nevada's casinos. This was largely accomplished by the late 1960s. In 1971, Harrah's casino became the first to be listed on the US stock exchange, marking the beginning of the shift from casinos being stand alone family businesses to multi-unit corporate businesses closely regulated by federal and state governments.

License, Tax and Regulate

The legalizing of casinos in Nevada in 1931 was largely ignored by other US states until the 1970s. By then, the Nevada experiment had yielded two outcomes that set the scene for expanding commercial legal casinos in other states. First, the expanding casino industry in Nevada was generating a steadily increasing flow of tax revenues in a state without even an income tax. Second, Nevada didn't become a place with an unreasonable amount of crime, problem

gamblers, bankrupt businesses and other negative consequences commonly associated with legal commercial casinos. Many began to perceive casinos' benefits as exceeding their costs. In addition, Americans were increasingly reporting in national surveys that they visited casinos themselves or didn't care if others visited them. Only a small minority (17% in a recent national survey; American Gaming Association, 2010) reported being opposed to casino development. Given the relative success of the Nevada experiment, broader public support for casino development, and the potential for more tax revenue, more states began to legalize casino gaming.

The approach states that legalize gaming follow is to: license, tax and regulate. Other than Nevada, where obtaining a gaming licence is not especially difficult or expensive, other US states have set limits on the number of licences they issue, and they charge as much as they think they can to issue them. Thus, other than in Nevada, legal casinos in the USA can be likened to state-operated monopolies. The gaming tax rate in Nevada is about 7% and ranges to a high of 55% in Pennsylvania.

Regulations, like tax rates, vary across the states that have legalized casino gaming. All states, including Nevada, take mitigating problem gaming seriously and invest significantly in programmes to reduce the incidence of the addiction and to treat those who fall victim to it. They all also carefully monitor the games offered to ensure their fairness. Fairness in this context means only that the games operate as advertised, and the casino must pay when a customer wins. In general, states do not regulate the house advantage of the game offered, which can range from almost 40% for some games (e.g. Keno) to about 2% for the average Black Jack player. It would appear that the states weigh generating tax revenue from casino gamblers more heavily in framing regulations than ensuring that gamblers receive good entertainment value from what they spend gambling in casinos.

In 1977, New Jersey was the second state to legalize casino gaming. Its goal was to generate tax revenue and reverse the decline of a once popular tourist destination – Atlantic City. Its experience with gaming was initially very successful, but recent increases in competition in its prime markets are severely threatening the survival of many Atlantic City casinos.

Beginning in 1991 in Illinois and Iowa, the riverboat casino model was introduced in the USA. The obvious question here is: why develop these relatively small and inefficient gaming venues? The not so obvious answer is that elected officials in these states, and the four others that quickly joined them, were afraid that many state residents would not favour their state becoming known as a Nevada with a dominant land-based casino gaming industry. On the other hand, riverboat gaming was deemed acceptable since residents associated it with the states' heritages. Thus, riverboat casinos resulted from a compromise: some new tax revenue with less political risk than with full-scale land-based casinos. Their downside is that they tend to only attract local residents who gamble and return home the same day. They don't attract tourists, especially those on overnight trips; hence they don't have significant positive impacts on the local economies where they are located.

Voters in the state of Michigan refused to support developing casinos in economically depressed Detroit on three occasions over a 10-year period. Michigan residents voted in favour the fourth time it was put to them on the statewide ballot. While the basic goal for the casinos was the same as that set for Atlantic City, another goal was emphasized by supporters the fourth time the issue was presented to Michigan voters. That issue was that a casino across the river in Windsor, Canada was collecting on average one million dollars a day in gambling profits from Detroit and area residents. While Michigan voters seem to have been less than enthusiastic about 'saving' its largest city, 'Stopping the leakage of dollars from the Michigan economy' combined with the 'Save Detroit' campaign message to garner enough votes to pass legislation authorizing developing three large-scale casinos in Detroit. Keeping residents'

gaming dollars home is now central in promoting commercial casino development across the USA.

The racino is the last model employed to introduce casino gaming in states without legal, commercial casinos. Strangely perhaps, many states legalized gambling on horse and dog races even though most other forms of gaming were not legal. Their rationale seemed to be that horse and dog racing are desirable 'sporting' events tied to tradition and the local agriculture industry. Revenue from gamblers' bets on races was needed to sustain horse/dog racing and generated a modest sum of revenues for government.

Race track attendance and gambling have been declining across the USA for about 20 years, thereby reducing state tax revenues, race track profits and the earnings of all those associated with the horse/dog racing industry. This turn of events has become a concern of state governments, and they have been searching for a solution to the problem. Legislators in West Virginia were the first to authorize racinos, essentially adding gaming machines to the race track venue. The rationale for the model was that the availability of gaming machines at tracks would attract more people to the races. In addition, a portion of the gaming machine revenues would be allocated to the track side of the combined gaming venue. The increase in volume of visitors plus the 'subsidy' from gaming machine revenues were projected to put the racing industry on the path back to sustainable growth. Only part of this projection has been realized. The gaming machine subsidy to race venues has substantially helped that industry; however, attendance at races and betting on their outcome continue to decline. State governments have been clear winners of racino developments because of added tax revenues from gaming machines. Could it be that added tax revenue was the true goal behind authorizing racinos and not the stated goal of sustaining the horse/dog racing industry?

One mission of governments is strangely absent in all of the above discussion: that is providing 'the best deal' for consumers.

In most cases, legalized casinos operate as monopolies. Monopolies rarely function in the best interests of consumers. Of course, governments require casinos to manage problem gaming, but is this out of concern for problem gamblers or is it primarily a policy required to mitigate voter concerns with establishing casinos? Governments also ensure that the games offered are 'fair', but their definition of fair doesn't ensure an optimal recreation experience for gamblers. Finally, governments have rigorously driven the criminal element out of casino operations and management. Could this be to ensure that governments can extract the maximum amount of tax revenue from the casinos in their jurisdiction? There are certainly a host of reasons for questioning the desirability of governments relying on casino tax revenues to support the services the public expects them to provide.

Development of Native American Indian Casinos in the USA

A Supreme Court decision in 1987, California versus Cabazon Board of Mission Indians, materially changed the casino landscape in the USA. In that case, the court ruled that the state could not prohibit gaming on Indian reservations. The US Congress in the following year passed the Indian Gaming Regulatory Act (IGRA), which provided guidance for how the states and Indian tribes should interact in establishing gaming venues on tribal lands. In combination, the court's ruling and the IGRA created the opportunity for tribes to open casinos in all but two US states (Hawaii and Utah). A brief historical context follows which will explain how this landmark decision came to be.

When old world immigrants began to establish colonies in America, it was already inhabited by Native American Indian tribes. Early on, relations between the tribes and the trickle of settlers from the old world were generally friendly, with both benefiting from trading goods and 'technologies'. As the flow of settlers became a flood and rivalries between old world countries crossed the sea with them to America, relations between and among different tribes and settlers from different countries soured and open warfare became common place. These conflicts, largely over 'ownership' of land, expanded as settlers advanced from the east coast into the interior of America. Some tribes waged war with the whites invading their territories while others, recognizing the inevitable, sold their lands for a pittance to the US government. In either case, the outcome was the same: the tribes were pushed from their lands by white settlers. They not only were forced from their lands but were also forced to abandon their traditional way of life based upon a combination of hunting and gathering, primitive agriculture and trading. The cultural, family and 'economic' ties that had sustained them for centuries were severed. Today, the consequences are still evident. Native Americans are poorer, sicker and less educated than most other Americans, and live in broken families in inferior housing and often survive on minimal welfare payments from the government. Colonization of America has been a disaster for its indigenous peoples.

California versus Cabazon is proving finally to offer tribes the opportunity to capture their fair share of the American Dream. Interestingly, that opportunity was created in the treaties forced upon the tribes by the US government when they relinquished their lands. The language in the treaties refers to the tribes as 'sovereign nations'. At the time the treaties were negotiated, these were meaningless words inserted in the treaties as a 'no cost' means to entice tribal leaders to accept 'contracts' containing minimal benefits to them. In its 1987 decision, the US Supreme Court assigned meaning to the tribes' sovereign nation status granted in their treaties with the US government. As such, the states could not control tribal activity on their reservations. Only the federal government is empowered to enter into substantive agreements or disagreements with other nations, including recognized Indian sovereign nations.

Since tribal sovereign nations exist within the states, the interests of both are more intertwined than they are among most other nations in the world. The IGRA was enacted by the US Congress to balance the interests of the parties in developing casinos on tribal lands. The essence of the IGRA is that the states can negotiate compacts (essentially contracts) with tribes concerning specifics such as how to share casino profits (states can't directly tax Indian casinos). Each compact is unique, resulting from give and take between a state and a tribe.

Today, tribal casinos exist in 29 states, and their total revenue approaches the level of that generated by all other legal commercial casinos in the USA (American Gaming Association, 2010). There is a great divide in the impact Indian casinos have had on individual tribes. Revenues aren't shared across tribes, thus those with casinos are better off economically than those without casinos. Small tribes with casinos earn more per capita and are benefiting more than larger tribes with casinos. Some tribes distribute the bulk of their casino profits on a per capita basis to tribal members while others allocate profits primarily to tribal infrastructure projects such as schools, healthcare and housing. The more foresighted tribes are investing some of their casino profits in projects to diversify their businesses, recognizing that their casino 'monopoly' is unlikely to be sustainable in the long run. Overall, tribal casinos are benefiting some of the most destitute (and deserving) citizens in the USA.

Casino Gaming Issues

An overview

Like other forms of tourism development, gaming has both positive and negative consequences for communities (NGISC, 1999). Gaming researchers have demonstrated that social, cultural, political and environmental impacts are equally likely to occur following casino development (Stokowski, 1996). From a public policy standpoint, most of the debate about the development of casino gaming hinges on the following four central issues: economic contribution to the community, crime in the community, social pathology and impact on people and businesses, and bankruptcy. The main questions related to these four issues centre on: does the establishment of casinos attract new dollars to the community, affect crime rates, increase social problems, and affect bankruptcy filings? Like any other controversy, casino gaming advocates find arguments to substantiate their claims and so do adversaries (Table 9.1).

Reviewing the literature on the impact of casino gaming, two most popular model gaming destinations reflect the controversy surrounding casino development. Las Vegas is one of the few places where casinos are recognized as beneficial to the economy and the economic impact issue is not debated (Thompson, 1999). Atlantic City is the place where casinos are recognized as not successfully contributing to the plight of the city. On the other hand, Heneghan (1999, p. 113), for example, proposes that to 'fully understand the magnitude of the revolutionary changes following casino development, one has to study what Atlantic City was before casinos and how it got there'. Atlantic City reached its height of popularity as a regional seaside resort in the early 1980s, but 30 years later tourist arrivals to the city decreased tremendously. Gaming was sought as an economic and urban development strategy that effectively created jobs and generated taxes for the city. According to Braunlich (1996, p. 15) the 'most disappointing lesson from Atlantic City experience is the failure of the casino hotel industry's economic success to translate into a comprehensive physical redevelopment of the city'. What Braunlich is suggesting is that Atlantic City must be viewed in a fuller context if the impacts of casino development are to be properly understood. Other gaming ventures and their hosting communities have also come under scrutiny and criticism regarding, for example, economic contributions, crime and problem gambling, the concern of the upcoming discussion.

Table 9.1. Example of casino gaming development issues/arguments: three different perspectives.

Issues	Casino gaming opponents' selected arguments	Casino gaming advocates' selected arguments	National Gambling Impact Study Commission's findings
Tourism	The gambling population is a local resident population (Kindt, 1994)	Legal casino gaming is viewed as a means to increase the number of tourists and the amount that they spend (Cabot, 1996)	The largest casinos reported that more than 90% of their patrons travelled more than 50 miles to the casino. The corresponding percentages for the smaller non-tribal and tribal casinos were 57% and 56%, respectively.
Jobs	Employment is taken away from traditional businesses that may provide a community benefit to an addictive activity that produces only social costs (Goodman, 1994)	Gaming jobs have a multiplier of 1.7, meaning that for every one casino job there are 1.7 other jobs created, many in support businesses that serve the casino (Cabot, 1996)	
Taxes	The costs of externalities caused by casino gaming such as dysfunctional gambling will exceed the expected tax revenues (Grinols and Omorov, 1996)	Jurisdictions may extract large sums of tax money from casino gaming (Cabot, 1996)	Larger and smaller non-tribal casinos paid about 13% in taxes and tribal casinos paid 18% of revenues to tax authorities (much of the higher percentage among the tribal casinos may be due to payments to tribal units)
Bankruptcy	The 298 US counties that have legalized gambling within their borders had a 1996 bankruptcy filing rate 18% higher than the filing in counties with no gambling. The bankruptcy rate was 35% higher than the average in counties with five or more gambling establishments (SMR Research, in AGA, 2000)	The majority of states with the highest bankruptcy rates are those with no casino gaming. Of the 24 counties in the USA with the highest bankruptcy filing rates, none has casino gaming (AGA, 2000)	The casino effect is not statistically significant for bankruptcy
Crime	The introduction of casino gaming in Wisconsin is associated with increased crime. The rates of major crimes in counties with casinos were 6.7% higher that they would have been in the absence of casinos (Williams *et al.*, 1996)	Communities with casino gaming are as safe as communities that do not have casinos (Margolis, 1997)	The casino effect is not statistically significant for any of the crime outcome measures

Continued

Table 9.1. Continued.

Issues	Casino gaming opponents' selected arguments	Casino gaming advocates' selected arguments	National Gambling Impact Study Commission's findings
Prevalence of pathological gambling	10,000–80,000 tax dollars are spent on a pathological gambler per year (Kindt, 1994). Problem and pathological gamblers create social costs of US$110–340 per adult per year when averaged over the entire population (Grinols and Omorov, 1996)		900 tax dollars per year are spent on a pathological gambler
Total social costs	At least 8 billion dollars are spent per year to cover social costs associated with gambling (Kindt, 1994)		5–6 billion dollars are spent on social costs attributed to gambling (National Opinion Research Center, 1999)
Substitution	Gambling only diverts dollars from existing businesses to gambling enterprises (Goodman, 1994)	There is no tangible evidence of the alleged substitution effect when applied to the casino gaming industry, because findings point to an overall increase in recreation spending of US$54.2 billion between 1990 and 1993. Of that, 3.2 billion was attributed to casino gaming. Casino gaming is not merely replacing other industries, because other recreation sectors are growing as well (AGA, 2000)	'The preponderance of empirical studies indicate claims of complete cannibalization of pre-existing local restaurants and entertainment facilities by a mere shift in resident spending is grossly exaggerated'

Economic Contribution to the Community

Supporters of gaming maintain that casinos are a key attraction that can stimulate and revitalize a community's economy, particularly its tourism industry (Cabot, 1996). According to Eadington (1996), the opening of a casino or casinos in a region that previously had no legal casino gaming 'has tapped a substantial latent demand for the activity' (p. 4). Many recently legalized casino jurisdictions, such as Windsor and Montreal, the Gulf Coast and Tunica County in Mississippi, Foxwoods in Connecticut,

or Joliet and Elgin in Illinois, he explains, have experienced surprising revenue and visitation rates. On the other hand, opponents (e.g. Grinols and Omorov, 1996) argue that 80–90% and more of the bulk of casino revenues come from residents. Assessing the direct economic impacts of two temporary Detroit casinos on the local area, Moufakkir (2002) found that only about 21% of casino patrons came from outside the study area, but concluded that these contributed significantly to the local economy. The study, however, did not consider the probable costs. Considering the added costs of casino gaming, Grinols and Omorov

(1996) argue, it appears that the costs of casino revenues outweigh the benefits, and thus maintain that casinos are not a viable option for economic development. Dovel (1996), for example, submits that casinos cannibalize sales from cinemas, restaurants and other community businesses that depend on discretionary dollars. Restaurants in many states have reported a decrease in revenue in response to the opening of a nearby casino, and many restaurants have closed. Grinols and Omorov (1996) found that casinos are associated with a drop in general merchandise and miscellaneous retail and wholesale trade within ten miles from the gaming establishments. On the other hand, Moufakkir (2002) found that 51% of the patrons of the casinos surveyed participated in other community-based businesses and activities (see also Moufakkir and Holecek, 2002a; Moufakkir et al., 2004). The end result is that while those who support casino gaming maintain that this development activity is a good economic impact catalyst, opponents maintain that casinos do not seem to have a positive impact on regional economic development and thus communities should not turn to gaming as a saviour. The caveat is that several interacting variables make generalizing about the economic impacts of casinos unfeasible, and thus judgement disregarding this complexity can be shortsighted if not hazardous and risky.

Economic impact studies

Opponents of casino gaming argue that most of the economic impact studies were commissioned by the gaming industry (e.g. Goddman, 1994), with a majority focusing exclusively on the positive impacts while ignoring or minimizing the negative impacts that are also associated with a gaming establishment (Gazel, 1998). Furthermore, several assumptions are made in estimating the economic impacts of a casino. Differing assumptions are in general a major cause for very large differences observed in estimates developed by different researchers (Gazel, 1998). The discrepancies result in a matter

that haunts not only gaming researchers but researchers in other fields. For example, when measuring the economic impacts of visitors to sports tournaments and special events Crompton (1999, p. 17) notes that:

> There is a temptation to adopt inappropriate procedures and assumptions in order to generate high economic impact numbers that will position an agency more favorably in the mind of elected officials. Sometimes such errors are the result of a genuine lack of understanding of economic impact analysis and the procedures used in it, but in other instances they are committed deliberately and mischievously to generate large numbers and mislead stakeholders.
>
> Crompton (1999, p. 17)

Gazel (1998) argues that positive and negative factors must be included in economic impact studies. The net economic impact of the presence of a casino in the local economy is thus the result of subtracting the negative impacts from the positive ones. For a comprehensive listing of impacts see Gazel (1998). Furthermore, comprehensive economic impact studies are costly, time consuming and therefore rare (NGISC, 1999). Moreover, analysts believe that the costs of casino development have been unequally discussed, particularly those costs that emerge over time or which are difficult to quantify are not fully considered. Often, a significant lag period exists between the beginning of casino development and the provision of expected gains. Such impacts are rarely considered in traditional, short-term economic impact analyses (Stokowski, 1999). Oddo (1997) and Kindt (1994), for example, maintain that, when the added costs of gaming are included in the economic impacts equation, the costs appear to outweigh the benefits, concluding that casino gaming is not a sound or desirable option for economic development. Moreover, the magnitude of economic impact generally depends on the context selected. For example, single areas boasting a positive impact can readily be found, but their concerns usually do not extend to surrounding areas where negative consequences 'of this good fortune' may surface (NGISC, 1999). In other words a gaming community may be benefiting from casinos, but, if the economic impact analysis is extended to include neighbouring communities, the magnitude of economic impact may decrease. This is because it is generally argued that neighbouring non-gaming communities may experience import externalities such as gambling addiction, crime and other costs without having gaming tax money to offset those costs.

In sum, three main reasons make the divergent perspectives about the magnitude of the economic impact of casino development possible. Stokowski (1999, p. 157) summarizes these as:

- Research about economic impacts tends to be supported through funds provided by agencies (industry or government) that have an interest in the outcome of the research.
- Not all economic benefits or costs are likely to be included in any single research study.
- Not all data are comparable in their original form, thus introducing many sources of error into the models.

Casino gaming can be viewed as an economic development in different guises as follows (Felsenstein and Freeman, 1998):

1. A redistributive effect: this effect happens when a local service that serves local demand is simply redistributing existing economic activity. In the case of gaming, if a casino attracts only local gamers, new money is not generated and therefore the casino does not contribute to the local economy.
2. An expansionary effect: this happens when a casino serves in an exporting gaming service capacity, and therefore by serving non-local demand attracts new money to the local community.
3. A substitution activity: this occurs when local casinos prevent local gaming money from leaking out of the local economy to other gaming jurisdictions.
4. An extractive activity: when a casino serves only external demand, it generates

very little positive benefit locally but leaves behind a legacy of local negative externalities.
5. Casinos that focus on local residents will probably not be the economic panacea that communities envision.

These guises will draw discretionary spending from other community entertainment areas, such as theatres and restaurants (Milanowski, 1996). Dovel (1996) explains that casinos cannibalize sales from cinemas and other businesses that depend on discretionary dollars. Restaurants in many communities reported a decrease in sales following the opening of a nearby casino, and several others went bankrupt. Moufakkir (2002) identified four types of gamers based on primary trip purpose, each with different gaming trip characteristics and impacts. For example, 59% of the intercepted patrons indicated that the casino was their primary reason to visit Detroit, suggesting that in this case the casino acts as a nucleus attraction for more than half of the patrons or that in the absence of the casino these patrons would not have come to the city. More than 50% reported that they would visit more often because they can visit the community's casino. About one half of the total sample participated in other non-casino-related activities in the community, such as dining, shopping, attending a sport event, exploring the city, and visiting friends and relatives. Over one-quarter stayed at least one night in the Detroit area. Despite these seemingly positive findings, it would be premature to support or reject casino development either in the study area or in general, not only because of the parsimony of the results but also because of other variables including crime and associated social costs.

Crime in the Community

Besides economic development, the other most frequently considered gaming development issue on the public policy agenda is crime (NGISC, 1999). Studying the legalization of casinos in the USA, Dombrink and Thompson (1990) found that crime potential was a central issue in more than half of the 22 state gaming campaigns examined. In the late 1980s when the operation of riverboat casinos was approved in Iowa and Illinois, and in 1990–1999 when small casinos opened in South Dakota and Colorado, there was not much debate on the relationship between casinos and crime. In 1992, the debate about this relationship was brought to centre stage when Chicago's mayor approved a proposal to build a casino in downtown Chicago. In the resulting debate, opponents of the project raised the crime issue in order to generate public support for their opposition to the initiative (Margolis, 1997). Gaming opponents have since raised the crime issue in other jurisdictions, including Missouri, Indiana, Florida, Maryland, Massachusetts, Louisiana, New York, Ohio, Pennsylvania and Michigan.

On a national level, organized opposition to casino gaming has made the crime issue a major point on the political agenda. Opponents claim that gaming development increases crime in three principal ways. First, people steal to support dysfunctional gambling habits. Second, gambling may attract criminals because it is a cash industry. As such, it can be used to exploit people. Third, criminal activity may increase because crowds draw petty thefts (Cabot, 1996). Street crime near casinos has been the concern of several studies. It involves crimes against the person or property of citizens and casino patrons, such as robbery, burglary, assault, rape, theft, murder and similar crimes (Miller and Schwartz, 1998). Environmental criminologists refer to places that attract criminal activities as 'hot spots'. The hot-spot theory originated by Spring and Block (1988) argues that certain places are more crimogenic than others. Because of the associated criminal activities casinos are considered hot spots. On the other hand, it is argued that casino gaming may lower street crime if it reduces unemployment in the area surrounding the casino, if it reduces illegal gambling or increases visitor security (Albanese, 1997). Proponents suggest that the legalization of gambling can help eliminate illegal gambling, thereby allowing the police to reallocate resources toward other crime prevention and law enforcement (Cabot, 1996).

Empirical studies (e.g. Albanese, 1985; Fridman et al., 1989; Hakim and Weinblatt, 1989) have found that total criminal offences and property crimes in particular increased after casinos opened in Atlantic City. In the more rural gaming areas of Deadwood, South Dakota; Black Hawk, Central City; and Cripple Creek, Colorado, residents perceived that crime had increased when casinos were introduced (Long et al., 1994). Stokowski (1996) found that the total number of criminal offences and arrests increased after gaming began, contrary to crime patterns across the State of Colorado during the same period. Cabot (1996) argues that unadjusted crime statistics show increases in crime incidents with the introduction of casinos in many but not all jurisdictions. According to him, jurisdictions considering casino development should recognize the likelihood that casino gaming, like any other tourist activity, may result in more street crime simply because of the increase in the number of visitors in the jurisdiction. An increased volume of criminal acts occurs in other tourist jurisdictions where a new tourist industry creates major attractions. Miller and Swartz (1998) argue that 'there is no reason to believe that gambling casinos are different from any other tourist attraction' (p. 8). Other studies (e.g. Margolis, 1997) found little evidence to support the notion that the presence of casino gaming in a community has any meaningful impact on crime rates. Similarly, Moufakkir (2005, p. 17–18) reviewed the gaming- and crime-related literature and found differences between studies. He also examined crime volume in Detroit and neighbouring communities before, during and after MGM Grand and MotorCity opened in the city, and found that most crimes did not increase, except for prostitution (arrests) and arson offences. Although it was concluded that there is no clear indication to suggest that crime volume increased when the casinos opened, Moufakkir maintained that caution needs to be taken when using and interpreting crime data independent of other variables.

Problem Gambling

Other researchers (e.g. Volberg, 1994; Thompson *et al.*, 1996) have indicated that there is an association between compulsive gambling crime and other social ills. It is argued that addiction to gambling may lead to crime. Compulsive gamblers may turn to illegal activities to support their addiction, finance gambling or pay gambling debts (Lesieur, 1992). Compulsive or pathological gambling remains the most real and serious side effect of gambling (NGISC, 1999). Proponents argue that gaming is generally a form of entertainment practised responsibly by millions of Americans (American Gaming Association, 2000). But gaming opponents argue that the vast majority of those who gamble have problems related to gambling, and a large portion of the revenues from expanded casinos come from problem and pathological gamblers (Grinols and Omorov, 1996). According to adversaries, the proliferation of casinos increases the percentage of people with gambling problems in a given population. Studies of problem gambling provide varying estimates of its incidence (NGISC, 1999).

It is estimated that 1–2% of the US population has the potential to become pathological gamblers (American Psychiatric Association, 2004). Their addiction to gambling is the most severe classification of problem gaming. They will go to almost any means (e.g. stealing from family, friends and employees) to obtain money to gamble. Unless someone (e.g. family member, casino employee) intervenes, pathological gamblers often can't break their addictive gambling behaviour and risk losing their families, jobs and all their assets (e.g. life insurance policies, retirement monies and personal possessions). Another 2–3% of the US population is classified as 'at risk' gamblers. They display similar but less severe problem gaming symptoms (e.g. gaming more often than desired, losing much more than intended or choosing to gamble rather than participate in desirable family activities). The net result for them is diminished 'quality of life' and a strong sense of guilt because they gamble more than they know

they should. Fortunately, most of these problem gamers are not so addicted that they can't recognize that they have a problem with gaming. Some are able to 'self-treat' to mitigate their addiction or are willing to seek professional help to manage it. Problem gaming researchers have found that problem gamers are also likely to display other addictive behaviour (e.g. drugs, shopping and alcohol). In layman's terms, the mental high they receive from gaming overcomes the downside consequences that they know exist from excessive gambling. Their brains are 'wired' differently than the majority of the rest of the population.

Problem gaming presents an interesting challenge for the casino industry, which prefers to view itself as being in the business of providing entertainment to its guests. Problem gamers are very good casino customers, but, unlike other businesses, casinos aggressively try to discourage problem gamers' patronage. This is in part voluntary since serving problem gamers often leads to tragic incidents leading to negative publicity that is bad for a casino's desired reputation as a socially responsible entertainment venue. It is also because governments require casinos to identify and remove problem gamers from their premises. Governments deem problem gaming as a serious issue in part because of the negative social consequences of the addict's behaviour but also because it reflects badly on governments themselves who are after all responsible for legalizing and regulating casinos in their jurisdictions.

There is no question that a significant percentage of any population is prone to become problem gamers and that some of them will become gambling addicts. But, banning casinos is not necessarily an optimal policy decision designed to protect those vulnerable to a problem gaming addiction. Such a policy would not eliminate peoples' exposure to opportunities to gamble legally (e.g. play the lottery) or illegally. Furthermore, anyone with a computer can gamble online with no supervision or little, if any, government regulation. Gary Loverman (2010) recently noted that, while the numbers and distribution of casinos across America have increased significantly over the last 20 years, the percentage of the US population that is classified as being problem gamers has not changed. Casinos do not seem to increase the incidence of problem gaming, although they surely provide alternatives to other gaming venues that are available to gaming addicts.

The casino industry in the USA invests significant monies to support problem-gaming research, employ education to identify problem gamers and provide treatment for addicts. Given that most people enjoy gambling as a form of entertainment, government-regulated casinos operated by responsible management are more socially desirable gaming venues than the majority of the others that are available to the public.

Discussion

The literature is divided on the social and economic benefits and costs a casino brings to a given community. Several differences across the studies in the literature may account for the inconsistent conclusions drawn from their results including the following:

1. The nature of the gaming community: is the community rural or urban, large, mid-sized or small, or in close proximity to a large population or not? Is the community a gaming destination with a cluster of casinos or does it offer only one casino?
2. The nature of the casino: does the casino offer only gaming or is it a full resort–conference centre complex with gaming?
3. Is it an Indian casino, a land-based commercial casino, a racino or a riverboat casino?
4. Is the casino location in close proximity to population centres, considered as a stop-over or primary destination/attractions?
5. What is the research methodology employed to conduct the study?
6. The gaming position of the researcher: does the researcher generally oppose or support gaming?
7. Who is sponsoring the study: is it a private research firm, a non-profit agency, or a public organization such as a university?

8. What is the purpose of the study: is it to measure the economic impacts, social impacts or a combination?

Gaming communities differ from one another. Their success may depend, to a large extent, on whether the community's casino(s) constitute(s) a destination casino resort that offers gambling along with a mega-resort containing overnight accommodations, retail businesses, meeting rooms, and expensive dining and entertainment opportunities. Furthermore, not all casinos are equally successful business ventures. Some have gone bankrupt and others are struggling to cope with the competition. Others are highly profitable, expanding or considering expansion. Based on this review, it would not make much sense to present more studies that support or reject casino gaming development. In a meta-analysis, Shaffer and Korn (2002, p. 178) concluded that 'it can appear that gambling causes social problems, and it even might be that gambling is a cause of these social problems. However, the current state of scientific research simply does not permit this conclusion.' What is important to acknowledge is that like many other tourism developments, casino gaming is neither a panacea nor a blight. Simply because some casino ventures provide economic benefits does not mean that they are appropriate or could serve as models for future development elsewhere. Very few generalizations are valid when considering the economic benefits and costs of casino development. The NGISC (1999, p. 7) concluded: 'No reasonable person would argue that gambling is cost free'. Almost every beneficial claim has its negative counterpart, and therefore, each case must be decided on its merit (Gartner, 1996). Any tourism development must be guided by a carefully planned policy. Legislators, investors and decision makers must weigh the economic benefits against the costs, bearing in mind that, in fact, the most sophisticated projections remain questionable. If potential costs and benefits are identified early in the planning process, it is often possible to exploit the benefits and mitigate the costs when the development project is implemented (McIntosh et al., 1995).

Communities form no common front: 'one community may welcome gambling as an economic salvation; while its neighbor may regard it as anathema. As such, there are few areas in which a single, national, one-size-fits-all approach can be recommended' (NGISC, p. vii). Despite obvious economic and social benefits and costs, and in spite of the claims and arguments by supporters and opponents, it would be ludicrous to even try to settle the controversies surrounding gaming by fixating on one case, a multitude of cases, one model or different models. While one can expect similar issues to surface around new casino development or expansion proposals, how each of these is processed and weighted will vary widely across individual cases. This is due to the complexities involved, variations across individual cases, and taste and preferences of communities. It is not unusual for a community via referendum to strongly reject a proposed casino three or four times before subsequently approving it.

The successes or failures of casinos are also the result of several interacting factors including management practices, marketing and positioning activities, acceptance or rejection of gaming by the host community, competition, and government regulations. The case for supporting gaming development will then rest on enlightened decisions and policies based not only on the benefits and costs of the proposed gaming development, but also on the consideration of other development alternatives, and surely on keeping the promise to the community. Finally, because of all the cost and benefit projections and accompanying assumptions and ambiguities, the final decision for establishing casinos will depend on the eyes of the beholders. The controversies can only help us to learn from the mistakes and successes of others, a key to informed decisions.

Conclusion

In 2009, the vast majority of Americans did not have to travel far to gamble at a casino; additional casinos were built in 2010 and others are expected to become available in the next couple of years. Casinos are no longer scarce or novelties across most of America. In fact, it has been reported that 90% of the US population resides within a 4-hour drive of a casino (Durham and Hashimoto, 2010). Recent events shed some light on the future for casino gaming in the USA. Leading into the 'Great Recession' in the USA in 2008, the casino industry was widely viewed as being 'recession proof' or at a minimum 'recession resistant'. Neither has proven to be correct in many casino markets. Although gaming revenues in some markets have expanded or not declined significantly, the situation in others is catastrophic. Several properties in Atlantic City and Las Vegas are in or near bankruptcy. Those in the worst financial straits are over-leveraged investments in expansion or new developments based upon what has proven to be overly optimistic projections of consumer demand and cash flow. Investors in these developments are not being repaid at all or are receiving only a small fraction of the amount that they loaned. Given this experience investing in casinos, access to capital for future casino developments is tight and will likely remain so for some time into the future.

The movie 'Field of Dreams' was released in 1989. It has an adult fantasy theme involving an Iowa corn farmer, an avid baseball fan, who is struggling to survive financially. In his dreams, he repeatedly hears a voice saying: 'Build it and they will come'. He eventually determines that 'it' is a ball diamond, which he builds, and which attracts baseball fans and the farm is saved. The line from the movie 'Build it and they will come' is a fitting descriptor underlying the rapid expansion of the casino industry during the past couple of decades. During the next couple of decades, the investment climate will be materially different: 'Build it in the right place at the right time and they will come'. 'It' will need to be a casino that is unique in the market and scaled to fit that target market. 'Right place' will be where there are limited existing and planned competitors, and it will be close to major population centres. The 'Right time' will be when investment capital is readily available at average or below average costs and when the probability of an economic recession is low. Nevertheless, to a certain extent, gaming development will always remain a gamble.

In summary, the casino market in the USA is entering a period of much slower expansion (maturity), and the casino gaming experience is shifting from being a novelty to a commodity. Governments and the tribes will continue to exploit their monopoly positions to the disadvantage of casino customers, but growing competition will result in an improved casino product and a better value for customers. Finally, expansion of casino gaming will be most rapid and profitable outside the USA. Countries in Asia are emerging as the new frontier for casino gaming. For example, Macau in China recently passed Las Vegas as the world's casino gaming revenue king, and the Chinese potential gaming market is only beginning to be tapped. Two major and very profitable casinos recently opened in Singapore. These successful developments will serve to expand casino gaming across Asia just as the success of Las Vegas casinos fuelled rapid and major expansion of casino gaming across the USA.

References

Albanese, J. (1985) The effect of casino gambling on crime. *Federal Probation* 49, 39–44.

Albanese, J.S. (1997) Predicting the impact of casino gambling on crime and law enforcement in Windsor, Ontario. In: Eadington, W.R. and Cornelius, J.A. (eds.) Gambling: Public Policies and the Social Sciences. Institute for the Study of Gambling and Commercial Gaming, University of Nevada, Reno, Nevada, pp. 351–366.

American Gaming Association (2000) State of the States: the AGA survey of casino entertainment. Available at: http://www.americangaming.org/assets/files/AGA (accessed 03 December 2003).

American Gaming Association (2009) State of the States: the AGA survey of casino entertainment. Available at: http://americangaming.org/survey/ (accessed 18 May 2010).

American Gaming Association (2010) State of the States: the AGA survey of casino entertainment. Available at: http://americangaming.org/survey/ (accessed 18 May 2010).

American Psychiatric Association (2004) *Diagnostic and Statistical Manual of Mental Disorders,* 4th edn. American Psychiatric Association, Washington, DC.

Boger, C.A. Jr (1994) The effects of Native American gaming on other tourist business. *Gaming Research and Review Journal* 1, 25–34.

Braunlich, C.G. (1996) Lessons from the Atlantic City casino experience. *Journal of Travel Research* 34, 46–56.

Cabot, A.N. (1996) *Casino Gaming: Policy, Economics and Regulation.* Nevada International Gaming Institute, Las Vegas, Nevada.

Chadbourne, C., Walker, P. and Wolfe, M. (1997) *Gambling, Economic Development, and Historic Preservation.* American Planning Association, Washington, DC.

Crompton, J.L. (1999) *Measuring the Economic Impact of Visitors to Sports Tournaments and Special Events.* Division of Professional Services, National Recreation and Park Association, Ashburn, Virginia.

Dombrink, J. and Thompson, W. (1990) *The Last Resort: Success and Failure in Campaigns for Casinos.* University of Nevada Press, Reno, Nevada.

Dovel, M.W. (1996) Gambling: more states are folding. *Kiplinger's Personal Finance Magazine* 50 (7), 14.

Durham, S. and Hashimoto, K. (2010) *The History of Gambling in America.* Prentice Hall, Upper Saddle River, New Jersey.

Eadington, W.R. (1996) The legalization of casinos: policy objectives, regulatory alternatives, and cost/benefit considerations. *Journal of Travel Research* 34, 3–8.

Felsenstein, D. and Freeman, D. (1998) Stimulating the impacts of gambling in a tourist location: some evidence from Israel. *Journal of Travel Research* 37, 145–155.

Fridman, J., Hakim, S. and Weinblatt, J. (1989) Casino gambling as a 'growth pole' strategy and its effect on crime. *Journal of Regional Science* 29, 615–623.

Gartner, W.C. (1996) *Tourism Development: Principles, Processes, and Policies.* Van Nostrand Reinhold, New York.

Gazel, D. (1998) The economic impacts of casino gambling at the state and local levels. *Annals of the American Academy of Political and Social Science* 556, 66–84.

Grinnols, E.L. and Omorov, J.D. (1996) Who loses when casinos win? *Illinois Business Review* 53, 7–17.

Goodman, R. (1994) *Legalized Gaming as a Strategy for Economic Development*. United States Gambling Study, Northampton, Massachusetts.

Hakim, S. and Buck, A. J. (1989) Do casinos enhance crime? *Journal of Criminal Justice* 17, 409–416.

Heneghan, D. (1999) Economic impacts of casino gaming in Atlantic City. In: Hsu, K.H.C. (ed.) *Legalized Casino Gaming in the United States: The Economic and Social Impacts*. The Haworth Hospitality Press, Binghamton, New York, pp. 113–133.

Kindt, J.W. (1994) The economic impacts of legalized gambling activities. *Drake Law Review* 43, 51–95.

Lesieur, H. R. (1992) Compulsive gambling. *Society* 49, 43–50.

Long, P., Clark, J. and Liston, D. (1994) *Win, Lose or Draw? Gambling with America's Small Towns*. The Aspen Institute, Washington, DC.

Loveman, G. (2010) Keynote address at the G2E Conference, November 17, Las Vegas, Nevada.

Mallach, A. (2010) Economic and social impact of introducing casino gambling: a review and assessment of the literature. Available at: http://www.philadelphiafed.org/community-development/publications/discussion-papers/discussion-paper_casino-gambling.pdf (accessed 18 May 2010).

Margolis, J.D. (1997) *Casinos and Crime: An Analysis of the Evidence*. American Gaming Association, Washington, DC.

McIntosh, R.W., Goeldener, C.R. and Ritchie, B. Jr (1995) *Tourism: Principles, Practices, Philosophies,* 7th edn. John Wiley and Sons, New York.

Milanowski, J. (1996) The economics of gambling. In: University of Nevada Las Vegas International Gaming Institute (ed.) *The Gaming Industry: Introduction and Perspectives*. John Wiley and Sons, New York.

Miller, W.J. and Schwartz, M.D. (1998) Casino gambling and street crime. *Annals of the American Academy of Political and Social Science* 556, 123–137.

Moufakkir, O. (2002) Changes in Selected Economic and Social Indicators Associated With the Establishment of Casinos in the City of Detroit. Unpublished dissertation. Michigan State University, East Lansing, Michigan.

Moufakkir, O. (2005) An assessment of crime volume following casino gaming development in the city of Detroit. *UNLV Gaming Research & Review Journal* 9, 15–28.

Moufakkir, O. and Holecek, D.F. (2002) How important is a casino to a community and how important is a community to a casino: an empirical basis for cooperative marketing between casinos and community tourism promotion agencies. Proceedings of the 2002 Northern Recreation Research Symposium, GTR-NE-301, 184–189. Available at: http://nrs.fs.fed.us/pubs/gtr/gtr_ne302/gtr_ne302_184.pdf (accessed 18 May 2010).

Moufakkir, O., Singh, A.J., Moufakkir-van der Woud, A. and Holecek, D. (2004) Impact of light, medium, and heavy spenders on casino destinations: segmenting gaming visitors based on amount of non-gaming expenditures. *UNLV Gaming Research & Review Journal* 8, 59–71.

National Gaming Impact Study Commission (1999) *Final report*. US Government Printing Office, Washington, DC.

National Indian Gaming Association (2009) *The Economic Impact of Indian Gaming in 2008*. National Indian Gaming Association, Washington, DC.

Oddo, A.R. (1997) The economics and ethics of casino gambling. *Review of Business* 18, 4–8.

Shaffer, H.J. and David, A.K. (2002) Gambling and related mental disorders: a public health analysis. *Annual Review of Public Health* 23, 171–212.

Spring, J.W. and Block, C.R. (1988) *Finding Crime Hot Spots: Experiments in the Identification of High Crime Areas*. Paper Presented at the 1988 Annual Meeting of the Midwest Sociological Society, Minneapolis.

Stokowski, P. (1996) Crime patterns and gaming development in rural Colorado. *Journal of Travel Research* 3, 63–69.

Stokowski, P. (1999) Economic impacts of riverboats and land-based non-native American casino gaming. In: Hsu, K.H.C. (ed.) *Legalized Casino Gaming in the United States: The Economic and Social Impacts*. The Haworth Hospitality Press, Binghamton, New York, pp. 155–174.

Thompson, W. (1999) Casinos in Las Vegas: when impacts are not the issue. In: Hsu, K.H.C. (ed.) *Legalized Casino Gaming in the United States: The Economic and Social Impacts*. The Haworth Hospitality Press, Binghamton, New York, pp. 93–112.

whereas for the same year international tourist arrivals worldwide increased by only 175% (Witt, 1991).

Nonetheless, the development of the tourism industry was unexpectedly cut in 1974 when the Turkish invasion of the island and the illegitimate occupation of the northern part of it (37.3% of its surface) led to political instability, the collapse of the economy, social problems, the loss of many infrastructural and superstructural elements, and to a decrease of tourist arrivals to 47,000 in 1975 (Witt, 1991; Ioannidis, 2001; Sharpley, 2002). After 1974 and until 1983, the northern part of the island was controlled by Turkey and, since 1983, it is self-declared and recognized only by itself as the Turkish Republic of Northern Cyprus (Barkey and Gordon, 2001). From that period, the Cyprus government concentrated its efforts on the free un-occupied southern part of the island.

The Cyprus government had to deal with many political, economic and social problems. Regarding tourism there was a vast damage both in terms of infrastructure and image; 65% of the total bed capacity and 96% of beds under construction (Saveriades, 2000), as well as 40% of the restaurants and bars, were located in the occupied north part of the island (Witt, 1991). Moreover, Nicosia International Airport, the main entrance point for international tourists now located in the United Nations Buffer Zone, closed (Saveriades, 2000), leaving the island without access by air until February 1975 when Larnaca International airport was completed.

This grave situation brought about the need for a series of decisions to be made by the government, with many of them often been taken hastily and without much foresight. The estimation of the positive (mainly economic) impact of tourism that was probably necessary for the survival of the island that time created a mass tourism development, based on misrule and without taking into account environmental and sustainability issues (EIU, 1992). Nevertheless, all these efforts led to the recovery of the tourism industry, to the re-establishment of Cyprus as a competitive Mediterranean

destination, and gradually to the increase in the number of visits to the island.

During the 1980s, tourism became a powerful industry for the Cypriot government. In 1980, tourist arrivals on the island were 348,530 and provided CYP71 million (EUR121 million) (Cyprus Tourism Organization Information Centre, 2005) (Table 10.1). The growth continued to increase rapidly. In 1990, around 1.5 million tourists visited the island (an increase of 448% in comparison to 1980) and generated CYP573 million (EUR979 million).

The peak point in terms of arrivals was, however, noted in 2001 when approximately 2.6 million tourists arrived in the country and generated CYP 1.27 billion (EUR 2.2 billion). After that year, the arrivals of international visitors in Cyprus started to decrease. In 2009, the arrivals reached the lowest level of the decade (2.1 million tourists) and EUR 1.51 million revenues. Tourist arrivals kept decreasing during 2010, despite the optimistic forecasts of the Strategic Plan for Tourism 2000–2010 put forward by the Cyprus Tourism Organization that indicated that for 2010 the number of arrivals would reach 3.5 million tourists and an increase of expenditure per visit would also be noticed (Cyprus Tourism Organization Information Centre, 2005).

This decrease continues for several reasons. Among the main problems that the

Table 10.1. Tourist arrivals and revenues.

Year	Arrivals	Revenues (EUR million)	Revenues (CYP million)
1980	348,530	121	71
1985	769,727	439	257
1990	1,561,479	979	573
1995	2,100,000	1,384	810
2001	2,696,732	2,182	1,277
2005	2,470,063	1,733	1,014
2006	2,400,924	1,772	1,037
2007	2,416,081	1,878	1,099
2008[a]	2,403,750	1,810	
2009	2,141,193	1,510	

[a]Since 1 January 2008 the official currency of Cyprus is the EURO.
Courtesy of the Cyprus Tourism Organization Information Centre (2005) and Cyprus Tourism Organization (2010).

country currently faces are its competitiveness and the lack of application of an organized tourist strategy. During the the past
decade Cyprus has been competing with
other destinations (e.g. Turkey and Egypt)
that offer multifarious tourist elements at
much more attractive prices (Archontides,
2007). Cyprus is an expensive destination
that offers similar or fewer characteristics
than other destinations. Therefore, the only
solution for its long-term stability and
growth is to turn towards more desirable
forms of development that emphasize quality, based on a specific planned strategy.

It is obvious that the tourist development model that revitalized the Cypriot
economy during the previous decades has
reached a level of saturation and needs significant changes. Indeed, for years, the
Cypriot tourist product has a seasonal character, and is based on heliocentric elements,
the visual consumption of sea and sun, while
it is characterized by regional imparity,
attracting the majority of tourists to mostly
coastal areas and leaving inland rural areas
significantly out of the focus (Sharpley,
2002). Furthermore, even if the need for
diversification of the tourist product of the
island to deal with the situation was underlined by the authorities years ago
(Andronikou, 1986; Archontides, 2007), still
the overdependence on mass tourism is obvious. As a consequence, the Cypriot tourism
product for many years was exchangeable
more by its price and less by its quality, creating an image for the island as a sunny destination for summer vacations. Nowadays,
this image is not valid anymore. Cyprus is an
expensive sunny destination but it continues
to offer elements of questionable quality,
where other competitive destinations excel
both in quantitative and qualitative terms.

Furthermore, the recent economic crisis affected the tourism industry of Cyprus
as well. Tourist arrivals were reduced by
11.1% during August 2009, the peak month
of tourism arrivals (Rostanti, 2009), while
the forecasts for 2010 are still negative.
According to the Minister of Commerce,
Industry and Tourism of Cyprus it is estimated that the arrivals of British tourists
(the leading market in tourism) will be

reduced by 10% this year (International
Travel Report, 2009). To deal with the situation, several practices of the tourism policy
of the island have been suggested and/or
adopted. These practices were based on the
axis 'emphasis on quality' and included
several solutions such as the construction of
marinas, sports tourism development, creation of convention centres, qualitative
improvement of hospitality operations, and
general enrichment of the current tourism
product (Archontides, 2007).

The construction of golf courses on the
island was argued to be one of these
enhancements that focus on quality, at least
in terms of competition. The development
of golf courses was considered by the tourism policy as one of the most appropriate
means for diversification and the revitalization of Cyprus as a contemporary and competitive destination. However, it raised a
series of conflicts and contradictions in the
Cypriot society. These issues will be discussed in this chapter.

The Chronicle of Golf Course Development in Cyprus

The development of golf courses in Cyprus
was judged, by tourism officials, to be an
effective way to the improvement of the
tourism product of the island, in terms of
quality. This step, aimed at maximizing the
tourist revenues, mostly focused on the
North European markets and the harmonization of the seasonality problem that
threatens tourism on the island. Hence, the
revised version of the Strategic Plan for
Tourism 2000–2010, the Strategic Plan for
Tourism 2003–2010, prepared by the Cyprus
Tourism Organization (CTO), recommended
allowing the development of 14 golf courses
for the following two reasons:

1. The fulfilment of quantitative goals based
on the anticipated increase of arrivals,
increased money spent, attraction of a
'higher spending' clientele.
2. The fulfilment of goals that focus on
quality, based on the re-positioning of
Cyprus in the tourism market.

The chronology to date of the development of golf courses in Cyprus portrays three major milestones. The need for golf tourism development has been mentioned since the 1990s (Archontides, 2007). Archontides (2007) reports that, in 1993, the council of Ministers established a policy for golf-course development that also justified the construction of 750 bed spaces per course. The interest was, however, limited mostly because the potential investors did not find that the specific number of bed spaces was an attractive incentive for further development and there was no progress. Hence, only three golf courses were developed by the beginning of the new century (Archontides, 2007).

In 2003, however, the government judged that the previous policy should be reviewed. The review was completed in 2005. Incentives were given by the government for the development of 11 more golf courses in Cyprus under the framework of the readjustment of the existing tourism product (Archontides, 2007). A main plank of the updated policy was that the development of new golf courses should be in line with the simultaneous development of property and tourism.

In 2009, the council of Ministers decided to readjust the policy for the development of golf courses in Cyprus (Ministry of Finance, 2009). The final number of golf courses allowed was stabilized at 14 and each investor should pay a licence fee of EUR 5 million. Given that Cyprus has been facing a water shortage for a number of years, queries regarding the appropriateness of the construction of golf courses as a solution for both the economic recovery and the long-term sustainable development of the island were generated. For this reason, the same decision also included the condition that the water required for the golf course and associated operations should not come from the government tanks and the draining system. Instead, the provision of water for the golf courses should come solely from desalination plants that will produce the necessary amounts of water via renewable means.

The financial incentives from the development of golf tourism were enough to attract many investors. As Archontides (2007) states, since 2005, 28 investors have shown interest in the construction of golf courses on the island and nine of them had already moved to the next steps for approval. At the time of writing, four golf courses operate on the island, all of them located in the Paphos area. Two of them have operated since 2010. Archontides (1997) also mentions that the competitors of Cyprus in terms of golf tourism are Spain, Portugal and Turkey.

Contribution of Golf Tourism

Golf is a well-developed form of sports tourism. In fact, its popularity is so great that it could be characterized as a major tourism activity. Golf tourism is considered as the largest sports travel market (Tassiopoulos and Haydam, 2008). It is a distinct form of tourism that brings 60 million golfers (Readman, 2003) to 32,000 golf courses in 140 countries worldwide (Hudson and Hudson, 2010). Those golfers spend almost EUR14.5 million per year (Markwick, 2000), making golf tourism one of the most important markets within the global industry.

Readman (2003) states that golf tourists include those who travel to destinations to partake in golf activities for non-commercial purposes as well as professionals. Hudson and Hudson (2010) suggest that three types of tourists can be defined as golf tourists: those that are primarily motivated by golf and therefore travel mostly for active participation in golf activities; those that consider playing golf as an adjunct to their main travel activity; and those that have a role either as a spectator of golf tournaments or a visitor to attractions related to golf. In any case, golf is a niche market of the tourism industry that can have remarkable impacts for travel destinations.

The impacts of golf activities for a destination are multidimensional. As Hudson and Hudson (2010) point out, golf tourism is only one cluster of a whole economy that they name 'golf economy'. They mention that other clusters/subsectors are also evident in this economy: golf facility operations, golf course capital investment, golf supplies, and media tournaments, associations and charities that compose the core industries of the economy; and hospitality and tourism as real estate that compose the enabled industries of the golf economy. These subsectors are interrelated and contribute directly and indirectly to employment and general economy of a place (Hudson and Hudson, 2010).

In terms of tourism, golf has significant positive impacts for destinations. Butler (2005) suggests that golf tourism can contribute positively to the development and growth of a destination. Golf is so powerful that it can transform a place into a golf destination, such as in the case of St Andrews in Scotland. As Markwick (2000) states, golf tourism can minimize the seasonality problem of many 'warm' destinations (such as the case study Malta), and therefore can lengthen the tourist season, since many golfers that cannot play golf during the winter months in northern countries, can move to the south where the weather conditions are more appropriate. Palmer (2004) also argues that golf tourism can be developed on degraded or derelict areas that are difficult to develop for any other activity and therefore this helps in their rejuvenation. Obviously, golf tourism adds value to the tourism products of a destination by diversifying and enhancing them with new activities, facilities and services, and hence creates more competitive destinations and projects their image further (Markwick, 2000; Palmer, 2004).

Another aspect of golf tourism mentioned in the literature is related to the characteristics of golf tourists. As Henessey *et al.* (2008) suggest, golf tourists can be categorized into three types: infrequent, moderate and dedicated. Dedicated golf tourists tend to be people of older ages, dedicated players with higher income levels, who are less sensitive to price and are more significant spenders than those in the other two categories. This category of golf tourists can create significant growth in an area's tourist industry (Henessey *et al.*, 2008). Hudson and Hudson (2010) agree with the previous

authors and add that golf tourists spend more on their vacations in comparison to leisure tourists and generally are of higher-spending social groups. Finally, Correira *et al.* (2007), trying to describe the golf tourist in Algarve, Portugal, state that golf tourists in the destination are males of older ages that keep visiting Algarve repeatedly for golfing activities, mostly because of the good weather conditions and the quality of the courses.

To conclude, the above information indicates that golf tourism is a high-spending activity that attracts tourists of higher income levels and spending capability who seek quality (Tassiopoulos and Haydam, 2008). In this regard, golf tourism could be characterized as a form of tourism development that can enrich the tourism product of a destination with new infrastructure, can generate income in it, and consequently revitalize it. Hence, golf tourism, under the appropriate directions, can contribute to the competitiveness of a destination.

There are, however, also negative impacts that are related to golf tourism. For instance, golf tourism leads to an increase in road traffic and is highly characterized by elitism (Hudson and Hudson, 2010). Nonetheless, the most important negative impacts of golf tourism development are related to environmental and sustainability issues (Markwick, 2000; Gössling *et al.*, 2002; Sharpley, 2003; Dodson, 2005), and are the basis for the creation of contradictions from different stakeholders in an area, in this case Cyprus.

Sustainability and Golf Tourism in Cyprus

It is thought by some authors that the word 'sustainable' and the words 'golf course' should not even be in the same sentence (Dodson, 2005). Elements most often included in sustainability comprise ecology, society and economy. Based on this categorization, golf courses, by default, are on the list of non-ecological man-made creations. It is unknown, however, what are the social and economic dimensions and how these create (or not) a positive impact locally, in this artificial equation. If sustainability in golf courses was an equation made of equally weighted ecological, economic and societal parameters, the solution to this equation could be either balanced or heavily weighted to one or two parameters and less weighted to the other.

The economic variable in the previous sentence creates a paradox; if financial growth (and subsequently societal wealth) is emphasized, golf courses become a really positive alternative to the tourism portfolio of a country. If, on the other hand, ecology and 'environmental correctness' are of primary concern, golf does not become an option. There is indeed, therefore, a need to create sustainable golf courses that equally promote wealth and social cohesion while, at the same time, treating local and regional natural resources with respect. Cyprus is a typical illustration of the paradox mentioned above. Drought, desertification and its political problem create a mixture of environmental and land management problems that are unique to the issue of golf-course development.

Critics of golf-course development, usually from the ecological and green movement, non-governmental organizations (NGOs), professional and scientific associations, local groups and individuals, have publicized their concerns on a number of occasions (Tatnall, 1991; Pleumarom, 1992; Pearce, 1993; Platt, 1994; Schwanke, 1997; Terman, 1997; Warnken *et al.*, 2001; Farrally *et al.*, 2003; Bramwell, 2004). Most importantly, the consumption and competition for scarce resources are discussed (land, water, soil and energy) between golf developments and other activities, as are soil and water pollution, ecosystem degradation, socioeconomic inequalities and induced, often unplanned, tourism and residential development (Briassoulis, 2002). Regarding sustainability, the chapter concentrates mainly on water and land management issues as they are the most important for Cyprus.

In 2009, the Government of Cyprus gave approval for the development of golf courses, on the condition that all these developments will obtain their water resources from their own-built desalination plants powered by renewable energy sources. At the same time, it was stressed that in accordance with the decision 'no water supplies will be given over by the government to meet the needs of these facilities' (Ministry of Finance, 2009, p. 102). On the 7th of May 2010 in his opening speech of the 35th Annual Cyprus Trade Fair, the President of the Republic of Cyprus Dimitris Christofias (Cyprus Presidency, 2010) stated that 'the aim of his Government is to have fourteen golf courses developed'.

Markwick (2000), in a case study, presents Malta as far as golf tourism is concerned. The parallel between Cyprus and Malta is direct. Markwick (2000) mentions that the major negative impacts that are associated with the golf courses are connected with the amount of land required for their development, especially in a place where land is already limited. For instance, the author argues that:

> It is estimated that an 18 hole golf course requires approximately 350 tumoli or 50–60 hectares of land (the upper limit applying where steep slopes, wetlands, wooded areas or rock must be avoided); while a further 25 hectares would be needed to expand to a 27 hole course.
>
> Markwick (2000, p. 516)

Moreover, Markwick continues, the courses need a considerable amount of water for the purposes of irrigation for greens and tees. In a Mediterranean island like Cyprus, each golf course requires 1 million cubic metres of water for its maintenance (Ministry of Agriculture, Natural Resources and the Environment, 2007). Markwick (2000) also adds that other adverse impacts from the development of golf courses include the disturbance of the landscape and the natural ecosystems of an area. Dodson (2005) adds that there could be the restraint of certain countryside activities such as agriculture because of the limitation of land areas. Also, in order to maintain the quality of the green in golf courses, large amounts of fertilizers, herbicides and pesticides are needed, and of course these can harm the environment by polluting the ground and the groundwater (Hudson and Hudson, 2010; Markwick, 2000). Cyprus, being in a similar geographic location to Malta, faces the same water restrictions and the same problems.

According to Warnken *et al.* (2001), in terms of negative impacts, the greatest concern was, and still is, pollution of ground and surface waters from nutrients and pesticides (Balogh, 1992). On average, a modern golf course requires the application of around 200 kg nitrogen/ha/year and 40 kg phosphate/ha/year (Petrovic, 1990), and 2.2 kg active ingredient (a.i.) of pesticide ha/year (Kendall *et al.*, 1992). Regarding water, De Stefano (2004) reports that the average tourist in Spain consumes 440 litres per day; this value increases to 880 litres if swimming pools and golf courses exist (Gossling, 2002). Water is a particularly precious resource in Cyprus. Water protection therefore features prominently in Cyprus' environmental policy. Rainfall in Cyprus has dropped by 15% since the 1970s. Since then the country has been parched by long droughts broken briefly by occasional downpours. The Government has decided to tackle the issue through desalination; the first plant started to operate in 1997, in Dhekelia (Marangou and Savvides, 2001).

Undoubtedly, golf courses require large quantities of water (Foley and Lardner LLP, 2005). Tourist and residential water use may reach 850 litres per person per day during the summer (De Stefano, 2004; Essex *et al.*, 2004). Water consumption on golf courses may be up to 10,000 m³/ha/year, equivalent to that of 12,000 people (Mastny, 2001; Briassoulis, 2002; De Stefano, 2004). The problems become dramatic during the summer, and especially during droughts, which are very common in South-eastern Europe, with Cyprus being a representative case.

Moreover, the continuous occupation of almost 40% of the Republic, coupled with almost 10% occupied by the British Sovereign Military Bases, dramatically limits Cyprus' available space for development. Wind energy is considered to be Cyprus' best bet in increasing its renewable energy

production (despite having a lower potential than most other countries) but a range of different objections have been raised by the people living in the area concerning issues such as impact on tourism, health and the safety of their farms and family, and existence of wildlife (Ioannou and Theocharidis, 2009). This has become evident through the Government's effort to create the first wind farms in Cyprus.

In an attempt to acknowledge society's environmental concerns, the European Golf Association Ecology Unit (a branch of a golf industry association) promotes the 'Committed to Green' label, introduced in 1997 (Buckley, 2002). To date, 80 of an estimated 5200 European golf courses are involved in this pilot scheme. Accreditation criteria have not been formalized, and the scheme appears somewhat embryonic (Buckley, 2002). The European Golf Association Ecology Unit has produced several useful publications in the 1990s, leading to the Valderrama Declaration of 1999, which is an agreement between international golfing bodies and several conservation NGOs to collaborate towards common goals (Hammond *et al.*, 2007). The Valderrama Declaration recognizes the link between nature and golf, while at the same time it mentions that 'growth of the game has spread golf far beyond its original climatic region, which has led to the need to confront new challenges in the field of course design and construction, and the management of turf grass and water resources' (Golf Ecology, 2010). The agreement identifies the advantages of golfers and stakeholders working together and specifies long-term goals towards sustainability.

Of course, the existence of golf courses does not mean only negative impacts on the environment. For instance, Tanner *et al.* (2005) conducted an experimental study on the effect of golf creation on biodiversity. Based on the findings of this study that was conducted in existing golf courses, golf courses can enhance the diversity of three indicator groups (birds, ground beetles and bumblebees), relative to adjacent pasture farmland. Nonetheless, the development of golf tourism in an area with limited natural resources raises many questions and leads to a series of contradictions. These contradictions are presented below.

Contradictions for Golf Tourism in Cyprus

The decision of the Cypriot government to allow the construction of 14 golf courses in Cyprus for enhancing, in terms of quality, the existing tourism product resulted in a series of contradictions. The issues mentioned in this section are based on findings from previous research that took the form of in-depth interviews with four principal representatives of various important bodies that deal with tourism, development and environmental subjects in Cyprus. Specifically, one respondent was a representative of the hotel sector of the island and an expert on the tourism development of Cyprus since its independence. The second respondent was a representative of a construction/development company that specializes in the development of golf courses in Cyprus. The third respondent was an official from the tourism policy in Cyprus. Finally, the last respondent was an official from the environmental bodies of Cyprus and an expert on the development of golf tourism in Cyprus. The interviews took place during the first months of 2010.

From the findings of the interviews as well as through the scanning of the literature and press/review concerning golf tourism on the island, three levels of contradictions were raised and discussed below. Two of the three contradictions are related to sustainability concerns. These contradictions are interrelated since the impacts of golf tourism development are woven through all aspects of the island: societal, environmental, economic and political.

First contradiction: agriculture and golf tourism

The first contradiction mentioned in the research is related to the conflicts between the agricultural sector and the golf developers. From the findings, it was mentioned that this conflict is derived by the fact that both activities demand large land areas and high volumes of water. The respondent that supports the development of golf courses stated that before analysing the subject of the land, someone must question its possible uses apart from the development of golf courses. He asserted that the agricultural sector in Cyprus is declining for several reasons, such as labour cost, in comparison to other countries. Moreover, he considered that even if there is agricultural development in Cyprus, questions regarding the wise and productive use of resources are raised. For instance, he continued that, if agriculture needs 75% of the water supplies and contributes only 5% to the Gross Domestic Product (GDP) of the Republic, while on the other hand if tourism (including golf tourism) needs 10% of the water supplies and contributes 30% to the GDP, then it is wiser to use this resource for tourism. He added, however, that the agricultural sector is needed for the economy of the country, but there is a need to define the level that this sector contributes to the economy. He concluded that the use of the land is a strategic point and needs to be addressed by the government.

Conversely, the representative from the environmental side disagreed with the above suggestions. He argued that the percentages mentioned above come from old studies of previous years and do not represent the reality nowadays. He added that the subject of resources, especially water issues, do not have only economic impacts. Attention should also be paid to its social and environmental aspects. He added that the agricultural sector on the island is dying and not considering its support will lead to important social problems. For instance, he stated that it is preferable to give the water to many farmers in order to support their crops, and therefore have activity, than giving it to the one or two businessmen of the golf industry for watering the grass.

Another respondent, supporter of golf tourism development in Cyprus, contradicted the position of the environmentalists by arguing that agriculture indeed uses large areas of land and volumes of water but it does not contribute highly to the economy of a country. It is a fact that the agricultural sector in Cyprus is shrinking (Papadavid, 2008). Characteristically, according to Papadavid (2008), there has been a notable decrease in agriculture: in 1960 the contribution of the sector to the GDP of the country was 16% while in 2004 it was only 3%. In parallel, he continues that this decrease also occurred because of the increase of the secondary and mainly the tertiary (including tourism) sectors of production. Additionally, the respondent indicated that the cost of production per unit is very high, a point also noted by Papadavid (2008), and the challenge is how this cost can be minimized. He mentioned that, under this scope, the problems of agriculture in Cyprus are not related to the development of golf tourism per se. He underlined that the Cypriot farmers need to understand that they will have to use the new technologies to minimize the cost of production. In this regard, Papadavid (2008) suggests that there is a need for sustainable methods to be applied to agricultural development in order to manage this minimization. In conclusion, the principal representative argued that, in fact, tourism (including golf tourism) supports the agricultural industry in Cyprus by providing demand for the local agricultural products (e.g. wine).

The antithesis between the environmentalists and the supporters of golf tourism development is obvious. The main point of conflict is the use of the limited resources of the island, a problem evident in Cyprus, especially in the past few years. However, this is only one layer of the contradictions resulting from the golf tourism development in the island of Cyprus. The second layer of contradictions is associated mostly with competitive terms rather than sustainable issues, and includes the existing hospitality industry and tourism development on the island and the development of golf tourism.

Second contradiction: hospitality, real estate development and golf tourism

The second contradiction is related to real-estate developers and the hospitality sector, largely the existing tourism industry of the island. There are some people who believe the development of golf courses for tourism purposes is just an excuse to justify the huge construction movements relating to this development. For instance, Yacoumis (2005) argues that golf course development is actually a real-estate development. He points out that each golf course in Cyprus will have its own residential capacity and that the on-site residents will have special treatment and priority for participating in golf activities, in comparison to the tourists of the island, creating limited space for tourists' participation. Yacoumis (2007) recognizes that indeed golf could be a potential means for diversification of Cyprus' existing tourism product, but this will happen only with the close cooperation of beach hotels (that comprise the majority of the hotels in Cyprus) and the golf industry. Nonetheless, he continues that since each golf course will develop its own residential units and resort/s, it will automatically raise the demand for the golfing facilities internally (residents/guests of golf properties), leaving those tourists who are recreational golfers residing in beach hotels and wishing to play golf, without spare playing capacity or with playing capacity at expensive prices. Yacoumis (2007) concludes that the development of golf for tourism purposes is just an excuse for satisfying the interests of real-estate developers, leaving the actual tourism industry (and its demand) out of focus.

Obviously, the golf developers have a different opinion about the above argument. As mentioned by one respondent representing the construction side of golf courses, the owners of properties in golf areas have some privileges such as a discount on the price for playing golf and 20% of the rounds played. However, he mentioned that the remaining 80% of golf space is provided to tourists. Golf tourists can book space through several distributors such as travel agents abroad or through hotels; therefore, the facilities are available to everyone. He concluded that, in fact, golf tourism supports tourism development in terms of quality, and increases the average spend per day, while at the same time minimizing the seasonality problem. The hospitality sector benefits from the golf courses development because they can have guests – golf tourists – even during the low period in winter months.

Another respondent representing the hotel and tourism sectors of the island indicated that without a doubt the real-estate industry supports the development of golf courses. However, he pointed out that many hotels in Cyprus have been upgraded in order to offer services of better quality. Since golf tourism attracts people of higher income levels with more sophisticated demands, those hotels can meet their expectations by offering what they need. However, he mentioned that the tourism model has been changed and/or expanded. Besides those residing in hotels, there are also more tourists with second homes in the destination. Some tourists decide to use the real-estate units for second homes or they rent them for a specific period of time through timesharing, single or multiple ownership. These variations are an evolution of tourism since the traditional tourism product with people residing only in hotels has been changed. In these circumstances, therefore, the developers operate in synergy with tourism and they are not necessarily 'enemies'. To conclude, there is interdependency between these two industries as well as mutual benefits.

Third contradiction: environment and golf tourism

This is perhaps the most noticeable contradiction. The fundamental dilemma critics and supporters face, when it comes to golf development, has to do with the contradiction between profit and environmental intervention. Indeed a successful and carefully planned golf development will generate profits for the owners /managers as well as the government but as one of the respondents put it: 'any building, let alone a golf development becomes an irreversible intervention' (in the environment).

The golf development critics raise a number of concerns related to sustainability and the environment. While a representative from the golf developers side reported that: '9,000 olive trees were planted, 3,000 more than those promised and 21,000 bushes in total, to counterbalance the environmental intervention we had to make', a representative from the other side, the environmentalists argued that: 'the olive trees will not be planted but they will merely be moved from other parts of the country as an olive tree to grow will require a number of years'. Therefore, there is no actual contribution from the developers' side rather than the shifts of trees from one place to another.

The number of golf courses is also a point of concern for those against golf development. The official of the tourism policy stated that with the existing mass model of tourism development, Cyprus loses: there is an environmental cost because the island is too small for accepting millions of tourists annually and, in parallel a cultural deterioration, the expenses for meeting of the needs of masses of tourists would be very high, high seasonality problems, low average spending per tourist, and so on. All these problems required turning towards a model of tourist development that would attract fewer numbers of tourists but higher income levels, with greater average spending, and during the whole year in order to balance the demand between the high and low periods. As the same respondent argued, golf tourism was an option to provide these benefits to the tourism industry of Cyprus and could operate successfully during the winter months because of the mild weather conditions. Considering that in order for golfers to play golf during the winter months they travel to distant 'exotic' destinations that can provide better weather conditions, Cyprus was judged to be an ideal sunny golf destination that is not so far from the Northern European markets. To meet the expectations of the golf tourists for variations in courses and to make Cyprus a competitive destination on the map of golf destinations, the number of golf courses was judged to be at least eight and even more. Hence, the government has announced plans to permit the development of 14 golf courses.

Obviously, as mentioned earlier, the construction of golf courses should be accompanied by a series of measures for minimizing their negative impacts as far as sustainability and stewardship is concerned. However, this decision is highly criticized by those representing the environmental point of view. As a respondent of those against golf developments stated: 'no golf courses! If we have to have them anyway, let's only have one or two of them'. The environmentalists argue that for maintaining 14 golf courses there is a need for water that equals one sixth of the average quantity of water in all the water tanks of the island (Cyprusgreens, 2010). The need for watering golf courses is dependent on the current climatologic conditions of an area. In Mediterranean climates, the maximum water consumption of a golf course is 1 million cubic metres per year (Ministry of Agriculture, Natural Resources and the Environment, 2007). Considering that the Water Development Department of Cyprus (2010) states that the water consumption for water services in the island (annual average for 2005–2007) was 79,899,054 cubic metres, then indeed the environmentalists' argument is correct. Hence, this number of golf courses, even if it will give revenues from golf tourism, potentially may harm the water resources of the place.

It is evident that water is a sticking point, especially given the scarcity of water resources in Cyprus. According to the critics: 'a single stay tourist consumes twice the amount of water the average Cypriot does'. The representative of the environmentalists argued that: 'the government promised to enforce the provision of water for the golf courses through desalination plants but this is done without conducting an environmental assessment'. In this regard, the respondent from the development of golf courses argued that the government set a series of conditions for constructing golf courses with the most significant the desalination schemes based on renewable sources of energy. According to him, despite the fact that desalination plants are quite a costly investment, they guarantee the needed quantities of water for the courses through-

out the year. Therefore, they can provide the amounts of water for maintaining the quality of the grass at the desirable (for the golfers and for the sport itself) level. Moreover, the use of alternative sources of energy is also a costly investment but, again, developers are willing to invest that money for providing the necessary quantities of water. Finally, he concluded that in order to obtain the licence to construct their golf course, the government obliged them to conduct a series of environmental impact studies.

Regarding the use of water, the representative from the tourism policy argued that in every project someone has to measure the negative and the positive points: 'in absolute terms I don't believe that there is development that is environmentally friendly'. We should therefore also consider the needs of each tourist among millions of them annually, in terms of water or energy consumption. As he argued, in the case of golf, desalination is a solution and, despite its high energy requirement, it could be an efficient way to provide water for the courses. Besides, the operation of the desalination units is based on renewable sources of energy. However, he suggested that tourism policy should focus on the introduction of a large central desalination hub that would provide water to every golf course on the island, instead of having the current situation where each golf course has its own independent desalination station. More desalination stations mean further use of energy and more cost to each investor. Nevertheless, even in this case, the environmentalists argue that the environmental danger is great and there will always be the need to monitor the sea and the coast (Cyprusgreens, 2010).

For the renewable sources of energy and the limitation in space that makes their installation difficult, the tourism expert pointed out that the government should give incentives to the developers in order for them to devote a part of their space to constructing renewable forms of energy such as solar panels and windmills: 'you need to allow the investor to build with his own cost on his land the wind or solar parks'. He concluded that the government does not give incentives to the investors and hence both of the parties lose.

Another point of contradiction between the environmentalists, tourism policy and developers is the deterioration of the landscape. As one of the respondents representing golf development critics stated: 'there are no aesthetic parameters included in the design of the new developments; there will be electricity provision, new roads and impact on nature'. The tourism policy official recognized that indeed, the development of golf courses has impacts on the environment. The aim, however, is to minimize these negative impacts. In this respect, the respondent representing the developers' point of view emphasizes that in their golf area all the buildings must respect the architecture of the landscape by using specific materials that will be in harmony with the surrounding natural and cultural environment of the area, and all the cables are located below ground.

What about the opinions of the host community for the development of golf courses in Cyprus? Apparently, it was mentioned that the host communities want the development of golf courses because they see a growth in their area from their operation. In fact, there is another contradiction between the local communities and environmentalists. The local communities consider the development of golf courses in their areas as a chance for further development, and thus economic growth (Ioannou, 2010). On the other hand, the respondent of the environmentalists' side argued that the local communities just want money and therefore will give their land for the purposes of golf development.

In conclusion, all the contradictions mentioned above justify that where there is any type of development being considered, there are also conflicted interests. In the case of Cyprus, it is evident that a development like golf tourism has and will have several impacts, positive and negative. Since this action has already been adopted, the aim is to focus on the harmonization of the contradictions so that a balance in golf-tourism development can be found.

Conclusion

The case of golf tourism development in Cyprus is a representative paradigm where the need for competitiveness and economic growth through tourism development battles against the need for stewardship and balanced use of the limited resources. Many stakeholders contribute to the formation and implementation of the promising plan to transform the eastern Mediterranean island into a competitive golf destination. Furthermore, the government of Cyprus has already decided to operate 14 golf courses on the island and licences have been given to the interested parties. Since the construction of the remaining golf courses is a matter of time, efforts have to be made to neutralize the negative impacts that this development already has caused or will result in.

For this reason, the tourism policy must focus on monitoring these impacts and when it is necessary to limit 'harmful' activities. In effect, this monitoring must be systematic and periodical, and should include environmental indicators not only prior to the construction of any golf course but also during its operation by tactically measuring the use of resources and supervising any procedure. The aforementioned, centralized desalination plant would probably be an effective solution for the appropriate management and dissemination of water resources. The plant could provide more potential for the minimization of the environmental cost, by operating more sustainably and providing water to every golf unit on the island (therefore controlling water use more efficiently). Moreover, the renewable sources of energy in the golf courses areas should also be an alternative option for their operations.

In addition, the golf course developers and managers should proceed through a series of thorough and structured best management practices as far as water usage is concerned. These management practices should focus on the appropriate use of any deposits of water available in a country where water is precious. As Dodson (2005) argues, the best management practices must include preventative and structural controls. The preventative measures will need to have a defensive character in an integrated storm management system. The structural controls, on the other hand, should be interventions 'designed to remove, filter, detain, or reroute potential contaminants carried in surface water' (Dodson, 2005, p. 127). The best management practices should operate in harmony with the environmental standards.

The appropriate management of golf courses could be aided by the application of a formal, accredited system of management such as ISO 14001 for golf courses (Hammond and Hudson, 2007). Hammond and Hudson (2007) argue that not many golf courses have developed this system, mostly because it requires a relatively high cost in terms of auditing, training and accreditation. However, they mention that there are representative examples of the successful adaptation of these systems to golf courses such as the Dubai-based Tower Links Golf Club, which is the first grassed golf club to be constructed north of Dubai that received ISO 14001 certification, in 2003. The ISO 14001 certification would be an opportunity for Cypriot developers to prove to their critics that indeed they take seriously the sustainable development of golf tourism in Cyprus and that they consider the environment by using green practices. Additionally, it would contribute to the branding of their operations and to the enhancement of their image.

Another, important point is the harmonization of the contradiction between the 'suspicious' hoteliers and the developers of golf courses. The tourism policy needs to have a strategy that would guarantee and ensure to the hospitality industry of the island that the golf course developers need to work closely with them

for their own long-term survival and growth. This strategy should be more than a communication tool; it should actively contribute to the synergy between these two stakeholders since one generates demand to the other.

Future research needs to focus on the optimization of water use. Despite the efforts of the policies in warm destinations to collect water for the summer seasons, still vast quantities of water stay unutilized and remain, in the case of Cyprus, in the sea. Hence, the challenge is how this water should be collected and used for the needs of golf tourism. Furthermore, renewable sources are a promising way to produce energy for the development of golf tourism, but still their adaptation is at a relatively early stage. Future research should concentrate on the reasons that this is happening, and on the lost potential and opportunities that the appropriate utilization of the sun and the wind (both of them dominate in Cyprus) would offer for golf tourism.

Finally, the case study of Cyprus demonstrates that micro-political interests play a pivotal role in any decision taken, including those of tourism development. While many people who recognize that mass tourism is no longer a solution for the island still wonder if the option of golf tourism development is a viable solution, emphasis must be given to how these decisions are taken and if there is short- or long-term planning behind them. Future analysis is vital for understanding the role of each stakeholder in the decision-making process and must focus on the relative importance of each decision taken and who should be taking it. Clearly, the policy bodies are the responsible decision makers but are these decisions made on the basis of solid viability studies, or do they just serve the interests of various stakeholders? Obviously, this question is a sensitive matter and comprises the basis of many contradictions in many places worldwide; more research would offer a valuable insight into how issues of economic development, social growth and environmental stability work together.

References

Andronikou, A. (1986) Cyprus - management of the tourism sector. *Tourism Management* 7, 127–129.

Archontides, Y.K. (2007) *Review of Cypriot Tourism: Through a Series of Articles, Interviews and Speeches.* A.A. Livani, Athens, Greece.

Balogh, J.C., Gibeault, V.A., Walker, W.J., Kenna, M.P. and Snow, J.T. (1992) Background and overview of environmental issues. In: Balogh, J.C. and Walker, W.J. (eds) *Course Management and Construction: Environmental Issues.* Lewis Publishers, Boca Raton, Florida, pp. 355–439.

Barkey, H.J. and Gordon, P.H. (2001) Cyprus: the predictable crisis. *The National Interest* 66, 83–94.

Bramwell, B. (2004) Mass tourism, diversification and sustainability in southern Europe's coastal regions. In: Bramwell, B. (ed.) *Coastal Mass Tourism: Diversification and Sustainable Development in Southern Europe.* Channel View Publications, Clevedon, UK, pp. 1–31.

Briassoulis, H. (2002) Sustainable tourism and the question of the commons. *Annals of Tourism Research* 29, 1065–1085.

Buckley, R. (2002) Tourism ecolabels. *Annals of Tourism Research* 29, 183–208.

Butler, R. (2005) The influence of sport destination development: the example of golf at St Andrews, Scotland. In: Higham, J. (ed.) *Sport Tourism Destinations.* Elsevier Butterworth-Heinemann, Oxford, UK, pp. 275–282.

Correia, A., Barros, C.P. and Silvestre, A.L. (2007) Golf tourism repeat choice behaviour in the Algarve: a mixed logit approach. *Tourism Economics* 13, 111–127.

Cyprusgreens (2010) Water and Golf Courses. Available at: http://www.cyprusgreens.org/golf.htm (accessed 19 June 2010).

Cyprus Presidency Official Website (2010) Opening speech of His Excellency the President of the Republic of Cyprus Mr Dimitris Christofias of the 35th Annual Cyprus Trade Fair. Available at: http://www.presidency. gov.cy (accessed 17 October 2010).

Cyprus Tourism Organization (2010) Cyprus tourism in figures, report, p. 1–4. Available at: http://www.visitcyprus. biz/wps/wcm/connect/83ea3a0041b24860980fbb96df2798e0/Cyprus+Tourism+in+Figures+2009.pdf? MOD=AJPERES&CACHEID=83ea3a0041b24860980fbb96df2798e0 (accessed 29 July 2010).

Cyprus Tourism Organization Information Centre (2005) Tourism. In: Dew, P. (ed.) *Doing Business with the Republic of Cyprus.* Global Market Briefings, London, pp. 26–33.

De Stefano, L. (2004) Freshwater and Tourism in the Mediterranean. WWF, Mediterranean Programme. Available at: http://assets.panda.org/downloads/medpotourismreportfinal_ofnc.pdf (accessed 18 September 2010).

Dodson, R.G. (2005) *Sustainable Golf Courses: A Guide to Environmental Stewardship.* Wiley, New Jersey.

EIU (1992) Cyprus, *International Tourism Reports* 2, 43–64.

Essex, S., Kent, M. and Newnham, R. (2004) Tourism development in Mallorca: is water supply a constraint? *Journal of Sustainable Tourism* 12, 4–28.

Farrally, M.R., Cochran, A.J., Crews, D.J., Price, R.J., Hurdzan, M.J., Snow, J.T. and Thomas, P.R. (2003) Golf science research at the beginning of the twenty-first century. *Journal of Sports Sciences* 21, 753–765.

Foley and Lardner LLP (2005) Golf survey: results and industry outlook. Available at: http://www.foley.com/ files/tbl_s31Publications/FileUpload137/3471/Golf%20Industry%20Outlook%20Survey%20Report.pdf (accessed 16 February 2010).

Golf Ecology (2010) The Valderrama Declaration. Available at: http://www.golfecology.co.uk/articles/valdec. html (accessed 17 December 2010).

Gössling, S. (2002) Global environmental consequences of tourism. *Global Environmental Change* 12, 283–302.

Gössling, S., Hansson, C.B., Hoörstmeier, O. and Saggel, S. (2002) Ecological footprint analysis as a tool to assess tourism sustainability. *Ecological Economics* 43, 199–211.

Hammond R.A. and Hudson M.D. (2007) Environmental management of UK golf courses for biodiversity-attitudes and actions. *Landscape and Urban Planning* 83, 127–136.

Henessey, S.M., MacDonald, R. and MacEachern, M. (2008) A framework for understanding golfing visitors to a destination. *Journal of Sport & Tourism* 13, 5–35.

Hudson, S. and Hudson, L. (2010) *Golf Tourism.* Goodfellow Publishers, Oxford, UK.

International Travel Report. (2009) British tourist arrivals are estimated to be reduced by 10% on 2010. Available at: http://www.intravelreport.gr/?p=5177 (accessed 23 December 2009).

Ioannides, D. (1992) Tourism development agents: the Cypriot resort cycle. *Annals of Tourism Research* 19, 711–731.

Ioannides, D. (2001) The dynamics and effects of tourism evolution in Cyprus. In: Apostolopoulos, Y., Loukissas, P. and Leontidou, L. (eds) *Mediterranean Tourism: Facets of Socioeconomic Development and Cultural Change*. Routledge, London and New York, pp. 112–128.

Ioannou, G. (2010) Blocking golf courses. Available at: http://www.sigmalive.com/simerini/news/258487 (accessed 14 June 2010).

Ioannou, I. and Theocharidis, D. (2009) Agripolicy: analysis of renewable energy and its impact on rural development in Cyprus. Available at: http://www.euroqualityfiles.net/AgriPolicy/Report%202.2/AgriPolicy%20WP2D2%20Cyprus%20Final.pdf (accessed 15 January 2010).

Kendall, R.J., Brewer, L.W., Hitchcock, R.R. and Mayer, J.R. (1992) American widgeon mortality associated with turf application of diazinon AG500. *Journal of Wildlife Disease* 28, 263–267.

Koutsakos, E. and Moxey, D. (2008) Larnaca desalination plant, Cyprus – from an efficient to an effective plant operation. *Desalination* 221, 84–91.

Koutsakos, E., Savvides, K. and Savva, K. (2005) Larnaca desalination plant operation – a client and contractor perspective. *Desalination and the Environment* 184, 157–164.

Marangou, V.S. and Savvides, K. (2001) First desalination plant in Cyprus product water aggressivity and corrosion control. *Desalination* 138, 251–258.

Markwick, M.C. (2000) Golf tourism development, stakeholders, differing discourses and alternative agendas: the case of Malta. *Tourism Management* 21, 515–524.

Mastny, L. (2001) *Travelling Light: New Paths for International Tourism*. Worldwatch Institute, Washington, DC.

Ministry of Agriculture, Natural Resources and the Environment (2007) Study of environmental impact assessment for the desalination plant of the company Medgolf Properties. Available at: http://www.cyprus.gov.cy/moa/agriculture.nsf/All/5F377582BB4A0B8BC22577A000274EA8/$file/5-2007.%CE%B2.pdf?OpenElement (accessed 16 November 2010).

Ministry of Finance (2009) *Official Newspaper of the Cypriot Democracy*. Decisions of the Council of Ministers, Appendix 4, Part 1, No. 4214, Nicosia, Cyprus.

Palmer, C. (2004) More than just a game: the consequences of golf tourism. In: Ritchie, B.W. and Adair, D. (eds) *Sport Tourism: Interrelationships, Impacts and Issues*. Channel View Publications, Clevedon, UK pp. 117–134.

Papadavid, G. (2008) Review of agricultural economy and the integration of agricultural trade of Cyprus in the wider European agricultural market. Available at: http://www.ari.gov.cy/content/pdf/ANASKOPHSH%20agr%20econ.pdf (accessed 16 October 2010).

Pearce, F. (1993) How green is your golf? *New Scientist* 139, 30–35.

Petrovic, A.M. (1990) The fate of nitrogenous fertilizers applied to turf grass. *Journal of Environmental Quality* 19, 1–14.

Platt, A.E. (1994) *Toxic Green: The Trouble with Golf*. Worldwatch Institute, Washington, DC.

Pleumarom, A. (1992) Course and effect: golf tourism in Thailand. *The Ecologist* 22, 104–110.

Readman, M. (2003) Golf tourism. In: Hudson, S. (ed.) *Sport and Adventure Tourism*. The Haworth Hospitality Press, Oxford, UK, pp. 165–201.

Rostanti, N. (2009) New decrease in tourist arrivals. Available at: http://www.politis.com.cy/cgibin/hweb?-A=895524&-V=archivearticles (accessed 23 December 2009).

Saveriades. A. (2000) Establishing the social tourism capacity for the tourist resorts of the east coast of the Republic of Cyprus. *Tourism Management* 21, 147–156.

Schwanke, D. (1997) *Resort Development Handbook*. The Urban Land Institute, Washington, DC.

Sharpley, R. (2002) Rural tourism and the challenge of tourism diversification: the case of Cyprus. *Tourism Management* 23, 233–244.

Sharpley, R. (2003) Tourism, modernisation and development on the island of Cyprus: challenges and policy responses. *Journal of Sustainable Tourism* 1, 246–265.

Tanner, R.A. and Gange, A.C. (2005) Effects of golf courses on local biodiversity. *Landscape and Urban Planning* 7, 137–146.

Tassiopoulos, D. and Haydam, N. (2008) Golf tourists in South Africa: a demand-side study of a niche market in sports tourism. *Tourism Management* 29, 870–882.

Tatnall, T. (1991) How 'green' is your golf course? *Parks and Recreation* 26, 30–32.

Terman, M.R. (1997) Natural links: naturalistic golf courses as wildlife habitat. *Landscape and Urban Planning* 38,183–197.

Warnken, J., Thompson, D. and Zakus, D.H. (2001) Golf course development in a major tourist destination: implications for planning and management. *Environmental Management* 27, 681–696.

The concept of 'residential tourism' has been used since the late 1970s (Jurdao, 1979) to explain the transformations brought about by the construction of property in tourist areas, and the configuration of two types of human mobility closely related to each other in the Mediterranean world: tourism and lifestyle migration. 'Residential tourists' are usually identified with second-home users. In fact, many dwellings evolve from being a holiday home to being something closer to a primary residence, as their users go from a tourist status to a status resembling that of an immigrant. Over the past few years, this concept has been used to refer to very different situations (Casado, 1999; Leontidou and Marmaras, 2001; Rodríguez, 2001; Salvà, 2002; Mazón, 2006; Haug et al., 2007; O'Reilly, 2007a, 2009; Mantecón and Huete, 2008; Benson and O'Reilly, 2009; Huete, 2009; Mazón et al., 2009; McWatters, 2009; Mantecón, 2010). When they delve into this reality, researchers question the worth of an expression that categorizes as tourists those people who intend to stay indefinitely in the tourist destination, and who often own property and are registered with their local council. Tourism involves an escape from the daily routine but the protagonists of residential tourism often do not seek to get away from the everyday life associated with their jobs. They are mainly retirees trying to redefine their daily life (in one, two or more homes) in an environment other than that where their working life took place. Consequently, explaining this requires approaches that place these processes on a continuum with a wide range of mobility types, whose nature – tourism or migration – is sometimes unclear (Williams and Hall, 2000, 2002; King, 2002; O'Reilly, 2003; Hall and Müller, 2004; Urry, 2007; Benson and O'Reilly, 2009; Huete, 2009; Janoschka, 2009; O'Reilly and Benson, 2009).

The concept of residential tourism itself is debatable since it comprises two contradictory terms. For instance, Karen O'Reilly (2007a) accepted the notion of residential tourism after acknowledging that the semantic contradiction of this expression enables researchers to highlight the tensions that appear in a social system where different types of mobility and residential strategies converge. The complexity of these new social realities has led her to use in her latest publications the notion of 'lifestyle migration', which provides a conceptual framework that helps her to explain the new migration forms. These forms have more to do with self-realization projects, and the search for an intangible 'good life' than with strictly productive activities. Lifestyle migration transcends and encompasses the usual umbrella concepts: second-home ownership, retirement migration, seasonal migration, international counter urbanization or leisure migration. In this respect, residential tourism is the best known of the different types of 'lifestyle migration', and Spain, the country where it has left a more profound mark (Benson and O'Reilly, 2009; O'Reilly and Benson, 2009). Mason McWatters (2009) also defends the concept of residential tourism in terms of its being useful to include different temporary situations, and, above all, because it takes into account the wishes of those who move to settle in their new home indefinitely.

The conceptual problem of residential tourism is linked to the development of modern multi-residential strategies, emergent transnational lifestyles, and intra-European migration patterns, the dynamics of which have become very complex (Williams et al., 1997, 2000; King et al., 1998; Rodríguez et al., 1998, 2004; Gustafson, 2001, 2008, 2009; King, 2002; O'Reilly, 2003, 2007b; Oliver, 2007; Benson, 2010). In the end, it is a matter of deciding how we are going to consider these people who spend more or less extended periods of time in property located in tourist areas, or their areas of influence, motivated by reasons more related to their search for a place where they can enjoy their leisure than a place to carry out an economic activity. Retirees make up the largest and most thoroughly studied group (International Retirement Migration). However, it is worth noting that during the past few years, and particularly in the case of Spain, the debate has intensified because of the increasing number of young British families that move to Spain to start a new life, and also because of the movements of actual transnational citizens that travel frequently between Spain and their home country (O'Reilly, 2007b).

A Case Study on Spain's Mediterranean Coast

The fact that residential tourism has spread in the past few years over so many different places in the world has brought about numerous effects (as a consequence of the cultural, economic, legal, geographic, environmental (etc.) characteristics of each region). However, our explanation is based on a case that, in our opinion, illustrates clearly this phenomenon, since the dynamics (and contradictions) of residential tourism have shown in this region with more intensity and for longer than anywhere else. Spain may be the country with more experience about the consequences of this phenomenon because the socio-economic modernization of Spain has partly been based on residential tourism (Mantecón, 2010), particularly on the Mediterranean coast. Thus, our explanation refers to the Mediterranean region where, for 50 years, the effects of residential tourism are clearly visible: the Costa Blanca. The coastal area of the Alicante province (south-east Spain) is known as Costa Blanca. It had, in 2010, a registered population of 1,921,988 inhabitants living in an area of 5,817.5 km². These are the official figures but it is estimated that the actual population during summer peak periods exceeds 2,500,000 inhabitants. Of the registered population, 15% comes from within the EU, but this figure goes up to 25% among the population aged over 65. According to official figures, there are 130,286 British nationals (34% of all the British citizens who reside in Spain) and 36,531 German nationals (19%) living on the Costa Blanca. In several towns there are more European citizens than Spanish nationals registered. An extreme case is the town of San Fulgencio: 78% of the registered population are foreign citizens and 92% of those come from other countries

within the EU. In fact, the Costa Blanca is the Spanish region where more houses were sold to foreign citizens in the first decade of the 21st century.

This region is a prime example of the mass tourism development paradigm. The tourism industry has been, for more than 40 years, the leading economic activity in most of the province's towns. Here we must consider tourism as an industry related, to a large extent, to the property development business. Thus, we cannot distinguish between tourism and urbanization processes when talking about this region's development. The urbanization initiatives have traditionally been focused on foreign, residential tourists, particularly from the Scandinavian countries, Germany and the UK.

The evolution of second-home property in the Alicante province is enlightening. There were 41,297 second homes in 1960. In 1981 the number had risen to 686,332 houses, and 20 years later, in 2001, the province had 1,008,909 second homes. An association created by Spain's best-selling real estate agents, specialized in holiday homes, estimates that approximately 1,200,000 dwellings are currently used as second homes on the Costa Blanca.

Social problems Linked to the (non-) Definition of the Situation

The development of residential tourism in Spain has led to two main types of problems: environmental and social. Among the environmental impacts we must draw attention to the excessive exploitation of the region's scarce water resources, and the destruction of natural areas of immense value due to the aggressive process of urbanization of the territory (Vera and Ivars, 2003). However, the purpose of this chapter is to focus on the social impacts of residential tourism, mainly associated with socio-demographic changes, and the lack of definition of a complex social situation.

Defining the situation is crucial to area and land-use planning. Local management is determined by the resources available to local councils, which are justified through the information gathered by official statistics regarding population and housing. In Spain, this problem is exacerbated by the central government's tendency to devolve powers to local governments. The country's legal system sometimes gives rise to baffling situations. For instance, the act that regulates the funding of local councils establishes certain conditions that a town must meet to be categorized as a 'tourist town' and thus have access to specific funding: it cannot be the capital of a province or a region (known in Spanish as *comunidad autónoma*), it must have between 20,000 and 75,000 registered inhabitants, and second homes must outnumber primary residences. Only 21 towns in the country meet these criteria.

The presence of European retirees on the Spanish coasts has contrasting consequences. On the one hand, they generate an important economic activity (real estate, trade/consumption, facilities, etc.) that stimulates the offer of personal, health and elderly care services; they also contribute to the urbanization and vitality of relatively neglected areas. On the other hand, under-registration is an obvious problem (since there are not exact figures about the actual number of residents), which has become a challenge for the administration, and particularly, for local and health authorities. The fiscal problem is also an economic one, as many of these immigrants usually keep their productive investments (and tax payments) outside the region and Spain, although no data to quantify this impact are available.

The healthcare question

The Spanish Health Act 1986 establishes the free and universal coverage of healthcare services. In implementing the Act the country's healthcare system guarantees a wide access to it for the foreign population. The Spanish media point out that the public healthcare system recoups only a part of the cost of the healthcare provided to tourists and residents. An ageing population, as a result of the arrival of senior tourists and migrants, generates costs that local Spanish authorities find difficult to meet. This situation becomes more complex when we consider the different political and administrative levels involved. Currently, the regions are responsible for healthcare planning, public health, and healthcare services through their own Health Service, which may lead to conflicts about the amount to be transferred (Schriewer and Rodes, 2006). At the time of writing this chapter, the health ministers of the EU member states, through the initiative of the Spanish government, passed a resolution to restrict what is known as 'healthcare tourism', that is, the practice of travelling to another EU country to obtain healthcare according to the different advantages offered by each national healthcare system. With new measures that derive from this recent resolution, the patient's home country and country of residence will share the cost of the treatment.

At the same time, we have insufficient empirical evidence to help determine the extent to which these foreign residents go back to their home countries when they become ill, although some researchers have shown an interest in analysing this question (Giner and Simó, 2009). As Janine Schildt (2010), and Klaus Schriewer and Joaquín Rodes (2006) have pointed out in regard to the case of German and British lifestyle migrants in southern Spain, a great number of these citizens are not included in official statistics because they are reluctant to regularize their status as residents. They fear that they might no longer be eligible for social services in their home country, and that a change in their tax residence might have a negative impact on their finances. Schildt distinguishes two types of dependent lifestyle migrants. Obviously, we can find different cases between both types. At one extreme there is a privileged group of migrants that are reluctant to use Spanish services (because they have difficulties in communicating or they do not trust the quality of the services), and have enough economic resources to access private healthcare services, or healthcare at home provided by competent professionals from their home country. At the other extreme, Schildt identifies a type of residents in a situation of risk, who live alone, receive a low retirement pension, have no contacts (relatives or friends) in their home country, and do not take part in social networks in Spain, all of which ends up isolating them. La Parra and Mateo (2008), and Huber and O'Reilly (2004) have warned about the gradual increase in the number of lifestyle migrants that experience such isolation associated with the proliferation of residents with mental health problems (anxiety/depression), and the increase in alcohol intake and tobacco use.

In this respect, one of the most obvious culture shocks happens when northern European retirees realize that social assistance directed at the elderly (linked to the Spanish Welfare State) is only effective when it is complemented with informal (but significant) help from relatives. Connected to this, the creation of jobs meant to meet the specific demand for social and healthcare services is expected to grow in the next few years. As a matter fact, new legal and consultancy services, specially directed at foreigners, are appearing, while young immigrants arrive and try, with no knowledge of Spanish, to set up property maintenance companies.

Political implications

Another increasingly important issue is the extension of political representation and participation rights in local elections to the citizens of all the EU member states. The proportion of foreign voters could, in some towns, decide the result of a local election. The increasing electoral weight of these groups, the appearance of volunteer organizations that carry out neighbourhood watch tasks (unusual in Spain) in coordination with the police, the emergence of environmental groups against property speculation, etc., show a reality that transcends what is considered 'tourism' in the strict sense of the term.

As Janoschka (2009) has reported in the context of Latin America, the collective social action of lifestyle migrants is an attempt to become a body of social actors able to influence the decision-making process in the local political agenda of their new (sometimes only temporary) place of residence. The action of these groups of residents eventually transforms the local political dynamic, and gives rise to new systems of alliances and influences. Over the past few years there has been an increase in the number of towns located in the tourist regions of southern Spain where the main political parties have included European citizens in their organization. In fact, 25 local councils in the Alicante province have a councillor working exclusively on matters related to this group of residents. In some towns, the associations of European residents have organized themselves politically. In San Fulgencio, for instance, they managed to win 7 out of 14 council seats (three went to British nationals) in the local elections held in 2007. With these new political associations, northern European citizens are trying to leave behind their image among the Spanish of mere consumers, heterogeneous and confused, of a tourist space. They are attempting to achieve a functional reorganization of the human relationships in an urban space whose morphology does not often meet the needs of its residents. This is determined by the creation of a dual or parallel space, where the urban centre of management is geographically and culturally apart from the social reality in which the interactions take place. Thus, the perception of the problems experienced by the peripheral housing estates, and the decision to set up associations to try to solve them reinforce the sense of belonging to the community.

The political organization of European residents, aimed at claiming their rights more effectively, may give rise to different reactions within the host society. However, as long as they are regarded as tourists (or residential tourists) Spanish society will not be aware of this new reality. Spaniards perceive European residents (regardless of whether or not they are retirees) as tourists or foreigners, but not as immigrants, a term applied only to citizens from countries with worse working conditions (Mantecón, 2010). Local, regional and central governments will have to accept the new multi-national and multi-cultural reality that these new migration patterns, either residential or related to the labour market, entail. Moreover, they will have to be capable of implementing integration policies more active than festivals and occasional meetings.

The EU member states struggle over the ideal of 'European citizenship' and social Europe, on the one hand, and their resistance to lose control of social policies, health systems and social security expenditure, on the other (Ackers and Dwyer, 2004; Schriewer and Rodes, 2006).

Limited interaction

The infrequent interactions between Spanish and European citizens, caused by the lack of communication resulting from their ignorance of their respective languages, and their socio-spatial separation, emphasize the perception of EU citizens as 'visitors'. Nevertheless, the frequency with which European residents use public services allows us to infer that there are different interaction patterns, particularly, a fluid relationship between European retirees and Spanish public institutions, and a weaker relationship between European citizens and Spanish ones. The low level of daily interaction between European residents and Spaniards, together with the low level of integration that the latter demand from these residents, facilitates their being regarded as a group difficult to categorize, but easily identifiable, and in any case, as an unproblematic social group. The relative isolation of European residents that Spanish society perceives as deliberate, feeds back into this insight, which is close to a stereotype. The media play a key role in the construction of the social image of the European residents. They generally refer to them with the terms residential tourist or European resident. The word

'immigrant', as mentioned above, is applied to people who come from a poor country, usually looking for work, and is rarely applied to the other European residents (except those from eastern Europe and Portugal) living in the Alicante province, irrespective of whether or not they are retirees. Furthermore, the connotations of the word 'tourist' among the Spaniards (related to the temporary stays of visitors, with economic benefits for the towns) create a lack of interest in the difficulties of interacting, and suppress prejudices and possible conflicts (Barke, 1999).

The situation is, however, in certain cases much more serious than we may think. An enlightening paper (O'Reilly, 2007b), based on the results from a sociological and ethnographic study carried out in the province of Málaga, highlights the unsuspected social exclusion faced by many lifestyle migrants and long-term tourists that reside in private dwellings in southern Spain. O'Reilly describes how, as well as transnational elites, there are other groups of British nationals that are not easily identified because of the complex system of mobility forms and residential strategies typical of some of these regions. As a result of the exacerbation of the above-mentioned interaction and social integration problems, the following groups (extremely difficult to quantify) find themselves in a precarious situation: middle-aged families with children who do not go to school, or who attend international private schools with fees their parents can hardly afford, people who work in the informal economy (so they do not pay taxes or contribute to the social security system), people who seek medical treatment through inadequate private health insurance or in hospitals' emergency rooms, other people lack the information needed to regularize their status as residents, people who do not know which person or institution they should go to when facing certain problems, residents who have practically no knowledge of the language so they are unable to make a phone call in case of an emergency to get an ambulance or the police, etc.

Developing an Analytical Tool that will Help to Justify the Implementation of Public Policies

Several researchers have developed criteria and typologies to explain the residential strategies that ambiguously range from tourism to migration (Jaakson, 1986; Thumerelle, 1986; Williams *et al.*, 1997; Betty and Cahill, 1998; Bell and Ward, 2000; King *et al.*, 2000; O'Reilly, 2000, 2007b; Williams and Hall, 2000; Rodríguez, 2001; Dehoorne, 2002; Gustafson, 2002; King, 2002; Müller, 2002; Aronsson, 2004; Duval, 2004; Breuer, 2005). These studies are a significant effort to clarify the theoretical framework and the context where public policies should be implemented. However, we have identified the need for a classification based on the statistical tests necessary to guarantee the empirical consistency of the proposed types. Using surveys to research into tourist movements and lifestyle migration shows methodological difficulties mainly due to the lack of a sampling frame. Previous surveys on this population were conducted with non-probability sampling: convenience sampling (Casado, 1999; Williams and Hall, 2002; Breuer, 2005), or ad hoc quotas sampling (Rodríguez *et al.*, 1998). It is precisely the lack of a classification based on criteria that could be operationalized to become objective and general variables that encouraged our research. We will now put forward a classification based on our own survey research.

The intention of conducting representative research is a significant step forward in our knowledge of international residential tourism. The sampling method and the face-to-face interviews in the respondents' homes support the survey's validity. For the selection of sampling units, towns in the Alicante province were grouped into three clusters, according to their geographical location with respect to the coast, and the four towns in each cluster with the highest number of houses built in previous years were selected. In this way, we tried to obtain a sample of those towns that had recently experienced the most intense residential

growth. A simple sampling method with proportional allocation was used. Our sample comprised citizens from all of the 25 EU state members (except Spain), non-working and residing in a private dwelling. A total of 872 interviews were conducted: 406 in coastal towns (Denia, Benidorm, Santa Pola and Torrevieja), 409 in towns within 20 km of the coast (Pedreguer, La Nucía, San Fulgencio and Rojales), and 57 in towns further away from the coast (Hondón de los Frailes, Aspe, Castalla and Biar). The sample is statistically representative of the area population, with a margin of error of ± 5%, a 2Ω (95%) confidence level, and a population variance of 50%. Fieldwork was carried out during the first quarter of 2005. The houses were selected by the random route method based on grids. The complexity of the matter forced us to make methodological decisions that would enable us to encompass the different residential strategies. Consequently, we did not set any limit regarding the length of the stay, or the age of the interviewees (except their having reached legal age). We assumed the existence of a seasonal variation, so we decided to conduct the fieldwork during the low tourist season. The questionnaire was applied in Spanish, French, English and German. It was divided into three main groups of questions: socio-demographic profile, reasons for moving, and definition of the lifestyle as a motivating factor when choosing the destination. To strengthen internal reliability, the questionnaire was pretested on a convenience sample of 30 respondents. All statistics were computed using the SPSS 16© software.

Proposing a Typology

Analysis of the socio-demographic data (age, nationality, job, level of education) and the residential patterns (months spent yearly in Alicante, frequency of visits to home country), shows that there is not a statistically significant relationship between these variables. However, being registered with the local council, the possession of property in the home country, and the possession of property in Spain appear as explanatory variables.

Approximately 68% of the respondents state that they are registered with their local council. This percentage is consistent with the estimates of other researchers (Casado et al., 2004; La Parra and Mateo, 2008). Almost four out of ten citizens keep a house in their home country. This is an important matter, since one cannot consider that these citizens are semi-residents in Alicante, or residents of two countries, and even less tourists, when they do not have a home in their country of origin. In this respect, it is worth noting that many retirees finance their relocation with the proceeds from the sale of their high-value homes, generally located in large European cities (Warnes et al., 2004). With this capital they purchase property in their destination, and also save some of it, which enables them to improve their quality of life. Faced with the evidence that many of these citizens do not keep a house in their home country, a relevant question is: what is the type of possession of their home on the Costa Blanca? 85.5% own it, 10.9% rent it, 3.4% use the dwelling of relatives or friends, and 2.2% have a timeshare.

There is no significant relationship between having previously visited the Costa Blanca as a tourist and owning property. It may be surprising that 26.9% (190) of the homeowners report never having visited the area as tourists. These data challenge the usual analyses, which assume that the purchase of property is in most cases the result of a previous process through which tourists became loyal to the destination. This has led us to examine the relationship between the type of possession on the Costa Blanca and the fact of having a dwelling in the home country. As expected, there is a significant relationship (χ^2=46.220; p<0.0001) between both variables, which shows that homeowners tend not to keep another home to a greater extent than those who do not own property in Spain. Up to 66.6% of homeowners do not keep a house in their home country, compared with 42.1% of residents renting their home,

35.5% of residents in timeshares, and 34.5% of those using the house of relatives or friends.

Thus, we put forward the hypothesis that the typology resulting from the cross-tabulation of the variables 'being registered' and 'possession of property' is the association that best represents the relationship between tourism and migration. We have named the new variable 'type of lifestyle migration', the categories of which are:

- Type 1. Permanent residents: foreign citizens who own a home and are registered on the *Padrón Municipal de Habitantes* (Council Register).
- Type 2. Temporary residents: foreign citizens who live in a home that they do not own (it is rented, a timeshare or owned by relatives or friends) and are registered.
- Type 3. Second-home owners: foreign citizens who own a home but are not registered.
- Type 4. Tourists: foreign citizens who do not own a home and are not registered.

The categories 'rental', 'timeshare' and 'relatives and friends' have been grouped into a single category equivalent to 'no ownership'. The type named 'permanent resident' (registered owner) is the largest group, since it comprises 61.7% of the respondents. At the other extreme, the 'tourist' (neither owner nor registered) barely includes a tenth (10.3%) of these citizens. The remaining types have been labelled 'temporary resident' (registered non-owner) and 'second home owner' (not registered owner; Table 11.1).

The distribution of these types according to nationality (see Table 11.2) shows that ownership is more frequent among British citizens, while the citizens from the rest of EU member states are more likely to rent their homes, and even likelier to rent without registering. German citizens are more evenly distributed across the four situations, although their highest score is among the temporary residents.

The percentage of foreign citizens who keep a house in their home country, despite

Table 11.1. Lifestyle migration typology.

	Possession of property		
	Ownership	Timeshare, rental or friends	Total
Registered	61.7%	6.2%	67.9%
	(531)	(53)	(584)
	Permanent residents	Temporary residents	
Not registered	21.7%	10.3%	32.1%
	(187)	(89)	(276)
	Second home owners	Tourists	
Total	83.5%	16.5%	100.0%
	(718)	(142)	(860)

$\chi^2 = 71.768$; $p < 0.0001$. N = 860

Table 11.2. Lifestyle migration typology and nationality.

	Nationality			
	Germany	Rest of EU	UK	Total
Permanent residents	14.9 %	22.0%	63.1%	100%
	(79)	(117)	(335)	(531)
Temporary residents	17.0%	45.3%	37.7%	100%
	(9)	(24)	(20)	(53)
Second-home owners	13.4%	25.1%	61.5%	100%
	(25)	(47)	(115)	(187)
Tourists	12.4%	49.4%	38.2%	100%
	(11)	(44)	(34)	(89)

Registered: $\chi^2 = 16.026$; $p < 0.0001$.
Not registered: $\chi^2 = 16.912$; $p < 0.0001$.
N = 860

being owners and registered in Spain, falls short of 25%, a figure similar to the percentage of citizens who do not have a house in their home country, or on the Costa Blanca, and are not registered (Table 11.3).

An open question was used to ask interviewees their main reason for choosing the Costa Blanca as a residential destination. The responses were fully transcribed by the interviewer, and later coded. This way, different expressions referring to the good weather or sunny days were coded under the category 'climate'. Statements related to health, lifestyle, environment, peace and quiet, and Spanish people were included in the category 'quality of life'. The fact of being familiar with the area on account of previous

Table 11.3. Lifestyle migration typology and possession of property in home country.

	Do you keep a house in your home country?		
	Yes	No	Total
Permanent residents	23.8%	76.2%	100%
	(124)	(398)	(522)
Temporary residents	43.4%	56.6%	100%
	(23)	(30)	(53)
Second-home owners	60.9%	39.1%	100%
	(112)	(72)	(184)
Tourists	76.1%	23.9%	100%
	(67)	(21)	(88)

Registered: $\chi^2 = 9.754$; $p = 0.002$.
Not registered: $\chi^2 = 6.166$; $p = 0.013$.
N = 847

holiday visits was included in a third category. Different responses referring to the low prices of property or the standard of life, knowing people in the area, or having the opportunity to play golf were included in the category 'other'. Climate is the reason for moving most frequently mentioned by second-home owners and tourists. However, the quality of life seems to be more important for residents (Table 11.4). Familiarity with the region, derived from previous tourist visits, or from having relatives or friends living there, is more relevant for temporary residents than for any other type.

Furthermore, 71.8% of the permanent residents agree with the statement 'Here I enjoy a higher standard of living than in my home country', compared with 62.9% of the second-home owners, 55.8% of the temporary residents and 51.2% of the tourists ($\chi^2 = 24.113$, p<0.0001). It could be said that those foreign citizens with closer ties with the Costa Blanca, considering the basic variables 'being registered' and 'possession of property', are the ones who claim to enjoy a higher standard of living in this area.

Table 11.5 shows the main characteristics of the four types of lifestyle migration defined in our research and based on the relationships between the possession of property, being registered with the local council, and other variables associated with motivations, length of stay, nationality and social relationships. A complete explanation of the statistical validity of our classification goes beyond the scope of this chapter,

but a detailed statistical analysis can be found in Huete (2009).

Conclusions

Several authors have developed typologies to define lifestyle migration and residential tourism. Some researchers have used the same variables, registration and possession of property, that we take into account to elaborate our typology, but have not performed the statistical tests necessary to obtain empirical evidence to support their hypotheses. Our approach to the discussion about the relationship between tourism and migration tries to determine the limits of the terms immigrant and tourist. It should be noted, however, that the delimitation of concepts that we have put forward is not the consequence of a process of deduction based on a set of premises. It is instead the result of inductive reasoning, which means that the categories that make up our typology derive directly from our empirical research.

The term immigrant, since it implies a change of residence and the context in which people carry out their daily activities, may be applied to the types of citizens who are registered, whether or not they own a home, but not to second-home owners (not registered), who in many cases spend short periods of time in Spain, and keep their primary residence in their home country. Neither could it be applied to those who

Table 11.4. Lifestyle migration typology and main reason for moving.

	Main reason for moving				
	Climate	Quality of life	Previous visit	Other	Total
Permanent residents	50.9% (266)	38.9% (204)	3.4% (18)	6.7% (35)	100% (522)
Temporary residents	39.6% (21)	32.1% (17)	17.0% (9)	11.3% (6)	100% (53)
Second-home owners	65.3% (120)	25.0% (46)	5.7% (10)	4.0% (7)	100% (184)
Tourists	54.2% (48)	32.7% (29)	6.6% (6)	6.6% (6)	100% (88)

$\chi^2 = 72.071$; p < 0.0001. N = 847.

Table 11.5. Main characteristics of the typology.

	Owners	Live in timeshare, rented property or friends' property
Registered	**Permanent residents** Majority group Do not keep a house in home country Spend almost the whole year on the Costa Blanca Better quality of life is their main motivation Choice of town based on price Would stay in Spain in case of illness Want to learn Spanish Believe the Spanish public administration is complex State to enjoy a better quality of life than in home country more often than other types British	**Temporary residents** Distributed across those who keep a house in home country and those who do not Spend more than 6 months a year on the Costa Blanca Diverse motivations, but previous knowledge is important Choose town following recommendations given by fellow citizens, and to live near them Do not want to learn Spanish Least worried about crime than other types Group least bothered by house construction More Germans here than in other groups
Not registered	**Second-home owners** Keep a house in home country Spend 4–9 months a year on the Costa Blanca Better quality of life is their main motivation Choice of town based on price Would go back to home country in case of illness Do not want to learn Spanish Lack information to manage on their own Believe the Spanish public administration is complex Most worried about crime than other types Neither British nor German	**Tourists** Minority group Keep a house in home country Spend 3 months a year on the Costa Blanca Climate is their main motivation Choice of town based on landscape and services available Do not need to know Spanish Believe tourism is good for the landscape Neither British nor German

make use of a private dwelling, but do not own it and are not registered, in spite of spending a certain time in the area. In this sense, we suggest limiting the use of the term tourists to those persons who intend to return to their home country, that is, they are passing through and enjoying their holidays in a second home of their own (or with other type of possession), while the citizens who do not want to return to, or do not know whether they will, their country of origin in the foreseeable future (which they show by registering with their local council in Spain) should be called 'immigrants', or at any rate, 'residents'.

Citizens who purchase a home and register with the local council develop stronger bonds with the place than those who rent a house and do not comply with bureaucratic regulations. Keeping a house in the country of origin, ownership of property and registration have proved to be operational variables that could be used in further research, instead of variables difficult to measure such as the sense of attachment to the place and the reasons for moving.

Foreign citizens who buy property to use it as a second home, or to move in after their retirement, are attracted to the town by the same reasons as those who come to spend their holidays: a climate beneficial to health, affordable prices, and a good mix of natural and social environment. This chapter has analysed and presented these types as an operational classification to be used in the research on the complex residential framework that characterizes many of the Mediterranean tourist towns, or the areas nearby. This classification could become a useful tool in resource management and regional planning, as well as in future studies about this increasingly important social phenomenon. It is worth noting that the towns where such process has been more intense experience great difficulties in explaining the complex system of residential mobility types with which they deal on a daily basis. The description of the mobility types here identified can also help to justify the resources necessary for the local administration of these areas.

If public institutions conducted surveys similar to the one described in this chapter, they would probably have a better knowledge of the characteristics of the groups that make up the social conglomerate of tourist towns in many Mediterranean regions. This would definitely help them to identify the specific needs of each one of these groups. The planning of local development seems very difficult without such approaches, especially when it comes to managing basic infrastructures with regard to important aspects such as healthcare provision. In this sense, some Spanish authorities seem not to have understood the actual cultural, economic and political consequences associated with a constantly erratic or inadequate planning.

References

Ackers, L. and Dwyer, P. (2004) Fixed laws, fluid lives: the citizenship status of post retirement migrants in the European Union. *Ageing and Society* 24, 451–475.

Aronsson, L. (2004) Place attachment of vacation residents: between tourists and permanent residents. In: Hall, C.M. and Müller, D.K. (eds) *Tourism, Mobility and Second Homes: Between Elite Landscape and Common Ground*. Channel View Publications, Clevedon, UK, pp. 75–86.

Barke, M. (1999) Tourism and culture in Spain: a case of minimal conflict? In: Robinson, M. and Boniface, P. (eds) *Tourism and Cultural Conflicts*. CABI Publishing, Wallingford, UK, pp 247–267.

Bell, M. and Ward, G. (2000) Comparing temporary mobility with permanent migration. *Tourism Geographies* 2, 87–107.

Benson, M. (2010) The context and trajectory of lifestyle migration: the case of the British residents of Southwest France. *European Societies* 12, 45–64.

Benson, M. and O'Reilly, K. (2009) Migration and the search for a better way of life: a critical exploration of lifestyle migration. *The Sociological Review* 57, 608–625.

Betty, C. and Cahill, M. (1998) Consideraciones Sociales y Sanitarias Sobre los Inmigrantes Británicos Mayores en España, en Particular los de la Costa del Sol. *Migraciones* 3, 83–115.

Breuer, T. (2005) Retirement migration or rather second-home tourism? German senior citizens on the Canary Islands. *Die Erde* 136, 313–333.

Casado, M.A. (1999) Socio-demographic impacts of residential tourism: a case study of Torrevieja, Spain. *International Journal of Tourism Research* 1, 223–237.

Casado, M.A., Kaiser, C. and Warnes, A.M. (2004) Northern European retired residents in nine southern European areas: characteristics, motivations and adjustment. *Ageing and Society* 24, 353–381.

Dehoorne, O. (2002) Tourisme, travail, migration: interrelations et logiques mobilitaires. *Revue Européenne des Migrations Internationales* 18, 7–36.

Duval, D.T. (2004) Mobile migrants: travel to second homes. In: Hall, C.M. and Müller, D.K. (eds) *Tourism, Mobility and Second Homes: between Elite Landscape and Common Ground*. Channel View Publications, Clevedon, UK, pp. 87–96.

Giner, J. and Simó, C. (2009) El retorno de los retirados Europeos: estudio sobre la Marina Alta. In: Mazón, T., Huete, R. and Mantecón, A. (eds) *Turismo, Urbanización y Estilos de Vida. Las Nuevas Formas de Movilidad Residencial*. Icaria, Barcelona, pp. 383–398.

Gustafson, P. (2001) Retirement migration and transnational lifestyles. *Ageing and Society* 21, 371–394.

Gustafson, P. (2002) Tourism and seasonal retirement migration. *Annals of Tourism Research* 29, 899–918.

Gustafson, P. (2008) Transnationalism in retirement migration: the case of North European retirees in Spain. *Ethnic and Racial Studies* 31, 451–475.

Gustafson, P. (2009) Your home in Spain: residential strategies in international retirement migration. In: Benson, M. and O'Reilly, K. (eds) *Lifestyle Migration: Expectations, Aspirations and Experiences*. Ashgate, Aldershot, UK, pp. 69–86.

Hall, C.M. and Müller, D.K. (2004) *Tourism, Mobility and Second Homes Between Elite Landscape and Common Ground*. Channel View Publications, Clevedon, UK.

Haug, B., Dann, G.M.S. and Mehmetoglu, M. (2007) Little Norway in Spain: from tourism to migration. *Annals of Tourism Research* 34, 202–222.

Huber, A. and O'Reilly, K. (2004) The construction of Heimat under conditions of individualised modernity: Swiss and British elderly migrants in Spain. *Ageing and Society* 24, 327–352.

Huete, R. (2009) *Turistas que llegan Para Quedarse. Una Explicación Sociológica Sobre la Movilidad Residencial*. Publicaciones Universidad de Alicante, Alicante, Spain.

Inglehart, R. (1997) *Modernization and Postmodernization: Cultural, Economic, and Political Change in 43 Societies*. Princeton University Press, Princeton, New Jersey.

Jaakson, R. (1986) Second-home domestic tourism. *Annals of Tourism Research* 13, 357–391.

Janoschka, M. (2009) The contested spaces of lifestyle mobilities: regime analysis as a tool to study political claims in Latin American retirement destinations. *Die Erde* 140, 251–274.

Jurdao, F. (1979) *España en Venta*. Ayuso, Madrid.

King, R. (2002) Towards a new map of European migration. *International Journal of Population Geography* 8, 89–106.

King, R., Warnes, A.M. and Williams, A.M. (1998) International retirement migration in Europe. *International Journal of Population Geography* 4, 91–111.

King, R., Warnes, A.M. and Williams, A.M. (2000) *Sunset Lives: British Retirement Migration to the Mediterranean*. Berg Publishers, Oxford, UK.

La Parra, D. and Mateo, M.A. (2008) Health status and access to health care of British nationals living on the Costa Blanca, Spain. *Ageing and Society* 28, 85–102.

Leontidou, L. and Marmaras, E. (2001) From tourists to migrants. Residential tourism and 'littoralization'. In: Apostolopoulos, Y., Lukissas and Leontidou, L. (eds) *Mediterranean Tourism. Facets of Socioeconomic Development and Cultural Change*. Routledge, London, pp. 257–267.

Mantecón, A. (2010) Tourist modernisation and social legitimation in Spain. *International Journal of Tourism Research* 12, 617–626.

Mantecón, A. and Huete, R. (2008) The value of authenticity in residential tourism: the decision-maker's point of view. *Tourist Studies* 8, 359–376.

Mazón, T. (2006) Inquiring into residential tourism: the Costa Blanca case. *Tourism and Hospitality Planning & Development* 3, 89–97.

Mazón, T., Huete, R. and Mantecón, A. (2009) *Turismo, Urbanización y Estilos de Vida. Las Nuevas Formas de Movilidad Residencial*. Icaria, Barcelona, Spain.

McWatters, M.R. (2009) *Residential Tourism. (De)Constructing Paradise*. Channel View Publications, Clevedon, UK.

Müller, D.K. (2002) German second homeowners in Sweden: some remarks on the tourism-migration-nexus. *Revue Européenne des Migrations Internationales* 18, 67–86.

Oliver, C. (2007) *Retirement Migration: Paradoxes of Ageing*. Routledge, London.

O'Reilly, K. (2000) *The British on the Costa del Sol. Transnational Identities and Local Communities*. Routledge, London.

O'Reilly, K. (2003) When is a tourist? The articulation of tourism and migration in Spain's Costa del Sol. *Tourist Studies* 3, 301–317.

O'Reilly, K. (2007a) Emerging tourism futures: residential tourism and its implications. In: Geoffrey, C. and Sibley, R. (eds) *Going Abroad: Travel, Tourism, and Migration*. Cambridge Scholars Publishing, Newcastle, UK, pp. 144–157.

O'Reilly, K. (2007b) Intra-European migration and the mobility-enclosure dialectic. *Sociology* 41, 277–293.

O'Reilly, K. (2009) Hosts and guests, guests and hosts: British residential tourism in the Costa del Sol. In: Obrador-Pons, P., Crang, M. and Travlou, P. (eds) *Cultures of Mass Tourism. Doing the Mediterranean in the Age of Banal Mobilities*. Farnham, UK, pp. 129–142.

O'Reilly, K. and Benson, M. (2009) Lifestyle migration: escaping to the good life? In: Benson, M. and O'Reilly, K. (eds) *Lifestyle Migration: Expectations, Aspirations and Experiences*. Ashgate, Farnham, UK, pp. 1–13.

Rodríguez, V. (2001) Tourism as a recruiting post for retirement migration. *Tourism Geographies* 3, 52–63.

Rodríguez, V., Fernández-Mayoralas, G. and Rojo, F. (1998) European retirees on the Costa del Sol: a cross-national comparison. *International Journal of Population Geography* 4, 183–200.

Rodríguez, V., Fernández-Mayoralas, G. and Rojo, F. (2004) International retirement migration: retired Europeans living on the Costa del Sol, Spain. *Population Review* 43, 1–36.

Salvà, P. (2002) Foreign immigration and tourism development in Spain's Balearic Islands. In: Hall, C.M. and Williams, A.M. (eds) *Tourism and Migration. New Relationships between Production and Consumption*. Kluwer Academic Publishers, London, pp. 119–134.

Schildt, J. (2010) The Sudden End of Amenity. Long-Term Care Dependency Among German Retirement Residents in Spain, *Workshop: Theorizing Lifestyle Migration*, 28–29 January, Spanish National Research Council (CSIC), Madrid, Spain.

Schriewer, K. and Rodes, J. (2006) Los cuidados médicos en un contexto transnacional. Jubilados Europeos en la región de Murcia. Available at: http://www.unavarra.es/migraciones/tallerCs2ryc.htm (accessed 10 July 2010).

Simó, C. and Herzog, B. (2005) El Asociacionismo de los Residentes Europeos en la Comunidad Valenciana. In: Mazón, T. and Aledo, A. (eds) *Turismo Residencial y Cambio Social. Nuevas Perspectivas Teóricas y Empíricas*. Aguaclara, Alicante, Spain, pp. 427–454.

Thumerelle, P.J. (1986) *Peuples en Mouvement. La Mobilité Spatiale des Populations*. Sedes, Paris.

Tuppen, J. (1991) France: the changing character of a key industry. In: Williams, A.M. and Shaw, G. (eds) *Tourism and Economic Development: Western European Experiences*. Wiley, London, pp. 191–206.

Urry, J. (2007) *Mobilities*. Polity, Cambridge, UK.

Vera, J.F. and Ivars, J.A. (2003) Measuring sustainability in a mass tourist destination: pressures, perceptions and policy responses in Torrevieja, Spain. *Journal of Sustainable Tourism* 11, 181–203.

Warnes, A., Friedrich, K., Kellaher, L. and Torres, S. (2004) The diversity and welfare of older migrants in Europe. *Ageing and Society* 24, 307–326.

Williams, A.M. and Hall, C.M. (2000) Tourism and migration: new relationships between production and consumption. *Tourism Geographies* 2, 5–27.

Williams, A.M. and Hall, C.M. (2002) Tourism, migration, circulation and mobility: the contingencies of time and place. In: Hall, C.M. and Williams, A.M. (eds) *Tourism and Migration: New Relationships between Production and Consumption*. Kluwer Academic Publishers, London, pp. 1–52.

Williams, A.M., King, R. and Warnes, A. (1997) A Place in the sun: international retirement migration from northern to southern Europe. *European Urban and Regional Studies* 4, 115–134.

Williams, A.M., King, R., Warnes, A. and Patterson, G. (2000) Tourism and international retirement migration: new forms of an old relationship in southern Europe. *Tourism Geographies* 2, 28–49.

12 Surrealist Pilgrims, Melting Clocks in Marble Halls: Dark Tourism for a Postmodern World

Don Craig[1] and Craig Thompson[1]
[1]*Stenden University, Leeuwarden, the Netherlands*

Introduction

Some months ago, a popular woman's magazine, in a glossy six-page spread that highlights intriguing travel destinations around the globe, teased readers with a feature titled 'the joy of cemeteries'. In the opening paragraphs on an article that touched on the New Orleans Cemetery, Père Lachaise in Paris and San Michele in Venice, readers were reassured that wanting to visit sites associated with death and bereavement is perfectly normal, and that a taste for visiting controversial final resting places is nothing to be ashamed of. After all, sites such as the Roman catacombs and the pyramids have been respectable tourism spots for centuries. The article goes on to discuss other 'places you wouldn't want to miss', including Ground Zero, Lockerbie, the Killing fields of Cambodia, various former concentration camps, and the scene of the accident where Diana, Princess of Wales was fatally injured.

The Origins

Dark Tourism 'speciality tours' have been offered for time immemorial. There is a theory that the first guided tour was a train trip in the late 1830s to Cornwall, which had been arranged for a blood-thirsty public to witness the execution of two convicted murderers. Even earlier than that, there is reference to groups of well-heeled individuals who travelled to Belgium at the time of the Battle of Waterloo in 1815, and suggested that they might even have been at the battlefield itself!

Earlier, the Romans staged fights between individuals and wild animals and, for that matter, between man and man to entertain the public at sites like the Colosseum in Rome and other amphitheatres of the Empire. During the medieval period, crowds gleefully flocked to public executions, whether hangings, burnings or simply run-of-the-mill tortures.

In the modern era, though, there has been a slight change. People have always been keen to visit places where battles, massacres and nasty deeds took place, generally provided these events happened within a reasonable time before their visit. Getting up close to a death site has always appealed to the sense of the macabre. Nowadays, however, phenomena such as global communications, social media and technology permit (if not encourage) death-related events to be reported, often in 'real time', as they happen. It is also through technology that these events may be replayed for repeated viewing. The gap between the event shown and when and where it took place therefore significantly narrowed. Thus, it is not unreasonable to assume that a visitor to a site where destruction and killings took place could well have been encouraged to be there by virtue of widespread media coverage, the so-called CNN phenomenon.

Traditionally tourism literature has placed its gaze on the marketing and consumption of 'pleasant diversions in pleasant places' (Lennon and Foley, 2000). More recently, however, academics and others have begun to explore the phenomenon of 'dark tourism', so providing a springboard for the study of the innate phenomenon of a fascination with the notorious and macabre (Lennon and Foley, 2000). In the opening years of this millennium, further terms ('thanatourism', 'black spot' tourism and 'atrocity heritage') were minted to explain and perhaps justify the packaging and consumption of death or distress as a tourist experience of both the distant and recent past (Rojek, 1993; Seaton, 1996; Tunbridge and Ashworth, 1996). Strange (2000) points out that the most studied places in these works are battle sites and death camps (Young, 1993; Seaton, 1999), which have literally and figuratively fixed the memory of collective violence to the places where suffering occurred. She develops a strong argument that the death sites of famous individuals (such as Marie Laveau, Mother Teresa, Jimmy Hendricks or President Kennedy) have also become both religious and secular tourism shrines (Rojek, 1993; Foley and Lennon, 1996). And although unusual disasters (such as the PanAm plane crash at Lockerbie or the destruction of the World Trade Center) draw the curious from around the world, it can be argued that commonplace crime scenes and traffic accident locations can also become impromptu attractions, where people pay their respects, often in the form of cemetery-like floral offerings, or simply come together to wonder at tragedy's aftermath (Foote, 1997).

Strange (2000) has argued that although such morbid destinations may

'give us a thrill', they also, by their very nature, provide opportunities for social, spiritual and political reflection. To put it another way, touring the more sombre destinations and sites may be 'gruesome' but is also, as with pilgrimage, 'good' (Dobbs, 1999, p. 35).

However, no study of dark tourism supply could ever be complete without acknowledging the tourist behaviour and demand for the product. Supporting this, Stone (2005a) argues that an ability to extract and interrogate the motives of so-called dark tourism is crucial to the understanding of this phenomenon. She goes on to say that this is particularly clear within a variety of socio-cultural and geographical contexts, and argues that it is perhaps this fundamental necessity of 'understanding the underside' and interpreting consumer motivation that both leads and steers the current dark tourism debate (Stone, 2005a).

Although Lennon and Foley (2002, p. 12) regard dark tourism as the 'commodification of anxiety and doubt', others employ wider definitions. Marcel (2003), for example, notes:

> ... when you think about it, people have always been attracted to sites where important or mass deaths have occurred. The early pilgrimages were to sites of religious deaths. The Via Dolorosa, the route followed by Christ when he was crucified, is only one of many early examples. The Tombs of the Pharaohs in Egypt and the Coliseum in Rome are major tourist attractions. So is the Tower of London, where historically important figures were beheaded. After the Battle of Waterloo in 1815, hotels and restaurants sprang up around the Belgian battlefield and changed the route of the 19th century British Grand Tour forever. Dark tourism may be identified as 'visitations to places where tragedies or historically noteworthy death has occurred and that continue to impact our lives'.
>
> Marcel (2003, p. 17)

Marcel (2003) goes on to write:

> Thanatourism seems to be the dirty little secret of the tourism industry. It thrives at

the Texas School Book Depository and the 'grassy knoll' in Dallas, where you can buy a coffee mug decorated with cross hair rifle-sights, at Auschwitz and in Holocaust museums around the world, in cemeteries where celebrities are buried, and at the site of Princess Diana's tragic car crash in Paris. Tourists visit places of public executions, like the Place De La Guillotine, sites of mass death like Pompeii and Dachau, places associated with celebrity deaths like Graceland, museums and memorials like the Vietnam War Memorial in Washington, and battlefields like ancient Troy, Gettysburg, Pearl Harbor and Omaha Beach. Does it sound crazy to think of death as a niche market? Then what do you make of the 'Titanic cruises' offered by charter companies, where tourists eat meals identical to those served on the ship, and hear music identical to the music played on the ship, as they travel to the precise spot where the ship lies at the bottom of the ocean.

Marcel (2003, pp.18ff.)

In much the same vein, Rojek (1993, p. 134) writes that although what one is consuming is not real, nonetheless the experience can be pleasurable and exciting even if one recognizes that it is also useless.

Interestingly, two years earlier, Mestrovic (1991, p. 4) had noted that 'the most important aspect of modernity is that it causes humankind to suffer from an excess of "mind" at the expense of the "heart": a virulent abstractionism that abhors anything permanent'. Now, either we could accept Mestrovic as correct, or we could view dark tourism as addressing the reverse side of Durkheim's concept of anomie (1895). So this therefore raises questions such as whether death is, in fact, the final frontier, whether our desire to confront death could be regarded as disgrace, since dark tourism compels the permanence of death to confront the 'ephemeral changes of the living' (Durkheim, 1895). Further, it challenges whether dark tourism is a way in which life renews itself from the unpleasant side of humanity.

Postmodernists (Derrida, Foucault, Lyotard, Baudrillard, Deleuze, to name but a few) have argued that we inhabit a world dedicated to fun. In line with this, authors such as Bell, Riesman and Rojek individually define modernity as looking for fun in the mundane. For example, Rojek (1993, pp. 133–134) suggests that the modern search for authenticity (particularly in leisure travel) and self-realization has ended. He further suggests that because of de-differentiation, leisure activity has assumed some of the characteristics of work activity. He develops his argument to suggest that the moral density of the State is called into question and that post-leisure and post-tourism celebrate fictive and dramaturgical values.

The Postmodernists therefore imply that the search for fun is often not as simple as it would at first glance appear. This seeming contradiction is highlighted by Mestrovic (1991, p. 25) who noted that 'postmodern vacations are usually stressful, few exotic places are left in the world and most vacation spots promise to deliver the same bland product-fun'. Agreeing with this in regard to cemetery tours, Rojek (1993, p. 141) writes:

> Bourgeois culture constructed the cemetery as a place of dignity and solemnity. Visitors were expected to show proper respect for the dead... However, the actions of Modernity operated to break down the barriers between sacred and profane, the closed world of the cemetery and the outside world of commerce..."

Rojek (1993, p. 141)

This peculiar and complex link between grief and evil, macabre and bizarre, and their various touristic representations has given rise to academic and ethical debate about the way that leisure and pleasure are intertwined with tragedy (Rojek, 1993, p. 170; Tunbridge and Ashworth, 1996, p. 112). Some heritage tourism commentators have argued that popularized 'theme park' history is inauthentic, and that tourism has become as an inappropriate and even immoral vehicle for the promotion of human suffering and tragic events (Hewison, 1987; MacCannell, 1992; Walsh, 1992; Urry, 1995). More recently, some have questioned these critics' distinction between 'bogus' and 'authentic' history by calling for more attention to the 'authorial intentions and authenticating devices at work in heritage sites' (Macdonald, 1997, p. 156–157). Thus commodification of history for mass consumption often leads to trivialization (the Amsterdam Dungeon is a case in point) but, as Seaton argues, this does not stop the presentation of counter-hegemonic stories or tales of misery, suffering or injustice. Also, as Seaton's work emphasizes, willing consumption of the more distressing aspects of the past are driven by tourists' demands and marketing strategies but are also subject to changes in political and cultural climates (1999, p. 155). Here, for example, Robben Island, off Cape Town, or Alcatraz, off San Francisco, comes to mind. The gaze of dark tourism continually shifts as new happenings (wars, falls of regimes and so on) take place, and as fresh influences (novels, memoirs, films, stage shows) lend a moral interpretation to sites of notoriety (Rojek and Urry, 1997, p. 53).

Although public remembrance of unpleasant or upsetting past events has been deeply and historically entrenched, the growing commercialization and consumer demand for this sector has been considerable. Many dark tourism authors note that places associated with 'death, disaster, and depravity' are now regular and indeed expected focal points on any international tourism itinerary (Urry, 1990; Seaton, 1996; Lennon and Foley, 2000, p. 3). Increasingly we find sites once used as places of imprisonment, where deliberate government-approved torture and deprivation were commonplace, have popular, if rather ghoulish appeal. Grizzly fascination with the occult aspects of punishment and torture may not be new; however, the demand for cemetery and prison history tourism (Alcatraz, Robben Island and so on) has dramatically increased. Paradoxically, penal reform in the modern world has resulted in a closing of old prisons and gaols, with the consequence that decommissioned places of incarceration have been redeveloped, for instance, as hotels and condominiums (Watson, 1997). Notable among these famous former prisons are

Pentridge in Melbourne, Breakwater Lodge behind the Victoria and Alfred in Cape Town, Pudu in Kuala Lumpur, and Port Blair on the Andamans. Significantly the conversion into museums and tourism sites, which caters to public demand, only occurred in the last 20 years.

Towards a Deeper Shade of Dark

Many tourists are instinctively attracted to dark tourism sites by the morbid fascination associated with death and dying. Marketing strategies capitalize on this most human of conditions, thereby commercializing dark tourism destinations, which in turn further underscores the attractiveness to tourists. Famously, the Elvis Presley website cajoles: 'If you're looking for fun things to do in Memphis and enjoy visiting celebrity homes, don't miss touring Elvis's 14-acre estate in Tennessee' (www.elvis.com). A cursory investigation reveals that Graceland offers several Elvis-related packages, with everything offered, from a simple tour to an 'Elvis wedding experience' in the 'Elvis chapel', as well as souvenir shopping to the 'Elvis Christmas celebration'.

As pointed out by Stone, myriad marketing efforts influence tourists in making their travel decisions. This is perhaps most obvious in the more highly commercialized dark tourism attractions, as shown in our Graceland example. Conversely at Auschwitz–Birchenau, with its accurate depiction of the atrocities and inhumane conditions, the commercial nature is not as immediately apparent. Because of regulations, no admission to the premises is charged. Obviously, some money-making initiatives are a part of the deal, including guided tours and the sale of publications and souvenir Holocaust-themed items. However, given the historical importance of the death camps further commercialization would be counterproductive. Not all such sites are, however, treated with equal sensitivity, a fact to which more than a million visitors annually to the Anne Frank House can attest.

One of the current debates on dark tourism suggests that there are degrees of darkness within tourism. According to this argument, the 'darkest' of dark tourism destinations are relatively little commercialized, for example, Chernobyl, whereas the 'less dark' death sites of popular icons like Elvis have a wide variety of support services and products. Of course, not all celebrity death sites or sites of a 'lighter' nature are heavily commercialized; however, an apparent link can be found between the historical and political sensitivity of the site and the level of commercialization. A poignant example is commemorative items manufactured from building detritus of Ground Zero, which assume almost religious significance to the visitors.

Further, Miles argues that there is an even deeper degree of darkness within the area of dark tourism. He proposes that a crucial difference exists between sites of death and suffering, as opposed to those associated with death and suffering (Miles, 2002, pp. 1175–1178). For example, the experience of the death camp site at Auschwitz–Birchenau is considerably darker than the one at the US Holocaust Memorial Museum in Washington DC (Stone, 2006, p. 151).

Dark Sun Resorts

Entering the picture are new destinations with all the characteristics of a holiday trip but that also have an underlying current of dark tourism. An example of this are the Pacific holiday paradises wiped out with enormous destruction by the tsunami in 2004. The Christmas holiday season was at its peak when, almost instantaneously, these glamorous oriental tourist attractions turned to watery graveyards. Nearly 300,000 people lost their lives, amongst them thousands of tourists, and the tourism infrastructure was destroyed.

Given the importance to the economies of these countries, the resorts were quickly rebuilt and, after a slow start, tourism is now almost back to normal. But these beautifully restored beaches remain places where thousands of people were tragically killed by the effect of the tsunami, and the spectre of the natural disaster still hovers close. In such locations, many people are still unaccounted for. And so, amongst the sun-seekers there are friends and relatives, coming to pay respect to the victims of the tsunami. There are others, however, for whom the prospect of 'dead corpses still to be found floating in the sea' (Beyette, 2006, in the Los Angeles Times) holds an appeal.

Would it then be correct to call such places 'dark'? On the one hand, while Lennon and Foley's criteria for dark tourism requiring answers about modern society are rendered invalid in this case, the fact remains that the tsunami brought about tremendous suffering, death and destruction. And while sun-seeking may be the main reason for tourism, there is an undercurrent of visiting places with death, suffering and disaster as the main theme, driven by both the supply of the destination and the visitors' interest in its extraordinary features.

Furthermore it is important to emphasize the multitude and diversity of dark tourism attractions, all of which by no means serve similar functions and share the same characteristics. As proved by our tsunami example, the tourist may indeed be a dark tourist, in spite of the destination not qualifying as a dark tourism destination.

Dark Tourism Supply

There are some physical destinations where atrocities and dying have actually taken place. Others are purposefully built in another location to commemorate such events. There are dark tourism products where the tragic event is being re-enacted with the tourist participating in the process (as is the case with the Tower of London). Some destinations, such as the Simon Wiesenthal Foundation, offer more educative value, some, such as Graceland, exist mainly for entertainment. We focus on plain distinguishable characteristics shared by a number of dark tourism destinations.

Destination Categories

An overview of contemporary dark tourism literature shows many different types of destinations (Dann, 2001; Stone, 2006).

In the first example of dark tourism, the sites of mass murder and genocide include Auschwitz and the Killing Fields of Cambodia where a large number of people have died. Ground Zero where the twin towers were struck down by terrorist attacks on September 11 2001 falls into this category, which is the darkest shade of dark tourism, with the closest contact to dying.

The second example includes museums and exhibitions with associations with genocide and wars. The Resistance Museums of Amsterdam and Copenhagen fall into this example, as do the US Holocaust Memorial Museum in Washington and the Yad Washem Holocaust Museum in Jerusalem, probably the best-known examples of these. The Imperial War Museum in London, which is dedicated to viewing the war history of the UK from the First World War until the present day, belongs here.

Example three is graveyards and cemeteries, which form an integral part of the itinerary. The presence of death and the related symbols, such as gravestones, sarcophagi and mausoleums, give the dark tourist pleasure that is rooted in Gothic or Romantic art and literature. Père-Lachaise in Paris is probably the most famous cemetery in the world. Beyond its primary function, this famous Romantic-inspired necropolis has become an open-air museum and pantheon garden.

Simulated dungeons, the fourth example, are generally rich in visual display and are built primarily for entertainment purposes. The London or Amsterdam Dungeons recall the horrors and atrocities from the darker sides of European history. They often include representations of punishments for crimes – just or unjust – from torture to executions and beheading.

Celebrity death sites can be regarded as a sub-division of this. Most visitors regard celebrities such as Elvis Presley, John Lennon, James Dean and Marilyn Monroe, Michael Jackson, Jim Morrison and Diana, Princess of Wales, as a personal part of their own lives.

Battlefields form our fifth example. The experience of standing on the actual ground where soldiers fell and blood was shed brings the dark tourist close to the reality of war. Veterans come to pay respects to their fallen comrades (as in Delville Wood – where, adding to the poignancy, the Last Post is played every sunset) and current members of regiments who distinguished themselves with valour in battles long past (such as Crimea, Rorke's Drift). Recalling the visits to Waterloo mentioned earlier, some dark tourists even visit active battlefields, such as those in the Middle East (www.dark-tourism.org.uk).

'Roots' (or Slavery) Tourism deals with the trans-Atlantic slave trade with destinations such as Cape Coast Castle and Elmina Castle in Ghana, and Gorée Island in Senegal, as well as destinations in Zanzibar, Liberia, Morocco and Eritrea being popular (www.dark-tourism.org.uk). Guided tours to these destinations focus on the tragedies and atrocities that slaves had to endure on the inhumane voyages to new destinations.

Re-enactments, where the dark tourist is part of the product itself, comprise our seventh and final category of dark tourism. The Isandlwana re-enactment commemorates the Anglo–Zulu conflict in South Africa and, similarly, the re-enactment of the Battle of Hastings is a yearly event at Battle Abbey in Battle, East Sussex. Another example of a dark tourism re-enactment is the re-enactment of the death of President John F. Kennedy. Foley and Lennon describe the experience, built around the assassination, in which a presidential limousine will take the dark tourist through the same route as it did on 22 November in 1963. The sounds, cheers of the crowd as well as the gunshot, are all played just as it happened. Even the speeding to the hospital is included in the experience (Foley and

Lennon, 2000, p. 98). True to the dark tourism definition, the tourist is brought close up to the death itself.

Dark Tourism on the Up

Dark tourism comprises only a small portion of the full spectrum. Paris, for example, is the most visited city in the world, and its theme park, Disneyland Paris, has around 12 million visitors annually. Compared to this, no dark tourism destination comes close. However, its importance to tourism as a whole cannot be underestimated. Valene Smith has argued that '...despite the horrors of death and destruction, the memorabilia of warfare and allied products...probably constitutes the largest single category of tourist attractions in the world' (1996, pp. 247–264). We can, however, arrive at some supporting figures.

Père Lachaise cemetery receives more than 1.5 million visitors annually, many of whom are drawn to the final resting place of such luminaries as Sarah Bernhardt, Oscar Wilde, Edith Piaf and Jim Morrison. There is some considerable dichotomy of visitors, ranging from elderly Parisian widows to rock fans to Goths.

Another cemetery that enjoys cult status and attracts all manner of people is the San Michele cemetery island in the Venice Lagoon. Home to many Venetian notables over the centuries and the final resting places of Ezra Pound, Sergei Diaghilev and Igor Stravinsky, it too attracts its fair share of visitors, some conventionally respectable, others less so. Some authors regard Isola San Michele as a chilly metaphor for Venice itself: all decay and fey despair. Unlike other great cemeteries, which attempt to deny mortality with creativity and neatly trimmed gardens, San Michele seems to wallow in death and putrefaction.

A third cemetery that has become a huge tourism attraction is the Louis I Cemetery in New Orleans. Though now home to the living homeless, it also has the mausoleum of Marie Laveau, the high priestess of voodoo, and attracts many occult visitors. More recently, some Hurricane Katrina victims have been buried here.

The Holocaust Memorial Museum in Washington DC averages around 1.7 million visitors per annum, with, strangely enough, more than 90% of these not being Jewish (di Natale and Breschi, 2009).

In 2010, more than a million people visited the Anne Frank memorial museum in Amsterdam, Holland. The same year, Auschwitz–Birchenau received more than half a million registered visitors (di Natale and Breschi, 2009)

Graceland welcomes more than 600,000 visitors each year, and contributes more than US$150 million annually to the Memphis economy (*The Guardian*, 26 July, 2002). The London Dungeon, also belonging to the less dark end of destinations, welcomes yearly more than 750,000 visitors. Other dungeons affiliated to the London Dungeon have been built elsewhere in Europe to cope with the demand and to capitalize on its success, for example, one in Hamburg and, most recently, one in Amsterdam. Madame Tussauds in London, with its waxwork chamber of horrors, proudly boasts that more than 500 million people (more than the population of the USA and Australia combined) have visited since it opened.

To some extent, dark tourism may be financially beneficial to any destination. The extent to which each benefits depends largely on its commercialization. What is significant about dark tourism, however, is that it delivers an educational component. In many cases, this aspect is central to the destination. For example, 34% of the visitors to the US Holocaust Museum are school-aged children.

Having examined the tenets of dark tourism, we have come to acknowledge that death has come to occupy a central place in society's consciousness. This would then suppose that a curiosity and fascination and, indeed in some cases a preoccupation, with death becomes a motivation for dark tourism.

The Intrigue of the Dark Side

Historically there has always been a fascination with death, whether our own or others, through a combination of respect and reverence or morbid curiosity and superstition. Stone (2006, p. 147) strongly maintains that it is society's apparent contemporary fascination with death, whether real or fictional, media inspired or otherwise, that is seemingly driving the dark tourism phenomenon.

A number of theories about the appeal of death and dying to the mind of the dark tourist have been drafted. Perhaps chief among these theories is the role of the contemporary media as it thrusts itself into your living room.

The Contribution of Media

From the 18th century, the public perception of death had become unfashionable and had faded from public view. No longer immediate, it was considered to be happening somewhere else. By the mid-19th century, death had become largely invisible to the public. Popular authors responded, through the gothic novel, by creating not only more lurid accounts of death but depictions which were more secular, violent and essentially uninstructive. This meant that death had come to take on an entertainment value.

For the average person in the street, the rise of illustrated newspapers, with their depiction of accidents and natural disasters, brought death graphically to the fore. While these sensational stories, with their gruesome coverage of train crashes, shipwrecks, floods and explosions, held no religious significance or redemptive force, they contributed to general and unspecified increases in anxiety. Though disasters are undeniably news, the press was only responding to a fascination with accounts of violent death that ran alongside the Victorian sentimentalization of death, which tried, if not to entirely wipe it out, at least to some extent to beautify the end of life.

Thus news headlines, with descriptions and images of violent death from these mid-19th century beginnings, remain sensational; the general opinion today is that it has gone ever farther in the same direction (Goldstein, 1998, pp. 39–40). So the media feeds the public's fascination with death, and the fascination grows the more it is fed. Television viewers get used to seeing death in their own living room; imagery becomes increasingly violent when closer and more powerful encounters with scenes of death are sought after. This brings us to the question of what makes scenes of death and violence so appealing in the first place.

The Dark Tourist Experience

Guards are assaulting the prisoners: beating them, spitting on them, slicing their skin with their Hitler Youth-knives. The prisoners are begging: please, stop, no more! They are wondering what in God's name they had done to deserve it. They are beaten with tycoons all over the body until there is no single solid bone in their bodies. They wither in great pain and finally drift away to silence. The guards have them thrown away outside to a ditch like dead animals. Only a pond of blood reminds the victims once were there.

di Natale and Breschi (2009)

Regardless of whether this incident was a film clip, part of a short story or a fictional portrayal, it would seem unlikely that there could be anything enjoyable in viewing it. Because the mind is naturally programmed to seek away from personal pain and suffering, it would seem anathema for a viewer to be excited by such scenes.

Goldstein's view is that attitudes to shows of violence specifically may be considered enjoyable and wholesome if they are deemed mediated by identification with a successful aggressor. In the extract above, the aggressor has almost divine power to decide on the fate of the prisoner. With no way for the prisoner to resist, the guard is able to walk away without fear of consequence.

Thus, in a safe setting like with sufficient removal from reality, the viewer is able to enjoy the show. Goldstein argues that '... people identify with fictional heroes, but also with the crudest of fictional villains, in order to attain "vicariously" the gratifications that these antagonists experience. Through such identification, it is said; people transcend their limited personal experience' (Goldstein, 1998, p. 163).

He takes this argument further and proposes that we are 'cleansed' through a dramatization of violence and death, and that watching a tragedy unfolding provides a catharsis. Whilst Goldstein stays with the realm of the fictional, this interest in the macabre is also becoming blurred with reality, with an ever-increasing number of real-life deaths (car accidents and the like) being displayed on the internet. Goldstein poses the difficult to answer question of whether empathy is possible.

But, so long as dark tourists feel excitement in an experience, it is worth attempting to quantify pleasure in observing depictions of death or violence and finding the roots, however difficult it may be. Herein lies the explanation.

Pleasure in Observing Death

Many have attempted to explain away the causes for the enjoyment of observing depictions of violence and death. The enjoyment, it must be said, does not necessarily arise from observation of death itself, but rather from identification with the victims and villains involved.

Huxley (1971) explains this dichotomy by dividing the world into good and evil. He argues that this gives us the opportunity to feel a 'oneness with all of humanity', a togetherness with both good and evil. He claims that normal existence can be transcended and that one may experience the satisfaction of believing oneself to be greater than evil.

Another theorist, Dickstein, has argued that, as we grow from childhood through adolescence to adulthood, we are taught to suppress our fears and superstitions and taught that society will protect us. 'But', Dickstein argues, 'in some level we never really believe this'. It is his belief that literary and cinematic fear makes us vicariously look for ways of coping with our insecurities caused by this inherent mistrust in the security provided by society (Dickstein, 1884).

A third argument, and perhaps the most primal, is that we need to enact displays of violence in order to confront our fears and insecurities. Such displays are presumed to 'help audiences to confront [perceived] personal guilt indirectly, so that they might break free from real or imagined sins through the controlled trauma of the experience' (Rockett, 1988, p. 3). This allows the viewer to walk away, control the situation to an extent, but yet 'live' the experience.

Thus, while we are afraid of death, the ability to observe depictions of suffering and dying enables us to confront these fears and walk away unscathed. In this way we control the experience ourselves and remain safe, much in the same way we control our actions while thrill seeking by driving fast and bungee jumping. Perhaps in this way we can experience some relief at such displays.

So perhaps this thrill seeking in some way explains the commodification of dark destinations. Physical and mental stimuli create a feeling of contentment. Perhaps, as Stone argues, 'the level of stimulation in the past will not be sufficient to satisfy the need in the future'.

Personal Interpretation

We all see things differently, and the way in which we view violence and death depends on our own experience and on the context within which we interpret it. To illustrate, depending on what angle (based on our own experiences) we view the characters in a film, we draw our own conclusions and interpretations, whether sympathetic or not, and experience emotions accordingly. In the same way, survivors of a death camp would view an Auschwitz exhibition differently to a teenager. And so it is with sensitivities. Some of us deal with violence differently to others. While some may react with revulsion, others may see entertainment.

So it must be argued that for each dark tourist, many different experiences are possible when visiting a dark tourism destination, depending on their pasts, their connection to the event in question, the company they are travelling with, as well as their own personalities. Further, dark tourism experiences are not only framed by psychological factors. Time and maturity can also alter attitudes and re-shape our understanding of past events.

From a Distance

Lennon and Foley, have argued that dark tourism is an intimidation of the very foundations of modernity (2000, p. 11). As such, we view dark tourism through the lenses we have at our disposal, and against the backdrop of the world we live in and the lives we lead. Our lives are framed by human rights struggles, and rapid advances in science and technology. We live in a world where violence has a different form to those known by our ancestors of centuries ago, and our vision of the world is markedly different to those of people living 500 years ago. A visit to a medieval site will result in different emotions, different fears, to a visit to a Second World War battlefield. A visit to where Henry VIII delivered a speech and a visit to where Martin Luther King delivered a speech will cause different emotions and address different concerns. Events far in the past do not touch us as directly as events in the immediate past.

Conclusion

There is much that is interesting to us only because it is rare or unusual. In a discussion on people's desire for violent entertainment, the sociologist Carroll suggests that horror films do not so much discharge negative emotions as appeal to our curiosity: 'horror attracts because anomalies command attention and elicit curiosity' (1990, p. 195). He argues that horror movies as a genre present society's norms only to violate them, and that this violation of norms holds a fascination for people to such an extent that they rarely see these violations in everyday experience.

Many of the norms that prevail in contemporary society support, among others, freedom of speech, equality and individual rights. Many events that dark tourism memorials and sites stand for were to violate these and many other norms, and often ended up with the loss of many lives or even mass murder. Hence dark tourism destinations could be thought of as sites that simply satisfy our curiosity above all.

When discussing dark tourism motivation, the term morbid curiosity is often used; indeed, we've used it in this chapter. It is a compulsion, a drive fixed with excitement and fear to know about macabre topics, such as death and horrible violence. In a milder form, however, this can be understood as a cathartic form of behaviour or as something instinctive within humans. This aspect of our nature is also often referred to as the 'Car Crash Syndrome', arising from the fact that is seems impossible for passersby to ignore such accidents.

We are fascinated by scenes of unimaginable destruction and disaster; we're drawn to the ghoulish and the bizarre. And at some stage, we all like to squirm in horror. So, somewhere, in amongst all of this, one thing stands out: there is something of the dark tourist in all of us.

References

Aitkenhead, D. (2000) Rough Justice. *The Observer* (28 May 2010).

Baker, B. (2001) Taking the law into their own hands: fighting crime in South Africa. Paper presented at the 29th Joint Sessions of Workshops, ECPR, Grenoble, France.

Bennett, T. (1995) *The Birth of the Museum: History, Theory and Politics*. Routledge, London.

Bluecloud, P. (1972) *Alcatraz is not an Island*. Wingbow, Berkeley, California.

Bologna, S. (1999) The construction of South African heritage: a study of tourism to Robben Island and Cape Town townships. Unpublished Paper. Department of Anthropology, University of Cape Town, Cape Town.

Buntman, F. (1997) The politics of conviction: political prisoner resistance on Robben Island, 1962–1991, and its implications for South African politics and resistance theory. PhD Thesis, University of Texas, Austin, Texas.

Buntman, F. and Juang, T. (2000) The role of political imprisonment in developing and enhancing political leadership: a comparative study of South Africa's and Taiwan's democratisation. *Journal of Asian and African Studies* 1, 43–66.

Champion, D. (1973) Alcatraz goes public. *San Francisco Chronicle* (October 26).

Deacon, H. (1996) Introduction. In: Deacon, H. (ed.) *The Island: A History of Robben Island 1488–1990*. Mayibuye Books, Cape Town, pp. 1–8.

Deegan, H. (2001) *The Politics of the New South Africa: Apartheid and After*. Longman, Harlow, UK.

DeNevi, D. (1991) *Riddle of the Rock: The Only Successful Escape from Alcatraz*. Prometheus Books, Buffalo, New York.

Di Natale, M. and Breschi, S. (2009) Ritualism, Realism and Revolt. Annual Sociology Symposium, University of Natal, South Africa.

Dlamini, M. (1984) *Hell-Hole Robben Island: Reminiscences of a Political Prisoner*. Spokesman, Nottingham, UK.

Dobbs, K. (1999) Good gruesome: the joy of prison museums. *Canadian Airlines Inflight Magazine* (June), 35–40.

Durkheim, E. (1895) *Rules of the Sociological Method*. The Free Press, New York.

Fine, E. and Haskell, J. (1985) Tour guide performance as site sacralization. *Annals of Tourism Research* 12, 73–95.

Foley, M. and Lennon, J. (1996) JFK and dark tourism: heart of darkness. *Journal of International Heritage Studies* 2, 195–197.

Foote, K. (1997) *Shadowed Ground: America's Landscapes of Violence and Tragedy*. University of Texas Press, Austin, Texas.

Glassberg, D. (1996) Public history and the study of memory. *The Public Historian* 18, 7–23.

Hewison, R. (1987) *The Heritage Industry*. Methuen, London.

Hutton, B. (1994) *Robben Island: Symbol of Resistance*. Mayibuye Books, Bellville, South Africa.

Irwin-Zarecka, I. (1994) *Frames of Remembrance: The Dynamics of Collective Memory*. Transaction Publishers, New Brunswick, New Jersey.

Johnson T., Nagel, J. and Champagne, D. (1997) *American Indian Activism: Alcatraz to the Longest Walk*. University Press, Urbana, Illinois.

Kathrada, A. (1997) Opening address: the Robben Island Exhibition, Esiqithini. In: Deacon, H., Penn, N., Odendaal, A. and Davison, P. (eds) *Robben Island Timeline*. Mayibuye Books, Cape Town, South Africa, pp. 5–11.

Kempa, M. (2003) Prisons: recent trends and problems. In: Srivastava, A., Singh, A. and Tiwari, R. (eds) *Encyclopedia of Criminology*. Fitzroy Dearborn Press, Chicago, Illinois, pp. 109–111.

Leman-Langlois, S. (1999) Constructing post-conflict justice: the South African truth and reconciliation commission as an ongoing invention of reconciliation and truth. PhD Thesis. University of Toronto, Toronto, Canada.

Lennon J. and Foley, M. (2000) *Dark Tourism: The Attraction of Death and Disaster*. Continuum, London.

Loo, T. (1998) *Fragments of the Rock: Representations and Rule on Alcatraz Island*. Paper presented at the American Law and Society Association, Aspen, Colorado.

Loo, T. and Strange, C. (2000) Rock prison of liberation: Alcatraz Island and the American imagination. *Radical History Review* 78, 27–56.

Lowenthal, D. (1985) *The Past is a Foreign Country*. Cambridge University Press, Cambridge, UK.

MacCannell, D. (1992) *Empty Meeting Grounds*. Routledge, London.

Macdonald, S. (1997) A people's story: heritage, identity, and authenticity. In: Rojek, C. and Urry, J. (eds) *Touring Cultures*. Routledge, London, pp. 155–176.

Mandela, N. (1994) *Long Walk to Freedom*. Abacus, London.

Mankiller, W. and Wallis, M. (1993) *Mankiller: A Chief and Her People*. St. Martin's Press, New York.

Naidoo, I. (1982) *Island in Chains: Ten Years on Robben Island*. Harmondsworth, Cape Town.

N.A. (1994) *Unlocking Alcatraz – Curriculum Guide: Federal Penitentiary (1934–1963) and Native American Occupation (1989–1991)*. Fort Mason, US Department of the Interior, Washington, DC.

Pratt, J. (2003) The disappearance of the prison: an episode in the civilizing process. In: Strange, C. and Bashford, A. (eds) *Isolation: Places and Practices of Exclusion*. Routledge, London.

Rioufol, V. (1999) Making of a new past for a "new" South Africa: the commemoration of Robben Island. MS thesis. Department of Political Studies, University of Cape Town, South Africa.

Rojek, C. (1993) *Ways of Escape: Modern Transformations of Leisure and Travel*. Macmillan, London.

Rojek C. and Urry, J. (1997) *Touring Cultures*. Routledge, London.

Ruth, D. (1996) *Inventing the Public Enemy: The Gangster in American Culture*. University of Chicago Press, Chicago.

Seaton, A. (1996) From thanatopsis to thanatourism: guided by the dark. *International Journal of Heritage Studies* 2, 234–244.

Shackley, M. (2001) Potential futures for Robben Island: shrine, museum or theme park? *International Journal of Heritage Studies* 7, 355–363.

Smith, P. and Warrior, R. (1996) *Like a Hurricane: The Indian Movement from Alcatraz to Wounded Knee*. The New Press, New York.

Strange, C. (2000) The Port Arthur Massacre: tragedy and public memory in Australia. Studies in law. *Politics and Society* 20, 159–182.

Tutu, D. (1999) *No Future Without Forgiveness*. Rider, London.

Urry, J. (1990) *The Tourist Gaze*. Sage Publications, London.

Urry, J. (1995) *Consuming Places*. Routledge, London.

Urry, J. (1992) *The Representation of the Past*. Routledge, London.

Watson, H. and Kopachevsky, J. (1994) Interpretations of tourism as commodity. *Annals of Tourism Research* 20, 643–660.

Watson, P. (1997) Anyone for a night behind bars? *Business Review Weekly* (December 8), p. 108.

13 The Golden Jubilee of Independence and Panafest in Ghana: 'All that Glitters is not Gold'

Edward Addo[1]

[1]*Tourism Department, Memorial University of Newfoundland, Grenfell Campus, Corner Brook, Newfoundland and Labrador, Canada*

Introduction

On 6 March 1957, the Gold Coast changed its name to Ghana when it became the first country in sub-Saharan Africa to gain independence from British colonial rule. When Ghana celebrated her golden jubilee of independence in 2007, one of the key objectives of the event was to strengthen Diaspora relations as the world also celebrated the 200th anniversary of the official abolition of the trans-Atlantic slave trade. Panafest, a biennial Pan-African arts festival, is also celebrated in Ghana to enhance the ideals of Pan-Africanism, African development and Diaspora relations. Primary activities of the two events in 2007 and Panafest in 2009 included visual arts display, performing arts, musical concerts, durbars and public lectures.

Both the golden jubilee of independence and Panafest have been characterized by political, economic and ethnocentric controversies that tend to overshadow their historical and cultural significance. The controversies are discussed in Ghanaian media, among Ghanaians at home and in the Diaspora. This chapter discusses the controversies in the context of cultural tourism and the political history of Ghana.

The research methodology used included an extensive literature review on Ghana's political history and tourism industry, participation in the golden jubilee of independence in 2007 and Panafest in 2007 and 2009, direct interviews with participants and stakeholders of both events in Accra, the national capital, and Cape Coast, the capital city of the Central Region and primary destination for Panafest. Secondary data and information (reports and comments) were also collected from the Ghana Tourist Board (GTB), and two media websites, Ghanaweb.com and Joyfmonline.com.

Conceptual Considerations: 'Celebrative Events' and Controversies in Cultural Tourism

'Celebrative events', such as festivals and anniversaries (Picard and Robinson, 2006), have been an integral part of cultural tourism since the era of modern travel. Gee *et al.* (1997) and Goeldner and Ritchie (2006) explain how tourism, through the ages, involved long journeys that offered visitors unique opportunities to experience exotic destinations, events and cultures. Africans/Egyptians, Syrians, Phoenicians/Lebanese, Polynesians, Chinese, Indians and Europeans (Romans, Greeks, English and French) were among the early travellers who participated in events such as the Olympics (beginning in 776 BCE) and the Grand Tour of the 17th and 18th centuries.

In recent years, celebrative events have become ubiquitous in the tourism industry. Destinations compete to host international events such as the Olympics, World Fairs and World Tourism Day partly because of their positive economic and socio-cultural impacts (Edwards *et al.*, 2004). The economic benefits include job creation, income generation and infrastructure development. The socio-cultural benefits include preservation of traditional norms and heritage, (re)affirmation of local identities and enhancement of destination image (O'Toole and Mikolaitis, 2002; Wendroff, 2004; Getz, 2005; Smith and Robinson, 2006; Goldblatt, 2008; Smith, 2009). The factors that account for successful events include political commitment and accountability, efficient organization and management practices, effective marketing, volunteerism, fundraising and coordinated planning at the micro (site), meso (destination) and macro (regional) levels (Armstrong, 2001; Gunn and Var, 2002).

The literature on cultural tourism also draws attention to the complexity of festivals and other events (Sandercock, 1998; Florida, 2002; Smith, 2009). Smith (2009) discusses some of the complexities and provides case study examples from different countries. She explains that flagship and urban regeneration projects, such as the Greenwich World Heritage project, tend to generate short-lived impacts and controversial legacies because of their insensitivity to the needs of small communities, and constricted approach to planning. She also points out that festivals and other celebrative events could attract investments and sponsorships, enhance the image of a destination, and provide alternative sources of revenue but could also undermine the cultural values of ethnic or minority groups.

Some event-related controversies have been discussed in the context of commodification, commercialization and globalization. Li (2000), Long *et al.* (2004), Picard and Robinson (2006) and Smith (2009) explain how globalization causes dissonance when external values and practices are superimposed on local communities by a few multi-national corporations. They further explain how short-sighted planning, political propaganda and flamboyant advertising could make an event popular but could be also deemed a failure in terms of social, cultural and economic impacts on local economies. This controversy is characteristic of events that are planned to attract international tourists who seek opportunities to experience other cultures. In recent years, different viewpoints on globalization such as 'Jihad' (protecting the uniqueness of cultural identity), 'McWorld' (hybridization, homogenization and standardization of culture) and 'Glocalization' (localizing the benefits of globalization) have surfaced in the cultural tourism literature (Smith, 2009).

Events pertaining to cultural attractions or landmarks could also create controversies in public policy, sustainable development, community participation, planning strategies, management, marketing, evaluation processes, international relations, ethics and etiquette (kickbacks, for example), sponsorship, security, and political ideologies and agenda (Allen, 2003; Long *et al.*, 2004; Beaven and Laws, 2007; Goldblatt, 2008). For example, a narrator may have a different perception or understanding of what a tourist attraction or product is. In other words, narratives could be value-laden, subjective and ethnocentric. Objective authenticity (relating to cultural sites or attractions), constructed authenticity (relating to performing and some forms of visual arts), and personal authenticity (relating to emotions and psychological experiences) are, therefore, subject to different values and interpretations that could be controversial (Goldblatt and Supovitz, 1999; Hoyle, 2002; Macleod, 2006).

In sub-Saharan Africa, celebrative events usually include festivals and independence anniversaries. These events are vehicles for reclaiming local and national identities. Discussions on controversies relating to such events in the sub-region would be incomplete without considering political economies and history. The traditional and critical theories in cultural tourism studies (Castro-Gomez, 2001) are, therefore, relevant. Smith (2009) reiterates Castro-Gomez's viewpoint that while the traditional theory naturalizes culture and focuses on concepts such as aesthetics and harmony, the critical theory emphasizes the socio-economic or conflictive aspects of culture. The critical theory, she explains, places culture in the context of political economies and focuses on concepts such as imperialism, post-colonialism, capitalism and globalization. Furthermore, she explains how tangible heritage and intangible heritage have created political, economic, ethical, social and psychological controversies in post-independence countries such as Malaysia and India, and how colonial sites or edifices that are preserved but used for different functions entail divergent values.

As discussed in the next section, Ghana inherited diverse tangible and intangible heritage at the dawn of independence for cultural tourism development. The country set the pace for others in the sub-region to follow. In the 1960s alone, Nigeria, Benin, Burkina Faso, Cameroon, Somalia, D.R. Congo, Madagascar, Central African Republic, Chad, la Cote d'Ivoire, Mali, Mauritania, Niger, Senegal, Togo and Gabon gained their political independence from European colonial rule (Lewin, 1991). The celebration of independence anniversaries in these countries underscores the economic, socio-cultural and political experiences with Europeans, particularly the Portuguese, Dutch, Danes, Swedish, English, French and Germans, for 500 years in the sub-region.

Ghana's Geography, History and Political Economy: Overview and Contextual Framework

Ghana is located on the Atlantic coast of West Africa between latitudes 4.5° N and 11° N and shares borders with three former French colonies: la Cote d'Ivoire, to the west; Togo, to the east; and Burkina Faso, to the north. The Gulf of Guinea, part of the Atlantic Ocean, stretches about 540 km (338 miles) along the southern border. The distance from the coast to the northern border is about 672 km (420 miles). The land area of Ghana measures about 238,540 km² (92,100 square miles), almost the same size as Britain or the states of Illinois and Indiana in the USA combined. The topography of the country changes from coastal plains and rolling land to mountain peaks and plateaus in the eastern and central areas (Briggs, 2002). The country has ten administrative regions.

The ten administrative regions more or less reflect the ethnic and tribal diversity of the country. The five major ethnic groups are Akan, Ewe, Guan and Ga-Adangbe in the southern and central areas, and Mole-Dagbane in the northern area. The Asante, Fante, Akim and Kwau are the major tribes of the Akan ethnic group (Library of Congress, 2007). The country's population increased from 6.7 million in 1960 to about 21.8 million in 1996. About 24.2 million people were counted in the 2010 population and housing census. There are regional variations in population distribution. Most of the people live in the southern half of the country. Regional capitals have high population densities in part due to urban-bias policies and development strategies encouraging rural–urban migration. This trend has persisted since the era of colonization (Boahen, 1975; Buah, 1998; Amenumey, 2008).

English is the official language used in government offices, large-scale businesses, national media and educational institutions. National culture is portrayed in diverse traditional, 'highlife' and 'hip-life' music and dance, funerals, festivals, durbars, folklore and religion. In terms of faith and religion, about 63% of Ghanaians are Christians, 15% are Muslims and 22% are indigenous or non-believers. Christianity predominates in the southern and central areas while Islam predominates in the northern area as a result of western European and trans-Saharan trade influences, respectively (Boahen, 1975; Buah, 1998; Amenumey, 2008).

The history of modern Ghana is linked with the ancient Ghana Empire that developed simultaneously with the Songhai and Mali empires between the 4th and 11th centuries. The presence of Portuguese, Dutch, Danish, Swedish, British, German and French merchants and missionaries in Ghana, beginning in 1471, and later British colonization resulted in intensive trans-Atlantic trade in commodities and slaves. British political influence in Ghana climaxed in the late 19th century after the signing of the Bond of 1844 in Berlin to partition Africa. In 1874 the British army, led by Sir Garnet Wolseley, captured Kumasi, the capital city of the Asante Empire in a war that the Asantes refer to as the 'Sagranti War'. In another Anglo–Asante war in 1899, the Asante King Prempeh I was captured and forced into exile. Consequently, British protectorate was declared over the Asantes. In subsequent years, the British government introduced a system of indirect rule allowing the institution of chieftaincy to play a major role in politics and public administration (Boahen, 1975; Buah, 1998; Amenumey, 2008).

The 1947–1956 period is very significant in Ghana's political history. In 1947, the United Gold Coast Convention (UGCC), a political party, was formed (Buah, 1998). The founders of the party included Obetsebi Lamptey, Ako Adjei, Ofori Atta, J.B. Danquah and Edward Akuffo Addo. Later, Kwame Nkrumah was invited to join the UGCC (Kellner, 1987). Some Ghanaians identify these men as 'The Big Six' and the architects of Ghana's independence. The agitation for independence gathered momentum when on 28 February 1948 Sergeant Adjetey and some ex-servicemen were shot as they marched to deliver a petition to the colonial government (Buah, 1998).

In 1949, Nkrumah deserted the UGCC to form and lead a new party, the Convention People's Party (CPP). His action created irreconcilable differences between him and his supporters, on one hand, and the rest of 'The Big Six' and their supporters, on the other hand. Political threats and imprisonment did not deter the CPP from exerting more pressure on the colonial government to grant independence to Ghana. In 1951 a new constitution led to general elections and the CPP won a two-thirds majority. The

constitution granted broad powers to Nkrumah and his party. In 1956 a plebiscite in British Togoland called for union with Ghana and the CPP passed an independence motion which was approved by the British Parliament. On 6 March 1957 the British colony of the Gold Coast became the first country in sub-Saharan Africa to gain political independence (Buah, 1998; Library of Congress, 2007). The independence celebration was attended by Harold Macmillan, the British Prime Minister, and Princess Marina, the Duchess of Kent who delivered a message from the Queen of England. The first Governor-General of Ghana, Sir Charles Arden-Clarke was sworn in on that day. The celebration underscored freedom and justice as key principles of Ghana's independence (BBC, 1957).

The political climate in Ghana became more hostile when in 1958 Nkrumah's government unilaterally repealed protection clauses of the constitution and passed the Preventive Detention Act (PDA) empowering the government to imprison political opponents without trial. Some of 'The Big Six' were thrown into jail and died there. The political tensions in the country intensified as Nkrumah's socialist and communist ideologies became more prominent. On 1 July 1960 Ghana became a Republic and in 1964 Nkrumah declared the country a one-party state. On 24 February 1966 while on a trip to Peking, China to attend a non-aligned conference, Nkrumah was overthrown by a military coup d'état. In 1972, he died in Romania. Some Ghanaians believe that Nkrumah's overthrow was orchestrated by the US Central Intelligence Agency (Agbodza, 2009).

Nkrumah's socio-economic development legacies in 1966 included investments in physical infrastructure (roads, the Akosombo dam, electricity and bridges), social infrastructure (education, health and housing), state-owned farms, and manufacturing industries, predominantly in the southern half of the country. His cultural and political legacies included the Diaspora relationships established with Dr W.E.B du Bois and George Padmore, two of the pioneers of Pan Africanism (Africa, 1974/75;

Killick, 1978). The former was the first African American to earn a doctoral degree from Harvard University. He died in 1963 at the age of 95 and was buried in Ghana. Padmore was a Trinidad scholar. The du Bois Center and Padmore Library in Accra attract many tourists from the Diaspora.

Nkrumah's era was followed by a series of military regimes led by Lt General J.A. Ankrah (1966–1967), Lt General A.A. Afrifa (1967–1969), General I.K. Acheampong (1972–1978), General F.W.A. Akuffo (1978–1979), and Flt Lt J.J. Rawlings (1979 and 1981–1992) interspersed with short-lived civilian governments led by Dr Kofi Abrefa Busia (1969–1972), Edward Akuffo Addo (1970–1972), and Dr Hilla Limann (1979–1981) (Hettne, 1990). The first era of Rawlings' military regime is considered the most brutal in Ghana's military governance because six military officers, including three former Heads of State (Afrifa, Acheampong and Akuffo), were executed by firing squad. Additionally, three Supreme Court judges, including a female judge who was still breastfeeding her baby, and two civilians were also abducted and killed.

In spite of the bloodshed and austerity economic measures introduced to clean the economy of corruption and mismanagement of public resources, Ghana's economy did not improve much as the prices of the country's major exports fell continuously, infrastructure deteriorated, and unemployment and inflation figures skyrocketed. The economic hardships led to growing dissatisfaction with both civilian and military governments in the 1970s and 1980s (World Bank, 1984; Ofori-Atta, 1988). In 1992, Ghana returned to a constitutional rule of the Fourth Republic under the presidency of J.J. Rawlings of the New Democratic Congress (NDC). President Rawlings was followed by Mr. John Agyekum Kufuor of the New Patriotic Party (NPP) for two consecutive terms, 2000–2008.

The NDC claims to be a social-democratic party flourishing on the principles of probity, accountability and transparency. The NPP, on the other hand, identifies itself as a party that champions the cause of property-owning democracy and the traditions of J.B. Danquah and the UGCC. The NDC is currently the ruling party led by President John Evans Atta Mills, a graduate and apostle of the Kwame Nkrumah Ideological Institute. He was also vice-president of Ghana in the second term of Rawlings' presidency. The CPP, a shadow of Nkrumah's party, has only one seat in parliament occupied by Nkrumah's daughter. The destiny of Ghana is still being shaped by the political ideologies and controversies surrounding 'The Big Six' and military personnel who overthrew democratically elected governments between 1957 and 1981 and ruled the country until 1992.

Growth and Development of Ghana's Tourism Industry

Different political, cultural and socio-economic events brought many tourists to Ghana after independence in 1957. However, the first indication of government interest in developing the tourism industry was a feasibility study in 1970 on the development of tourist attractions for a five-year (1972–1976) development plan (Obuan Committee, 1972). In 1973, the Ghana Tourist Board (GTB) was established to implement national tourism policies and to co-ordinate tourism activities. It was charged with the key responsibility to regulate tourism enterprises such as accommodation, catering, travel, transport and charter operations through registration, inspection, licensing, classification and enforcement of decisions. GTB was also charged with the responsibility to promote and market tourism in Ghana and abroad, conduct studies and research into trends in the tourism industry at home and abroad to aid decision and policy-making, promote the development of tourist facilities, and to carry out other functions that would be conferred on it by legislative instruments (GTB, 1998).

In the mid-1970s financial and technical limitations of the government necessitated more studies and evaluation of the country's tourism potential by international development organizations such as the United

Fig. 13.1. The Golden Jubilee of Independence: cultural and political significance.

a special secretariat to attract thousands of international visitors to the country to celebrate the anniversary from January to December, 2007. The Chief of Staff of the Office of the President of Ghana was also involved with its planning and management.

The three objectives of the event underscored the importance of Ghana's history, political economy, Diaspora relations and heritage: 'to celebrate and commemorate Ghana's landmark achievement as the first country in Black Africa to attain independence from colonial rule; to reflect on the evolution, development, achievements and drawbacks of our country over the past fifty (50) years; and to look forward to the future, to our vision of excellence in all fields of endeavour in the next fifty (50) years towards our centenary birthday as a nation' (Ghana @ 50, 2007).

The programmes and activities of the mega cultural event underlined the nationalistic sentiments and patriotism of Ghanaians. Moreover, the programmes and activities, which were centred on 12 monthly themes, accentuated the political struggle for independence, socio-economic and political achievements made since 1957, and Diaspora relations. The monthly themes were: January, *Reflections;* February, *Towards Emancipation*; March, *Freedom March*; April, *Our Nation, Our People*; May, *Our Wealth and Our Prosperity;* June, *Heroes of Ghana Month;* July, *African Unity Month;* August, *Diaspora Month*; September, *Service to the Nation*; October, *Knowledge and Ghana's Development*; November, *A Healthy People, A Healthy Nation*; December, *Final Curtain* (Ghana @ 50, 2007).

On 5 March 2007, a special parliamentary session featured speeches by His Excellency Olusegun Obasanjo, President of Nigeria, and the Duke of Kent who represented Her Majesty, Queen Elizabeth II. Both dignitaries praised Ghana for being able to withstand the political and economic storms that engulfed her in the 1970s and 1980s. References were made to the Peer Review Mechanism of which Ghana was the first country reviewed, and the improved relations that the country had had with the UK and the rest of the world. In his inaugural speech, Kofi Annan, a Ghanaian and former UN Secretary General, praised Ghana for her socio-economic achievements and reminded Africans of the need to tackle the three overarching challenges facing the continent: 'the need for more security, the demand for better development, and the rising cry for human rights and rule of law' (Annan, 2007).

Participant observations and interviews conducted on 6 March 2007 in the streets of Accra, at the Black Star/Independence Square, Kwame Nkrumah Memorial Park, W.E.B. du Bois Center, hotels and restaurants indicated that the 50th independence anniversary was worth celebrating in a grand style in spite of some prevailing political controversies and socio-economic challenges. The theme of the event, 'Championing African Excellence', was linked to Nkrumah's vision that Ghana would be the guiding light of African independence and solitary: the BLACK STAR, the lodestar of Africa. The official website for the event proclaimed that 'Ghana's attainment of independence and the subsequent ideological support it extended to other colonized countries on the continent, culminated in the emancipation of many of these countries from colonial rule' (Ghana @ 50, 2007).

In terms of achievements and what made Ghanaians proud of their country and citizenship, about 60% of the 100 randomly selected individuals indicated that they preferred hard-won freedom with problems to servitude in tranquillity. This notion was also declared in the anniversary speeches and programmes. An equally important attribute of the event was the constant reference to the link between Ghana's tourism industry and the Diaspora. The presence of the diplomatic corps, UN delegation, Heads of State, and visitors from the Diaspora, particularly the Americas and Caribbean, at the Black Star/Independence Square on the morning of 6 March 2007 was highly acknowledged by the government of Ghana. The American and Caribbean delegations included Rev. Jesse Jackson and some Rastafarians. The golden jubilee's monthly theme for August, 'Diaspora Month', provided impetus to Panafest 2007 activities, which included enactments of the slave march. Justifiably, the golden jubilee of independence was considered to be a viable driver of economic transition, diversification, and tourism growth and development.

Frequent recitation of the national pledge and singing of the national anthem emphasized the need to preserve and enhance Ghana's heritage, political freedom and Diaspora relations. National identity and patriotism were also portrayed in the anniversary songs, television advertisements in Ghana and abroad (on the BBC, for example), billboards, posters, locally manufactured textiles, arts, legacy projects and enactments like the slave march, Nkrumah's declaration of Ghana's independence, and special parliamentary sessions. Chieftaincy affairs, heritage, traditional music and dance, gold jewellery and 'kente' (Ghana's traditional textile) were showcased.

The nation's security personnel, school children/students, UN peacekeeping personnel and Ghanaians of all walks of life demonstrated great pride and enthusiasm in celebrating the 50th milestone of political independence. Undoubtedly, the event brought Ghanaians and the international community together to reflect on Ghana's socio-economic achievements, political history, heritage and culture. The specific achievements that the interviewees

mentioned included freedom from colonial rule, a functional democratic constitution, 50 years without a civil war, Ghana's simultaneous chairmanship of the AU and ECOWAS, and the Black Stars' first-time appearance and impressive performance at the 2006 FIFA World Cup tournament in Germany. The Black Stars, the national soccer team, beat the US team by two goals to one (2–1) and the Czech Republic team by two goals to nil (2–0). Additionally, Ghanaians celebrated a modest, but steady, economic growth and political stability in the past decade.

Experiential Controversies of the Golden Jubilee of Independence

In spite of its diverse and positive cultural, political and economic impacts on Ghana's economy, the golden jubilee of independence was, and still is, characterized by some controversies. On 6 March 2007 at the independence parade, the crowd was exhilarated when a marching band from the UK played pipes and marched in kilts. It was a different cultural performance that many Ghanaians witnessed for the first time. Contrarily, some Ghanaians were disappointed that their president wore a three-piece suit instead of Ghanaian attire for the unique independence parade. In response to criticisms, the president asked his critics to understand that the three-piece suit was international attire and explained that as much as he appreciated local traditions and cultures he also realized the need to conform to the dictates of a rapidly advancing world (*Daily Guide*, 2007). Some Ghanaians did not appreciate the president's exposition. The 'presidential dress code controversy' is still alive in some Ghanaian political discourse. Was it the concept of globalization that ultimately influenced the president's choice of attire for the unique event?

There have been some allegations of poor planning and management of the event. In his anniversary message to Ghanaians on 6 March, the president advised those who were not happy about the high public expenditures on the event not to portray themselves as people who knew the cost of everything but did not know the benefit of anything. As was expected, soon after the 2008 general elections, the NDC-led government accused the Chief of Staff of the previous NPP-led government and the Chief Executive of the Ghana @ 50 Secretariat of causing financial loss to the state. The alleged losses were associated with various contracts, vehicle purchases, infrastructure development, bank overdrafts, loans, procurements, memorabilia, etc. in excess of the initial US$20 million budgeted for the event. Some media reports claimed that the total cost of the event exceeded US$78 million. In response to intense outcry for public accountability, mainly by the NDC party and its supporters, a commission of inquiry was set up to investigate the alleged misappropriation and make recommendations to the government. Later, when the case was referred to a court, the defendants were vindicated on the grounds of 'inadmissible prosecution by the plaintiff' (i.e. the Government of Ghana), meaning the findings of the commission of inquiry could not be used to prosecute the defendants (Ghana News Agency, 2010).

Controversies over the political ideologies and socio-economic contributions of 'The Big Six' have also been associated with the golden jubilee of independence. Activists of Nkrumah's political ideology (unitary government and socialism) argued that the economic and political achievements of the first president of the country were underrepresented in the golden jubilee of independence. On the other hand, activists of Danquah's political ideology (federalism and capitalism) argued that the rest of 'The Big Six' were the real architects of Ghana's independence. Nkrumah was portrayed as a political opportunist and demagogue, who turned Ghana into a one-party state, flouted the principles of freedom and justice promised at the dawn of independence, and mismanaged the country's financial resources. Students of both schools of thought agreed, however, that Ghanaians such as Paa Grant, Mensah Sarbah, Casely Hayford, Komla Gbedemah,

Kojo Botsio, Nii Kwabena Boni, Seth Antoh, Kwegyir Aggrey, Philip Quarcoe and Sergeant Adjetey, one of the ex-servicemen who were shot in 1948, should also be rightfully recognized as national heroes and founding fathers of the nation.

Similar political controversies surrounding the golden jubilee of independence have been underscored in another study (Lentz and Budniok, 2007). The authors highlight the political squabbles that existed between NPP and NDC parliamentarians, procedural lapses in the special parliamentary session on 5 March 2007, restrictions and challenges that journalists and researchers faced, and poor planning and inadequate logistics for some activities of the celebrative mega event.

More recently, some political, economic and cultural controversies have cropped up in relation to a new presidential palace built by the NPP-led government to commemorate the golden jubilee of independence. The presidential edifice, a political and cultural landmark, like the White House in Washington, DC, USA, 10 Downing Street in London, UK, and the Kremlin in Moscow, Russia, is also a tourist attraction. Currently, the Osu Castle in Accra, a colonial edifice, is the seat of government offering a limited access to only invited guests and dignitaries. It could be seen afar by tourists or the public from the coast at Osu or the Independence/Black Star Square.

Interestingly, the wrangles between the two major political parties (NPP and NDC) developed along the ideological divide between Nkrumah and Danquah of 'The Big Six', have been extended to the estimated US$70 million presidential edifice, which was initially christened the 'Golden Jubilee House'. Without any official ceremony, the NDC-led government changed the name to 'Flagstaff House', a legacy of the British colonial government. Nkrumah used the colonial Flagstaff House as office and residence after using the Christianborg Castle for the same purposes in 1957. During the course of research, it became public knowledge that the actual dilapidated and abandoned colonial Flagstaff House was renovated and retained by the NPP-led government.

One reason given for dumping the name 'Golden Jubilee House' was that the NPP-led government did not have any legislative instrument backing its adoption. Another reason given was that the new name tarnished Nkrumah's political reputation. Some officials of the president's office complained that the location of the new presidential edifice did not provide adequate security. They also maintained that the main structure required some repairs and landscaping. Meanwhile, part of the edifice was being used by the Ministry of Foreign Affairs because its own office building was burnt down.

Finally, there was an established ethnocentric controversy surrounding the new presidential edifice. Some NDC supporters from the Greater Accra Region argued that the presidential edifice resembled a stool used mostly by the Akan ethnic group, particularly the Asantes who constitute the political backbone of the NPP. The stool-shaped presidential edifice was, therefore, considered to be a cultural eyesore to the non-Akan ethnic groups in the Greater Accra Region.

Some interviewees argued that if the seat of government was relocated to the new presidential edifice, the Osu Castle could become a UNESCO designated World Heritage Site like the Elmina and Cape Coast castles. Consequently, it would become a destination-based or latent cultural capital to attract many domestic and international tourists, especially those from the Diaspora. The interviewees contended that the local community and the Ghanaian taxpayer would benefit more from the colonial edifice as a tourist attraction instead of being the seat of government.

The divergent values entailed in Osu Castle and the controversial 'Golden Jubilee House'/'Flagstaff House' as the seat of government are mostly political, ethnocentric, cultural and economic. At the time of writing this chapter, the president was still reluctant to move from Osu Castle to the controversial 'Golden Jubilee House'/'Flagstaff House' and some Ghanaians belonging to the NPP and other opposition parties were strongly accusing the NDC-led government of using propaganda to humiliate the former president of Ghana, and the NPP and its supporters

Cultural and Political Significance of Panafest

The idea of Panafest was conceived by a Ghanaian woman, Efua Sutherland, in the late 1980s and was first launched in 1991. The founder invited all peoples of African descent to come to Elmina and Cape Coast, in the Central Region, in the final week of July and on the first day of August, to celebrate the history, heritage and beauty of Africa through artistic and cultural manifestations. Elmina and Cape Coast were considered ideal destinations for Panafest because of the St George and Carolusburg castles. As a Pan-African arts festival, Panafest welcomes support from all persons committed to the wellbeing of Africans on the continent and in the Diaspora (K. Yankah, Accra, 2007, personal communication).

The five core objectives of Panafest are: 'to establish the truth about the history of Africa and experience of its people, using the vehicle of African arts and culture; to provide a forum to promote unity between Africans on the continent and in the Diaspora; to affirm the common heritage of African peoples the world over and define Africa's contribution to world civilization; to encourage regular review of Africa's development objectives, strategies and policies; and to mobilize consensus for the formulation and implementation of potential alternative options for development' (K. Yankah, Accra, 2007, personal communication).

The African Union (AU), formerly the Organization of African Unity (OAU), endorses Panafest as an important celebrative event in Africa. The event is, therefore, held under the auspices of the AU, and GTB and MOT on behalf of the Government of Ghana. International organizations and private enterprises sponsor the event. Among the major stakeholders and sponsors are the Agricultural Development Bank (Ghana), Western Union, North American Airlines, Spacefon, United States Agency for

International Development (USAID), STAR Brewery Ghana Ltd, Telecom and the Commonwealth Secretariat. Other stakeholders are politicians, producers and vendors of traditional crafts and arts, musicians, tour operators, owners of hospitality facilities, and domestic and international tourists.

Panafest showcases a grand durbar of chiefs, rites of passage programmes, slave march re-enactment, midnight candlelight vigil at the Cape Coast castle, Emancipation Day commemoration, musical concerts and performing arts (Fig. 13.2). International performing and visual artists from across Africa and the Diaspora are regular and important participants. Stevie Wonder, the renowned American musician co-chaired Panafest 1994; NourbeSe Philip, a Canadian lawyer, poet and writer of Trinidad descent, was a special guest of honour in 1994; and in 1999, 2001 and 2003 the festival featured James Cannings, an international recording artist and businessman, accomplished guitarist, keyboardist, composer, arranger, songwriter, producer and studio engineer. Before his participation in Panafest, the Guyana-born artist had had a track record of volunteer work at hospitals, nursing homes, schools, colleges, libraries and international festivals, and had played his music in many countries.

Panafest 2007 marked the eighth edition of the festival and was highly significant because it coincided with Ghana's 50th independence anniversary, and the 200th anniversary of the abolition of the trans-Atlantic slave trade. It also heralded the Joseph Project, another Diaspora-related event that was later launched and had Rita Marley (widow of Bob Marley, the Reggae music legend), Julius Garvey (son of Marcus Garvey, a prominent Pan-Africanist), and Michelle Jones Galvin (a great-great-grandniece of Harriet Tubman, a celebrated African-American abolitionist) as special guests of honour. The dual themes for Panafest 2007 were 'Re-uniting the African Family' and '50 Years of Independence: Pan-Africanism Revisited – 21 Century Edition'. A colloquium theme for the event was 'Pan-Africanism in the Context of Africa's Political, Economic and Social Development' (direct interview with Yankah, Panafest Secretariat, 2007).

In a message delivered to mark the 2007 Panafest celebration, Mr Yankah, Chairman of Panafest Secretariat, called upon Ghanaians, Africans and all persons committed to the wellbeing of Africans on the continent and in the Diaspora to intensify their search for the re-emergence of African

Fig. 13.2. Panafest activities and attractions. Pictures courtesy of GTB and Panafest Secretariat.

civilization, which was trampled upon by many years of slavery, colonialism and imperialism. The message underscored the political contributions of African legends like Kwame Nkrumah of Ghana, Sekou Toure of Guinea, and Modibo Keita of Mali, and the influences of Marcus Garvey, W.E.B du Bois, and George Padmore on the political liberation of the continent and the 'Return to Africa Movement' (direct interview with Yankah, Panafest Secretariat, 2007).

Experiential Controversies of Panafest

Like the golden jubilee of independence, Panafest has been characterized by some administrative lapses, economic challenges and political controversies. In previous years, the festival suffered from a lack of sponsorship, late payment of entry fees and some communication problems (direct interview with Yankah, Panafest Secretariat, 2007). In Cape Coast in 2009, all the interviewees identified the same problems with Panafest 2007 and 2009. In addition, they mentioned poor advertisement and marketing strategies, insufficient logistics, dwindling public sector support and interest, partisan politics and controversies, expensive booth fees, and poor sales of African arts and crafts.

In 2009, some art and craft vendors from Nigeria, Burkina Faso and Mali wanted the destination for Panafest rotated from one African country to another, an indication of geopolitics and interest in commoditization/commodification and commercialization of Panafest, instead of emphasizing the event's unique cultural and historical significance to the European-built castles and forts in Ghana used for the slave trade. Some interviewees also pointed out that in previous years (before 2009) Panafest was better able to bring Africans on the continent and in the Diaspora together for a common course – to celebrate the history, heritage and culture of Africa. They also claimed that, on previous occasions, the event was better able to serve as a vehicle for promoting African unity and reconciling political, social and cultural differences. In spite of their frustrations and experiential challenges, the vendors

maintained that it would be worth celebrating the event in the future.

All the 40 vendors and 20 visitors interviewed at Panafest 2009 were not pleased with the declining government support for the event, decreasing sponsorship and publicity, and cancellation of the Joseph Project which was introduced by the NPP-led government to add more vigour to Panafest in order to attract more international visitors from the Diaspora. As indicated earlier, the launch of the Joseph Project in 2007 attracted tourists from the Diaspora including the widow of a prominent Reggae musician, and descendants of a renowned Pan-Africanist and a famous African-American abolitionist.

The greatest disappointment, however, was expressed about the high cost of booths or space used by vendors to sell their products, poor quality and inadequate sanitary facilities on site, and a declined number of attendees and buyers in 2009. The disappointment was also partly attributed to the declining publicity and financial support the government gave to Panafest 2009. Paradoxically, 80% of the vendors interviewed indicated that they wanted less government involvement in the planning and management of Panafest but more financial and technical support to facilitate their participation in the event.

Conclusion

The golden jubilee of independence in 2007 and Panafest in 2007 and 2009 underscored Ghana's history, political economy, development challenges and achievements since European contacts in the 15th century. In 2007, Ghanaians faced many socio-economic challenges such as unemployment, high cost of living, inadequate infrastructure, high cost of education, brain-drain of professionals and young educated citizens, corruption and public mismanagement of national resources. Nevertheless, some Ghanaians felt the two mega and cultural events were worth celebrating in a grand style.

The golden jubilee of independence continues to be characterized by political, ethnocentric and economic controversies. Suspicions and complaints about excessive expenditures, poor planning and ethnocentric politics have tainted the cultural significance of the event. In 2009, Panafest experienced a sharp decline in public sector support, logistics and attendance. Additionally, vendors were disappointed by poor sanitary facilities, and high cost of booths and space to exhibit their products.

Other countries in sub-Saharan Africa look up to Ghana for leadership in celebrating independence anniversaries and socio-economic achievements. Disappointingly, however, the political, financial and ethnocentric controversies surrounding the golden jubilee of independence and Panafest suggest that 'all that glitters is not gold' in Ghana. There is a need for more cooperation between the public and private sectors to better plan and manage celebrative events. There is also a need to seriously address the political and ethnocentric controversies surrounding the new presidential edifice. As some of the interviewees indicated, relocation of the seat of government to the new presidential palace could enhance the potential of Osu Castle as destination-based or latent capital to attract more tourists, especially from the Diaspora. This in turn could create additional jobs and generate some revenue for the host community and the tourism industry. Hopefully, further research might indicate different scope and dimensions of the controversies associated with independence and Diaspora-related celebrations in Ghana and other countries in sub-Saharan Africa.

References

Africa (1974/75) GHANA: 61–69. Available at: Africaonline.com.gh/tourism/flag 2007 (accessed 27 September 2007).

Agbodza, K. (2009) RE: Bagbin: Ghana had founding fathers. Available at: http://www.ghanaweb.com/GhanaHomePage/features/artikel.php?ID=158831 (accessed 10 October 2010).

Allen, J. (2003) *Event Planning Ethics and Etiquette: A Principled Approach to the Business of Special Event Management*. Etobicoke, John Wiley and Sons, Canada.

Amenumey, D.E.K. (2008) *Ghana. A Concise History from Pre-Colonial Times to the 20th Century*. Woeli Publishing Service, Accra.

Annan, K. (2007) Championing Africa's renaissance: peace, development and human rights. Inaugural speech, Ghana @ 50 Golden Jubilee Lectures. Available at: http://www.ghana50.gov.gh/events/ (accessed 26 March 2007).

Anquandah, J.K., Opoku-Agyemang, N.J. and Doortmont, M.R. (2007) Transatlantic Slave Trade: Landmarks, Legacies, Expectations. *Proceedings of the International Conference on Historic Slave Route*. Sub-Saharan Publications, Accra, Ghana, pp. 23–53.

Armstrong, J.S. (2001) *Planning Special Events. Excellence in Fund Raising Work Book Series*. Jossey-Bass, San Francisco, California.

BBC (1957) *Ghana celebrates independence*. Available at: http://www.BBC.co.uk/onthisday/hi/dates/stories/march/6/newsid_2515000/2515459.stm (accessed 20 October 2010).

Beaven, Z. and Laws, C. (2007) Service quality in arts events: operations management strategies for effective delivery. *Event Management: An International Journal* 10, 209–219.

Boahen, A. (1975) *Ghana: Evolution and Change in the Nineteenth and Twentieth Centuries*. Longman, London.

Bourdieu, P. (1984) *Distinction: A Social Critique of the Judgement of Taste*. Cambridge University Press, Cambridge, UK.

Briggs, P. (2002) *Ghana. The Bradt Travel Guide*. The Globe Pequot Press, Guilford, Connecticut.

Buah, F.K. (1998) *A History of Ghana. Revised and Updated*. Macmillan Publishers, Oxford, UK.

Castro-Gomez, S. (2001) Traditional vs. critical cultural theory. *Cultural Critique* 49, 139–154.

Curtin, S. and Busby G. (1999) Sustainable destination development: the tour operator perspective. *International Journal of Tourism Research* 1, 135–147.

Daily Guide Newspaper (2007) Why I was in suit. Kufuor speaks. *Daily Guide Newspaper* No. 1968, 1.

Edwards, J., Moital, M. and Vaughan, R. (2004) The impacts of mega-events: the case of EXPO'98-Lisbon. In: Long, P. and Robinson, M. (eds) *Festivals and Tourism: Marketing, Management and Evaluation*. Business Education Publishers Ltd, Sunderland, UK, pp.195–215.

Florida, R. (2002) *The Rise of the Creative Class*. Routledge, London.

Gee, C.Y., Makens, J.C. and Choy, D.J.L. (1997) *The Travel Industry*. International Thomson Publishing, New York.

Getz, D. (2005) *Event Management and Event Tourism*. Cognizant Communication Corporation, New York.

Ghana @ 50 (2007) Official website for the 50th independence anniversary celebration of Ghana. Available at: http://www.ghana50.gov.gh/ (accessed 02 March 2007).

Ghana News Agency (2010) Ghana Bar Association (GBA) expresses concern about criticisms on ruling. Available at: http://Ghanaweb.com/news (accessed 18 August 2010).

Ghana Tourist Board (1995) *The 15-Year National Tourism Development Plan*. GTB, Accra.

Ghana Tourist Board (1998) *Business Development Unit. First Draft of Project Document*. GTB, Accra.

Ghana Tourist Board (2007) *Facts and Figures on Ghana's Slave Castles, Forts and Lodges*. GTB, Accra.

Ghana Tourist Board (2010) *Tourism Statistical Fact Sheet on Ghana*. GTB, Accra.

Goeldner, C.R. and Ritchie, J.R.B. (2006) *Tourism: Principles, Practices, Philosophy*. John Wiley and Sons, New York.

Goldblatt, J. (2008) *Special Events: The Roots and Wings of Celebration*. John Wiley and Sons, Hoboken, New Jersey.

Goldblatt, J.F. and Supovitz, F. (1999) *Dollars and Events: How to Succeed in the Special Events Business*. John Wiley and Sons, New York.

Gunn, C.A. and Var, T. (2002) *Tourism Planning: Basics, Concepts, Cases*. Routledge, New York.

Hettne, B. (1990) *Development Theory and the Three Worlds*. John Wiley and Sons, New York.

Hoyle, L.H. (2002) *Events Marketing: How to Successfully Promote Events, Festivals, Conventions, and Expositions*. John Wiley and Sons, New York.

Kellner, D.A.M. (1987) *Kwame Nkrumah*. Chelsea House, New York.

Killick, T. (1978) *Development Economics in Action: A Study of Economic Policies in Ghana*. Heinneman, London.

Lentz, C. and Budniok, J. (2007) Ghana@50 – celebrating the nation: an account. *Afrika Spectrum* 42, 531–541.

Lewin, A. (1991) *Africa is Not a Country: It's a Continent*. Clarendon Press, Wotton-under-Edge, UK.

Li, V. (2000) What is in a name? Questioning globalization. *Cultural Critique* 45, 1–39.

Library of Congress USA (2007) Country Studies: Ghana. Available at: http://lcweb2.loc.gov/frd/cs/ghtoc.html (accessed 8 April 2007).

Long, P., Robinson, M. and Picard, P. (2004) Festivals and tourism: links and fevelopments. In: Long, P. and Robinson, M. (eds) *Festivals and Tourism: Marketing, Management and Evaluation*. Business Education Publishers Ltd, Sunderland, UK, pp. 1–14.

Macleod, N. (2006) Cultural tourism: aspects of authenticity and communication. In: Smith, M.K. and Robinson, M. (eds) *Cultural Tourism in a Changing World: Politics, Participation and (Re)presentation*. Channel View Publications, Clevedon, UK, pp. 177–190.

Meethan, K. (2001) *Tourism in Global Society: Place, Culture and Consumption*. Palgrave, Basingstoke, UK.

National Atlas Development Centre (1995) *Tourist Map of Ghana including a Plan of Accra*, 1995 edition. Council for Scientific and Industrial Research, Unimax Publishers, Accra.

Obuan Committee (1972) *Report of the Feasibility Study Committee on the Development of Ghana's Tourist Attractions for the 5-year Plan Period 1972–1976*. Government of Ghana, Accra.

Ofori-Atta, W. (1988) *Ghana: A Nation in Crisis*. The Ghana Academy of Arts and Sciences, Accra.

O'Toole, W. and Mikolaitis, P. (2002) *Corporate Event Project Management*. John Wiley and Sons, New York.

Picard, D. and Robinson, M. (2006) Remaking worlds: festivals, tourism and change. In: Picard, D. and Robinson, M. (eds) *Festivals, Tourism and Social Change: Remaking Worlds*. Channel View Publication, Clevedon, UK, pp. 1–31.

Ramerini, M. (2009) Dutch and Portuguese colonial history. European forts in Ghana. Available at: http://www.colonialvoyage.com (accessed 16 February 2009).

Sandercock, L. (1998) *Towards Cosmopolis*. John Wiley, Chichester, UK.

Smith, M.K. and Robinson, M. (2006) Politics, power and play: the shifting context of cultural tourism. In: Smith, M.K. and Robinson, M. (eds) *Cultural Tourism in a Changing World: Politics, Participation and (Re)presentation*. Channel View Publications, Clevedon, UK, pp. 1–17.

Smith, M.K. (2009) *Issues in Cultural Tourism Studies*. Routledge, New York.

Wendroff, A.L. (2004) *Special Events: Proven Strategies for Nonprofit Fundraising*. John Wiley and Sons, Hoboken, New Jersey.

World Bank (1984) *Country Study: Ghana. Politics and Programs for Adjustment*. World Bank, Washington, DC.

WTO (1999) *Tourism Marketing Trends: Africa. 1989–1998*. WTO Commission for Africa, Madrid.

14 The Ideological Role of Intergovernmental Organizations in the Promotion of International Tourism

Jorge Ferraz[1]

[1]*Escola Superior de Hotelaria e Turismo do Estoril (Estoril Higher Institute for Hotel and Tourism Studies), Estoril, Portugal.*

Introduction

The main purpose of our research has been to gauge the ideological dimension of Intergovernmental Organizations' (IGOs') discourse relating to tourism and the role it plays in moulding the relationship between the different societies involved in international tourism in the past 50 years, addressing issues and controversies about the role of the IGOs.

In the final declarations and conclusions of many of the meetings and international conferences on tourism organized by IGOs, the stated aim is to build a fairer world and combat international and global inequality (see the List of Declarations section). There are, however, some studies (see Lanfant, 1991, 1992, 1995; Mowforth and Munt, 2009) that call into question not only the benign side of international tourism but also the role played by the IGOs in building a fairer and more equitable world.

Our main empirical case study was a comprehensive analysis of the most significant declarations and propositions about tourism from the main IGOs, using content analysis methods. We analysed a set of 30 final declarations and final propositions from international meetings (documents that we will call 'declarations' in the wider meaning of the word; see the List of Declarations) produced and adapted by the IGOs, especially the World Tourism Organization (UNWTO). Besides UNWTO (the heir of the International Union of Official Travel Organizations [IUOTO] and, until 2003, when it became a United Nations specialized agency, known as WTO), other IGOs involved in meetings and international conferences and declarations about tourism (often in association with the UNWTO) include: the United Nations Development Programme (UNDP), the United Nations Environment Programme (UNEP), the World Bank (WB), the United Nations Conference on Trade and Development (UNCTAD), the United Nations Educational, Scientific and Cultural Organization (UNESCO), the Conference on Security and Co-Operation in Europe (CSCE). In some cases, there is also involvement by business associations or international business leaders' organizations such as the World Travel and Tourism Council (WTTC), or Non-Governmental Organizations (NGOs) such as the International Council on Monuments and Sites (ICOMOS), the International Institute for Peace through Tourism (IIPT) and the Earth Council.

Actually, tourism, whilst an international phenomenon, cannot be reduced to a geographic fact or tourism fluxes. It is a total social phenomenon, structural in the definition of unequal changes between peoples and societies far beyond the pursuit of leisure by participants from industrial and post-industrial societies (see Lanfant, 1991, 1992, 1995). In this process, tourism acquires the statute of an ideological substitute of the 'exchange theory' with consequences on the cultural matrix of the involved societies, in particular the receptor ones (Lanfant, 1991, 1992, 1995), and consequently participates in the configuration of an unequal and stratified interdependence between the different societies involved.

The importance of the IGOs comes from the fact that they constitute the main model of institutional formalization of an international regime (see Dougherty and Pfaltzgraff, 2003). Here, we see regime as a complex whole 'of mutual expectations, rules and regulations, organizational plans, energies and financial commitments that have been accepted by a group of states' (Ruggie, 1998, p. 56) inside a framework that ranges from a simple organization between national states to a model of organization of the international system that includes the supranational and the transnational.

The dependence of many countries on the IGOs is another relevant factor. The IGOs, such as the World Bank (WB), could finance projects or offer expertise in planning (in the case of the UNWTO), defining the type of project to be developed and thus conditioning the choices made by each country (see Lanfant, 1991, 1992, 1995; Hawkins and Mann, 2007). The Hawkins and Mann (2007) study on the financings of the WB for the development of tourism since the 1960s until the early years of the 21st century identifies four phases that correspond to different intervention models. These models have strong correlation with orthodoxies and theories about economic development in general and tourism in particular (for example, economic and tourism growth versus environmental preservation; see Hawkins and Mann, 2007) and ideological choices about the public and private sectors role. The promoted projects could even be presented as an important factor for a fairer international

system based upon scientific and technical arguments but, in fact, such projects and policies related to tourism are mainly political arguments that presume a selection of values (see Hall, 1994, p. 110).

The intergovernmental organizations' discourse contributes to the referred ideological phenomenon while promoting themes, products, practices and tourism models that, on behalf of the interest of all people and communities involved, correspond primarily to the ideologies, interests and preoccupations of those in the most developed[1] societies and are related to:

- Alterations in the organization of international tourist activity and the roles of those involved.
- Changes in the international regime and in the model of the relationship between societies.
- Changes in the most developed contemporary societies with respect to the meanings placed on leisure, respective practices and the role that tourism assumes on them.
- Different social, political and economic capacities of the implicated societies.

The declarations in question were then subjected to content analysis, a set of techniques and procedures constituting a 'controlled hermeneutic based on deduction: the inference' (Bardin, 1991, p. 9). A controlled interpretation that seeks to unravel the unspoken or not explicitly stated, where, as Vala (1986) says, we have to take into account the connection between the conditions of discourse and production analysis.

We interpreted the themes presented at the discourses (a thematic analysis, the categories of which were constructed using deductive and inductive procedures) and we also examined their structure and presentation (see Bardin, 1991; Vala, 1986). Likewise, we had in mind the significant absences: the implicit or muted issues, themes, perspectives and actors associated with international tourism and its understanding within the context of societal and tourism changes. In fact, the hidden and the implicit in the words are revealing components of the ideological phenomenon (Bourdieu, 1989).

Thus, besides the aforementioned inventory of contents and themes and how they are evaluated, we should then contextualize the discourse. It is not just looking at the text itself and its speaker, but also establishing the connection with the reality of the social phenomenon in question and its nature in a particular socio-historical context.

Finally, having in mind the degree of saturation and redundancy of the thematic categories in question, we also have to pay attention to the relative heterogeneity of how these categories present themselves in the different statements.

The thematic categories that were built are:

- The general thematic or the explicit subject of the statement.
- The role attributed to tourism (economic, social, cultural, political, environment protection).
- The types of tourism in terms of movements and flows, particularly with regard to the types of spaces and privileged societies.
- The types of tourism products.
- Tourism models relating to the practices and behaviours of those involved.
- Privileged collective actors.
- The nature and content of the roles assigned to different collective actors.
- The model of tourism development proposed.

Ideology and Discourse in the IGOs

For us, the concept of ideology is based on four pillars (see Gramsci, 1966, 1974 [written between 1910 and 1935]; Mannheim, 1979 [published in 1936]; Boudon, 1986; McLellan, 1987): an organized discursive system that is not reduced to a totalitarian 'logical-idea' nor to the field of politics or expression of irrationality; historical contextualization of the discourse and practices of its actors; guidance for

behaviour; and imposition of power and hierarchical relationships between actors, practices and values.

To these four pillars we add a fifth, the one that allows us to better cope with the hidden and not explicit dimension in the social reality and in its discourses, the ground which hosts the deepest dynamics of power relations; the discourse in question always states to report to a supra-individual concern and worldview. In its construction are involved not only the dominant actors, but also the dominated ones, assimilating as their interest what such discourse states, legitimizing particular views and interests, transfigured into the interests and views of all; an 'invisible power... [that] may be exercised only with the complicity of those who do not want you to know that they are subjected to it ...' (Bourdieu, 1989, p. 7–8), a phenomenon of cultural hegemony (see Gramsci, 1966, 1974). Thus, we see the arousal of practices and discourses that are more than a mere imposition of external violence or coercion gaining some historical durability and becoming somewhat organic (see Gramsci, 1966, 1974).

We do not endorse, therefore, a vision of ideology as 'arbitrary ideology' but rather as 'organic ideology' (see Gramsci, 1966, 1974), a set of ideas or beliefs associating a worldview to a corresponding conduct (Gramsci cited in McLellan, 1987). We see it as kind of total system of thought, ownership of determined social groups, which refers directly to struggles between dominants and dominated actors, bearing in mind their specific places in the social processes and in social struggles (Mannheim, 1979 [1936]).

In the IGOs' proposals we can see statements about the IGO formal attributions, infer relations of forces between IGO members and the institutionalization of an international multilateral regime, as Ruggie (1998) describes. We can also see the power effect produced by the words of an institutional discourse that claims to be supported by technical and scientific arguments. However, such arguments and proposals are not simple facts associated with expertise but political arguments in which the choice and implementation of the values involved depends on 'the relative power of *winners* and *losers*' (Hall, 1994, p. 110). This is indeed a characteristic of the power of scientific discourse; its apparent neutrality hides its ideological dimension.

Bourdieu (1989) says that understanding how the institutions represent themselves and the implications it has for the issue of power means analysing the word in its symbolic value: as capital of a 'field'; as power based on legitimacy that has to denote and connote and on the legitimacy of who utters them. Thus, a possible taxonomy constructed this way could be transformed on power relationships (comprehended in those social interactions and in these processes) that manifest themselves as 'relations of meaning' and assume the contours of a 'political classification system' (Bourdieu, 1989, p. 14–15). In the declarations of the IGOs a taxonomy is established and a worldview is legitimized which, constituting an act of power by the word, becomes symbolic violence.

However, the power of the IGOs comes also from the capacity to legitimize themselves as such. The IGOs are not mere passive components of an unequal international system, a sounding of a discourse completely lagged from the concerns of all those who are part of it and which they claim to represent, nor simply transmission belts of the interests of more powerful actors, be they states, multinational corporations or other powerful interest group. The question of the role they assume in international relations, particularly as formal dimension and rationalized and bureaucratic apparatus of the international regime (Archer, 1995; Ruggie, 1998), as well as the processes of legitimation – as 'legitimate domination' (see Weber, 1989) – are essential to confer capacity to the implementation of their proposals.

Ideology and Tourism

Taking into account the relationship between tourism and ideology, its connection with the issue of international exchanges and socio-historical changes, we have some assumptions as a starting point.

Firstly, tourism has to be understood in the field of the changing in the meanings and practices of leisure and its relationship to work, which also constitutes an important terrain for the assertion of new forms of social differentiation (see Boyer, 1972; Urry, 1990; Rojek, 1995; Rojek and Urry, 1997; MacCannel, 1999 [1976]; Santos, 2002).

Along with the traditional view of work versus leisure, recreational tourism versus existential tourism, to use the concepts of Cohen (1996), we see today a flexible overlap of time, space and practice of work and leisure, resulting from late capitalism processes that have obvious implications for tourism (see Rojek and Urry, 1997). For example, the meaning of some work and leisure practices needs no longer to be perceived as opposing spheres of social life. They don't need to rest upon a rigid dichotomy between production and consumption, such as was in the context of modernity, in which the work was at the centre of the premise of human existence and leisure was left as a donatory function of rewarding work, or romantic escapism from the conditions of daily life (Rojek, 1995). In the current context of post-modernity, leisure occupies a central place in the meaning of human existence (Rojek, 1995).

In addition, the tourist experience of the social actor appears as a complex whole of several motivations and practices, interconnected in a variety of products consumed by the same individual (Rojek and Urry, 1997; Prentice, 2007), some of them clearly associating leisure and work, as in some short city breaks occurring in the middle of work periods, or in the case of mega-events and contemporary urban tourism (see Roche, 1996).

In what concerns the type of tourism and tourists, we have gone from a model of 'old tourist' to the 'new tourist' (Poon, 2003). The 'old tourism' that has been the predominant model of tourism until the 1970s was characterized by mass organized travel and pre-purchased standardized package and tourists seeking the sun and sea (Poon, 2003), looking, as could be inferred from the typology and using the concepts of Cohen (1996), for experiences of diversionary and recreational types.

The 'new tourism', which would correspond to the transition from a Fordist society to a post-Fordist society, covers aspects such as market segmentation, the customization of products and travel, the use of new information technologies and communication, flexible use of space and time, diversification and creation of niche products, the search for novelty, refusal of the standardized travel, environmental concerns, pluralism of tastes and experiences and even tourist involvement with the local societies (see Poon, 2003; Mowforth and Munt, 2009).

Poon's approach is useful to state the relationship between changes in capitalism, contemporary societies and tourism (Mowforth and Munt, 2009). Our perspective, however, is not to endorse a dichotomous view that could represent any idea of historical radical shift. Besides, the 'new tourist' represents a social actor whose ethical discourse corresponds to a marketing trait and an ideological construction, what Mowforth and Munt (2009) call 'ego-tourist'. Today, the existential tourists or those for whom authenticity is really the equivocal issue (Cohen, 1995, 1996) coexists with the one who, for example, joins the experience of a sun-and-sea mass tourism with adventure tourism (see also Rojek and Urry, 1997; Prentice, 2007). Instead, we see the coexistence, in the consumptions and motivations of tourist, of the 'old tourist' and the 'new tourist'.

These types of 'old' and 'new' also have, in terms of products, their modes of embodiment, from which we can give some examples. As 'old' we can point out the prevalent images of the sun-and-sea mass tourism, the winter sports tourism (such as the alpine type), the tourism in cosmopolitan centres and in cities with historical or heritage interest, religious tourism and pilgrimages or even thermal tourism.

For 'new tourism', we can point out, among a myriad of classifications that are difficult to distinguish, rural tourism, ecotourism, new urban and metropolitan tourism, mega-events, MICE tourism and the meeting industry, theme park tourism (fre-quently based upon a strong technological component), residential tourism, city-break tourism, wellness tourism, golf, volunteer tourism, adventure tourism and a great deal of niche products. These products fit the logics of market segmentation, product customizing, new motivations and ideologies and could be understood in the context of increased global competition for tourism demand and supply involving all kind of countries, areas and societies (see Roche, 1996; WTO, 1998; Apostolopoulos et al., 2001; Hoffman et al., 2003; Bramwell, 2004; UNWTO & ETC, 2006; Mowforth and Munt; 2009). Some of these products are not exactly 'new' (some have been around 30 years) but could be presented as a type of tourism that addresses the 'new tourism' model and the 'new tourist' behaviour and motivations.

Secondly, tourism has the characteristic of a system of trans-local and international interactions and exchanges, encompassing economic, social, political, cultural and psychological dimensions, and contributing to the configuration model of the relationship between societies and of the way of life of their populations (see Urry, 1990; Lanfant, 1991, 1992, 1995; Hall, 1994; Britton, 1996; Crick, 1996; Mowforth and Munt, 2009).

For example, the Global South countries have little or no control over the process or benefits they could draw (see Britton, 1996; Crick, 1996). Even if they control the development tourism policies and plans, they do not control the tourism demand, the multinational corporations or the industry global processes of integration (see Knowles et al., 2004; Hjalager, 2007). We face a global industrial network that supports a tourism system that primarily responds to the needs of the tourist metropolitan centres (Nash, cited in Hall, 1994), under the form of an 'international division of the tourist sites' with areas of the world and countries specialized in certain types of products and markets, including the most industrialized societies (Urry, 1990).

Not invalidating the existence of relations of domination of the neo-colonial type in certain tourist areas (Britton, 1996), we cannot reduce the phenomenon to a simple one-dimensional hierarchical model. What we see is mainly a division and specialization of labour, services, products and spaces, intrinsically linked to a specialization of economies and to socio-cultural, ideological, economic and political changes affecting all countries (Urry, 1990; Mowforth and Munt, 2009), where tourism occupies a unique place in the complex system of asymmetric interdependencies between those involved in the international system and the different societies, often with a transnational logic. Dézert and Wackermann call it a network whose:

> ... structures develop in such a way that national societies are identified no longer essentially in terms of their place within hierarchies of domination/subordination, but by variable roles and functions.
> (Cited in Lanfant, 1995, p. 34).

Thirdly, the way business is managed and the identification of its key players tell us that we are dealing with principles of high expertise and planning in the context of an extraordinary and progressive process of global connection between major collective actors such as multinational corporations, states, the IGOs and non-governmental organizations (NGOs) (Lanfant, 1991, 1992, 1995; Hall, 1994; Britton, 1996; Mowforth and Munt, 1998; Knowles *et al.*, 2004; Hjalager, 2007). The tourism industry comes from the internationalization model of an ethnocentric matrix, as we have seen in the 1960s and 1970s, to the current transnational logic that implies flexible reorganization of the value chain (Hjalager, 2007), on which the local actors had always a limited capacity for intervention. In the internationalization model, corporations do not have a global intervention on the market nor are they engaged in multinational or transnational alliances, but they are in the international arena only to search for new markets for existing products, often in conjunction with national tourism boards (Hjalager, 2007). The transnational logic expresses the high globalization stage where the corporations see the world as a unique space.

Finally, we have to look at the discourse on tourism and leisure and how it conceals its ideological nature. Hall (1994) tells us:

> ... the dominant ideology of leisure and tourism in western capitalist societies which is increasingly being exported throughout the world through the modernization dynamic portrays leisure and tourism as essentially a private and individual choice. Such an ideology only serves to legitimize the relation between the culture industry and dominant ideology.
> (Hall, 1994, p.192).

IGOs, Contemporary Societies and Tourism

When discussing the role and significance of the IGOs, we begin by picking up the concept of *World System In Transition* by Santos (2001), since that allows us to make the connection between the approach of international relations and the comprehension of the dynamics of relations between societies and the role of IGOs, far beyond a formal dimension. Moreover, the nature of the concept overcomes mutually exclusive dichotomies between modern and postmodern societies, between a world-system and an era of globalization (see Santos, 2001). His model of 'constellations of practice' allows us to identify more easily the coexistence of different logics, actors and interests, which fit the local and the global, the international and the transnational, the multinational corporations, the states, the IGOs, the NGOs and other civil society actors, and where, along with a structure of asymmetric relations between the periphery/semi-periphery/centre, typical of modern society, we identify the logic of the network interactions and a new form of global/local hierarchy. Different powers, logics and actors interact in a complex web of interdependencies.

It is in this complex and multipolar context, and using the concept of 'international regime' – the institutionalized context of the IGOs (Ruggie, 1998) – that we see the action and discourse of the IGOs.

According to Ruggie, 'international regimes are commonly defined as social institutions around which states' expectations converge in different issues-areas' (1998, p. 89). However, the regimes are dialogic in nature, and one must include in its analysis the social interactions that result from effective communication between individual and collective actors (Ruggie, 1998), even because they also represent perspectives that are more than a mere sum of states interests and may assume a life of its own (Dougherty and Pfaltzgraff, 2003).

For Ruggie, the decentralized interstate principle where 'states are subject to no external earthly authority, and there exists no organization above states, only between them (…) has become partially but progressively modified', because of the emergence of spheres of influence, of supranational actors and 'an even more complex pattern of interconnectedness of decisions, events and developments [that] modifies the principle of independence' (Ruggie, 1998, p. 47–48).

Ruggie (1998) says that the institutional form of international contemporary life is the multilateralism. This implies that the coordination of national policies and agendas among several states is done on the basis of certain principles of ordering relations between them (Ruggie, 1998), formalized in international law and on the IGOs, without forgetting, however, that the institutional context not only relies on the interdependence between states but also on the inequality between them (Waltz, 1999).

Finally, Ruggie (1998) states that the possibility of any kind of understanding between the international players and the regularity and continuity in their interactions such as the ones we could find in IGOs, has to be based upon a Weberian perspective of authority and power, a model of legitimate domination. This is a crucial factor in determining the capacity of intervention of IGOs.

The IGOs legitimacy, the power to decide on investments, the expertise skills they could offer and the nature of the contemporary international system play a crucial role in giving strength to their discourse. Thus, the IGOs also express dynamics of power

and willingness and an understanding based on the principle of minimally shared values and meanings by the involved societies.

To avoid confusion between organization and institution, we say that organization is a form of an institution, and the term international organizations refers mainly to a system of rules and objectives associated with a rationalized administrative apparatus (Archer, 1995). From this perspective the IGOs are formal organizations with permanent bodies, subject to international law, constituted as an association of states, expressing the will to bring order to international relations, defending common interests and establishing ties beyond their national borders (see Fernandes, 1991). IGOs can be of two types: coordination or cooperation (such as the UNWTO) where there isn't any transference of sovereignty; or integration as is the single case of the European Union where there is some transfer of sovereignty from the member states to the organization (Fernandes, 1991).

Of all these, the most relevant for our purpose are the IGOs of cooperation and coordination. Accordingly, the UNWTO stands out, either by its objectives (focusing on tourism, in its varied dimensions of social, economic and cultural phenomena), the geographical dimension and the number of members (almost global), the areas of intervention (from technical planning to codes of ethics) and also for having recently acquired the status of the United Nations specialized agency for tourism.

The Declarations of the IGOs: Main Results and Discussion

Concerning the formal structure of discourse and the type of terminology used, each 'Declaration' usually begins by invoking the foregoing or any international legal framework on rights. The first 'Declarations' had a very programmatic speech, with terminology that refers to values and human rights. With the advance of this millennium, the speech began to lose the explicit enunciation of rights and values; a more technical and neutral language is presented, and the aim of exchanging experiences and knowledge dissemination and research becomes increasingly important and more frequently mentioned.

When we deal with the concrete issues and perspectives presented in the proposals of the IGOs we find, at first sight, remarkable overlaps and repetitions. On closer look, however, we see contradictions, silences, phases and paradigm shifts that reveal a strong consonance with societal changes within leisure meanings and practices, with changes in the types of issues and international concerns (primarily focused on the perspective of the emitter societies, in general the most developed) and with ideological changes, especially in matters related to the roles played by states and corporations in the tourism field.

Now, turning to the identification of the phases, it should be noted that, until the 1970s, the dominant discourse of IGOs emphasized the dimension of tourism as an international phenomenon related to the physical movement of large numbers of people between countries and continents and the stated aim imputed on tourism by the IGOs' discourse was to be an important factor in the economic development and modernization of the so-called less developed societies and in finding international peace. The holidays and the leisure time were associated with the right to move freely and should be extended to all, in the logic of continuous growth, with a major interventionist role reserved for the state, from planning to managing the financial loans coming from the IGOs (see Lanfant, 1995; Britton, 1996; Hawkins and Mann, 2007). The focus of the intervention was based on the idea that tourism in the societies acted primarily as an economic phenomenon.

Throughout the 1960s and 1970s, IGOs such as the United Nations Educational, Scientific and Cultural Organization (UNESCO), WB and IUOTO/UNWTO were very active in systematically promoting (and inducing) tourism in the Third World (see Lanfant, 1995; Hawkins and Mann, 2007). However, this developmental view

produced perverse effects. Lanfant says that international organizations orchestrated an intense campaign that led the least developed countries to adopt this development orthodoxy, seeking foreign capital and leading to the creation of 'huge tourism centers..., worlds set apart on the margins of everyday life...' (Lanfant, 1995, p. 27). In those cases, that process means the establishment of social, cultural and economic enclaves not necessarily responding to the needs of local societies.

In this international flux, the dominant interaction would be registered among people from emitter societies (industrialized societies) and individuals and structures of receptive societies (traditional societies or developing ones). As to the main tourist products of this era, we have the sun-and-beach type and winter sports alpine type, as well the historical heritage of cities (for example, in Italy and France[2]).

However, the phenomena of seasonality and massification led, in the late 1970s and in international meetings, such as the 'Conference on Security and Co-Operation in Europe' in Helsinki in 1975 and the Seminar on the Social and Cultural Impacts of Tourism sponsored by UNESCO and WB in 1976 (de Kadt, 1979), to the raising of the issue of degradation of the physical spaces and to the appearance of the first proposals relating to the protection of fragile areas.

We have still an emphasis on the development of international tourism and a strong belief in its economic virtues, but we see concerns about the issue of massification and saturation beginning to emerge.

The declaration in Manila in 1980 could be seen as turning point in the discourse on tourism, where the articulation of issues related to domestic tourism, rural tourism, diversification of tourism products, sustainability, environment or the theme of 'individualized' and responsible tourism associated with lifestyles. The centre of the discourse shifted to identity themes and environmental issues in a context of preservation and enjoyment of non-industrial cultures, which we see as an important factor in the production of an effect of immobilization of the natural and cultural environments of the non-industrialized societies.

It is true that the Manila Declaration says that 'world tourism can contribute to the establishment of a new international economic order that will help to eliminate the widening economic gap between developed and developing countries' and that, in point 4, invokes, as it has done at the Rome Conference in 1963, the Universal Declaration of Human Rights. Nevertheless, in 1963, such ideas were central and appear associated with the freedom to travel, with the growth of international tourism and with the development of the poorest countries, with impacts on peace and intercultural themes. In 1980, these objectives were less prominent than domestic tourism, being that domestic tourism is mainly a phenomenon and a concern of the developed countries.

Even international cooperation or the international development of tourism must be accompanied 'by a similar effort to expand domestic tourism', and where the right to holiday that would be taken from a declaration of human rights appears, in paragraph 8, connected to the 'opportunity for the citizen to get to know his own environment, a deeper awareness of his national identity and of the solidarity that links him to his compatriots and the sense of belonging to a culture and to the people are all major reasons for stimulating the individual's participation in domestic and international tourism...' (Manila Declaration).

There is another document to which could be assigned an exemplary status: the 'Global Code of Ethics for Tourism' (GCOEFT) presented in 1999. This is a code of conduct to be followed by all actors in the tourism process and it often seems to be a summary of the former declarations on tourism, although under the rule of four structural features: a sustainable and responsible practice, highlighting nature tourism and eco-tourism; a vision of a tourist consumption and practices more preservationist at socio-cultural and environmental levels, as opposed to preceding developmental logics; the defence of tourism as a phenomenon of human rights and as a way to fulfil existential needs (rather than the expression of hedonistic leisure); the repeated emphasis on liberalization and deregulation of business activity and on industry self-regulation, while acknowledging some of its perverse effects, such as job insecurity and excessive repatriation of profits.

In fact, since 1980, in a progressive manner, the speech of the IGOs started rejecting the logic of growth, and the discourse about the motivation for tourism acquired a mainly 'psycho-cultural' meaning, beyond the mere right to leisure and travel. On behalf of a new orthodoxy, the preservation of identities gains 'a normative, prescriptive value' (Lanfant, 1995, p. 31).

All this discourse seems to speak less about the development of poorer societies and more about the problems or concerns of developed societies. It seems that it is concerned more with the motivations of the new 'middle-class' tourist than with the needs of host communities, in a process of immobilization of the cultural and natural characteristics of the traditional (and poorer) societies.

The enunciation of these concerns is accompanied, throughout the 1990s, by the decline of the state and the growing advocacy of economic deregulation, of public–private partnerships and appeals to industry social responsibility in a framework of self-regulation. These are discourses in line with the 'Washington Consensus' and with the neo-liberalism of the 1990s (see Santos, 2001) and of the new millennium.

On the international dimension of tourism, what stands out is the issue of institutional cooperation and harmonization assured by the states and the IGOs, focused on planning sustainable policies in a coordinated manner, mainly speaking about the need for regulatory mechanisms for environmental protection and about initiatives to promote the awareness of those involved.

Here and there, references are made to international inequalities, inferred mainly from the issue of the socio-economic benefits to local communities. However, the question of international inequality as a characteristic of the international system does not deserve the status of recurrent concern, except in the 'Amman Declaration on Peace through Tourism', in 2000, and in the 'International Conference on Tourism, Religions and the Dialogue of Cultures', in Cordoba, 2007. In the GCOEFT there is a reference to this problem, when the aim of promoting sustainable world tourism order is stated, benefits of which could be shared by all members of society; nevertheless, that concern is presented in the context of an open and liberalized economy.

As for the problem of interculturalism, peace and international security the scene is similar: decades of near invisibility revived by the 'Declarations' resulting from the conferences that took place in Amman and Cordoba and by the GCOEFT. In the GCOEFT, to be more precise, the question is not really interculturalism, but mainly the contribution of tourism 'to mutual understanding and respect between peoples and societies' (Article 1, Global Code of Ethics for Tourism).

Following the declaration of the 'Millennium Development Goals' in 2000, the issues of poverty reduction and the redistribution of economic benefits, now associated with the encouragement of small local ownership, are back (see 'Hue Declaration', 2004; 'Harnessing Tourism for the Millennium Development Goals', 2005). However, the principle of economic deregulation and international liberalization of business services and investment is not in question, it is only a request for 'liberalization with a human face' (see 'The Sustainable Tourism – Eliminate Poverty (ST–EP) Initiative', 2002).

In the IGOs' discourse of the past 10 years there is a relative reduction in the primacy of environmental preservation, but it does not disappear. This is now accompanied by a need for a contribution from tourism to reduce poverty and injustice; the elected products and practices continue to be cultural tourism and ecotourism associated with motivations related to identity issues, now legitimized by the claim that they have economic virtues for local people, encouraging them to make the most of their activities, products and traditional crafts (see 'The Québec Declaration on Ecotourism', 2002; 'Hue Declaration', 2004; 'Harnessing Tourism

for the Millennium Development Goals', 2005). The communities of the most disadvantaged societies are therefore still seen as objects of glorification while they maintain their traditional way of life, frozen in time, in space and in their aspirations. The aestheticization of poverty is a possible result (see Mowfort and Munt, 2009).

Finally, and more recently, three new themes have emerged: climate change, urban tourism and the dialogue of civilizations. The meetings of Djerba in 2003 and Davos in 2007 added the concern of climate change and the impact on tourism activity and industry, stating, in addition, the need to reduce poverty. The same was also said in the conference of Kuala Lumpur, 2007. Besides that, we don't see major differences with what you can find in other recent declarations.

As for metropolitan tourism (the name used by UNWTO), the emergence of two conferences in the space of a year, in 2006 and 2007, in Shanghai and Busan, agree with the (re)emergence of the previously low profile urban tourism. This is a phenomenon that covers cultural tourism, business tourism, urban policies and regeneration of cities, creation of mega-events, development of creative industries and the connection between the cultural and the economic (see Page, 1995; Roche, 1996); the political, economic and ideological process of tourist urbanization affects mainly the most developed societies (see Hoffman et al., 2003). Furthermore, these conferences were held in cities of Asian countries that are important economic and financial actors in the global economy and (along with Kuala Lumpur) are in a geographical area of repeated significance for UNWTO, territories of the most explosive growth in tourism for the next decade (see WTO, 1998; Knowles et al., 2004).

To conclude we mention the issue of peace and dialogue of civilizations. When we look at the conference 'Tourism, Religions and the Dialogue of Cultures' in Cordoba, 2007, it seems that a circle closes. Coupled with the novelty of the economic opportunity offered by religious tourism, it seems that what is at stake here is the return of the vision of tourism as a factor in inter-culturalism, dialogue and peace.

But the problem stated now is no longer the Cold War, nor the issue of development and poverty as a cause of violence or advocating modernization and growth. The current problem is the dialogue and/or conflict between religions and civilizations[3]. The 'Amman Declaration on Peace through Tourism' in 2000 set the tone with the great concern of obtaining 'Peace through Tourism'. The International Conference of Cordoba took place after the September 11, 2001 and the Madrid train bombings in 2004, which gave more relevance to the issue. Besides the relevant presence of the High Representative of the 'United Nations – Alliance of Civilizations' at the conference, the final declaration text itself expresses the notion that tourism, if it brings development and reduces the distance between societies, will contribute to the dialogue too. The summary of the report (point 1.a.) refers to 'tourism's potential to stimulate and facilitate the dialogue among different civilizations'. The conflict of civilizations, in this perspective, is thus a cultural, ideological, religious and socio-economic problem.

We end this part of our chapter by saying that, from the results that we have reached and bearing in mind the nature and role of IGOs, it makes sense to subscribe to the idea that these tend 'to create a shared and overall vision of the development of tourism. [However]... its involvement in tourism varies according to the organizations, eras and countries, in a process in which the IGOs perceive tourism as a function of its political agenda' (PNUE/PAM, 2005, p. 76).

Conclusions and Suggestions for Future Research

In analysing the contents of the various IGO declarations we conclude that there is a connection between civilizational changes and mutations in leisure, as well as a strong consonance with themes, interests and problems of emitter societies and of the most powerful players. However, this connection is not the only content or concern at stake, because the IGOs also have to meet the actual needs of the disadvantaged, framed as they are in an international regime, supported in processes and contents of legitimate domination that could respond in some way to problems of the world as a whole. The choice of topics and subjects of the declarations reflects an uneven variety. That is, there is inequality and asymmetry but not the reduction to a simple phenomenon of one-dimensional domination.

The structuring logic of international tourism is characterized by an interdependent asymmetry between different societies and actors, an unequal exchange, where the idea of a socio-cultural encounter and of mutual social and economic benefits that would follow is primarily an ideological formulation that the IGOs ultimately legitimize. Moreover, the definition of those objectives and how to achieve them appear as a technical scientific discourse, making it more difficult to decipher the ideological dimension.

The logic and content of the discourse on international tourism, especially in its ideological content and when it promotes contact between the industrial and post-industrial societies with the traditional societies (the former being mainly the emitter societies and the latter, the receptive societies), 'forces' the host societies to 'want' a particular place in an international specialization of tourist sites and products, offering a unique product. The non-industrial cultures and lifestyles and/or a luxuriant nature untouched by industrialization become a tourist product ready for the leisure needs of the people from the emitter societies.

This also happens because receptive countries from the Global South are frequently very dependent on the income obtained from international tourism and have few resources for endogenous financial investment. They also lack expertise, don't have the appropriate cultural, political and social framework to play the game and need to gain more access to the mechanisms that affect the tourism development process. They have little control on the global–local nexus referred to by Milne and Altejevic (2001). Furthermore, we see that the discourse on tourism hides the unequal social, political and economic processes behind the satisfaction of leisure needs, in which the issue of leisure as a human right appears free from social contexts and interests.

So the social, economic and ideological and political factors and the role of industry in leisure and tourism choices remain largely unspoken. In this process, leisure acquires an intrinsic 'goodness' because it is connected with human rights and is a response to real profound human needs. Tourism is then associated with interculturalism, peace and economic development (mainly in the IGOs' earlier declarations) or with the defence of culture and nature (more strongly in more recent declarations). It addresses simultaneously (however, not equally) the needs and concerns of the emitter and receptive societies. The defence of culture and nature that is made in the declarations (from the preservation of traditional identities to the climate change problems) becomes even more powerful and acquires the status of a universal dogma. It appears as a common heritage that asks for our urgent attention, in the face of a world on the brink of real major disasters but never questioning whether it is a choice of local societies.

Tourism politics, which is what is proposed in the 'Declarations', are neither mere facts nor neutral judgements, but choices and political arguments that involve values and options that are difficult to uncover. The uneven nature of the relationship between the involved actors, the matrix of ideological invisibility that is attributed to tourism, and the ideological and legitimating power of the technical scientific discourse are part of the nature of tourism politics.

In conclusion, it must be said that a better determination of the ideological dimension of discourse of the IGOs also implies an analysis of the processes of choosing themes and decision making, bearing in mind the correlation of forces between the different actors involved in the IGOs and their concrete interactions in the organizations' everyday life. This is work that still needs to be done.

Notes

[1] We refer to development in the holistic perspective presented by Burns and Novelli (2008), who, without neglecting the importance of economic growth, technological advancement and the issue of wealth distribution, integrate in a systematic way the societies, social and political structures and dynamics.
[2] See, in addition to statistics of UNWTO, PNUE/PAM (2005), Cazes (1989) and Fúster (1991).
[3] See the different views and perspectives on the problematic nature of current relations between the West and Islam and the significant weight it has on the concerns of those involved in international relations (Huntington, 2001; Keppel, 2003; Khader, 2005)

List of Declarations

'Convention on Customs Facilities for Tourism', New York, 1954, United Nations.
'United Nations Conference on International Travel and Tourism', Rome, 1963, United Nations.
'International Charter for the Conservation and Restoration of Monuments and Sites (Venice Charter)', 1964, International Council on Monuments and Sites (ICOMOS) (Latter Recalled by the United Nations Educational, Scientific and Cultural Organization [UNESCO] Declarations).
'Convention Concerning the Protection of the World Cultural and Natural Heritage', 1972, UNESCO.
'Conference on Security and Co-Operation in Europe (CSCE). Final Act' Helsinki, 1975, CSCE.
'Policy Recommendations Adopted by the Seminar on the Social and Cultural Impacts of Tourism (Tourism: Passport to Development?)', Washington, 1976, World Bank and UNESCO.
'Charter for Cultural Tourism', 1976, World Tourism Organization (WTO) and ICOMOS, Among Others.

'Recommendation Concerning the Safeguarding and Contemporary Role of Historic Areas', Nairobi, 1976, UNESCO.

'The Manila Declaration on World Tourism', 1980, WTO.

'Acapulco Document', 1982, WTO Meeting.

'Tourism Bill of Rights and Tourist Code', 1985, WTO.

'The Hague Declaration on Tourism', 1989, WTO (among others).

'The Charter for a Sustainable Tourism', World Conference on Sustainable Tourism, Lanzarote, 1995, WTO, UNESCO and the United Nations Environment Programme (UNEP).

'Agenda 21 for the Travel and Tourism Industry: Towards Environmental Sustainable Development', 1996, WTO, World Travel and Tourism Council (WTTC) and the Earth Council.

'International Conference on Sustainable Tourism in Small Island Developing States and other Islands', Lanzarote, 1998, UNEP and WTO.

'Global Code of Ethics for Tourism', 1999, WTO, (2001, United Nations).

'Amman Declaration on Peace Through Tourism', 2000, International Institute for Peace Through Tourism (IIPT), United Nations and WTTC.

'The Québec Declaration on Ecotourism', 2002, WTO and UNEP.

'The Sustainable Tourism – Eliminate Poverty (ST-EP) Initiative'. Presentation at the World Summit on Sustainable Development (WSSD), Johannesburg, 2002, WTO.

'Sahara Cultures and Peoples. Towards a Strategy for the Sustainable Development of Tourism in the Sahara, in the Context of Combating Poverty', 2002, UNESCO.

'Agenda 21 – Sustainability in the European Tourism Sector. Discussion Document', 2002, European Union (EU).

'Seven Mechanisms of Sustainable Tourism – Eliminating Poverty Programme (ST-EP). (Tourism and Poverty Alleviation: Recommendations for Action)', 2004, UNWTO.

'The Djerba Declaration on Climate Change and Tourism', Djerba, 2003, WTO, UNESCO and UNEP (among others).

'Hue Declaration on Cultural Tourism and Poverty Alleviation', Hue, 2004, UNWTO.

'Harnessing Tourism for the Millennium Development Goals', 2005, UNWTO

'International Conference on Metropolitan Tourism', Shanghai, 2007, UNWTO.

'Climate Change and Tourism. Responding to Global Changes. (Davos Declaration)', 2007, UNWTO, UNEP and World Economic Forum (Among Others).

'International Conference on Tourism, Religions and the Dialogue of Cultures', Cordoba, 2007, UNWTO.

'International Conference on Metropolitan Tourism', Busan, 2007, UNWTO.

'World Tourism Conference. Tourism Success Stories and Shooting Stars', 2007, Kuala Lumpur, UNWTO.

References

Apostolopoulos, Y., Loukissas, P. and Leontidou, L. (2001) *Mediterranean Tourism. Facets of Socioeconomic Development and Cultural Change.* Routledge, London.

Archer, C. (1995) *International Organizations,* 2nd edn. Routledge, London.

Bardin, L. (1991) *Análise de Conteúdo.* Edições 70, Lisbon.

Boudon, R. (1986) *L'Idéologie. L' origine des Idées Reçues.* Fayard, Paris.

Bourdieu, P. (1989) *O Poder Simbólico.* Difel, Lisbon.

Boyer, M. (1972) *Le Tourisme.* Seuil, Paris.

Bramwell, B. (2004) Mass tourism, diversification and sustainability in southern Europe's coastal regions. In: Bramwell, B. (ed.) *Coastal Mass Tourism: Diversification and Sustainable Development in Southern Europe.* Channel View Publications, Clevedon, UK, pp.1–31.

Britton, S. (1996) Tourism, dependency and development. In: Apostolopoulos, Y., Leivadi, S. and Yiannakis, A. (eds) *The Sociology of Tourism: Theoretical and Empirical Investigations.* Routledge, London, pp. 155–172.

Burns, P. and Novelli, M. (2008) Introduction: The majority world development and tourism. In: Burns, P. and Novelli, M. (eds) *Tourism Development: Growth, Myths and Inequalities.* CABI Publishing, Wallingford, UK, pp. 17–30.

Cazes, G. (1989) *Le Tourisme International: Mirage ou Stratégie d'Avenir.* Hatier, Paris.

Cohen, E. (1995) Contemporary tourism – trends and challenges: sustainable authenticity or contrived post-modernity? In: Butler, R. and Pearce, D. (eds) *Change in Tourism: People, Places, Processes*. Routledge, London, pp. 12–29.

Cohen, E. (1996) A phenomenology of tourist experiences. In: Apostolopoulos, Y., Leivadi, S. and Yiannakis, A. (eds) *The Sociology of Tourism: Theoretical and Empirical Investigations*. Routledge, London, pp. 90–111.

Crick, M. (1996) Representations of international tourism in the social sciences. In: Apostolopoulos, Y., Leivadi, S. and Yiannakis, A. (eds) *The Sociology of Tourism: Theoretical and Empirical Investigations*. Routledge, London, pp. 15–50.

de Kadt, E. (1979) *Tourism – Passport to Development? Perspectives on the Social and Cultural Effects of Tourism in Developing Countries*. Oxford University Press for the World Bank and UNESCO, New York.

Dougherty, J.E. and Pfaltzgraff Jr, R.L. (2003) *Relações Internacionais – As Teorias em Confronto. Um Estudo Detalhado*. Gradiva, Lisbon.

Fernandes, A.J. (1991) *Relações Internacionais. Factos, Teorias e Organizações*. Editorial Presença, Lisbon.

Fúster, L.F. (1991) *Historia General del Turismo de Masas*. Alianza Editorial, Madrid.

Gramsci, A. (1966) *Concepção Dialética da História*. Editôra Civilização Brasileira, Rio de Janeiro.

Gramsci, A. (1974) *Obras Escolhidas - Volume I e II*. Editorial Estampa, Lisbon.

Hall, C.M. (1994) *Tourism and Politics: Policy, Power and Place*. John Wiley and Sons, Chichester, UK.

Hawkins, D.E. and Mann, S. (2007) The World Bank's role in tourism development. *Annals of Tourism Research* 34, 348–363.

Hjalager, A.M. (2007) Stages in the economic globalization of tourism. *Annals of Tourism Research* 34, 437–457.

Hoffman, L., Fainstein, S. and Judd, D. (2003) *Cities and Visitors: Regulating People, Markets and City Space*. Blackwell Publishing, Malden, UK.

Huntington, S. (2001) *O Choque das Civilizações e a Mudança na Ordem Mundial*, 2nd edn. Gradiva, Lisbon,

Keppel, G. (2003) Fronteras políticas y religiosas en el Mediterráneo. *Tribuna Mediterrània* 5, 17–28.

Khader, B. (2005) Euro-Mediterranean partnership or Euro-Arab partnership? *Anuario del Mediterráneo* 2005, 98–103.

Knowles, T., Diamantis, D. and El-Mourhab, J. (2004) *Globalization of Tourism and Hospitality*. Thomson Learning, London.

Lanfant, M.F. (1991) *Tourisme International Reconsidéré: Milieu Exclu, Tiers Exclu? Le Principe de l'Alternative*. Centre des Hautes Études Touristiques, Aix-en-Provence, France.

Lanfant, M.F. (1992) L'identité en jeu dans l'echange touristique international. *Sociologia Urbana e Rurale* 38, 171–176.

Lanfant, M.F. (1995) International tourism, internationalization and the challenge to identity. In: Lanfant, M.F., Allcock, J. and Bruner, E. (eds) *International Tourism: Identity and Change*. Sage Publications Ltd, London, pp. 24–43.

MacCannel, D. (1999) *The Tourist: A New Theory of the Leisure Class*. University of California Press, Berkeley, California.

Mannheim, K. (1979) *Ideology and Utopia*. Routledge and Kegan Paul, London.

McLellan, D. (1987) *A Ideologia*. Editorial Estampa, Lisbon.

Milne, S. and Ateljevic, I. (2001) Tourism, economic development and the global local nexus: theory embracing complexity. *Tourism Geographies* 3, 369–393.

Mowforth, M. and Munt, I. (2009) *Tourism and Sustainability: Development, Globalisation and New Tourism in the Third World*. Routledge, London.

Page, S.J. (1995) *Urban Tourism*. Routledge, London.

PNUE/PAM (Programme des Nations Unies pour l'Environment. Plan d'Action pour la Méditerranée – Plan Bleu) (2005) Dossier sur le tourisme et le développement durable en Méditerranée. Available at: http://195.97.36.231/acrobatfiles/MTSacrobatfiles/mts159.pdf (accessed 14 October 2010).

Poon, A. (2003) Competitive strategies for a new tourism. In: Cooper, C. (ed.) *Classic Reviews in Tourism*. Channel View Publications, Clevedon, UK, pp. 130–142.

Prentice, R. (2007) Motivação do turista e tipologias. In: Lew, A.A., Hall, C.M. and Williams, A.M. (eds) *Compêndio de Turismo*. Instituto Piaget, Lisbon, pp. 297–315.

Roche, M. (1996) Mega-events and micro-modernization: on the sociology of the new urban tourism. In: Apostolopoulos, Y., Leivadi, S. and Yiannakis, A. (eds) *The Sociology of Tourism: Theoretical and Empirical Investigations*. Routledge, London, pp. 315–346.

Rojek, C. (1995) *Decentring Leisure: Rethinking Leisure Theory*. Sage Publications, London.

Rojek, C. and Urry, J. (1997) *Touring Cultures*. Routledge, London.

Ruggie, J.G. (1998) *Constructing the World Polity. Essays on International Institutionalization*. Routledge, London.

Santos, B.S. (2001) Os processos da globalização. In: Santos, B.S. (ed.) *Globalização: Fatalidade ou Utopia?* Edições Afrontamento, Porto, Portugal, pp. 31–106.

Santos, F. (2002) *Turismo Mosaico de Sonhos: Incursões Sociológicas Pela Cultura Turística*. Colibri, Lisbon.

UNWTO and ETC (World Tourism Organization and European Travel Commission) (2006) *City Tourism & Culture – The European Experience*. World Tourism Organization, Madrid.

Urry, J. (1990) *The Tourist Gaze: Leisure and Travel in Contemporary Societies*. Sage Publications, London.

Vala, J. (1986) A análise de conteúdo. In: Silva, A.S. and Pinto, J.M. (eds) *Metodologia das Ciências Sociais*. Afrontamento, Porto, Portugal, pp. 101–128.

Waltz, K. (1999) Globalization and governance. Available at: http://www.mtholyoke.edu/acad/intrel/walglob. htm (accessed 26 February 2003).

Weber, M. (1989) Tipos de dominação. In: da Cruz, M.B. (ed.) *Teorias Sociológicas. I Volume – Os Fundadores e os Clássicos*. Fundação Calouste Gulbenkian, Lisbon, pp. 681–723.

WTO (World Tourism Organization) (1998) *Tourism 2020 Vision: A New Forecast From the World Tourism Organization*. OMT-WTO-BTO, Madrid.

15 The Paradoxes of Tourism Encounters in the Mass Tourism Spaces of the Gambia

Helen Pattison[1]

[1]Lancaster Environment Centre, Lancaster University, UK

Introduction

The tourism industry has been dubbed the vanguard of globalization; a major global economic force. Tourism involves flows of people, capital, policy, information, images, technology and organizations connecting disparate cultures and societies in a converging and 'shrinking' world (Dirlik, 1994). To research tourism spaces involves exploring the complex interaction between the global, national and local that creates postcolonial global places. The field of tourism is a potentially rich site from which to examine the fluidity of identity, the multiple discourses involved in identity construction and the competing modes of representations, all within an interconnected and interacting world (King 2008). Tourism studies have, however, been critiqued for failing to conceptualize in any great depth the complexity of tourism spaces and experiences. A lack of meaningful engagement with the agency of the subaltern 'host' and their position in the postcolonial global moment has resulted in a simplistic binary of the host–guest relation that overlooks the paradoxes, parallels and micro-controversies inherent in tourism encounters. Within this chapter I present the case for utilizing a postcolonial (global) framework of Foucauldian relational power as an epistemology and methodology to re-inscribe meaning to the experience of the 'host'. I explore how local people become 'hosts' within the mass tourism industry of The Gambia, reconfiguring power and identity to create a host–tourist (direct or indirect) encounter that generates its own micro-controversies.

The Trouble with Tourism Studies

Tourism studies have attempted to chart the implications of the rapid rate of tourism development as concerns arise over the neo-colonial nature of tourism and the impact(s) that this may have on the destination country. Until recently, however, tourism studies research has rested on a narrow theoretical and methodological base and has been unable to conceptualize (in great depth) the complexity inherent in tourism (Franklin and Crang, 2001). Franklin and Crang (2001, p. 5) believe part of the problem is that tourism studies researchers do not have 'the tools necessary to analyze and theorize the complex cultural and social processes that have unfolded'. Phillimore and Goodson (2004) explored the paradigmatic influences and use of methods within tourism research by reviewing academic articles published in eight tourism and leisure journals between 1996 and 2003. They found that the overwhelming majority of research was framed by a positivist and post-positivist paradigm. This approach is scientific, rational and technical. The researcher is perceived to be an 'expert'; the voice of the researched is often invisible as they become the disembodied objects of the researcher's gaze. Universalizing and totalizing explanations for social phenomena are sought for and/or applied, which has resulted in tourist and host typologies (Humberstone, 2004). As Pernecky (2010, p. 2) argues, 'one would presume that after forty years of tourism scholarship the field would have achieved a certain degree of maturity and a plethora of issues would have been explored, theorised, and conceptualised. Yet the opposite appears to be the case'. Similarly, Pritchard and Morgan (2007, p. 13) believe that 'we still know too little about tourism identities, relationships ... and much of the new work on identity, difference, the body ... which has forced a rethinking of the social science intellectual universe remains on the margin of our subject'. Pernecky (2010, p. 5) agrees that there is a lack of critical approaches in tourism studies and any real theoretical (and practical) engagement with ontology, epistemology and methodology. Thus, there exists a growing body of tourism researchers 'that call for innovative approaches to tourism', as 'the old ways of knowledge production may not be satisfactory any longer'.

The absence of a sophisticated engagement with ontology, epistemology and methodology within tourism studies has implications for knowledge constructed about, or perhaps more often *for*, non-Western 'hosts'. Tucker and Akama (2009, p. 513) say of tourism researchers: 'In their discussions ... in relation to tourism the same imperialist imagery that is employed in tourism promotions has unfortunately been maintained by many commentators on tourism, thus showing a desire by them also to fix the "ethnic" identities of peoples in tourism destinations into perpetual

"otherness"'. This simplistic viewing of the 'other' has set rigid frameworks within which to interpret tourism experiences, such as the host–guest paradigm[1]. Stronza (2001), Evans-Pritchard (1989) and Martinez (1996) focus on the host within the host–guest framework but whilst they attempt to describe host–guest interaction they only serve to reinforce the binary opposition of 'host' and 'guest'; the host as the dominated 'other'. In more recent years Cheong and Miller (2000) have attempted to describe the complexity and fluidity of power within the host–guest relationship by using a Foucauldian concept of relational power. Cheong and Miller (2000) argue that rather than a binary host–guest relationship the hosts act as middlemen between local people and tourists; this tripartite system is not fixed as the identities of local people, hosts and tourists can shift. Cheong and Miller, however, miss the (often subtle) complexity and dynamism of these relations as the tourist is reduced to a largely passive role. Maoz (2006) discusses how hosts perceive tourists (the local gaze) and how this perception can influence the tourist gaze, or the actions and behaviour of the tourist. Maoz (2006) suggests that the tourist gaze and the local gaze exist side-by-side; 'the local gaze is based on a more complex, two-sided picture, where both the tourist and the local gazes exist, affecting and feeding each other, resulting in what is termed "the mutual gaze"' (Maoz, 2006, p. 222). Maoz (2006), Cheong and Miller (2000) and the previous works cited locate their work within a host–guest paradigm that Aramberri (2001, p. 741) believes is defunct; a myth; 'the host-guest model does not help to explain the nature of modern mass tourism; obscures the complex interactions between local cultures and their environments, and favors a static and exclusionary vision of cultures'. Similarly, McNaughton (2006, p. 660) describes: 'The host-guest paradigm has not only framed the way researchers think about the interactions that occur in tourism, its application predetermines the researcher's understandings of the very relationships they are there to observe, describe and interpret'. McNaughton's (2006) empirical research in Pakaram, India, on the position of handicraft traders within the tourism industry led her to acknowledge 'the complexity of life-on-the-ground'. McNaughton (2006) found that some groups, such as the handicraft traders, have been marginalized by both the tourist industry and academia because they do not fit into the role of 'host', but rather, are 'uninvited interlopers' (McNaughton, 2006, p. 659). McNaughton (2006) argues that this says a lot more about the discourse of tourism than what is actually happening on the ground, in tourism spaces.

Ladson-Billings and Donnor (2005, p. 294) believe that it is the responsibility of the tourism studies scholar to 'transcend narrow disciplinary boundaries if it is to have any impact on people who reside in subaltern sites or even on policymakers'. An engagement with the actions and interactions between (host) agency and (Western) discourse (Bianchi, 2009) and a focus on the transitional spaces of tourism development will avoid the reinforcement of colonial binaries and 'unhelpful dichotomies' (Tucker, 2010, p. 983). Tourism studies have focused on either the local, and its difference and diversity, or macro-hierarchical structures of power and inequality. The agency of the subject within the local and its negotiation of macro power has been largely neglected (Bianchi, 2003). Bianchi (2009, p. 491) sets a future research agenda: 'What is needed, as elsewhere in the social sciences of our moment, is more systematic analysis of the actions and interactions between agency and discourse, and theorization of such defensive struggles in relation to the reproduction of institutional complexes and structures of power'.

Osagie and Buzinde (2011, p. 211) argue that a critical approach to tourism studies 'coupled with the critical structures of postcolonial research offer a lens through which the nuances and complexities of tourism, especially in developing nations, can be better articulated and embedded within a decolonizing agenda'. Postcolonial theory is useful as it both emphasizes 'the pervasiveness of the legacies of colonialism in

tourism' and also 'the ways in which tourism might act as a medium for offering postcolonial counter-narratives of resistance to those colonial relationships' (Tucker and Akama, 2009, p. 504)[2]. Treacher (2005, pp. 44–45) defines postcolonial theory as:

> A body of work that attempts to explore the inextricably linked relations between the western people and those from the non-West. It is a way of conceptualizing, understanding and speaking about the complex relations between the colonized and the colonizer, and these psychological and political inscriptions mark us all whatever our history of colonization. Critically, it is committed to opening up a space in which those without a voice can speak and be heard, to extending theoretical viewpoints and analysis, to encompass knowledge and understandings developed outside of the West.

Listening to the subaltern leads to the possibilities of alternative discourses to that of Western/colonial discourse (Dirlik, 1994). Indeed Loomba (2005) believes postcolonialism to be involved with recovering the views of previously colonized subjects and as such engages us in debates over authenticity, hybridity and colonial identities, to name a few. Although postcolonial theory is involved with recovering the voices of the subaltern, the discipline has been criticized for reproducing Western (colonial) discourse, through homogenizing and 'othering' the postcolonial subject, condition and experience (Finnstrom, 1997; Loomba, 2005). Appiah (1996, p. 62) has pronounced Western intellectuals to be 'otherness machines' and postcolonial authors to present a 'dark vision' of the 'other' as it is suffocated by Western discourse. Through her seminal essay 'Can the subaltern speak?', Spivak (1988) asks the question of whether the voices of the subaltern are condemned to be forever distorted through representation, or whether they can speak for themselves. One of Spivak's conclusions is that it is not the inability of the subaltern to speak that is the problem but the inability of the dominant West to listen (McEwan, 2009). In the following section I argue that combining postcolonial theory with Foucault's notion of relational power enables me to re-centre the agency of the subaltern.

An Alternative Theoretical and Methodological Base; a Postcolonial (Global) Framework of Foucauldian Relational Power

The framework positions the subaltern within macro-structures of asymmetrical power (Western discursive and non-discursive practices) but also enables me to recognize that power is not static but 'mobile, reversible and unstable' (Foucault 1996, p. 442). Foucault (1982a, 1982b) presents a complex, dynamic and localized form of agency and resistance (of the subject) through his description of power as a relation; every subject is an object of power but also has the capacity to exercise power through acting upon another; acting upon the actions or conduct of a subject. Furthermore, the subject is constituted through this possibility of resistance within power relations. Butin (2001, p. 169) explains, 'The individual is not passively made by power, but makes herself by being able to resist within power relations'. I argue that this enables me to conceptualize the dynamics of power in the tourism spaces of The Gambia by positioning the 'host' as an active agent within the macro-structures of discursive and non-discursive practices. As power is relational, diffuse and multi-directional the 'host' is not passive but is able to act, resist and negotiate the many influences inherent to tourism spaces; the host becomes both the object and agent of power and Western colonial binaries of 'subject' and 'object', 'active' and 'passive' are deconstructed.

Whilst presenting the case for a post-colonial Foucauldian framework for tourism research it must be recognized that a relatively new global order has emerged that conditions the development of tourism. Hardt and Negri (2000) argue that this is an age of global flows (of capital, information, technology and people) that connect geographically and socio-culturally

disparate spaces and places within a de-centred, de-territorialized 'Empire'. As such, 'globalization represents a new way of perceiving the world that distinguishes the present from the world of colonialism and neo-colonialism at the moment of decolonization in the aftermath of World War II' (Dirlik, 2002, p. 429). I argue that both postcolonial theory and globalization theory can learn from each other, in order to better understand the complex configurations of power within place(s). For example, despite this insistence upon a new world order that has radically transformed global systems of power, the contemporary moment is not ahistorical; it is not rootless. As such, 'the shift from "colonial" to "postcolonial" to "global" [is] much more problematic than Hardt and Negri ... named' (Ganguly, 2007, p. 31). It can be argued that globalization has brought into existence new forms of colonialism/imperialism (Dirlik, 2002; Ganguly, 2007) and also 'intensified pre-existing global asymmetries, particularly those that were produced by modern colonialism (Loomba, 2005, p. 215). By engaging with globalization theory, postcolonial theory can be made even more relevant to the contemporary moment.

A major criticism levelled at postcolonial theory is its preoccupation with texts, discourses and the 'cultural' to the neglect of the persistence of colonialism/imperialism through the non-discursive/material (Cook and Harrison, 2003; McEwan, 2009). Postcolonial theories are not easily translated into action on the ground, or the 'real' world (McEwan, 2009). As Cook and Harrison (2003, p. 298) state 'contemporary postcolonial criticism leaves largely undiscussed the articulation of imaginative and material geographies, "culture" and "economy", and "postcolonialism" and global capitalism'. Schwarz (2000, p. 7) calls for a 'materially grounded postcolonial studies' whilst according to Dirlik (2002) part of the problem is that postcolonial theory is too focused on past legacies to the extent that it is largely oblivious to contemporary configurations of power. Whilst colonialism/imperialism persists, it can often appear differently as it is refracted through a contemporary reconfiguration of global relations, presenting 'new questions both of politics and of cultural identities' (Dirlik, 2002, p. 445). Thus, postcolonial theory must place old and new imperialisms/colonialisms in a globalizing, re-materializing frame.

Whilst postcolonial theory needs to be brought into the present, globalization must be re-historicized in order to recognize the persistence of colonialism/imperialism within global configurations. Colonialism created bonds/binaries between the colonized and the colonizer, constructing identities and stereotypes that remain entrenched in contemporary discourses, structures and practices, in a form of latent orientalism. Contemporary identities are influenced by a history (that includes colonial history) of racial and cultural 'othering', and mixing, to produce complex plural contemporary identities (Ganguly, 2007). Ganguly (2007, p. 38) believes that concentrating on the 'now' of the global order dislocates and flattens out complex, dynamic identities and experiences. Instead, there needs to be an 'opening up of the temporality of the "now" to reverberations of other times that co-exist with it … pasts-and-futures-in-the-present that co-exist with late capital'. Postcolonial theory can help to bring the past into the present and historicize changing social relations.

A postcolonial (global) framework of Foucauldian relational power will enable me to focus on the experiences of the 'host' whilst also recognizing that the 'host' is part of an interconnected web of power. This allows me to grasp a more comprehensive understanding of contemporary configurations of power and identity – embracing temporal (local, national and global) and spatial (past-and-futures-in-the-present) dimensions – that are manifest in, and also expressed through host–tourist encounters.

A postcolonial framework of Foucauldian relational power can also be used as a methodology that opens up a space within the field of tourist studies from which to uncover the voices of the subaltern 'host'. By providing the 'hosts' with cameras and listening to

their voices through photo-elicitation interviews (PEIs) I aim to enable them to 'speak'; they are the 'experts' of their own lives and the researcher should not presume to 'know' for them. I pay particular attention to the use of cameras as, whilst visual methods have been used as a research technique within the social sciences, in tourism research they are 'simply not on the agenda' (Feighey, 2003, p. 78). I argue that cameras are more than just a research tool; they become inextricably bound up with their owner's personal subjectivities, enmeshed in micro- and macro- power relations, and can frame the dominant discourse of a society; they can be both colonizing and decolonizing. The visual is a significant element of tourism; the tourist gaze is premised on the visual nature of tourism as images represent (and signpost) people and places to be consumed by the gaze (Urry, 2002). Such images often construct 'imaginary' people and places in a (re)colonizing gaze. Through the lens of the camera 'hosts' are able to represent the multiple, complex identities of 'self', 'other' and place and reveal the paradoxes and parallels between the host gaze and the tourist gaze and how these are manifested through encounter.

Researching the Tourism Spaces of Kotu and Senegambia

Tourism research has not fully conceptualized the multiple interconnecting influences that constitute place, thus has been unable to comprehensively understand the agency and (possibilities for) resistance of the subaltern 'host'. I briefly describe the wider socio-political context of tourism development in Kotu and Senegambia, The Gambia so that the paradoxes, ambiguities and parallels that are inherent in host–tourist encounters can be better understood.

Since 1974 (with the establishment of a Tourism Development Area [TDA] along the North West coastline) the Gambian government has sought to combine socio-economic development with foreign investment in tourism. A series of five-year plans integrated national development policies and tourism policies within a framework of national objectives. This approach to development reflects the Eurocentric values of linear progress and modernization that, with respect to The Gambia, is not considerate of the postcolonial local context. As part of the TDA, Kotu/Senegambia has experienced heavy investment in tourism development by Western transnational corporations resulting in many foreign-owned tourist resorts. The tourist industry within these spaces is characterized by a high percentage of economic leakage, high levels of foreign imports and poor links between the tourist industry and other sectors of the local economy (agriculture, manufacturing/industry). This equates to a lack of tourism revenue to invest in socio-economic development and the exclusion of local people/businesses from the tourist industry. In addition, there are few Gambians employed in managerial positions within the industry and in at least one tourism resort, the employees are not paid a wage. In general, many local people (in Kotu/Senegambia) feel that their country is being run by foreigners and that they are being placed on the margins; this is not helped by the lax immigration policy as ex-pats and non-Gambian Africans are perceived to have colonized Gambian spaces. The sense of alienation and exclusion is exacerbated by the presence and actions of the tourist police; the government commissions them to 'clean up' the area of any unwanted 'hosts' that threaten the West's image of a paradise. This gaze of the government and the tourist police is internalized within the tourist gaze; the 'hosts' become the dangerous 'other' from which they need to be protected by gun-wielding security units.

On the micro-scale the materialities, practices and policies of the tourist resorts and the tour companies who operate within, reinforce the stereotypes of 'African' people and place (that are preconceived through Gambian tourist brochures), and create a division between the 'inside' space of the resorts and the uncertain space 'outside'. For example, certain stereotypical images, or signs, are utilized within Palm Beach Hotel to create an exclusive place for tourists to consume with their gaze; a European Africa with a hint of the exotic; an imaginary Gambia. The space is designed and controlled (through aesthetics, facilities and entertainment) to keep the tourists inside, whilst security guards and tourist police keep the local people out. The practices of the tour operators (such as the introductory welcome talks) exclude and homogenize local people who do not work in purified spaces nor conform to the romantic notion of the 'other'. The tour operators portray themselves as the 'hosts' whilst many of the local people in the outside 'other' space are 'unwanted nuisances' (own observation of a welcome talk).

Whilst local 'hosts' appear to be positioned within an asymmetrical power relation with the tourism industry and the government – as they are excluded and labelled the dangerous 'other' or unwanted nuisances – the 'hosts' are able to resist, negotiate and transform this power, to become the vehicle of power (and not just its object). The 'host' 'becomes' through forms of micro-resistance to the macro structure of the tourist industry, the politics of the tour-operators/resorts and the approach of the government. The 'host' also 'becomes' through being enmeshed in micro-politics within the 'host community'; there is constant conflict and competition amongst many local people in the area to become a 'host', to prove that they are a 'host' and to sustain their position as a 'host'. The meaning of a 'host' is fluid and the sectors of the industry – formal, informal and bumsters – are interchangeable. The multiple meanings that underpin 'host' are manifested in the host–tourist encounter, and these encounter(s) also contribute to the creation of the identity and meaning of 'host'. Host–tourist encounters (of the 'intimate enemy' involving friendship and sex/crime and violence) represent the ambivalent relationship the hosts have with the Western tourism industry. The 'hosts' actively resist the Western tourism industry so they can open up opportunities to be included by the West and embody Western wealth. Through active resistance 'hosts' constitute and reconstitute their 'self', to become multiple 'selves', and multiple 'others' to different people (which may either reinforce or deconstruct stereotypes). The actions of the 'host' upon the actions of the tourist also influences tourist behaviour and how they perceive and experience the 'inside' (resort) and 'outside' 'other' spaces of Senegambia and Kotu. The following three sections highlight a few of the paradoxes and parallels in host–tourist encounters within tourism spaces. Each section is based on the nature of the photographs (and the associated information collated through PEIs) taken by the Kotu/Senegambia 'hosts'.

'Intimate Enemy³'; The Paradoxical Relationship between the Host and the Tourist

For many of the 'hosts' in Kotu/Senegambia, hospitality and friendship are key traits of a good 'host' and they base their encounters with tourists on such sentiments. However, the 'hosts' image of the tourists as the rich Western 'other' along with their exclusion from the tourist industry by the resorts, tour operators and the Gambian government creates a somewhat ambiguous relationship with the tourists. The tourists become the paradoxical 'intimate enemy'. Foucault (Foucault 1982a, 1982b) believes that actions (and the potential for actions to influence other people's actions and behaviour) are a form of power and resistance. In Senegambia local people's actions are underwritten by ambiguities; local people resist exclusion from the tourist industry and the tour operators by including themselves, and creating friendships with tourists based on materialism. The local people seem to dislike and disrespect the tourists, calling then 'lazy crocodiles' and 'beach potatoes', and believe they are ignorant for expecting 'Africa' to be another Europe. As Alieu, the front of house manager at Palm Beach tells me, 'tourists sometimes do not understand they are not in Europe anymore ... they forget they are in Africa. So they want to see all things like Europe. That is not possible. There is a big difference between

Europe and here'. Despite this perception of tourists, however, the 'hosts' embrace them and their lifestyle in a paradoxical relationship. They desire what they dislike for the benefits it can bring them. The tourists are perceived in binary opposition to the local people in terms of material wealth and money and for the difference in culture but the tourists are not necessarily civilized or superior (as colonial legacy would have it).

The 'hosts' become 'other' to their 'selves' in order to secure the tourists friendship; they conform to a pre-constructed identity of an exotic, poor 'African' but also demonstrate that they aspire to a Western sense of progress/development and lifestyle, in order to gain a tourist's trust and friendship. If they do not internalize the tourist gaze they become a hassling nuisance, or a negative 'other'. As Foucault (1982a) would have it this internalization is still a form of resistance as the local people choose to act this way, and these actions open up alternative possibilities for material benefits. In the long term, resistance may become stronger as the local person chooses to discard the friendship. Local people may also choose not to conform to the tourist gaze from the first encounter and use hassling and aggression to take what they want from the tourist. Whichever alternative they choose, local people have the power to influence the tourists' behaviour to make them choose to act in a certain way, to create a certain place in which the tourists act.

For many tourists, Kotu/Senegambia is an uncertain, disturbing and undisciplined place; a paradise confused, where local people force embodied encounters by invading the tourist's personal space. The tourists are not used to such physical proximity with 'strangers', such embodied encounters. An English boy on holiday with his parents commented, 'Hassling is not aggressive but the locals are too friendly. They put their arms around mum and won't let go'. Such experiences are manifested through tourists' movement through space: rushed. Heads are down to avoid eye contact with local people, so they cannot easily be approached. Bodily movements become a defence mechanism for many tourists.

A Romantic Liaison with an 'Intimate Enemy'

The majority of photographs taken of host–tourist encounters and interaction within Kotu/Senegambia were of young Gambian men and white Western women (Fig. 15.1). Various names are given to The Gambian coast by the media, in which sexual innuendos abound, 'Sex Paradise', 'Haven of Sex', 'The lovers paradise' to name but a few (Nyanzi *et al.*, 2005).

   The nature of the encounter is different for each character; for the Gambian it is a material encounter, for the Westerner it is an emotional encounter, of love and companionship. They are each other's 'other'. However, the host and the tourist do not stay in their stereotypical roles but by embracing the 'other' they attempt to align themselves with the 'other' and in part, become the 'other'. The men desire Western materialism and a Western lifestyle and the women want to become more exotic, carefree and sexy.

   The women enjoy sexual encounters with Gambian Rasta as they are charmed, chased and 'loved'; they are desired by young, attractive men. The women become sexual 'objects' themselves, something which they gain power from and invite. As Taylor (2000, p. 46) says 'Sex tourism allows some Western women to sexualize their bodies in ways that would be difficult to achieve back home'. The women rediscover their sexuality through the attention of male Gambians; they want to become different and 'other' from the 'selves' that they associate with in the West. Power comes through the women discovering their 'self' as 'other' and discovering the power, or lure, of their body; to be able to 'hook' an exotic man and to own his body. There are Western women who project their fantasies on the Gambian male body, who, through their gaze, inscribe the body with Western discourse. The black African man has sexual prowess; a larger penis and greater stamina than the white Western man. The African is primitive, with an animal-like quality, 'an Other who is endowed with a primitive masculinity' (Phillips 1999, p. 189). The women want to feel desired and protected by the primitive instincts of the African but they also want to tame (to make the 'other' more like 'self'); to conquer and consume the 'noble savage'. The women also wish to care; to provide for

Fig. 15.1. Photograph taken by Gupta, a shopkeeper.

their man by paying for food and drinks, and buying gifts.

Many Gambian men inscribe the bodies of Western women with their own fantasies, the image of wealth and an affluent Western lifestyle; there are Gambians who believe all Western tourists to be rich. These images are reinforced by the behaviour of tourists, who often flash their money around; some females doing so on purpose in order to seduce men into a relationship with them. Tourists are 'using their economic power to obtain sexual experiences' (Taylor, 2000, p. 41).

The Western female and Gambian male both have power in the reciprocal tourist–host encounter; power is relational. 'Hosts' internalize the female tourist gaze to become the 'other'. By conforming to stereotypes, however, the Gambians do not consider themselves as powerless, but rather that they have control over their own 'otherness'; it is purposeful 'otherness'. This 'otherness' is used as a form of resistance to the exclusion of the tourism industry. The male Gambians use their bodies as a form of power to attain their aspirations of a Western lifestyle and to take control of their livelihoods. Appearance is important in terms of the construction of identity of the Gambians. The 'boys' deliberately grow long dreadlocks to fit the image of the Rasta, in the belief that women find them exotic, 'rugged' and masculine. They wear tight vests to show off their muscular bodies.

For the Gambian male the power comes not necessarily through sex, but what the seduction of the Western women represents. Many Gambians feel empowered by the conquest of rich, Western women. The sex is a form of power and resistance to the exclusionary nature of the tourism industry; the Gambian is able to manipulate the tourist industry, an industry perceived to suppress and exclude them. The material, sexual encounter gives a Gambian power over his social peers: through the conquering of the rich Western foreigner, through acquisition of wealth and through image. There are high expectations and peer pressure for a young local male to get into a relationship with a white foreign female. There is a certain respect or social standing given to those local people in such a relationship. This varies with the type of tourists they are with and the nature of the relationship. Gambian men often have several wives. The greater the number of wives, the greater the respect for the husband; he gains a higher social status. The wives are a symbol of power and wealth for the man; the women represent status symbols. Alongside this cultural and religious tradition has grown an alternative practice, albeit one which embraces a similar attitude to the aforementioned. Many Gambian males use white, Western women as symbols of wealth, respect and power. For the Gambians, the older and richer the female is, the greater the respect for the male amongst his peers. The richer, older woman is also more likely to take the 'boy' back to Europe. And as Richard from ASSET (Association of Small Scale Enterprises in Tourism) reveals, 'a few think going to Europe is heaven; they make women fall in love with small boys'.

Power and control also emerges in the way some 'boys' treat the women; the women are seduced for their sex and money and then left in the cold. Carlos, a tourist policeman, sees the aftermath of such treatment. He gives an example of a woman who had been on holiday with her family and had stayed on longer to be with her Gambian boyfriend, who 'ate' all her money and the money her family sent her, to leave her with nothing and no way of getting home.

For many of the women seduced by romance encounters, the actual experience can unmask the projected fantasies/myths. Modou says that once the Gambian men get to Europe they leave the woman for a younger girl whom they can start a family with. Comments left on an internet forum entitled 'British Women who love Gambian men??! (Topix, 2008)' attest to disillusionment with the romance encounter and the realization that they are the 'intimate enemy'. Laura M from the UK says:

> Any British woman wanting the fairytale believe me it only exists for so long, Gambian men know how to sweep you off your feet and get you hooked but oppose

Notes

[1] The traditional host–guest paradigm was introduced through Smith's (1989) seminal edited collection *Hosts and Guests: the Anthropology of Tourism*.

[2] However, thus far the tourism studies field has not meaningfully engaged with postcolonial theory to uncover the voice of the subaltern host (Osagie and Buzinde, 2011).

[3] A term borrowed from Nandy's (1983) '*Intimate Enemy: Loss and Recovery of Self Under Colonialism*'.

References

Appiah, K.A. (1996) Is the post in postmodernism the post in postcolonialism? In: Mongia, P. (ed.) *Contemporary Postcolonial Theory: A Reader*. Arnold, London, pp. 55–71.

Aramberri, J. (2001) The host should get lost: paradigms in the tourism theory. *Annals of Tourism Research* 28, 738–761.

Bianchi, R.V. (2003) Place and power in tourism development: tracing the complex articulations of community and locality. *PASOS* 1, 13–32.

Bianchi, R.V. (2009) The 'critical turn' in tourism studies: a radical critique. *Tourism Geographies* 11, 484–504.

Butin, D.W. (2001) If this is resistance I would hate to see domination: retrieving Foucault's notion of resistance within educational research. *Educational Studies* 32, 157–176.

Cheong, S. and Miller, M. (2000) Power and tourism: a Foucauldian observation. *Annals of Tourism Research* 27, 371–390.

Cook, I. and Harrison, M. (2003) Cross over food: re-materializing postcolonial geographies. *Transactions* 28, 296–317.

Dirlik, A. (1994) The postcolonial aura: third world criticism in the age of global capitalism. *Critical Inquiry* 20, 328–356.

Dirlik, A. (2002) Rethinking colonialism: globalization, postcolonialism, and the nation. *Interventions* 4, 428–448.

Enwezor, O. (2006) *Snap Judgments: New Positions in Contemporary African Photography*. Steidl, New York.

Evans-Pritchard, D. (1989) How 'they' see 'us': Native American images of tourists. *Annals of Tourism Research* 16, 89–105.

Feighey, W. (2003) Negative image? Developing the visual in tourism research. *Current Issues in Tourism* 6, 76–85.

Finnstrom, S. (1997) Postcoloniality and the postcolony: theories of the global and the local. Working Papers in Cultural Anthropology, 7. Department of Cultural Anthropology and Ethnology, Uppsala University, Sweden.

Foucault, M. (1982a) Why study power: the question of the subject. In: Dreyfus, H. and Rabinow, P. (eds) *Michel Foucault, Beyond Structuralism and Hermeneutics*. University of Chicago Press, Chicago, Illinois, pp. 208–216.

Foucault, M. (1982b) How is power exercised? In: Dreyfus, H. and Rabinow, P. (eds) *Michel Foucault: Beyond Structuralism and Hermeneutics*. University of Chicago Press, Chicago, Illinois, pp. 216–226.

Foucault, M. (1996) *Foucault Live: Interviews, 1961–1984*. S. Lotringer (ed.), 2nd edn. MIT Press, New York.

Franklin, A. and Crang, M. (2001) The trouble with tourism and travel theory. *Tourist Studies* 1, 5–22.

Ganguly, D. (2007) From empire to empire? Writing the transnational Anglo-Indian self in Australia. *Journal of Intercultural Studies* 28, 27–40.

Hardt, M. and Negri, A. (2000) *Empire*. Harvard University Press, Cambridge, Massachusetts.

Humberstone, B. (2004) Standpoint research: multiple versions of reality in tourism theorizing and research. In: Goodson, L. and Phillimore, J. (eds) *Qualitative Research in Tourism: Ontologies, Epistemologies and Methodologies*. Routledge, London, pp. 119–136.

King, V.T. (2008) Tourism in Asia: a review of the achievements and challenges. *Journal of Travel Issues in Southeast Asia* 22, 104–136.

Ladston-Billings, G. and Donnor, J. (2005). The moral activist role of critical race theory scholarship. In: Denzin, L.K. and Lincoln, Y.S. (eds) *The Sage Handbook of Qualitative Research,* 3rd edn. Sage, Thousand Oaks, California, pp. 279–301.

Loomba, A. (2005) *Colonialism/Postcolonialism (New Critical Idiom)*. Routledge, London.

Maoz, D. (2006) The mutual gaze. *Annals of Tourism Research* 33, 221–239.

Martinez, D.P. (1996) The tourist as deity: ancient continuities in modern Japan. In: Selwyn, T. (ed.) *The Tourist Image: Myths and Myth Making in Tourism*. Wiley, London, pp. 163–178.

McEwan, C. (2009) *Postcolonialism and Development*. Routledge, Oxford.

McNaughton, D. (2006) The "host" as uninvited "guest": hospitality, violence and tourism. *Annals of Tourism Research* 22, 645–665.

Nandy, A. (1983) *The Intimate Enemy: Loss and Recovery of Self Under Colonialism*. Oxford University Press, Delhi.

Nyanzi, S., Rosenberg-Jallow, O., Bah, O. and Nyanzi, S. (2005) Bumsters, big black organs and old white gold: embodied racial myths in sexual relationships of Gambian beach boys. *Culture, Health & Sexuality* 7, 557–569.

Osagie, I. and Buzinde, C.N. (2011) Culture and postcolonial resistance: Antigua in Kincaid's A Small Place. *Annals of Tourism Research* 38, 210–230.

Pernecky, T. (2010) The being of tourism. *The Journal of Tourism and Peace Research* 1, 1–15.

Phillimore, J. and Goodson, L. (2004) Progress in qualitative research in tourism: epistemology, ontology and methodology. In: Goodson, L. and Phillimore, J. (eds) *Qualitative Research in Tourism: Ontologies, Epistemologies and Methodologies*. Routledge, London, pp. 3–29.

Phillips, J.L. (1999) Tourist-oriented prostitution in Barbados: the case of the beach boy and the white female tourist. In: Kempadoo, K. (ed.) *Sun, Sex, and Gold: Tourism and Sex Work in the Caribbean*. Rowman & Littlefield, New York, pp. 183–200.

Pritchard, A. and Morgan, N. (2007) De-centring tourism's intellectual universe, or traversing the dialogue between change and tradition. In: Ateljevic, I., Pritchard, A. and Morgan, N. (eds) *The Critical Turn in Tourism Studies: Innovative Research Methodologies*. Elseiver, Amsterdam, pp. 11–28.

Schwarz, H. (2000) Mission impossible: introducing postcolonial studies in the U.S. Academy. In: Schwarz, H. and Ray, S. (eds) *A Companion to Postcolonial Studies*. Blackwell, Malden, Massachusetts, pp. 1–20.

Smith, V.L. (1989) *Hosts and Guests: The Anthropology of Tourism*. University of Pennsylvania Press, Philadelphia.

Spivak, G.C. (1988) Can the subaltern speak? In: Nelson, C. and Grossberg, S. (eds) *Marxism and the Interpretation of Culture*. Macmillan, Basingstoke, UK, pp. 120–130.

Stronza, A. (2001) Anthropology of tourism: forging new grounds for ecotourism and other alternatives. *Annual Review of Anthropology* 30, 261–283.

Taylor, S. (2000) Tourism and 'embodied' commodities: sex tourism in the Caribbean. In: Clift, S. and Carter, S. (eds) *Tourism and Sex: Culture, Commerce and Coercion*. Pinter, London, pp. 41–53.

Topix (2009) British women who love Gambian men. Available at: http://www.topix.com/forum/world/the-gambia/TLSV02K4NEU0EM8HL (accessed 14 August 2009).

Treacher, A. (2005) On postcolonial subjectivity. *Group Analysis* 38, 43–57.

Tucker, H. (2010) Peasant-entrepreneurs: a longitudinal ethnography. *Annals of Tourism Research* 37, 927–946.

Tucker, H. and Akama, J. (2009) Tourism as postcolonialism. In: Jamal, T. and Robinson, M. (eds) *The Sage Handbook of Tourism Studies*. Sage, London, pp. 504–520.

Urry, J. (2002) *The Tourist Gaze*. Sage Publications, London.

16 Tourism or Conservation? A Controversy in Chitwan National Park, Nepal

Kalyan Bhandari[1]
[1]*School of Interdisciplinary Studies, University of Glasgow, Dumfries Campus, Scotland, UK*

Introduction

Tourism in Nepal relies on nature-based attractions. Trekking and mountaineering have remained one of the most-liked tourism attractions in Nepal and are well known all over the world. But a lesser known fact is that about 45% of Nepal's half a million tourists visit various national parks and protected areas (NTS, 2009). Chitwan National Park (CNP) is the most visited national park, receiving 40% of the total national park visitors, which is three times more visitors than the famous Mount Everest region (NTS, 2009). The CNP is popular for jungle safari and 'is recognized as the best preserved conservation area in all Asia with a fascinating range of wildlife roaming free' claims the Nepalese Tourist Board (NTB) (NTB, 2010). There are well-served hotels and other tourist service providers located outside the national park. Additionally there are seven high-cost concessionaires (Eco-lodges) inside the park. The presence of these concessionaires recently became a national controversy and the nation's biggest obsession.

The main issue of the controversy was whether the national park should or should not allow tourism businesses to operate within it. The primary arguments put forward by conservationists were that allowing any commercial business within the national park boundary is against the very principle of conservation; and the businesses were less sensitive to the conservation issues and that this is one of the reasons behind increased poaching within the park, allegations refuted by the tourism entrepreneurs. This controversy involved local stakeholders, tourism entrepreneurs, government ministries, departments and ultimately parliamentary committees: and left the seven concessionaires inside the park shut for 6 months. This chapter deals with this controversy that arrested the entire country's attention in the latter half of 2009.

In this chapter we will see that the licence controversy is an extension of the conflict within the park. It emanates from the park politics, business interests and local communities' antipathy towards the concessionaires, and is less grounded in the real conservation issue alone. The businesses inside the park enjoy more privilege on park resources than other stakeholders adjoining the park, which has brought a common resentment against these businesses. The controversy is thus a reaction against this disparity in access to park benefits. This chapter suggests that an integrated approach to park management that ensures equitable distribution of park benefits can help establish harmony between tourism and conservation in the future.

The Founding of Chitwan National Park

Wildlife hunting can be identified as one of the earliest forms of tourism in Nepal. Nepal was closed to outside visitors until 1951 because the country was run by the dictatorial Rana oligarchy that was apprehensive of outsiders' presence in the country. Any visit by outsiders was forbidden except if they were the British missionaries on whom the Rana regime (1846–1951) relied for their political survival (Bhandari, 2004). One of the most effective political means the Ranas exercised to remain in power was by appeasing the British East India Company. Inviting British dignitaries to Nepal for wildlife hunting in the dense forest in the southern plains was a popular diplomatic practice. Chitwan remained the favourite one for the purpose, a trend that continued even after the end of the Rana regime in 1951 (Piessel, 1990); for example, the then king in 1961 hosted a tiger hunt in the area for Queen Elizabeth and Prince Philip when they were on a state visit to Nepal (Thapa, 2009).

The establishment of the CNP was the initiation of a few devoted affluent conservationists close to the royal family. During the Rana regime Chitwan was protected as a royal hunting reserve. After the reinstatement of monarchical rule (1951–1990), the excellent hunting environment in Chitwan made it a favourite one for the king and other members of the royal family for their recreational activities. Members of royal families were above the law and hunting for them was organized by government employees. *Tiger Warden*, a memoir written by the wife of the country's leading conservationist who served as the first warden of the CNP, reveals that the national park staff had to assist fulltime when a royal hunt was on (cited in Thapa, 2009). Preparations for these hunts got underway months before the royal family arrived. The king's interest

in hunting, and Chitwan as his favourite hunting location, was adroitly maneuvered by the king's associates in getting the royal nod to declare the area a national park in 1973.

Despite being declared a national park, even after 1990 when the country adopted constitutional monarchy, the royal family enjoyed impunity and hunting expeditions by royal family members continued unabated. The strong royal presence and the idea of a national park that laid emphasis on the separation of human society from the natural environment was one of the reasons that created a local resentment to the park, writes Thapa (2009):

> The people living near the national park came to view the park staff as guarding the jungles for the exclusive use of the royal family. It did not help that some of the army personnel guarding the parks indulged in hunting, and even poaching and the smuggling of wildlife contraband. The Royal Nepal Army, for its part, behaved as though the people of the area were menaces to be kept away by the use of force. This led to parks-vs-people conflicts and, more generally to an erosion of trust regarding the entire concept of conservation.
>
> Thapa (2009, p.101)

There is another source of conflict in the CNP. Nepal's dense southern forests were protected during the Rana regime as a defence against external invasion, as these forests were malaria infested. Tharus were the native inhabitants in the region and their livelihood depended on the exploitation of forests and grasslands (Guneratne, 2001). The eradication of malaria in the 1950s gave rise to mass migration from the hills and as a result there was mass forest clearing to provide human settlements and crop cultivation. The establishment of a national park by displacing a large number of the local population created resentment among local people, as it put on hold forest encroachment and severely restricted their access to park resources (Nepal and Weber, 1995). Around 22,000 local people were evicted to establish the park (Thapa, 2009).

Wildlife Tourism in Chitwan

Chitwan is Nepal's most popular tourist destination after Kathmandu and Pokhara. The number of foreign tourists to the CNP has increased from fewer than 1000 in 1974 to 83,000 in 2008 (NTS, 2009). Additionally, about 35,000 local visitors visit the park every year (NTS, 2009). The main activities in the park are wildlife watching from elephants' backs, four-wheel-drive tours, canoe trips, fishing and bird watching. Some 50 species of mammals are recorded in the park. The principal attraction of the park is the last Nepalese population of the one-horned rhinoceros. According to the wildlife census of Nepal in 2008, out of the total of 435 rhinos in Nepal, 408 were in the CNP (Nepal National Rhino Count, 2008). There are more than 70 low-budget lodges and guest houses outside the Park, mostly at Sauraha, in addition to the seven luxury Eco-lodges within the Park. The park is served by an airport at Bharatpur 20 km to the north and is accessible from Kathmandu by road.

Chitwan is Nepal's first national park. Its importance in the global biodiversity preserve recognized, the CNP was declared a World Heritage Site by UNESCO in 1983. The CNP is situated in southern central Nepal and covers a total of 932 km^2 in area. An area of 750 km^2 surrounding the park is declared a buffer zone, which consists of forests and private lands, including cultivated lands. More than 200,000 people inhabit the buffer zone area. It is also one of Nepal's earliest developed tourism destinations. The first wildlife safari lodge was established in the 1960s before the area was declared a national park. Nepal's conservation movement has achieved a remarkable feat since the establishment of the CNP. By 2009, Nepal had designated more than 23% of its total area as national parks and conservation areas. It has 10 national parks, 3 wildlife reserves, 1 hunting reserve, 6 conservation areas, and 12 buffer zones – all covering an area of 34,186.62 km^2, which is more than the entire size of Belgium. The park and the local people jointly initiate community development activities and manage natural resources in the buffer zone.

The government has made a commitment of providing at least 30–50% of the park revenue for community development and natural resource management in the buffer zone.

Conflict in Conservation Areas

Parks versus people conflict is widely researched and debated in conservation discourse. The root of this conflict, to an extent, goes back to the very philosophy on which the establishment of the national park is founded. The idea of conservation started from the west as a reaction against the transformation of nature and increasing capital accumulation (Akama, 1996; Boyd and Butler 2000). According to Akama (1996), these pioneer conservationists, composed of the gentry and affluent members of society, started to campaign against the destruction of pristine nature areas, both at home and in the colonies. These were people who were not living at the economic margin and wanted the remaining pristine nature areas to be preserved and protected against what they perceived as the 'greed and rapacity' of their fellow countrymen. They campaigned for the remaining pristine nature areas to be demarcated and fenced off to form protected nature sanctuaries, which led to the establishment of national parks. Thus, the rural communities surrounding protected natural areas have little or no influence on decision making or the institutions of wildlife conservation and tourist management (Akama, 1996). According to Macleod (2001), the Western attitude towards local people and the deeply rooted intellectual separation of human society from the natural environment has created much of the park–people conflict. He pinpoints that this separation can be witnessed in the 1975 definition of 'national park' by the IUCN, which specifically lays down the condition to isolate the park from the people.

> Where one or several ecosystems are not materially altered by human exploitation and occupation, whose plants and animal species, geomorphologic sites and habitants,

are of special scientific, educative and recreative interest, or which contains a natural landscape of great beauty. Where the highest competent authority of the country has taken steps to prevent or eliminate as soon as possible, exploitation or occupation in the whole area and to enforce effectively, the respect of ecological, geomorphologic or aesthetic features that have led to its establishment.

West and Brechin (1991)

The need for a people-centred approach to national park management is widely reiterated for reducing the conflict (Hannah, 1992; Wells *et al.*, 1992; Nepal and Weber, 1993; Ghimire and Pimbert, 1997). Nepal (2000a, p. 73) argues that, '...if parks and protected areas are to remain viable in future, local communities must be given a greater role in park management, and livelihood issues must be adequately addressed in park policies'. According to him, tourism can be one of the significant ways to enhance a positive relationship between parks and people. He notes that programmes that are based on revenues generated by or through parks-based tourism have had positive impacts on local people, which not only offer employment opportunities but also develop in them positive feelings towards protected areas.

Tourism has always been a major feature of national parks in most countries (Butler, 2000). McNeely (1995) views tourism as a resource that is capable of expanding a partnership between local people and national parks. It can play the role of mediator to strengthen the conservation capacity of the park authority and at the same time influence local attitudes towards conservation (Nepal, 2000b). In developing countries, tourism can have a greater role as it can provide economic support to communities that have lost access to natural resources as a consequence of national park creation (Liliholm and Romney, 2000). But the relationship between tourism and conservation has not been as easy (Kenchington, 1989). Boyd (2000) notes that with increased promotion of tourism in the park, the focus of priority is shifting towards a 'protection' mandate, as opposed

to use. This discourages tourism in national parks.

But the best option to tackle a tourism or conservation mandate can be sought after considering the varied level of interactions between them. Budowski (1976) identifies three different relationships between tourism and nature conservation: conflict, coexistence and symbiosis. He notes that poorly planned tourism can lead to conflict in conservation areas, whereas better thought out plans and effective management can help in achieving a balance between tourism and conservation. The ideal symbiotic relationship between the two can be achieved with some attitudinal change by both the parties, writes Budowki (1976). Getz and Jamal (1994) believe a symbiotic relationship develops where stewardship of the ecological environment becomes a necessity not only for long-term habitat preservation, but also in order to preserve the quality of life desired by local inhabitants. According to them, the type, scale and pace of tourism and resort development must consider impacts on the ecological environment and on the socio-cultural environment of the local communities in the region.

Chitwan occupies an important place for both conservation and tourism. Its conservation value is well acknowledged. Because of the large amount of human habitation surrounding the park, Chitwan has remained at the forefront of park–people conflict in Nepal. Most of the earlier conflicts in the park concerned the contrasting priorities of the park administration and local people (Nepal and Weber, 1995), specifically agricultural land use (Milton and Binney, 1980) versus grazing and fodder (Sharma and Shaw, 1993). Mishra (1982) has outlined the four basic areas of conflict in the park, namely, loss of life, loss of livestock and crops to wildlife and difficulties due to resentment arising from the park regulations. Nepal and Weber (1995) have identified five causes of park–people conflict in Chitwan: illegal transactions of forest products from the park, livestock grazing, illegal hunting and fishing, crop damage by the park's wild animals, and threats to human and animal life. The effects of tourism on the national park and its conservation goal have not been well studied except for the impact of wildlife tourism on animal communities (Curry *et al.*, 2001). The presence of concessionaires inside the park was not part of any of the above conflicts. It never occurred before that these concessionaires were detrimental to the park's conservation goal. There was no reported conflict between the concessionaires, the conservationists, the national park authorities or the local people. The issue came up suddenly after the government failed to renew their contract; then a much deeper conflict between tourism businesses inside the park and the conservationists was exposed.

Controversy in Chitwan National Park

Whereas all past conflicts in Chitwan remained limited to a clash over the use of park resources, the concessionaires' conflict graduated into a full-blown controversy. Conflicts exist when incompatible activities occur (Deutsch, 1973, 1980). But controversy is a special kind of conflict and occurs when one person's ideas, opinions, conclusions, theories and information are incompatible with another's when they discuss problems and make decisions (Tjosvold, 1985). According to Tjosvold, decision makers disagree when they define problems, outline alternatives, make choices and implement solutions. Controversy involves differences of opinion that at least temporarily prevent, delay or interfere with reaching a decision. Persons in controversy have opposing views about how they should proceed, and face the pressure to resolve these differences in order to reach a decision and move forward (Tjosvold, 1985).

The Chitwan controversy began in July 2009 when the latest 15-year contract that allowed seven concessionaires to operate inside the park came to an end. In 1993, the government had issued an operating licence to seven resorts for a span of 15 years. The government did not renew their operating licence before their term expired

in 2009 and neither gave any advance notice of its intention nor furnished any reason for its failure to renew the licence. This leads to uncertainty over the future of these concessionaires, the businesses inside the park were closed temporarily and guests were evacuated until the issue was to be resolved. But what lay ahead was more controversy, and deeper divisions started to arise between the various stakeholders in the ensuing days.

The difference of opinion initially came from within the government. The Minister for Forest and Soil Conservation was reportedly in favour of renewing the licences of the hotels, whereas his top civil servant, the Forest Secretary, was against the renewal. The divergent views within the government meant indecision on licence renewal, as the Forest Secretary declined to recommend their renewal. The failure to renew the seven eco-lodges raised disputes between the entrepreneurs and government officials. The government, mainly the bureaucracy, and wildlife activists argued the hotels hurt the environment inside the park and were detrimental to conservation goals. On the other hand, the resort owners argued their hotels have actually helped raise awareness about conservation and helped fund the national park through royalties. 'It is clear that the smugglers and poachers active in the park find our presence there a threat to them and want us closed,' said one of Nepal's pioneer tourism entrepreneurs and owner of a concessionaire in the park.

The intensity of the conflict started to reach a higher level and the Nepalese Parliament's Public Accounts Committee (PAC) intervened. Initially the PAC decided to stop the hotels operating within the park. Later, it formed a sub-committee to look into the environmental impact inside the CNP due to the presence of the hotels and asked it to submit the findings within 15 days. The sub-committee recommended three options. The first was that hoteliers will be given 6–7-year contracts to run the hotels outside the park in the buffer-zone area of the CNP if they relocate outside the national park within 6 months. In the second option, the contract will be for the next

4 years if they take about a year to relocate the hotels. The third alternative was that the hotels will be allowed to operate inside the park for 2 years but they will not be given permission to operate them anywhere after that period. 'We recommended these options as Nepal is celebrating Nepal Tourism Year (NTY) in 2011 and we don't want to create a serious impact on the tourism sector of the country', it was said (Nepalnews, 2009).

While the government was considering the PAC options over the issue, another parliamentary committee – Natural Resources and Means Committee (NRMC) – challenged the PAC decision, arguing that the PAC has no jurisdiction over the issue. The NRMC's argument was that the issue over the use of the natural resources falls under its jurisdiction and the PAC has no authority to decide the case. The NRMC directed the government not to arrive at any decision before it took the final decision, after initially ruling that the resorts needed to be shut down immediately. It formed another subcommittee to look into the matter. The subcommittee held interactions at various levels, which became a platform for heated discussions between hoteliers and their opponents, where the hoteliers faced humiliation and accusations of looting and smuggling wildlife, as reported by a national newspaper (Republica, 2009). For example, citing an earlier report, a government bureaucrat complained that most of the rhinos and tigers in the park have been found killed near the hotels. 'Was the national park made for biodiversity conservation or hotel operations?' he questioned. A local conservation activist accused the hoteliers of looting by evading tax while enjoying exclusive rights of operating hotels inside the park at the cost of wildlife. Most of the lawmakers in the meeting opined that the hoteliers should be immediately evicted from the CNP as the law bars anyone from enjoying exclusive rights to public property. 'It will be unfair to allow them to enjoy exclusive rights to operate hotels inside the CNP, while barring the locals from using the resources there. They should immediately pack up,' said a lawmaker. The hoteliers were infuriated by the accusations. An owner of a concessionaire

asked, 'Were we invited to the meeting to be humiliated?' The subcommittee chairman had to apologize to the hoteliers about some remarks in the meeting. Despite all this, the NRMC members were divided over the matter and delayed their final recommendation.

The most contentious of the issues in the park has been the poaching of wild animals, especially the endangered one-horned rhinos, in the vicinity of the concessionaires inside the park. Chitwan is the home to Nepal's successful project to conserve the endangered one-horned rhinos. The large number of rhinos in the park has been targeted by poachers and there have been quite a few instances of rhino poaching inside the park. A government report claimed that most of this poaching was found to be done near the concessionaires, and this has remained a central issue in the relationship between conservationists and businesses inside the park. Nepali media raised this issue constantly while covering the news on the licence row. To raise awareness about wildlife concerns, a cartoon published in Nepal's national English daily showed a minister voting for the hotels and all the animals voting a 'No' to hotels inside the park.

The minister concerned was under pressure from the big business communities, and said he was confused as the two parliamentary committees had taken up the issue. There was a demand from the business fraternity to renew the contract for which some intense lobbying was done by the hoteliers. The business chambers were of the opinion to let the hotels operate at least until 2011, the year the government is celebrating as NTY. Nepal's nodal tourism promotion body that also aims to achieve national conservation goals through its tourism effort was on the hoteliers' side, though it seldom tries to expose itself openly on such matters. 'The CEO wanted them to be renewed if not for a longer term then at least till the end of 2011 since NTY was approaching', said an NTB official.

Seeing the divergent views and contradictory opinions of the parliamentary committees, the government formed its own taskforce headed by the Finance Minister to make recommendations to the cabinet. The task force made a vague recommendation to the government to decide on the basis of the directives of the parliamentary committees, whilst also keeping in view the statutory obligation to provide licences on the basis of open tender. The National Park and Wildlife Conservation Act, 1973 says the government may contract through sealed tender to operate hotel, lodge, public transport or other services within the protected area for its wider benefit.

While the two parliamentary committees were still fighting over jurisdiction on the matter, the cabinet finally decided to allow the seven hotels to operate for another 3 years, keeping in view Nepal's preparation for celebrating 2011 as NTY. Though there were some reservations from the conservationists about this decision to temporarily allow the businesses to operate, for now the issue has been shelved until the next renewal in July 2012.

The dimensions of the controversy

Though the controversy seemed to be primarily concerned with the conflict of the priority of conservation over tourism in the park, there were other dimensions that were more importantly driving the whole episode. Most important of them was Nepal's changed political context.

Nepal's changed socio-political context

Nepal has witnessed an enormous political change in recent years; in particular, the past 20 years have been the most tumultuous period in Nepal's history. The communist war led by the Maoist Party intensified in recent years and the political parties finally agreed to abolish the 250-year-old institution of monarchy and adopt a new Republican constitution through a constitutional assembly. Since then Nepal is on an interim constitution and a transitional government is in place. There has been an intense demand for federalism and power devolution for the exploitation of regional or local resources.

Most of these demands have been informed by leftist ideology and increased ethnic movements.

The monarchy was formally abolished in 2008 and since then there have been assaults against royals (Bhandari, 2010) and even against those who are viewed as monarchists. During the past decade of Maoist insurgency, the Maoists systematically spearheaded propaganda against the royal family, their businesses and the Nepalese army. Nepal deploys army personnel to provide the park with security and there were frequent skirmishes between the army and the Maoists in the past (Baral and Heinen, 2006). The Maoists' propaganda was largely successful in creating resentment against the royals and the army amongst the general public and the local communities.

Nepal's changed political context was highly relevant in this case. If there was genuine concern about conservation, it was possible for conservationists to raise the issue because of the recent political change. Nepal's conservation movement is largely dominated by conservationists employed in government institutions. 'Conservationists were always against the licensing of hotels inside the park but kept themselves quiet on earlier occasions due to their job insecurity, but the present timing made it easier for them to speak up', believed a conservationist (LPD; respondents are designated by initials), who had been a senior conservation official with the Nepal government. According to him, the changed political context and fluid political dispensation made it easier for them to raise the issue this time.

Many respondents this author talked to opined that the practice of allowing the concessionaires inside the park served royal interests during the earlier regime. Their view was that this was why licences were issued without holding any consultation on their possible impact on the park environment, and no tender process was carried out. There was no consultation within the Department of National Parks and Wildlife Conservation (DNPWC) or with conservationists. Due to this lack of consultation on earlier occasions, no one within the DNPWC was taking the ownership of earlier agreements with the concessionaires, said a conservationist (KT). Although the latest licence was issued just after the political change that ended the monarch's direct rule in 1990, it was done largely because of the royal regime's precedence, favouring those considered close to political power. It must also be noted that the government formed after the political change of 1990 strongly pursued capitalist policies and tourism was given a foremost priority in achieving the country's economic goals. This favoured big companies getting the licence. Some of the concessionaires were believed to be related to Nepal's ex-royals or closely associated with them. Quite a few of them had been ardent supporters of absolute monarchy in the past. This obviously made some political parties oppose them, such as the ultra-leftist Maoist Party that had fought for the abolition of the monarchy in the past and which has emerged the largest party now. To an extent the licence case metaphorically became a conflict between the new order and the old order in Nepali politics. For example, the political careers of both the Minister of Forest and Soil Conservation and Minister of Tourism and Civil Aviation were groomed during the erstwhile monarchical rule of the pre-1990 era and they were front-running supporters for licence renewal. For the majority of the local communities, the concessionaires inside the park represented Nepal's elite class and were seen as rightists and thus were opposed.

Different Mandates between Tourism and Conservation

The convergence of tourism in a conservation area is definitely a source of conflict because of different mandates between tourism and conservation. Boyd (2000) identifies this presence of dual mandates within a park system, namely the protection of natural and cultural heritage, and the provision of the opportunities to enjoy and benefit from the parks as problems national park managers face. The nature of the bipolarities between tourism and conservation can be understood from Burns' (2004) dichotomy between the 'Tourism First' (rightist) school and 'Development First' (leftist) school (Burns, 2004). According to Burns (2004), the Development First school is concerned about economic and social dualism, core-periphery relationships, and concomitant underdevelopment. The Tourism First school has as its key concerns economic growth on trickle-down or multipliers of development; however, the main beneficiaries of this approach are the international tourism industry and local elites. As mentioned before, the concessionaires or the big businesses were the proponents of the Tourism First school, whereas the conservationists and the local businesses represented the Development First school. This conflict represented a confrontation between them, metaphorically between the political leftist and the rightist.

The division of mandate between tourism and conservation was clearly visible in the opinions expressed by respondents this author contacted. For the conservationists the presence of hotels inside the park can be viewed as a serious breach of the purpose of conservation. 'It marginalizes conservation efforts and is against the welfare of animals', viewed one respondent (ERS). He continued:

> From a conservation point of view, I am totally against it. Based on past experiences and research, it has been reported that much wildlife is being killed around hotels. In addition, as the hotels are located at strategic locations, mainly in biodiversity hot spots, there remains a chance of a threat to tourists and locals by wild animals, mainly tigers.

Conservationists have used the report that claimed that a significant number of rhinos were poached near the hotels inside the park. To most conservationists, it was not clear why these businesses had to be located within the park and even some of the tourism people were critical of the idea of having businesses inside. A respondent (BKS) who is with the national tourism board believed:

The hotels should be allowed to operate inside the park only on condition that their activities are being closely monitored and that the resorts are complying with the rules of the park in matters of conservation. Since poaching, use of firewood, noise, disturbances and other nuisances are widespread and the monitoring part is very poor in Nepal fuelled by rampant corruption, it is advisable not to have the resorts inside the park.

The allegations of conservationists are not baseless. These Eco-lodges are private companies and there tend to be various contentious issues by virtue of their nature. There is a wide range of criticism of their low level of accountability and transparency in their operation elsewhere (Hannah, 2006). The main emphasis of the private companies is on their clients or market demands, not on the broader segments of society; they do not seek a broad social sanction (Kwan et al., 2008), and little is known about the private sector's role in protecting biodiversity (Krug, 2001). But despite this, concessionaires are important intermediaries in achieving parks' economic goals and many pioneering countries have favoured them. For example, the National Park Service (1998) of the USA has 600 profit-oriented concessionaires under contract. New Zealand relies heavily on commercial enterprises for providing visitor services, with 1134 concessionaires, and has seen a rapid growth in the number of concession operators (Cessford and Thompson, 2002 cited in Eagles, 2009). In Chitwan's case, 'it must be noted that the concessionaires play an important role in the promotion of Nepalese tourism abroad, particularly Chitwan's jungle safari is exclusively promoted by them internationally', acknowledged a respondent (LBB) from the Nepalese tourism board. This makes it imperative to accommodate concessionaires alongside the park's conservation goals.

Rivalry between Businesses
Inside and Outside the Park

Burns (2004) believes that local politics in many countries, developed and developing, can be characterized by petty-mindedness and internal factions of various interest groups, not to mention corruption. Interestingly, among those who were singing the conservation tune were also a section of tourism business and hotels themselves. These were the businesses located outside the park that were in competition with the concessionaires inside the park. It has more to do with their business interests than any serious conservation commitment. 'Though on the surface it seems that the conflict is associated with conservation as conservationists are raising their voice in its favor, it is strongly associated with economic perspectives', suggested a respondent (ERS).

There is a deep-rooted conflict between businesses inside and outside the park. Outsiders are demanding with the government to be given access to their elephants (for Jungle Safari) inside the national park. The park prohibits elephants from outside to enter the park. Businesses outside the park can offer jungle safari to the tourists in the community forest in the adjoining buffer zones but not inside the park. There are currently 45 elephants outside the park. The concessionaires enjoy the exclusive right to offer jungle safari inside the park on their elephants. The local businesses have been demanding access to their elephants for jungle safari inside the park. The park authorities have been refusing this by arguing that permitting outside elephants inside the park can spread contagious diseases to park animals.

There are other issues. The hoteliers operating outside the park believe that during the off season these concessionaires who are supposed to cater to high-end tourists accommodate budget tourists, which is against their contract and not acceptable to hoteliers outside. Likewise, there is another debate concerning labour used in the park hotels: most of the labour and consumables are not locally hired and locals get minimum benefits from them. There is even some corruption at the policy level, a respondent (ERS) alleged. Being situated inside the park was itself a special privilege that gives a comparative advantage to the licence holders over the ones who are outside the park. Most of the high-paying tourists were monopolized by the hotels inside the park because of their privileged location. A respondent (BKS) took the view:

> It [the controversy] is a combination of both the genuine concern and the disparity of location from a business point of view. The resorts located inside the park are always using that factor as a USP for promoting their business at the cost of others. Besides these ingredients for conflict, the poaching of rhinos has aggravated the situation to boiling point and attracted national concern.

Local Antipathy Towards the Concessionaires

Since the local communities were not benefiting substantially from the businesses inside the park, these businesses were seen as benefiting themselves without being serious about conservation or the welfare of the local communities. A credible and extensive review of the CNP was done in 1996 and no such assessment since then has been carried out. The 1996 report to assess the value, threat and evaluation of the national park categorically said that fewer than 2% of 290,000 people around the park were employed by the local tourism businesses: most of them were working temporarily on a daily wage basis. There was a very marginal use of local agricultural products by the businesses (KMTNC, 1996). There have been no significant policy measures to improve local access to tourism benefits apart from introducing a policy of ploughing back the revenue generated by them.

The concessionaires were not abiding by their contractual duty. There were millions of payments in arrears by these concessionaires at the time of the licence renewal row. The government collects royalties and conservation fees from the concessionaires. Some concessionaires stopped paying their royalty and conservation fees a few years ago, asking the government to waive their liability. They claimed that they had suffered a huge loss during the period of heightened Maoist conflict when Nepal's

tourist arrivals nose-dived, that is, during 2000–2005. Lack of revenue to government meant that there was no revenue ploughed back to the national park area and to the local communities. This resulted in general antipathy against the concessionaires.

Importantly, the excluded group in the entire controversy was the local community. Although the parliamentary subcommittees reached the area to get the local peoples' opinion on the matter, no proper representation of local voice was evident in the entire debate. It was widely believed that most of the locals were against these concessionaires as the local benefit to them was minimal. The absence of local people from the entire debate is unfortunate but not new, however. There was no local consultation while issuing licences to the hotels on earlier occasions. All respondents this author reached believed that the national park was established at the cost of local people who have been denied the use of their forest resources, and it is equally important to respond to their demands. Sharing of hotel income with the local community would be a wise strategy, so it is important to allow hotels inside the park if that were to mean benefit to the local community. This also makes it imperative to find a long-term and sustainable solution to this issue.

Conclusions

In this chapter we have seen how contested tourism and conservation can be at times. The mandate with which both of them work is often fraught with contradictions and it is a challenge for authorities to achieve a fine balance between the two. Even if there is any balance between the two, it tends to fail at times because of its intricacies brought about by both internal and external factors. The failure of the concessionaires to meet their contractual obligations and questions over their conservation commitment has led to local stakeholders' antipathy towards them. The change in the political regime additionally posed an important question as to their significance in the country's new political context.

This case also brings forth the issue of the ideological dilemma between tourism and conservation and the difficultly it poses to tourism planners. Tourism existed in the CNP before the park was established and there should be no reason that they cannot co-exist in the future. Butler (2000) argues that no attempt to delete tourism's role in national parks, either unilaterally or globally, can be realistic. It would certainly be counter-productive to the parks movement as it would remove a great deal of public sympathy and support for the parks concept (Butler, 2000). With such a scenario, planners face a great challenge to effectively accommodate both tourism and conservation goals in the national park system. Burns' (2004) proposal of middle-ground in planning can be relevant here. He notes that traditional tourism planning has failed to achieve the development of the poor marginalized people who are the target beneficiaries; and thus local communities see little or no benefit from what is going on around them. According to him, the relatively newer ideas of the alternative model that lays more emphasis on 'leave only footprint' exhortations does not bring in dollars to develop the industry, or supply large-scale employment, or a reliable stream of tax revenues to government. Burns (2004) proposes a more integrated approach that can balance tourism systems and institutions by taking into account local–global partnerships/networks, consumption patterns and the effect of the culture.

The integrated approach can be a wise strategy for the CNP. Both tourism and conservation people would be happy if the hotels could be licensed under a stringent quality regime. That is, there should be an effective and efficient monitoring mechanism. Only high-end tourists should be catered for by these concessionaires and smooth channelling of hotel revenues to local development should be ensured. This requires effective implementation of the government's plough-back policy. The strategy could address economic benefit to the local community, whilst maintaining the very objective of biodiversity conservation.

This controversy teaches us some important lessons that can be useful to other conservation parks thinking of opening their territory to tourism businesses. It lays out the complexities that can come with different mandates between conservation and tourism. Though Nepal's case of political instability can be atypical in this case, a need for a balanced approach between tourism and conservation, understanding of local business interests, and importance of stakeholder consultations in policy planning is a lesson for others in the policy-making process in similar cases.

Acknowledgements

The author thanks Dr Shant Raj Jnawali, Kiran Timalsina and Deepak Raj Joshi (NTB) for their assistance in the preparation of this chapter.

References

Akama, J.S. (1996) Western environmental values and nature-based tourism in Kenya. *Tourism Management* 17, 567–574.

Baral, N.M.S. and Heinen, T.J. (2006) The Maoist people's war and conservation in Nepal. *Politics and Life Sciences* 24, 2–11.

Bhandari, K. (2004) Nepalese tourism – crisis and beyond: Nepal's endeavour for tourism recovery. *Tourism* 52, 375–383.

Bhandari, K. (2010) Tourism in Nepal: post-monarchy challenges. *Journal of Tourism and Cultural Change* 8, 69–83.

Boyd, S. and Butler, R. (2000) Tourism and national parks: the origin of the concept. In: Butler, R. and Boyd, S. (eds) *Tourism and National Parks*. Wiley, Chichester, UK, pp. 13–27.

Boyd, S.W. (2000) Tourism, national parks and sustainability. In: Butler, R. and Boyd, S. (eds) *Tourism and National Parks*. Wiley, Chichester, UK, pp. 161–186.

Budowski, G. (1976) Tourism and environmental conservation: conflict, coexistence, or symbiosis? *Environmental Conservation* 3, 27–31.

Burns, P. (2004) Tourism planning a third way. *Annals of Tourism Research* 31, 24–43.

Butler, R. (2000) Tourism and national parks in the twenty-first century. In: Butler, R. and Boyd, S. (eds) *Tourism and National Parks*. Wiley, Chichester, pp. 324–335.

Cessford, G. and Thompson, A. (2002) Managing tourism in the New Zealand protected area system. *Parks* 12, 26–36.

Curry, B., Moore, W., Bauer, J., Cosgriff, K. and Lipscombe, N. (2001) Modelling impacts of wildlife tourism on animal communities: a case study from Royal Chitwan National Park, Nepal. *Journal of Sustainable Tourism* 9, 514–529.

Deutsch, M. (1973) *The Resolution of Conflict*. Yale University Press, New Haven, Connecticut.

Deutsch, M. (1980) Over fifty years of conflict research. In: Festinger L. (ed.) *Four Decades of Social Psychology*. Oxford University Press, New York, pp. 46–77.

Eagles, P.F.J. (2009) Governance of recreation and tourism partnerships in parks and protected areas. *Journal of Sustainable Tourism* 17, 231–248.

Getz, D. and Jamal, T.B. (1994) The environment–community symbiosis: a case of collaborative tourism planning. *Journal of Sustainable Tourism* 2, 152–173.

Ghimire, K. and Pimbert, K. (1997) *Social Change and Conservation*. Earthscan, London.

Guneratne, A. (2001) Shaping the tourist's gaze: representing ethnic difference in a Nepali village. *Royal Anthropological Institute* 7, 527–543.

Hannah, L. (1992) *African People, African Parks: An Evaluation of Development Initiatives as a Means of Improving Protected Area Conservation in Africa*. Conservation International, Washington, DC.

Hannah, L. (2006) Governance of private protected areas in Canada: advancing the public interest. PhD thesis. Department of Geography, University of Victoria, Victoria, British Columbia, Canada.

Kenchington, R.A. (1989) Tourism in the Galapagos Islands: the dilemma of conservation. *Environmental Conservation* 16, 227–236.

KMTNC (King Mahendra Trust for Nature Conservation) (1996) *Royal Chitwan National Park: An Assessment of Values, Threats, and Opportunities*. KMTNC, Kathmandu.

Krug, W. (2001) Private supply of protected land in South Africa: a review of markets, approaches, barriers and issues. Workshop paper presented at the International Workshop on Market Creation for Bio-Diversity Products and Services, World Bank/OECD, Paris.

Kwan, P., Eagles, P.F.J. and Gebhardt, A. (2008) Eco-lodge patrons' characteristics and motivations: a study of Belize. *Journal of Ecotourism* 7, 1–25.

Liliholm, R.J. and Romney, L.R. (2000) Tourism, national parks and wildlife. In: Butler, R. and Boyd. S. (eds) *Tourism and National Parks*. Wiley, Chichester, UK, pp.137–151.

Macleod, D.V.L. (2001) Parks or people? National parks and the case of Del Este, Dominican Republic. *Progress in Development Studies* 1, 221–235.

McNeely, J.A. (1995) *Expanding Partnerships in Conservation*. Island Press, Washington, DC.

Milton, J.P. and Binney, G.A. (1980) *Ecological Planning in Nepalese Tarai: A Report on Resolving Resource Conflicts Between Wildlife Conservation and Agricultural Land Use in Padampur Panchayat*. Threshold, International Centre for Environmental Renewal, Washington, DC.

Mishra, H. (1982) Balancing human needs and conservation in Nepal's Royal Chitwan National Park. *Ambio* 11, 246–251.

Nepalnews (2009) PAC panel forwards three options to jungle resorts. Available at: http://www.nepalnews.com/home/index.php/business-&-economy/1337-pac-panel-forwards-three-options-to-jungle-resorts-.html (accessed 14 July 2010).

Nepal, S. (2000a) Tourism, national parks and local communities. In: Butler, R. and Boyd, S. (eds) *Tourism and National Parks*. Wiley, Chichester, UK, pp. 73–94.

Nepal, S. (2000b) Tourism in protected areas: the Nepalese Himalaya. *Annals of Tourism Research* 27, 661–681.

Nepal, S.K. and Weber, K.E. (1993) *Struggle for Existence, Park–People Conflict in Royal Chitwan National Park, Nepal*. Asian Institute of Technology, Bangkok.

Nepal, S.K. and Weber, K.E. (1995) The quandary of local people–park relations in Nepal's Chitwan National Park. *Environmental Management* 19, 853–866.

Nepal National Rhino Count (2008) Rhino count – 2008, Nepal. Available at: http://www.dnpwc.gov.np/publication/Rhino_Count_2008_Nepal.pdf (accessed 14 June 2010).

NTB (Nepal Tourism Board) (2010) Jungle safari. Available at: http://welcomenepal.com/promotional/submain.php?menuid=3&submenuid=58921462757&subpageid=173276679231 (accessed 24 August 2010).

NTS (2009) Nepal tourism statistics. Available at: http://www.welcomenepal.com/images/downloads/Nepal_Tourism_Statistics_2009.pdf (accessed 16 March 2011).

Piessel, M. (1990) *Tiger for Breakfast*. Time Books International, New Delhi.

Republica (2009) Chitwan hoteliers 'humiliated' at parliamentary discussion. Available at: http://www.myrepublica.com/portal/index.php?action=news_details&news_id10728 (accessed 28 July 2010).

Sharma, U.R. and Shaw, W.W. (1993) Role of Nepal's Royal Chitwan National Park in meeting the grazing and fodder needs of local people. *Environmental Conservation* 20, 139–142.

Thapa, M. (2009) *A Boy From Siklis*. Penguin, New Delhi.

The National Park and Wildlife Conservation Act (1973) (in Nepali). Available from: http://www.dnpwc.gov.np/npwc%20act%202029.pdf (accessed 30 July 2010).

Tjosvold, D. (1985) Implications of controversy research for management. *Journal of Management* 11, 21–37.

Wells, M., Brown, K. and Hannah, L. (1992) *People and Parks, Linking Protected Areas with Local Communities*. The World Bank/ WWF/USAID, Washington, DC.

West, P. and Brechin, S. (1991) *Resident Peoples and National Parks: Social Dilemmas and Strategies in International Conservation*. The University of Arizona Press, Tucson, Arizona.

17   Volunteer Tourism: Commodified Trend or New Phenomenon?

Angela M. Benson[1] and Stephen Wearing[2]
[1]*Tourism and Travel, University of Brighton, School of Service Management, Eastbourne, UK;* [2]*School of Leisure, Sport and Tourism, Faculty of University of Technology, Sydney, Kuring-gai Campus, Australia*

Introduction

> There is no overt criticism of volunteer tourism in the literature, in part because little research has been undertaken on this topic, but also because its laudable character and outcomes may render it more resistant to critical scrutiny.
>
> Weaver (2006, p. 46)

As indicated in the opening quote by Weaver (2006) and highlighted by Sin (2009) there is a dearth of academic literature that takes a critical perspective of volunteer tourism. The literature on volunteer tourism has predominantly been written from 2000 onwards, it has tended to describe the volunteer tourism phenomenon rather than understand or identify its potentially controversial nature. The focus has been, and still is to some extent, on the volunteer with a small and fragmented literature associated with host communities, the organizations offering volunteer tourism and other key stakeholders. Recently, however, volunteer tourism has come under scrutiny not only in the academic literature (see a series of research probes in the *Tourism Recreation Research Journal* by Butcher, 2011; Guttentag, 2011; and Raymond, 2011) but also in the media. This chapter will examine the criticism and engage in a critical evaluation of volunteer

tourism and, more specifically, look at its relationship to the projects it engages in and the communities in which many of its projects occur.

Volunteer Tourism

Volunteer tourism has become a global phenomenon with market predictions indicating growth in both size and value (Mintel, 2008; Tourism Research and Marketing (TRAM), 2008). In 2009, predicted growth indicated 62% of volunteer tour operators expected to send more volunteers abroad than the previous year, 16% expected to send a similar amount and 20% expected to send less (Nestora *et al.*, 2009). As of 2011, there are no clear statistics as to the size of the volunteer tourism market with the majority of figures being derived from website hits (e.g. Ingram, 2011), volunteer surveys and supply side operators. Mintel (2008) estimated that the market reached US$150 million in 2006; TRAM (2008) suggests that 'the total expenditure generated by volunteer tourism is likely to be between £832 million (US$1.66 billion) and £1.3 billion (US$2.6 billion)' (p. 42) 'with a total of 1.6 million volunteer tourists a year' (p. 5).

This growth has brought a proliferation of firms and organizations moving into this market, predominantly from Western countries. Whilst many volunteering opportunities are linked to charitable organizations, it is also evident that some of the growth in this sector is by profit-making companies. While some of these new entrants can be linked to social entrepreneurship, others are purely commercial. The market place is not static and whilst new firms enter the market, others change their status. For example, the volunteering company i to i was bought by First Choice Holidays, a profit-maximizing firm, for around £20 million in 2007. Trekforce Expeditions, a charitable organization offering volunteer opportunities ceased to trade in 2006; the former managing director took the opportunity of forming a new company in the name of Trekforce Worldwide, which is still operating today. The projects offered by such companies are wide ranging: social justice projects, teaching English, archaeology digs, community development, wildlife and conservation projects, care and health related. These projects are found in both terrestrial and marine environments. The market segmentation includes projects directed towards individuals, families, groups, students (in particular the gap-year students), career breaks and the corporate market. This growth and segmentation of the market has produced a range of resources, websites and publications, which are regularly updated, and are largely descriptive but offer information that outline the myriad of volunteer tourism projects available (e.g. Hardy, 2004; Ausender and Heyniger, 2007; Hindle et al., 2007; McCloskey, 2008). The message of some of this material has changed over recent years and now includes challenging the ethical status of volunteer tourism rather than the previous passive acceptance of volunteer tourism as a 'saving the world' concept (Benson, 2011).

Criticisms are also evident from organizations not directly involved with offering volunteer tourism per se, but who are situated within the voluntary sector:

> This week, Voluntary Service Overseas (VSO) opined that the 'charity tourism'

of many year-out programs was a new form of colonialism. Students who travel to developing countries risk doing more harm than good, argued Judith Brodie, UK director of VSO, criticizing the emphasis on volunteer enjoyment rather than on how to help the communities they work in.
> Bartham (2006)

This criticism refers to the consumption of volunteer tourism products as exotic adventures with an implied altruistic philosophy, but are designed more to cater to the needs of the tourists than the needs of the communities that they purportedly serve. The volunteer tourists inadvertently fetishize and regard the host communities as exotic or impoverished 'others', rather than making a meaningful connection with their hosts or developing any insight into cultural diversity. VSO continued to voice concerns in 2007:

> VSO has warned that gappers risk becoming the 'new colonialists' if attitudes to voluntary work in the developing world do not change, accusing gap year companies of increasingly catering to the needs of young people seeking to combine a little worthiness with a lot of travel, rather than the communities they claim to support.
> Ward (2007)

These sentiments are echoed by Patricia Barnet (Director of Tourism Concern, UK) 'It's a new form of colonialism; really...The market is geared toward profit rather than the needs of the communities' (Fitzpatrick, 2007).

Whilst this rhetoric does not specifically mention volunteer tourism, gap-year products often include a volunteer experience, and many of the companies offering volunteer tourism also offer gap years.

Academic research into volunteer tourism has grown significantly since 2000. Wearing (2001, p. 1) defines volunteer tourism as 'tourists who volunteer in an organized way to undertake holidays that involve aiding or alleviating the material poverty of some groups in society, the restoration of certain environments, or research into aspects of society or environment'. Since this definition, which is now considered to be fairly narrow in its focus (Lyons and Wearing, 2008), a number of other definitions have begun to emerge (Singh, 2002; Ellis, 2003; Uriely *et al.*, 2003; Singh, 2004; McGehee and Santos, 2005). Despite the emergence of these new definitions, there does not seem to be one that has captured the changing boundaries of volunteer tourism and Wearing's definition of 2001 still remains the most cited. The early definitions of volunteer tourism have tended to favour the altruistic side of volunteering. More recent debates, however, ask 'Is it (volunteer tourism) altruistic or ego-centric?' (or one of many positions along that continuum). A more common view is now being recognized that most forms of volunteer tourism (and indeed, modern volunteering) are not just about 'doing good for others' but also about 'doing good for self' (Matthews 2008, p. 111) which is echoed in the United Nations (UN) definition of volunteering (UN, 2001). Whilst the 'doing good for others' will be discussed in more detail later in the chapter, the 'doing good for self' can often be seen on university and first job application forms and volunteer curricula vitae.

Volunteer Tourism in the Context of Sustainability

Sustainable development became a prominent issue in the early 1980s at a general societal level. The World Conservation Strategy established sustainability as a foundational principle for a large number of projects based in developing countries. Sustainability is currently defined generally as development that is able to supply current needs without jeopardizing the needs of people in the future (World Commission on Environment and Development, 1987). Volunteer tourism is often associated with the concept of alternative tourism, ecotourism and sustainable tourism but while it is associated with these concepts, the discussion of volunteer tourism within the sustainable tourism development paradigm is limited and problematic. While there has been much theorizing about the concept of

sustainable tourism, the actual implementation and engagement into practice has taken a long time and even now is limited and piecemeal. A key barrier to this has been a shared vision between key stakeholders. Butcher and Smith (2010) echo this and highlight the gap between theoretically espousing, sustainable practices and actually implementing them in an effective manner. Even if implementation is happening within the context of volunteer tourism, it is difficult to determine whether all organizations, in all destinations and within all projects embody the ideals of sustainable tourism development all of the time. One of the main issues when trying to determine whether sustainability is taking place is the measuring and evaluation of it. Consequently, volunteer tourism is only associated with or measured against the three fundamental pillars of sustainability – economic, social and environmental – to a limited extent. This is true within both the volunteer tourism literature and the wider tourism literature. Most case examples have been undertaken by focusing on a single dimension (or impact) at one moment in time. This is due in part to different dimensions of impact evaluation requiring their own methodologies and capabilities. Consequently, tools, methodologies and capabilities for taking a holistic approach to evaluating the combined social, economic and environmental contributions are in their infancy. Despite this, the literature clearly indicates that balance between the three pillars is essential if sustainability is to be achieved (Cronin, 1990; Burns and Holden, 1995; Clarke, 1997; Swarbrooke, 1999; Hardy *et al.*, 2002; Ko, 2005; United Nations Development Programme, 2005). Any impact research conducted on just one element is insufficiently rich to create meaningful data upon which to engage in critical discussion or make informed management decisions. For volunteer tourism to succeed, it has to be sustainable for both the social and natural environments of the area visited while not becoming another form of tourism based mainly on economic development but rather a mixing of elements with community and the natural environment as key elements, while allowing the volunteer to return home and in turn engage and influence their original community.

Volunteer Tourism and the Mass Tourism Debate

There are criticisms inherent in attempting to discuss and compare volunteer tourism and mass tourism. One could argue volunteer tourism is yet another subset of mass tourism, as the proliferation of commercial volunteer tourism packages and products would imply (Wearing, 2001). Volunteer tourism experiences do tend to occur in communities that are living in marginal or environmentally threatened areas while more mainstream tourism tends to focus on established towns and centres. But does this also imply that the socio-cultural impacts of volunteer tourism are less harmful than mass tourism? Is not a footprint a footprint regardless?

We would argue that volunteer tourism can be differentiated at a more fundamental level through the approach that it attempts to take. Although this has been critiqued by Butcher and Smith (2010) as unrealistic with the number of NGOs and not-for-profit organizations engaged in this form of tourism, it is obvious that it has developed around a set of ideals that may or may not realize a more altruistic outcome. It could be argued, however, that new 'ethical' tourism practices (Butcher, 2005) emerging from a greater global awareness and a motivation that is counter to mass tourism are, arguably, more cosmopolitan in basis and altruistic in outcome. It can then be posited that volunteer tourism is one form of tourism that is growing in popularity and, as it has been presented in the literature, as a form of alternative tourism that creates the types of encounters that foster mutual understanding and respect (Wearing, 2001). This is a fundamental way of differentiating it.

There is a growing literature on volunteer tourism that questions its approach and foundation on social consciousness and cross-cultural understanding. For Raymond and Hall (2009), cross-cultural

understanding is by no means a given outcome. Similarly, Nyaupane *et al.* (2008, p.652) state that '...contact alone will not necessarily provide a positive cross-cultural experience...'. Simpson's work (2004, 2005) suggests that existing stereotypes may actually be reinforced, thereby deepening dichotomies. Others question the reciprocal benefits of such cross-cultural interaction given the inherent complexities of significant cultural (and economic) divides and, more importantly, the dearth of research on host community experiences (see McGehee and Andereck, 2009; Woosnam and Lee, 2011). Sin (2009) argues that volunteer tourists are motivated more by a desire 'to travel' than by a desire 'to contribute', and that they often regard aid-recipients as inferior. Sin found that 'many volunteer tourists are typically more interested in fulfilling objectives relating to the "self"' (Sin, 2009, p. 497). This particular finding critiques the altruistic motivations that earlier research had claimed as a key foundation of volunteer tourism (see Wearing, 2001). Butcher and Smith (2010, p. 33), although more positive, have also explored the notion of the 'self' in volunteer tourism, finding that 'the "desire to make a difference" ... [has become] connected to lifestyle ... [and] closely linked to a narrative of personal growth'. Some of these issues are fundamental to differentiating volunteer tourism. Table 17.1 sets out some means of examining this. It is set in the context of the ways volunteer tourism seeks to differentiate itself from mass tourism.

The Volunteer

The growing number of journal articles has focused heavily on the volunteer (Brown and Morrison, 2003; Galley and Clifton, 2004; Stoddart and Rogerson, 2004; McGehee and Santos, 2005; Mustonen, 2005; Brown and Lehto, 2005; Campbell and Smith, 2006) and more specifically the self (Wearing and Neil, 2000; Wearing, 2002, 2003; Wearing and Deane, 2003; Wickens 2011). Despite the

Table 17.1. Differentiating volunteer tourism from mass tourism.

Mass tourism	Volunteer tourism
Management of 'evolutionary' change (survival of the fittest) within a Western neo-liberal rationalist approach based on free-market economic principles	Focus is on co-operatives and community-based approaches where dominant free-market principles are relevant but secondary to principles associated with NGOs and volunteering
Maintaining social order, existing tourism systems unquestioned	Micro-level social systems, attempting to move beyond macro-assumed social order to community needs
Greater efficiency of current tourism systems hence increased profitability	More just and equitable systems that can expand the efficient tourism system to include social issues
Appearance of harmony, integration and cohesion of social groups involved in the tourism process	Contradictions between social ideals and reality, attempts to demonstrate this and find projects that alleviate it
Focus on ways to maintain cohesion and consensus to ensure the tourist experience is not disrupted	Ways to ensure a dialogue is created that allows need to become a part of the process and realized in the tourism experience
Expect homogenous host communities	Attempt to acknowledge difference in host communities
Identifying and meeting singular economic stakeholder needs within existing social system	Attempting to re-examine stakeholder needs and focus on basic human needs within and outside existing social system
Focused on actuality, discovering and understanding what is available and how it can be used	Focused on potentiality: providing a vision of what could be and building pathways to achieve it

focus upon the volunteer in the literature, there is no one profile that fits all. Case studies tend to outline demographics of a certain group, for example, youths are the volunteers in the Galley and Clifton (2004) study; however, this is more to do with the organization under study and their marketing to a specific target group (i.e. university students) than a generic profile of volunteers. This being said, the majority of volunteers are from industrialized, developed nations seeking an experience in a developing country or a country in transition. They tend to be affluent and free (albeit for periods of time, e.g. between college and university, between jobs, retirement). This gives the volunteer both time and money to engage in volunteer projects.

A number of the studies have examined volunteer tourists and the influencing factors of why they engage in volunteer activities. Wearing (2004) believes it is difficult to gauge the motivations of volunteer tourists. He continues by outlining that the internal

push motives (Crompton, 1979), such as discovery, enlightenment and personal growth, are important but features of a destination are more than simply pull motives. To this group, physical locations in developing countries also act as a motivation. Additionally, volunteer tourists are attracted by many of the elements that make up a mainstream tourist experience. In addition, due to their psychographic characteristics, pull factors may be ranked higher for volunteer tourists than mainstream tourists. In the study by Benson and Siebert (2009), however, the results did not show this and of the top five most important motivational factors – 'to experience something different, something new'; 'meet African people'; 'to learn about another country and cultures'; 'to live in another country'; and 'to broaden one's mind (cultural experiences)' – four were push factors. Brown and Lehto (2005) argue that the volunteer tourist is able to learn beyond the typical tourism platform and that volunteer tourism introduces a concept of making a difference. This is supported by Wearing (2001) who uses the term altruism. Lyons (2003), however, disputes this, arguing that altruism is not the main focus, as volunteers are not homogenous entities. Gazley (2001) examined the motivation of episodic (short-term) volunteers and noted that, although volunteering was the main reason for travel, other motivations such as fun, adventure and learning were also important. Learning and education are also seen as key components by Benson (2005). This was supported by Galley and Clifton (2004) who examined the motivations of research ecotourists and found the motives 'personal development' and 'academic achievement' were frequent responses made by volunteers as to why they engaged in volunteer tourism.

Volunteer Organizations and Management

Wearing *et al.* (2005) examined NGOs as a key stakeholder between volunteer tourists and communities. A small number of papers have engaged in research linked to the organizations: Wearing (2004) concentrated on conservation organizations; Coghlan (2007) examined a number of volunteer tourism organizations and offered an image-based typology. A further study by Coghlan (2008) explored the role of organization staff. Benson and Henderson (2011) conducted a strategic analysis of research volunteer tourism organizations. Holmes and Smith (2009) examined managing volunteers in tourism. More recent work by Blackman and Benson has been more management focused; they have examined the psychological contract within volunteer tourism (Blackman and Benson, 2010a), knowledge stickiness as part of knowledge transfer (Blackman and Benson, 2010b) and distributed leadership (Benson and Blackman, 2010).

Despite the limited academic research, organizations often appear to receive poor press; the lack of empirical evidence to support or refute these debates, however, remains an issue. Whilst organizations may only want their successes published rather than their failures, this does not seem to be different from organizations in any other sector. Organizations are often criticized for the short time a volunteer spends on a project; however, this does not appear to be balanced by how long the actual organization has been at a destination/project site. There are examples of organizations that have been engaged in projects for a number of years: for example, Operation Wallacea has been operating in Wakatobi Marine National Park, Indonesia since 1995, and the Malaysian Bat project has been supported by Earthwatch since 2001. What is not clear is the extent to which these projects have left lasting legacies, either for the country or local communities. Consequently, these examples are not given in order to defend organizations but to demonstrate that there is still much research to be undertaken. Longitudinal studies of volunteer projects are non-existent, at best there are a few studies that use a retrospective gaze (Mittelberg and Palgi, 2011; Zahra, 2011).

It is acknowledged in the literature that volunteer tourism is associated with payment. Volunteer tourists, just as with ecotourism, often pay a premium to participate in the projects that they engage in. Actual research in this area, however, is negligible. Despite this, discussions are evident in respect of how this profit is expended. The majority of the organizations in the volunteer tourism sector now publish some form of data on how the volunteer payment is distributed; however, this often lacks detail and is mostly unsatisfactory. A general understanding is that (depending upon the project) the money contributes to company administration, project staff, food, accommodations and financing the community projects, via payments to employ community members or to purchase materials, and so on. The debates about what does happen to the money and whether the additional payment actually contributes to the projects' front-line resources or to the profit of the organization involved, still needs to be addressed. This seems to be a fundamental issue in the evaluation of volunteer tourism.

Discordant views between academic research and organizations are evident. For example, recently Linda Richter and Amy Norman (2010) of the Human Sciences Research Council, South Africa, claimed that some volunteer overseas trips are detrimental, such as in the case of 'AIDS orphan tourism'. This criticism is based on the fact that the projects volunteer tourists work on are often short term, and the work is often low skilled and risks displacing locals who need the employment. In particular, when volunteers are working with children, Richter and Norman (2010) argue that the formation of an intense bond between a volunteer tourist and a child (who may have been abused or abandoned previously) can be devastating to the child when the tourist leaves. A follow up article by Peter Slowe, Founder of Projects Abroad, and Britain's largest gap-year organization stated 'Our experience… is entirely at odds with those findings. We hear hundreds of success stories every year about the work our volunteers have done in teaching, conservation and care projects in South Africa as well as many other countries' (Slowe, 2010).

These conflicting views of volunteer tourism highlight a need to avoid a generalized assumption that volunteer tourism is automatically good, just and altruistic. It is a layered phenomenon, with multiple stakeholders who have multiple needs and agendas, and continues to require a more critical analysis and the untangling of its components.

Volunteer Tourism and Communities

A number of studies have focused on volunteer tourism and host communities (Singh, 2002; Broad, 2003; Higgins-Desbiolles, 2003; Singh, 2004; Clifton and Benson, 2006; Gard McGehee and Andereck, 2009) and in particular cultural aspects (Lyons, 2003; McIntosh and Zahra, 2005; Raymond and Hall, 2008). Despite this small amount of literature, the debates surrounding volunteer tourism and host communities are extensive. Does volunteer tourism 'make a difference' to the host communities where

the project is taking place and whether it does or does not, what are the associated problems with having volunteers in communities, e.g. neo-colonialism. Whilst this section will discuss volunteer tourism and communities, it needs to be acknowledged that some volunteer tourism does not take place within a community setting; for example, two projects organized by the volunteer organization Earthwatch, (i) monitoring pink dolphins on a boat in Peru and (ii) determining the health of a bat colony in a jungle in Central Malaysia, were not directly associated with any local communities.

It is essential to recognize that a two-way interactive process between host communities and guests (the tourists) occurs in tourism. As Sofield (1991) states, 'the culture of the host society is as much at risk from various forms of tourism as physical environments' (p. 56). From definitions of volunteer tourism we can find a central aim of sustaining the well-being of the local community where tourism takes place. Consequently, it is possible that volunteer tourism can be viewed as a development strategy with the potential of leading to sustainable development and centring the conjunction of natural resource qualities, locals and the visitor that all benefit from tourism activity, albeit of a certain type.

There is a clear recognition at a community level of the threat that social and environmental degradation poses to community well-being when profit-by-any-means economics becomes the sole focus of outcomes from tourism (Guttentag, 2009). At the same time, communities perceive that tourism, if conducted carefully, can assist in their own efforts to maintain and enhance their local social environment; however, this can be exploited by the tourism system where communities are living subsistence lifestyles and will accept what might be considered inequitable outcome. The tourism sector is simultaneously developing an understanding that there is a significant and growing market for tourism products that not only presents the natural environment and community heritage but that demonstrably supports the maintenance of that heritage, but does not hinder community development.

Volunteer tourism is often positioned as an alternative to mass tourism when a local community is seeking a tourism solution that will generate local income while allowing the community to remain in control of managing and protecting their social lives and environment. Further research and a systematic evaluation is required across this sector to see if the outcomes are being reached; currently Guttentag (2009) and Butcher and Smith (2010) provide some examples of the negative impacts created through projects in host communities. We need to gain insight into how people can participate in the development of volunteer tourism as an aid to better mitigate the negative impacts of tourism and increase benefits to the local community. The two main premises underlying the need to undertake research and to establish a framework for sustainable environmental management for volunteer tourism are (i) that there is no mechanism for evaluating this area and the projects that are taking place without a frame of reference and (ii) continued anecdotal examples cannot allow comprehensive insights into how it can be changed and improved. For example, one issue that continually arises is that volunteer projects are more likely to succeed when active local-level support exists than when not. This chapter does not claim to establish that volunteer local-level participation in tourism is sufficient by itself to ensure positive outcomes for stakeholders but that more systematic evaluation is required to provide the basis for further discussion.

Specifically, the emphasis in much of the literature on sustainable development and participation has not been on people's initiatives as keys to finding solutions for environmental problems; rather it has been on people's lack of participation as an obstacle to the solution (by outsiders). In other words, there has been much more attention paid to ways in which local people can be persuaded to provide the necessary support for tourism projects designed outside the community and presented as capacity building than to ways in which community initiatives can be facilitated to inform and possibly create more successful tourism

projects. Of course, local people cannot and do not always provide solutions to their problems, but the argument made here is that the potential of community-based tourism has been unduly neglected, and that a wider recognition of the ways in which people can find solutions in volunteer tourism projects can only enhance the knowledge base of working on projects in the tourism field.

High economic leakage, little control over operations and relatively few local people being employed in the industry have often been the critique directed at the tourism industry. Volunteer tourism is presented as trying to change this profile but no evidence exists as yet to provide support to show that it has achieved this. Wearing's (2001) original work found that lack of skills and recognition of decision-making structures in local communities, particularly indigenous ones, is a major factor contributing to and perpetuating this occurrence. He demonstrates how the existence and recognition of the community's skills might provide a twining and symbiotic relationship for volunteer tourism projects, in that the volunteer (who generally has limited skills) needs to be taught by the community member (who generally has the skills required for the on-the-ground project). This could lead to a reversal of the roles where the skill of the community member is recognized and valued and required for success in the project. Through this, avenues to more successful community-based tourism development could be found and also allow the local people to educate tourists in both cultural and environmental aspects of the local area (initiated through the activities of work on the volunteer tourism project), thus meeting a fundamental goal of volunteer tourism.

In order for communities to become aware of the place and role volunteer tourism can have in community-based projects, it is important to make them aware of the differing needs of the various operators in the tourism industry and the tourism system. This can be achieved with training and education of local communities as well as empowerment of indigenous systems in larger planning structures. The different sectors such as governments, private enterprise, local communities, conservation organizations, non-governmental organizations and international institutions all need to be able to see the potential for linking this sector of tourism with local communities. It is recognized, however, that this is a tall order for all these key stakeholders to be engaged in a co-ordinated approach, but if communities can reach an understanding of where they fit within the broader framework of the tourism and conservation sectors there is a better chance of carefully designed volunteer tourism programmes. This would enable communities to have the opportunity to control where they fit in the tourism industry and enable a focus for fostering host communities' values while providing education for volunteer tourists. The principles of community-based tourism incorporate the facilitation of sharing ownership and control, of tourism and the associated resource. In the context of volunteer tourism, the application of these principles would allow indigenous communities self-determination and to halt the continuing appropriation of their culture by government and non-government, conservation and tourist agencies. We believe that volunteering and community-based tourism are not just activities undertaken by the volunteer tourist, but should be a partnership between the volunteer tourist, the company organizing the project and the community they are visiting. The project, whilst not outliving its usefulness to the community, should have longevity as indicated above. In creating a partnership experience, those involved not only attempt to reduce negative impacts on the community but put something back into the community.

Community-based tourism linked to volunteering has caught the imagination of many NGOs and local communities, governments, international organizations and the tourism industry. There is a current debate worldwide concerning how community-based tourism projects should be undertaken. This is generating increasing interest in the potential of community-based tourism, particularly by a range of NGOs operating in developing countries. For while community-based tourism is increasingly being seen as a way to promote sustainable tourism it is also seen as being able to provide valuable income. Volunteer programmes and community-based tourism potentially offer new paths towards sustainable development and new ways of doing tourism. A wide range of institutions and organizations do, and will continue to, play an important role in the development of the community-based tourism industry. The types of organizations vary considerably and a number provide international support and sponsorship for the implementation of research projects and community development. These organizations facilitate this process through the provision of necessary resources that may not otherwise be available. The international scope of these organizations can prove to be invaluable assistance in terms of their accumulated knowledge and experience.

The tourism industry may be able to embrace the concept of volunteer tourism as other NGOs and developing governments have done. The ideas of self-sufficiency are growing and local communities now face the dilemma of how their small-scale effort can be developed without being commodified and dominated by wider market forces.

Conclusions

In the past, there was value considered in the 'tourist gaze'; that is, that tourists visiting brought in economic benefit and could observe new and novel lifestyles and cultures, although primarily through the local service industries, the built and natural environment and less so from intimate interactions with local members of the community. Volunteer tourism has been positioned as having potential to shift the value to interactions with the members of the community. Value is defined here more broadly than its use in economics, which sees it as a monetary measure (Peterson *et al.*, 1988, p. 4) to which it embodies meanings important to the community (Australian Heritage Commission, 1992, p. 10). The future of the

Earth's biological diversity is dependent on improving the security and quality of life of many, so they are not forced to deplete natural resources (Boo, 1990, p. 3). Many developing countries require sustainable development to ensure the needs of the present communities are met without compromising the needs of future ones (World Commission on Environment and Development, 1987, p. 8), and this may be achieved with a shift to this way of valuing.

Volunteer tourism can offer some answers in response to these requirements. Volunteer tourism seeks to capitalize on the growth in tourism to different cultures in search of authenticity and return the benefits of this to the host community. Volunteer tourism is premised on the idea that it can only be sustainable if the natural and cultural assets it is reliant on survive and prosper. This chapter suggests a more systematic research agenda is required before any assessment can be made of the area of volunteer tourism and its success or failure. The chapter has raised and examined many of the concerns raised about volunteer tourism and finds that evidence is at best anecdotal as to the outcomes of volunteer tourism projects.

The chapter has suggested that a key area in need of research is that of the volunteer tourism project, with areas, such as the lack of opportunities for involvement in decision making relating to tourism by host communities engaging in volunteer tourism projects, being a key. The second area arises from what could be regarded as inadequate responses from governments and the tourism industry when administrative or legislative mechanisms are being established to enable the creation of these projects. The third relates to the lack of financial, social and vocational benefits flowing to these communities from projects that could now be considered to be commercially exploiting these communities. The fourth relates to the need to establish better tools for evaluating socio-cultural impacts in assessing outcomes of volunteer tourism projects.

These concerns embrace a wide range of issues relating to the management of community resources adjacent to these communities and arise from perceptions of inadequate levels of participation by these communities in the management of what they regard as their traditional domains. The area is a large and diverse one, and the main emphasis here is in regard to the dynamic social exchange between the tourist, the volunteer tourism organizations and the host community. It is obvious that if the social structure and context of the community is not sustained then the experience for the volunteer tourists themselves is threatened. Of interest here is how processes are set up to achieve this and the research required to engage in finding solutions that suit the objectives of volunteer tourism approaches rather than traditional tourism; one obvious area is the solutions that have been researched and found in the area of ecotourism.

The outcomes above present potential for stakeholders interested in establishing forms of community-focused volunteer tourism projects to rethink the way they seek to engage with others. Evidence from the literature indicates that very little research exists on the outcomes of these projects but it is suggested that these projects can have significant effects, both positive and negative, upon the host communities. Currently the underlying differentiation of volunteer tourism from mass tourism (see Table 17.1) would suggest that volunteer tourism, as with ecotourism, can seek to find different processes and mechanism to achieve its outcomes and that innovation and research is required to enable this, with some suggestion that the application of principles and process found in ecotourism and community-based tourism may provide some guidance. Despite the growing popularity of volunteer tourism, systematic academic research in this area is still in its infancy. There is no doubt that the concept of volunteer tourism and our understanding of it have developed over a relatively short period of time but there is still much work to be done in order to appreciate and understand fully the value of this area.

References

Ausender, F. and McCloskey, E. (2008) *World Volunteers: The World Guide to Humanitarian and Development Volunteering*. Universe Publishing, New York.

Australian Heritage Commission (1992) *What is Social Value? A Discussion Paper*. Australian Government Publishing Service, Canberra.

Bartham, P. (2006) Volunteer tourism and the gap year. Available at: http://www.worldvolunteerweb.org/news-views/viewpoints/doc/volunteer-tourism-the.html (accessed 21 September 2008).

Benson, A.M. (2005) Research Tourism: professional travelling versus useful discovery. In: Novelli, M. (ed.) *Niche Tourism: Contemporary Issues, Trends and Cases*. Elsevier, Butterworth-Heinemann, Oxford, UK.

Benson, A.M. (2011) *Volunteer Tourism: Theoretical Frameworks and Practical Applications*. Routledge, Abingdon, UK.

Benson, A.M. and Blackman, D. (2010) To distribute leadership or not? A lesson from the islands. *Journal of Tourism Management*, 32, 1141–1149.

Benson, A.M. and Henderson, S. (2011) A strategic analysis of volunteer tourism organisations. *The Service Industries Journal* 31, 405–424.

Benson, A.M. and Seibert, N. (2009) Volunteer tourism: motivations of German participants in South Africa. Special Issue on Volunteer Tourism. *Annals of Leisure Research* 12, 295–314.

Blackman, D. and Benson, A.M. (2010a) Research volunteer tourism: the role of the psychological contract in managing research volunteer tourism. *Journal of Travel and Tourism Marketing* 27, 1–15.

Blackman, D. and Benson, A.M. (2010b) Overcoming knowledge stickiness in scientific knowledge transfer. *Public Understanding of Science*. Available at: http://pus.sagepub.com/content/early/2010/09/23/0963662510379463 (DOI: 10.1177/0963662510379463).

Boo, E. (1990) *Ecotourism: The Potential and Pitfalls, Volume I*. World Wildlife Foundation, Washington, DC.

Broad, S. (2003) Living the Thai life – a case study of volunteer tourism at the Gibbon Rehabilitation Project, Thailand. *Tourism Recreation Research* 28, 63–77.

Brown, S. and Lehto, X. (2005) Travelling with a purpose: understanding the motives and benefits of volunteer vacationers. *Current Issues in Tourism* 8, 479–496.

Brown, S. and Morrison, A.M. (2003) Expanding volunteer vacation participation: an exploratory study on the mini-mission concept. *Tourism Recreation Research* 28, 73–82.

Burns, P.M. and Holden, A. (1995) *Tourism: A New Perspective*. Prentice Hall, Hemel Hempstead, UK.

Butcher, J. (2005) The moral authority of ecotourism: a critique. *Current Issues in Tourism* 8, 114–124.

Butcher, J. (2011) Volunteer tourism: may not be as good as it seems. *Tourism Recreation Research* 36, 75–76.

Butcher, J. and Smith, P. (2010) Making a difference: volunteer tourism and development. *Tourism Recreation Research* 35, 27–36.

Campbell, L. and Smith, C. (2006) What makes them pay? Values of volunteer tourists working for sea turtle conservation. *Environmental Management* 38, 84–98.

Clarke, J. (1997) A framework of approaches to sustainable tourism. *Journal of Sustainable Tourism* 5, 224–233.

Clifton, J. and Benson, A.M. (2006) Planning for sustainable ecotourism: the case of research ecotourism in developing country destinations. *Journal of Sustainable Tourism* 14, 238–254.

Coghlan, A. (2007) Towards an integrated image-based typology of volunteer tourism organisations. *Journal of Sustainable Tourism* 15, 267–287.

Coghlan, A. (2008) Exploring the role of expedition staff in volunteer tourism. *International Journal of Tourism Research* 10, 183–191.

Crompton, J.L. (1979) Motivations for pleasure vacation. *Annals of Tourism Research* 8, 187–219.

Cronin, L. (1990) A strategy for tourism and sustainable development. *World Leisure and Recreation Journal* Fall, 12–18.

Ellis, C. (2003) Participatory environmental research in tourism: a global view. *Tourism Recreation Research* 28, 45–55.

Fitzpatrick, L. (2007) Vacationing like Brangelina, TIME Magazine. Available at: http://www.time.com/time/magazine/article/0,9171,1647457,00.html (accessed 27 July 2007).

Galley, G. and Clifton, J. (2004) The motivational and demographic characteristics of research ecotourists: operation Wallacea volunteers in South-east Sulawesi, Indonesia. *Journal of Ecotourism* 3, 69–82.

Gazley, B. (2001) Volunteer vacationers and what research can tell us about them. *e-Volunteerism: The Electronic Journal of the Volunteerism Community* 1 (2). Available at: http://www.e-volunteerism.com/quarterly/01win/facintro

Guttentag, D. (2011) Volunteer tourism: as good as it seems? *Tourism Recreation Research* 36, 69–74.

Guttentag, D.A. (2009) The possible negative impacts of volunteer tourism. *International Journal of Tourism Research* 11, 537–551.

Hardy, A., Beeton, R.J.S. and Pearson, L. (2002) Sustainable tourism: an overview of the concept and its position in relation to conceptualisations of tourism. *Journal of Sustainable Tourism* 10, 475–496.

Hardy, R. (2004) *The Virgin Guide to Volunteering: Give Your Time and Get Work and Life Experience in Return*. Virgin Books, London.

Heyniger, C. (2007) The complete guide to volunteer tourism. Available at: http://www.bravenewtraveler.com (accessed 21 July 2008).

Higgins-Desbiolles, F. (2003) Reconciliation tourism: tourism healing divided societies. *Tourism Recreation Research* 28, 35–44.

Hindle, C., Miller, K., Wintle, S. and Cavalieri, N. (2007) *Volunteer: A Traveller's Guide to Making a Difference Around the World*. Lonely Planet, Footscray, Melbourne, Australia.

Holmes, K. and Smith, K. (2009) *Managing Volunteers in Tourism: Attractions, Destinations and Events*. Butterworth-Heinemann, Oxford, UK.

Ingram, J. (2011) Volunteer tourism: how do we know it is 'making a difference'? In: M. Benson (ed.) *Volunteer Tourism: Theoretical Framework and Practical Applications*. Routledge, Abingdon, UK.

Ko, T.G. (2005) Development of a tourism sustainability assessment procedure: a conceptual approach. *Tourism Management* 26, 431–445.

Lyons, K.D. (2003) Ambiguities in volunteer tourism: a case study of Australians participating in a J-1 visitor exchange programme. *Tourism Recreation Research* 28, 5–13.

Lyons, K.D. and Wearing, S. (2008) *Journeys of Discovery in Volunteer Tourism: International Case Study Perspective*. CABI Publishing, Wallingford, UK.

McGehee, N.G. and Andereck, K. (2009) Volunteer tourism and the "voluntoured": the case of Tijuana, Mexico. *Journal of Sustainable Tourism* 17, 39–51.

McGehee, N.G. and Santos, C.A. (2005) Social change, discourse and volunteer tourism. *Annals of Tourism Research* 32, 760–779.

McIntosh, A.J. and Zahra, A. (2005) Alternative cultural experiences through volunteer tourism. Paper presented at the Association for Tourism and Leisure Education (ATLAS), Catalonia, Spain.

Matthews, A. (2008) Negotiated selves: exploring the impact of local–global interactions on young volunteer travellers. In: Lyons, K.D. and Wearing, S. (eds) *Journeys of Discovery in Volunteer Tourism*. CABI Publishing, Wallingford, UK, pp. 101–117.

Mintel International Group Ltd (2008) *Volunteer Tourism – International – September 2008*. Mintel International Group Ltd, London.

Mittelberg, D. and Palgi, M. (2011) Self and society in voluntourism: a thirty year retrospective analysis of post trip self development of volunteer tourists to the Israeli Kibbutz. In: Benson, A.M. (ed.) *Volunteer Tourism: Theoretical Frameworks and Practical Applications*. Routledge, Abingdon, UK.

Mustonen, P. (2005) Volunteer tourism: postmodern pilgrimage? *Journal of Tourism and Cultural Change* 3, 160–177.

Nestor, A., Yeung, P. and Calderon, H. (2009) Volunteer travel insights, 2009. Bradt travel guides, Lasso communications, GeckoGo. Available at: http://www.geckogo.com/volunteer/report2009

Nyaupane, G.P., Teye, V. and Paris, C. (2008) Innocents abroad: attitude change toward hosts. *Annals of Tourism Research* 35, 650–667.

Peterson, G.L., Driver, B.L. and Gregory, R. (1988) *Amenity Resource Valuation: Integrating Economics with Other Disciplines*. Venture Publishing, State College, Pennsylvania.

Raymond, E. (2011) Volunteer tourism: looking forward. *Tourism Recreation Research* 36, 77–80.

Raymond, E.M. and Hall, C.M. (2008) The development of cross-cultural (mis)understanding through volunteer tourism. *Journal of Sustainable Tourism* 16, 530–543.

Richter, L.M. and Norman, A. (2010) AIDS orphan tourism: a threat to young children in residential care. *Vulnerable Children and Youth Studies* 5, 217–229.

Simpson, K. (2004) Doing development: the gap year, volunteer-tourists and a popular practice of development. *Journal of International Development* 16, 681–692.

Simpson, K. (2005) Dropping out or signing up? The professionalisation of youth travel. In: Laurie, N. and Bondi, L. *Working the Spaces of Neoliberalism: Activism, Professionalisation and Incorporation*. Blackwell Publishing, Malden, Massachusetts, pp. 54–76.

Sin, H.L. (2009) Volunteer tourism – "involve me and I will learn"? *Annals of Tourism Research* 36, 480–501.

Singh, T.V. (2002) Altruistic tourism: another shade of sustainable tourism: the case of Kanda community. *Tourism: An International Interdisciplinary Journal* 50, 371–381.

Singh, T.V. (2004) *New Horizons in Tourism: Strange Experiences and Stranger Practices*. CABI Publishing, Wallingford, UK.

Slowe, P. (2010) Gap-year volunteers fulfil a vital role abroad. Available at: http://www.telegraph.co.uk/travel/hubs/gapyear/8110847/Gap-year-volunteers-fulfil-a-vital-role-abroad.html (accessed 4 November 2010).

Sofield, T.H.B. (1991) Sustainable ethnic tourism in the South Pacific: some principles. *Journal of Tourism Studies* 2, 56–72.

Stoddart, H. and Rogerson, C.M. (2004) Volunteer tourism: the case of habitat for humanity South Africa. *GeoJournal* 60, 311.

Swarbrooke, J. (1999) *Sustainable Tourism Management*. CABI Publishing, Wallingford, UK.

Tourism Research and Marketing (TRAM) (2008) *Volunteer Tourism: A Global Analysis*. ATLAS Publications, Barcelona, Spain.

UN (2001) *United Nations Volunteers Report*. UN General Assembly Special Session on Social Development, Geneva.

United Nations Development Programme (2005) *The Sustainable Difference: Energy and Environment to Achieve the MDGs*. Development Programme, Energy Environment Bureau for Development Policy, Energy and Environment Group, United Nations, New York.

Uriely, N., Reichel, A. and Ron, A. (2003) Volunteering in tourism: additional thinking. *Tourism Recreation Research* 28, 57–62.

Ward, L. (2007) You're better off backpacking – VSO warns about perils of 'voluntourism'. Available at: http://www.guardian.co.uk/uk/2007/aug/14/students.charitablegiving (accessed 14 August 2007).

Wearing, S. (2001) *Volunteer Tourism: Experiences that make a Difference*. CABI Publishing, Wallingford, UK.

Wearing, S. (2002) Re-centring the self in volunteer tourism. In: Dann, G.M.S. (ed.) *The Tourist as a Metaphor of the Social World*. CABI Publishing, Wallingford, UK, pp. 237–262.

Wearing, S. (2003) *Volunteer Tourism*. CABI Publishing, Wallingford, UK.

Wearing, S. (2004) Examining best practice in volunteer tourism. In: Stebbins, R. and Graham, M. (eds) *Volunteering as Leisure/Leisure as Volunteering: An International Assessment*. CABI Publishing, Wallingford, UK, pp. 209–224.

Wearing, S. and Deane, B. (2003) Seeking self: leisure and tourism on common ground. *World Leisure* 45, 4–12.

Wearing, S. and Neil, J. (2000) Refiguring self and identity through volunteer tourism. *Loisir et Societe/Society and Leisure* 23, 389–419.

Wearing, S., McDonald, M. and Ponting, J. (2005) Building a decommodified research paradigm in tourism: the contribution of NGOs. *Journal of Sustainable Tourism* 13, 424–439.

Weaver, D. (2006) *Sustainable Tourism*. Elsevier Buttterworth-Heinemann, Oxford, UK.

Wickens, E. (2011) Journeys of the self: volunteer tourists in Nepal. In: Benson, A.M. (ed.) *Volunteer Tourism: Theory Framework to Practical Applications*. Routledge, Abingdon, UK, pp. 42–52.

Woosnam, K.M. and Lee, Y.J. (2011) Applying social distance to voluntourism research. *Annals of Tourism Research* 38, 309–313.

World Commission on Environment and Development (1987) *Our Common Future*. Oxford University Press, Oxford, UK.

Zahra, A. (2011) Volunteer tourism as a life-changing experience. In: Benson, A.M. (ed.) *Volunteer Tourism: Theoretical Frameworks and Practical Applications*. Routledge, Abingdon, UK.

Conclusion

The study of controversy is both complicated and complex. It is complex in that so many characters are involved in so many meanings and interpretations, and its complexity resonates in the difficulty of making sound judgements (which will of course mean different things to different people). Even where clarification of major points of disagreements between actors exist, lingering doubts remain, like sharks in the water waiting to attack our preconceptions and supposedly settled minds just as we thought it was safe to go back into the water! Whether we side with Prospero or Caliban in this 'Tempest' of a world, our job as teachers and students of controversy is to understand and present the situation from different perspectives. Certainly, a controversy is not a controversy if its nature does not cover the discourses representing opinions of those who support a strategy or policy and those who do not. In tourism, with its complex nature and multiple stakeholders (some willing some not), no decisions are easy, and very few can be made without controversy. Thus when decision makers are confronted with a controversial issue, even when they are provided with the most comprehensive picture, the granularity, the murkiness, the dark shadows, are ever present. However, in the case of tourism, with its extended supply/ value and interest chains, it is even more difficult for sound decisions to be made because sound analyses of the controversy are so often missing.

The contributors to the present book have selected a controversy based on their interest and expertise. Although it was difficult for some authors to remain neutral, or emotionless in their discussion and analysis, the reader might, in some cases, have found the discussion skewed to a particular viewpoint, which may not coalesce with mainstream opinion. Consequently, some readers may argue that studying controversy may be all well and good, but what about, they may ask, the truth? Is the study and analysis of controversy supposed to be a means to an end? Absolutely yes. We would not be offering this volume if *we* did not think that some views are more productive, pragmatic and, indeed, noble than others; if *we* did not believe in the critical and cultural contexts of tourism; if *we* did not believe in tourism as having the potential to shape our futures; if *we* did not believe in its potential for leading humanity towards the good life. Understanding the controversial nature of tourism is for us 'not the opposite of reaching resolution but a precondition of doing so' (Graff and Phelan, 2000, p. 101).

Where, then, do *we* stand in the debate between those who ask for more moralization of tourism and those who are irritated by it? Our own answer, for what it is worth, is that although in some cases we believe that there is merit to both positions, we nevertheless have no hidden meaning: the truth is out there and is reflected in the ways we have been doing tourism. In Chapter 1, Moufakkir argues against the invisibility of the moralization of tourism in tourism promotion and education, emphasizing the need for more education for freedom even if this education will set limits to our tourism freedoms. Where, then, do we stand in the debate about unity in diversity, or what Aykin addressed in Chapter 2 when discussing the conflicting views about a common European tourism policy? Where, then, do we stand in the debate about development and/or progress, as stressed in Chapter 3 by Papanicolaou in her discussion of the development of tourism and the 'development' of the Mayan culture in her region, or what Novelli and Tisch-Rottensteiner in Chapter 4 have observed about the increasing demand for authenticity and for development in their case study, and the ongoing contradiction between the promotion of pro-poor tourism and the demand on natural and cultural preservation? Where, then, do we stand in the controversies surrounding medical tourism as presented by Vequist and his colleagues in Chapter 5, who themselves have concluded that there are still many gaps to be filled to come to a conclusion about this emerging phenomenon? How are we to deal with supporters or adversaries of wildlife tourism and trophy hunting, when Dobson himself in Chapter 6 has left us perplexed, yet enlightened, but completely undecided? Where then do we stand when, despite 20 years of past research, we are still asked to comment on how 'eco' ecotourism is or how it benefits indigenous people, while we know from Boyd's excellent review and analysis of the topic (Chapter 7) that disagreements about its definitions, meanings, operations and implications still exist? Indigenous cultures are sold and bought, and to these ends both vendor and buyer are orchestrating the transformation of culture's authenticity in a mutually

dependent yet unequal partnership; one which is economically needed but culturally unwelcomed, although cultural commodification and change may, to some, seem unavoidable and transformational (Chapter 8). So, where, then, do we stand in relation to power and control over ethnic culture and its hybridization? Is culture hybridization a phenomenon that we should welcome, reject or just ignore, despite our consciousness of the realistic powers of culture fluidity? This is the complex question that Xie has left us with. We are left with so many questions that to take sides, sometimes, seems to us is nothing but a gamble.

Even with a growing phenomenon such as casino gaming (as presented by Moufakkir and Holecek in Chapter 9), we gain the impression that we have left the reader with the idea that any gaming development is a gamble. It is, however, clear to us that golf tourism, in some development contexts, is a clear indication that we are gambling with nature, the economy and the locals' long-term quality of life despite the recommendations offered by Boukas and his co-authors in Chapter 10. While discussing the controversies surrounding residential tourism in Chapter 11, Huete and Mantecón have left us with questions even more pressing than those directly related to this phenomenon, questions to make us think even beyond the European identity to consider the realities of global citizenship and the right to travel and tourism. Craig and Thompson's chapter (Chapter 12) brings us closer to death and makes us think about the dark side not only of tourism but of human behaviour, which, to some extent, lightens our existence and darkens our human realities. Discussing the impacts of cultural events on the local community, Addo (Chapter 13) confronts us with the disillusionment of economic benefits of such events, but more importantly leaves us thinking about postcolonial celebrations of independence and the exploitation of those celebrations for economic and political reasons.

Exploitation has also been manifested in the discourse and actions of intergovernmental organizations, whose raison d'être is to build a fairer and more equitable world. But events have travestied implicitly and explicitly into what Ferraz in Chapter 14 refers to as a phenomenon of cultural and economic hegemony, serving the interest of the more powerful actors. In another take on power, 'pleasure' tourists to less developed countries (the people of which are controversially called the 'bottom billion' by Paul Collier, 2007), as those depicted by Pattison in Chapter 15, are powerful actors who through their right to pleasure empower and please their powerless hosts. In this pleasure–power context, the powerless and powerful are both engaged in a mutually orchestrated power–resistance game relationship. To some, this topsy-turvy situation is rather a game of convenience; to others, the winners and losers are obvious. In Chapter 16, Bhandari discusses controversies related to tourism and conservation and his case illustrates vividly that despite reaching a consensus among the stakeholders involved, no matter how good or willing they may be, the question of who is losing and who is winning still resonates, and to some, its answer may depend less on pragmatism than on idealism. To others being pragmatic is a more realistic way to solve conservation and development issues. Even those volunteer tourists who are pragmatic in their idealism are not spared from criticism. Focusing on volunteer tourism, Benson and Wearing (Chapter 17) have left us with many questions and suggestions for further research. One question that can exemplify our struggle with writing about controversies is: does it matter that volunteer tourists are or are not altruistic, since they make a difference in their lives and in those they have touched?

The controversies presented in this volume can be used to re-emphasize the complexity of the tourism environment, and the realities of decision making in tourism policy, planning and development, which cannot be dissociated from who we are as people. The complexity of tourism is also manifested in the very nature of the diversity of tourism stakeholders, their roles, power and influence. The absence of debate can lead to myopic

understanding, limited vision and a 'business-knows-best', neo-liberal future where finance and profit dominate culture and social systems. The purpose of this volume is to expose our readers to conflicting views, broaden horizons and subject our views to a critical gaze. These controversies may also be valuable in fostering the pedagogical goal of building interest and aiding the formation of critical principles. It is our hope that the contents of this volume spark discussion in the classroom and tourism development office, with the view to building appreciation for the kind of research and reasoning on which good development can be built. The purpose of this book was to present a controversial view of tourism with the objective of providing the reader with a picture comprehensive enough to facilitate decision making with the capability of foreseeing the best possible scenarios for future tourism behaviour, development and outcome. Once evaluated, the controversies can provide important indications for a destination management organization.

> Learning by controversy offers a practical classroom solution to the angrily polarized debates of our time. Indeed, this strategy presents a model of how the quality of cultural debate in our society at large might be improved. It is a common prediction that the culture of the twenty-first century will put a premium on people's ability to deal productively with conflict and cultural differences. Learning by controversy is sound training for citizenship in that future.
>
> Graff and Phelan (2000, p. vii)

Our engagement with controversy can only deepen our engagement with tourism development. Our point here is when a community has to decide on a tourism policy and what type of development to embrace, 'you and your fellow citizens do not have the luxury of saying, "it's all a matter of subjective opinion (...)" Simply to opt out of a debate is to surrender one of the most important forms of action available to a citizen of a democracy' (Graff and Phelan, 2000, p. 106).

References

Graff, G. and Phelan, J. (2000) *A Case Study in Critical Controversy: The Tempest.* (William Shakespeare) Macmillan Press, Hampshire, UK.

Collier, P. (2007) *The Bottom Billion: Why the Poorest Countries are Failing and What Can be Done About it.* Oxford University Press, Oxford, UK.

Index